NAVAL RENAISSANCE

NAVAL RENAISSANCE
The U.S. Navy in the 1980s

Frederick H. Hartmann

Alfred Thayer Mahan Professor Emeritus
Naval War College

Naval Institute Press
Annapolis, Maryland

Copyright © 1990
by the United States Naval Institute
Annapolis, Maryland

The paper used in this publication meets
the minimum requirements of American
National Standard for Information Sciences—
Permanence of Paper for Printed Library Materials,
ANSI Z39.48-1984.

Library of Congress Cataloging-in-Publication Data

Hartmann, Frederick H.
    Naval renaissance : the U.S. Navy in the 1980s / Frederick H. Hartmann.
        p.   cm.
    Includes bibliographical references.
    ISBN 0-87021-591-4
    1. United States.   Navy—History—20th century.   I. Title.
VA58.4.H374   1990
359'.00973'09048—dc20   89-28475
                                                                     CIP

Printed in the United States of America

9 8 7 6 5 4 3 2

First printing

To the memory of
Admiral Richard G. Colbert
—they do not come better

CONTENTS

13 Naval Operations 231
14 The Strategic Defense Initiative................... 248
15 Changing the Watch............................. 264

    Appendices
    A Principal National Security Officials 277
    B A Typical Daily CNO Schedule 279
    C OPNAV in 1942............................. 281
    D OPNAV in 1985 282
    E The Ninety-Day Message 283

    Notes.. 287
    Index.. 325

LIST OF FIGURES AND TABLES

PREFACE

When Harold and Margaret Sprout began their studies of the U.S. Navy before World War II, there existed little scholarly analysis of the development of that major American institution. And despite the able contributions of a few dozen authors since then, the literature is scant. Particularly notable is how little political scientists have contributed, the work of Vincent Davis being a prominent exception. What there is comes mostly from historians and tends therefore to focus on earlier periods. The present study deals with the contemporary navy from a political science point of view—with documents whose ink is hardly dry and with participants who are, in almost every case, still alive. It relies heavily on interviews because, in the city of leaks that Washington is, so much has deliberately not been written down.

Admiral James D. Watkins, while still the chief of naval operations, became convinced that the story of the navy during the years in which it grew to almost six hundred ships should be written up. He asked Rear Admiral Ronald Marryott, then president of the Naval War College, to suggest an author, which is how I entered the picture. I agreed to write a book for the same reason Admiral Watkins suggested one: it had the potential to be of great value to career naval officers and to the wider military and defense community.

For initial analysis, Admiral Watkins ordered major documents from the time of his tenure to be collected and sorted into eighteen categories. This collection, plus certain materials requested by me during Admiral Carlisle A. H. Trost's first nine months in office, are the written materials I have used. They represent only a fraction of the mountain of paper "generated" during the years from 1982 through 1987.

The doors of the men who shaped recent navy history opened for

xi

me in almost every case, as the acknowledgments clearly show, and in almost all the interviews I taped—120—the material is frank and forthcoming. This tape collection, now in the hands of the contemporary history branch of the Naval Historical Center, Washington Navy Yard, will give historians a rich source of commentary and information to tap as they write more definitive accounts in later years. I was fortunate also to be in a position to interview senior admirals from nine allied or friendly nations, most of them chiefs of their navies. But these I did not tape.

There are a few deliberate omissions. On the intelligence side, I have stuck to commentaries already in the public domain when discussing, for example, the Walker case. And needless to say, any classified material has been removed in the security review. I have also refrained from discussing personalities, except where that is indispensable to the understanding of developments.

Despite my background as a naval reservist of some forty-five years and the senior civilian academician at the Naval War College between 1966 and 1986, there were gaps in my knowledge of the navy that needed filling before this work could be completed. I had never been under way in a modern nuclear aircraft carrier; I had never toured a modern supply center; I had never visited air tactical training facilities such as those at Fallon and Miramar; I had no real idea of the nature of U.S. space activities. Only after considerable traveling was I able to see the navy from a broader perspective.

This book is in no sense the story of Admiral Watkins's career to date. He did not want one, and in any event I have no talent for biography. It is, instead, a presentation of the navy's overall program from 1980 to 1987, especially 1982 to 1986, the "payoff" years culminating the efforts of many, stretching back at least to Admiral Zumwalt's time, to revitalize and modernize the U.S. Navy. Initially, the analysis discusses serious problems in leadership, management, and morale. Ultimately, it focuses on the great successes that followed, what some have called a naval renaissance.

This material is approached from the top down, my documents being mostly from the CNO's files and my interviews primarily with senior officials. There is also much more here about the uniformed navy than about senior civilian officials, not only because of access but also because a "blue suit" slant is rare and consequently valuable. I do not apologize for this, though I should point out that no downgrading of the civilian role is intended. In Congress, I interviewed only one key senator and two key congressmen, but their views are already largely on the public record. Four former navy secretaries and two undersecretaries—a fascinating group—provided me with a well-articulated but divergent set of views.

An account of the navy between 1980 and 1987 must include information on the tremendous defense effort made during the Reagan administration and on its results. It must point out the significant revision by Congress of the defense organization of the United States, especially the powers and duties of the Joint Chiefs. These wider concerns are covered primarily as they touch on the main subject.

Presenting material from congressional hearings posed a difficult organizational problem. I wanted a faithful account but had to distill it from literally thousands of pages of transcripts. Because both testimony and questions and answers tend at times to stray and at times to be repetitive, I compromised, imposing on my account some degree of order and eliminating much of the repetition, so as not to weary the reader, while at the same time retaining the flavor of the hearings.

It is hoped that this book will lead the way to additional accounts of successive periods of contemporary naval history. To encourage such a development, profits from its sale will go to the Naval War College Foundation, whose generous grant of travel funds made it possible in the first place.

Although the material that follows has gone through a security clearance, the navy made no attempt to push my conclusions in any direction. The judgments are my own.

ACKNOWLEDGMENTS

A whole host of people had a hand in this book; I hope I have not neglected anyone of central importance.

Many of those I interviewed have since been promoted or moved on to other positions. In most cases rank and position are given as they were on the day of the interview, sometimes with reference to past or subsequent assignments. Direct quotations from interviews were made with the approval and review of those interviewed.

My thanks go first to Admiral James D. Watkins for his patience during many hours of questioning. Rear Admiral J. M. Boorda, Admiral Watkins's executive assistant, was a mine of information. Captain Al Rudy, (OP-00J), special legal counsel, gave me insights into the CNO's attitudes about disciplinary problems. Captain Paul L. Gruendl, executive assistant to the assistant VCNO, guided me through the complicated organization of OPNAV and critiqued my first draft on it. Captain Charles H. Kinney, Captain Kathy Laughton, and Pat Talbot briefed me on the work of the navy's inspector general. Rear Admirals William T. Pendley (OP-60) and Paul Butcher (OP-06B) explained the substantive aspects of the joint side of the CNO's duties, while Rear Admiral W. O. Studeman (OP-009) discussed the intelligence side. Vice Admiral Lewis Seaton examined the navy's medical problems and Vice Admiral R. E. Kirksey described the work of OP-094. Rear Admiral Jerome F. Smith (OP-61) looked at the allied navy picture with me, Rear Admiral Roger Bacon (OP-65) commented on the strategic picture. Vice Admiral James R. Hogg (OP-095) indicated the problems in coordinating warfare efforts across navy "communities," and Vice Admiral A. J. Baciocco (OP-098) introduced me to some of the research and development complications. Rear Admiral John McNamara (OP-09G) gave a chief chaplain's view.

Vice Admirals Bruce Demars (OP-02), Edward H. Martin (OP-05), and Joseph Metcalf III (OP-03), the well-known OPNAV "barons," filled me in on submarine-, air-, and surface-warfare problems. Vice Admiral Daniel L. Cooper (OP-090) discussed the issue of the budget. Vice Admiral Tom Hughes gave me insights into contemporary logistics problems.

Captains Mike Hughes (OP-00K) and Linton Brooks (OP-65) gave generously of their time and together showed the great range of the OPNAV staff, Hughes speaking on the CNO's executive panel, Brooks on the genesis of such ideas as SDI.

Vice Admiral Cecil J. Kempf (OP-09R) and Mr. Bill Legg of his staff provided many insights into current reserve affairs. Vice Admiral Dudley L. Carlson (OP-01) shed light on the complex world of personnel requirements.

My old friend General P. X. Kelley, commandant of the Marine Corps, turned a thirty-minute interview into an hour and a half with many useful observations. Admiral Kinnaird R. McKee commented from his unique position in both the Energy Department and the Navy Department. Congressman Charles Bennett gave me a view from the legislative side, and Admiral Wes MacDonald, recently retired as supreme allied commander of the Atlantic, spoke from the perspective of a commander in chief. Rear Admiral Ronald F. Marryott, president of the Naval War College and formerly OP-06B, commented on Watkins's first years. John Cardinal O'Connor, archbishop of New York and a retired rear admiral, graciously reminisced about his years in service and his many associations with Watkins.

Retired CNO Admiral James L. Holloway III generously filled in the background that led up to the Hayward and Watkins years. Retired Admiral Sylvester Foley, Jr., assistant secretary of energy (nuclear) and formerly CINCPACFLT, gave the salty view of a commander in chief. Congressman Bill Chappell of Florida told me how he got the navy to take its reservists more seriously.

Commander Tom Hayes (OP-06C) reviewed navy procedures for working up agendas for the Joint Chiefs and took me to see "The Tank."

Mr. Robert C. McFarlane, former assistant to the president for national security affairs and currently at Georgetown's Center for Strategic and International Studies, discussed the beginnings of SDI, and Vice Admiral John Poindexter, then national security assistant, took time from a busy day at the White House to provide further details on SDI.

In Norfolk, Admiral Lee Baggett, Jr., and Admiral Carlisle A. H. Trost, now CNO, gave me their own evaluation of the 1982–87 period. Vice Admiral Scot McCauley, commander, naval surface force, Atlantic, was a great source on background, having served so long with Admiral Watkins. In Pensacola, Vice Admiral Ron Thunman, CNET, spoke about improvements to the 688-class submarine and its follow-on. Retired Vice Admiral Charles H. Griffiths supplied background on the submarine navy, while retired Admiral Ike Kidd gave a superb summary of logistics problems over the years.

Rear Admiral David E. Jeremiah, former executive assistant to Admiral Watkins, covered the first part of the Watkins years.

Mr. Robert Murray, head of Harvard's national security affairs program, former undersecretary of the navy, and first director of the Strategic Studies Group at Newport, commented on the origins of that group. Dr. Robert Wood, second director, looked at its continuation, and Marshall Brement, third and current director, its present tasking. Professor John Hattendorf of the Naval War College shared with me his detailed (but classified) work on the development of the maritime strategy.

Admiral J. B. Busey, VCNO, gave generously of his time in a lengthy interview, and former CNO and chairman of the Joint Chiefs Admiral Tom Moorer offered particularly useful insights.

Colonel Gilbert D. Rye, USAF (Ret.), key man in the internal National Security Council development of SDI and now president of COMSAT Government Systems, completed my understanding of the sequence of events leading to the concept's acceptance by the Joint Chiefs. In Annapolis Captain James Barber, director of the Naval Institute, and Captain Paul Schratz, a frequent commentator on the navy's recent past, spoke from their unique vantages.

In Virginia General Charles A. Gabriel, air force chief of staff during Watkins's tenure as CNO, was particularly forthcoming and helpful. In the Pentagon, Captain Jerome N. Burke, USN, senior military speech writer to the secretary of defense and former speech writer to ex-Secretary of the Navy Middendorf, not only furnished needed materials but made many acute observations. I also thank Normal Friedman for a very useful conversation at the Naval Historical Center in the Old Washington Navy Yard.

In Newport, a conversation with Ambassador J. William Middendorf II furnished a needed clue to President Carter's initial actions as chief executive.

Vice Admiral James A. Sagerholm, now retired, explained his part in directing the personal excellence program. Vice Admiral William P. Lawrence, also retired, reviewed his experiences as chief of naval personnel. General John Vessey, former chairman of the Joint Chiefs of Staff, gave an excellent appraisal of the role of that group.

In Newport Captain Jack Grunawalt, then holding the chair in international law, and Captain Ash Roach, both with experience in the Judge Advocate General Corps, spelled out chapter and verse on legal matters in the years 1980–87. Admiral Arthur S. Moreau, Jr., then commander in chief, south, NATO, gave the initial part of what was to be a series of interviews and then, to the regret of all, died unexpectedly. Captain George Allen reviewed the history of the Naval War College's integrated-warfare course, while Captain Robert Watts, deputy at the college, briefed me on the effects of the transition year into Admiral Trost's leadership. Rear Admiral John A. Baldwin filled me in on the "political" purpose of Sea Plan 2000; retired Vice Admiral Thomas Weschler went over his role in developing what became the *Spruance-*class destroyer. Captain Tim Somes, chairman of operations at the college, summarized the experiences behind his sponsorship of its present curriculum. Bud Hay went over the connection at the college between research and gaming, while Captain Jay Hurlburt, director of the War Gaming Center, and Captain Dave Klinger, assistant director, addressed in particular the increase in gaming analysis.

In Washington, Vice Admiral William H. Rowden spoke of NAVSEA, Captain William Owens, then executive assistant to the VCNO, of his experiences as an early member of the Strategic Studies Group. Vice Admiral Henry C. Mustin briefed me on the most recent revisions to the maritime strategy, and retired Admiral William N. Small took me back over his days as VCNO. Vice Admiral Lando Zech, now chairman of the U.S. Nuclear Regulatory Commission, reviewed the personnel problems he encountered at the Navy Annex. General Maxwell R. Thurman took an hour from a busy day as army vice chief to review army-navy interfaces. Rear Admiral John R. Seeholtz, at the Naval Observatory, went into the many ways oceanography and meteorology are growing in importance. Retired Admiral Robert L. J. Long provided valuable material.

At Palo Alto, Dr. Edward Teller reviewed his role in stimulating interest in SDI.

In Hawaii, Admiral James A. Lyons, CINCPACFLT, Admiral Thomas Hayward (Ret.), and Admiral Ronald I. Hays, USCINCPAC, discussed their roles in the years covered in this book. In Monterey, Vice Admiral Richard A. Miller (Ret.), former vice chief of the Naval Material Command, explained the problems that led to its dissolution. Rear Admiral Robert C. Austin, superintendent of the Naval Postgraduate School, reviewed this period years as it affected that school.

At the White House again, retired Rear Admiral William A. Cockell, on the staff of the National Security Council, took me through the Hayward years when he was executive assistant. General John A. Wickham, Jr., retired army chief of staff, amplified General Thurman's discussion of the Joint Chiefs and of army-navy cooperation. Vice Admiral Glenwood Clark, Jr., introduced me to the problems of SPAWARS, the newest of the systems commands. Former Navy Under-secretary James Woolsey told of his service, especially on the CNO's executive panel. Vice Admiral Dave Jeremiah (today with one more star), went over the *Achille Lauro* affair and "Libya I" from his vantage as at-sea commander. Admiral Elmo Zumwalt looked back on his tour as CNO with me. Retired Admiral Harry D. Train II gave his perspective on his tour as CINCLANT and as supreme allied commander, Atlantic. Captain Peter Swartz recounted OPNAV 603's role in the initial formulation of the maritime strategy.

In Fallon, Nevada, Dr. Roger Whiteway, senior civilian, explained how "Strike University" began and how it worked, electronic range and all. In San Francisco, Vice Admiral Robert R. Monroe, now senior vice president of defense matters for Bechtel, explained operational evaluation. Former Assistant Secretary of Defense Francis West went over his Sea Plan 2000 role, which account retired Captain James Patton complemented by discussing the Pacific planning that antedated it. In Seattle, Admiral Jack Williams, (Ret.), provided another view of the Naval Material Command. Retired Vice Admiral Staser Holcomb, now president of one of the USAA companies, sharpened my understanding of the evolution of the navy's systems analysis. Vice Admiral William E. Ramsey, vice commander, U.S. Space Command, recounted how the navy's space effort began and continued. Captain George O'Brien, skipper of the *Carl Vinson,* spent several hours at sea explaining carrier operations and super-CAG. Commander David Gibbs, the *Vinson* supply officer, took me into his specialized world, as did many other of that ship's senior officers.

Former Navy Secretary Graham Claytor, now head of Amtrak, described how he saw the secretary's role. Rear Admiral Richard C. Macke, at the navy's Space Command in Dahlgren, completed the picture on space. Rear Admiral James F. Dorsey, Jr., then OP-06B, showed how the European command's functioning affected navy operations. Captain Ernie Tedeschi and Commander Bill Willfong explained the progress of modular-construction systems in the new DDG 51–class destroyers.

Bill Wegner, at Admiral Watkins's request, gave me a valuable interview on his experience as Admiral Rickover's deputy. John Warner, between votes on the Senate floor, commented on his days as navy secretary. In Yorktown, Virginia, over a delightful dinner, former Secretary John Lehman answered all my questions fully and frankly.

In Newport once more, I had the pleasure of interviewing a number of admirals from other nations assembled for the Ninth International Seapower Symposium. I did not tape these sessions but have drawn upon my notes occasionally. These officers were Vice Admiral Maximo Eduardo Rivero-Kelly, vice chief of staff, Argentine navy; Vice Admiral Charles Thomas, commander, Canadian Maritime Command; Admiral Jose T. Castro Merino, commander, Chilean Navy; Vice Admiral Jean Betermier, director, French Naval War College; Vice Admiral Hans Joachim Mann, inspector general of the navy of the Federal Republic of Germany; Rear Admiral Aldo Gallo, commandant, Naval War Institute, Italy; Rear Admiral Bjarne Martin Grimstvedt, inspector general, Norwegian navy; Vice Admiral Fernando Martin Avorra, director, Spanish Naval War College; Vice Admiral Bengt J. Schuback, commander in chief, Swedish naval forces; and Admiral William Staveley, first sea lord and chief of naval staff, Royal Navy.

There are literally dozens of others who assisted me or who answered my questions patiently—the gun boss on the *Vinson*, the sailors below the waterline who assembled bombs so that I could judge the problem of timing in changing targets quickly, the three supply officers who took me through the depot at Miramar, the skipper who showed me around "Top Gun," to name only a few.

A dozen or so enlisted men in the CNO's administration "shop," under the adroit leadership of Chief Richard Bonner and later of Senior Chief Philip Clinton, handled many administrative chores for me: YN1 Gregory F. Bunten, YN1 Brian S. Kane, YN2 Carolyn Liebeck, YN2 Charlene Pangilinan, YN2 Mary Wadsworth, YN2 Virginia Jones, YN2 Colette Marguy, YN2 Gina Vyrostek, YN3 Rocky Bowman, YN3 Frank Tinney, YNSN Corinne Williams, YNSN Rex Murdock, CWO2 William Bergbauer, and Chief Chuck Yard. Bonner, Yard, and Clinton were all subsequently commissioned.

Lieutenant Junior Grade Erv Lhotka, in the CNO's office, did a superb job of collecting basic documents for the period under survey, and Captain Don Dvornik helped me over the early hurdles.

At my request, Richard Halloran of *The New York Times* sent his fine write-up of the CNO's week. I used it in chapter 3.

Air Force Lieutenant Colonel Donald R. Baucom, the historian of SDIO, informally reviewed chapter 14 and made several useful suggestions. Captain Elizabeth Wylie did the same for the origins of the maritime strategy.

Lieutenant Commander Don Marcotte did a computer analysis of some 1,500 CNO daily schedules while he was a student at the Naval War College.

John Hanley of the Strategic Studies Group staff at the Naval War College furnished statistics on the group's flag section.

Mary Guimond, executive assistant to the dean of academics of the Naval War College, deserves special thanks. She and the hard-working women in the college's word-processing center handled the manuscript and its successive revisions with efficiency and good will. Ian Oliver's graphic arts division reproduced the tables.

The Naval War College Foundation generously provided the funding for my travels.

In concluding a long list, let me thank once again the four flag officers who consistently encouraged and supported me: Jack Baldwin, Hunt Hardisty, Ron Marryott, and Jim Watkins.

LIST OF ACRONYMS

ABM	antiballistic missile
ASAT	antisatellite
BOSS	Buy Our Spares Smart
BUPERS	Bureau of Naval Personnel
CAG	commander, air group
CAR	Center for Advanced Research
CEP	CNO's executive panel
C^3I	command, control, communications, intelligence
CINCEUR	commander in chief, Europe
CINCLANT	commander in chief, Atlantic
CINCLANTFLT	commander in chief, Atlantic Fleet
CINCPACFLT	commander in chief, Pacific Fleet
CINCUS	commander in chief, United States
CINCUSNAVEUR	commander in chief, U.S. Naval Forces, Europe
CMR	contract management review
CNA	Center for Naval Analyses
CNET	commander, Naval Education and Training
CNO	chief of naval operations
CNOM	chief of naval operations memorandum
CO	commanding officer
CVN	nuclear aircraft carrier
CVV	VSTOL aircraft carrier
CWO	chief warrant officer
DCNO	deputy chief of naval operations
DMSO	director of major staff office for CNO
DSARC	Defense Systems Acquisition Review Council
ENWGS	enhanced naval war-gaming system

FY	fiscal year
IDC	independent duty corpsman
IFF	identification, friend or foe
ITAC	integrated trend analysis capability
JDA	Joint Deployment Agency
JRMB	Joint Requirements and Management Board
MAD	mutual assured destruction
MIRV	multiple independently targeted reentry vehicles
MPS	multiple protective shelter
NAVAIRSYSCOM	Naval Air Systems Command
NAVOP	headquarters memorandum
NAVSEA	Naval Sea Systems Command
NAVSUP	Naval Supply Command
NEWS	naval electronic-warfare simulator
OPNAV	Office of the Chief of Naval Operations
OPTEVFOR	Operational Test and Evaluation Force
OR	operational requirement
POM	program objective memorandum
PRM	presidential review memorandum
QRMC	quadrennial review of military compensation
ROC	reserve officer course
ROE	rule of engagement
SDI	strategic defense initiative
SDIO	Strategic Defense Initiative Organization
SIOP	Single Integrated (Nuclear Attack) Operations Plan
SLCM	submarine-launched cruise missile
SPAWARS	Space and Naval Warfare Systems Command
SUADPS	shipboard uniform automated data-processing system
TACTS	tactical air combat training system
TOR	tentative operational requirement
UNITAS	U.S. Latin American Fleet Tour
USCINCLANT	U.S. commander in chief, Atlantic
USCINCPAC	U.S. commander in chief, Pacific
VCNO	vice chief of naval operations
VSTOL	vertical takeoff and landing
YN	yeoman
YNSN	yeoman seaman

PART I

TOPPING OFF

Chapter 1

THE POST–
WORLD WAR II
NAVY

To describe and analyze an institution like the U.S. Navy as it exists at any one point in history is a difficult task. The navy is—has always been—more than the sum of its ships and shore stations, more even than the men and women who wear its uniform. The navy is all of that and more—a tradition of over two hundred years' standing. Behind every ship and sailor looms the ghost of a predecessor; even ships inherit names.

The navy carries on the age-old customs of the sea. All sailors, regardless of nationality or epoch, are in some sense alike, for life at sea cultivates certain character traits. No other profession competes with it in eliciting respect for the forces of nature and an instant readiness to deal with the unexpected. It can be a cruel life for the unprepared.

Those who sail in ships of war must be ready at a moment's notice to engage in operations, to encounter enemy fire. Most American combatant ships are deployed to their wartime stations in peacetime. This fact sets the navy aside from other U.S. services. And, again, it encourages certain attitudes of mind. To cite a small example, the navy has to know international law. Thus the navy is in one sense straightforward and unsophisticated—the sea is not deceived by concealed incompetence—and in another sense sophisticated ("Join the navy and see the world"). It is a complex institution, though it may look simple enough to some from the outside.

The U.S. Navy exists to protect and defend the American people and to serve the duly elected government, which defines specifically what that role entails. Yet it has often lacked the essential ingredients—money and men and supplies—for fulfilling such a role. Not too many years before Pearl Harbor the Pacific Fleet had only enough oil to sortie out of

3

San Pedro for one or two weeks at sea; a few years later, with the advent of World War II, budgets were unlimited. As Captain Edward L. Beach tells us in his book, *The United States Navy: Two Hundred Years,* fluctuation in financial support (and public regard) is nothing new: "In 1815 the navy was one of the objects of the nation's greatest pride. Only thirty years later it had sunk to a nadir of national regard."[1] The same roller-coaster situation was evident after World War II as the navy struggled to phase out obsolescent ships constructed for that war and replace them with modern platforms. Struggled to do so while simultaneously responding to the operational demands, first of the Korean War, then of the Vietnam War, which rapidly burned up modernization funds. Struggled to do so while being the service always called upon for a quick response, a peacetime presence. Henry Kissinger's first question in a crisis was always, Where are the carriers? And, ironically, it was the carriers—very expensive to be sure—that attracted the attention of budget cutters like a needle to a magnet in successive national administrations.

Whether or not support is adequate, however, the navy's response has almost always been an ingrained "can do." The ships and the men will be driven to match the task. In the Vietnam War, a fleet short of spare parts operated at sustained tempos instead of being replaced on an orderly schedule.

The seesaw of conflicting requirements during a period of rapid technological change had drawn the navy to dangerously low levels of readiness by the end of the Vietnam War, just as the Soviet Union ventured to sea in force with its first blue-water navy. Tired and disillusioned by that war and encouraged by the prospects for detente, the American people cut back financial support at the very time the navy needed it most to renovate and replace the aging World War II fleet. The Carter administration's view of the strategic role of the fleet, a truncated role, provided a rationale for not really trying. Add to this the disaffection of American youth with military service and the popularity of drugs in the 1970s—the problems confronting the navy's leaders became formidable.

The solution to these and similar problems, as far as the uniformed navy is concerned, is in the hands of the chief of naval operations. Any CNO, on assuming office, is one of a chain of relay runners; he carries the navy torch forward through his tenure, but he starts from the specific position—with a set budget and a set number of ships, people, and programs. He will take the navy four years into the future and, given the chance, change much in those four years. Wherever he starts his race, regardless of what his tour brings, fair weather or foul, he must keep the torch alight.

The ebb and flow in defense budgets after 1945, we shall shortly see, produced drastic results, and even when problems were fewer there was always a lot of work to be done—as in the 1980–87 period, which is the focus of this book. But seldom was the plunge from the crest so unexpected as in 1945.

HIGH AND DRY WITHOUT A STRATEGY OR AN ENEMY

When Admiral Chester Nimitz, the famed commander of World War II, became CNO on 15 December 1945, he might well have thought that the navy would bask in the warmth of public approval for its role in the Pacific war. Instead, he found himself caught in the middle of an intense battle over a proposed unification of the services. That battle took place in the shadow of Hiroshima and Nagasaki, for the atomic bomb did more than prod a reluctant Japan into its final decision to surrender. To the surprise of the U.S. Navy, the bomb threatened its very existence. Atomic weapons convinced many in the public (and therefore in the Congress) that ships were now highly vulnerable targets, and that the air force could handle any serious threat to American security. After all, there were no other powerful navies afloat and the United States had a monopoly on the bomb, which was expected to last longer than it did. By eliminating Japanese seapower the U.S. Navy had become victim of its own success. There were enough influential voices now to proclaim that the day of fleet clashes was over. The battleship was said to be obsolete, and the idea of paying for large carriers instead of B-36s was not appealing. What would one do with carriers? And so Nimitz, a principal architect of the effective Pacific war strategy, found himself embroiled in a fight for the navy's survival.

Unification, favored by President Truman, would inevitably subordinate naval views of warfare to the army and the air force, which approached military problems with substantially different perspectives. Nimitz fought instead for coordination, a battle he eventually won with the passage of the National Security Act of 18 July 1947. But that victory was, in a sense, a negative one—the axe wouldn't fall until later. Many today interpret that first battle (and the subsequent ones, for the bureaucratic war over unification-coordination was far from over) as an argument over "turf" and resources. And it was. But the navy would hardly have fought so long and so hard if nothing more had been at stake.

Even those who have served a long time in the military may not realize, unless thrown together with members of other services, how the services differ in attitude and outlook—in what might be called institutional character. Differences derive from the experiences of personnel and from the environment in which they carry on their profession. The key points about people who wear the navy blue are two: they live with and on the sea, and their peacetime activities, at least since the 1950s, are markedly similar to what they would be doing in the event of war.

Obviously, a fair percentage of the navy at any one time is not deployed at sea. Even so, its attention is always focused seaward and the shore establishment exists to serve the forces afloat. In allocating resources, if there is a choice to be made between afloat and ashore, the navy almost always favors the former. Deployed forces are 90 to 100 percent manned, while shore billets if necessary are held at 70 percent. This attitude makes sense; it is the sea forces, forward deployed, that in the twinkling of an eye have to be transformed into fully engaged fighting forces. If war breaks out, the army must begin an extended mobilization (though army and air force units deployed with NATO or in Korea are basically in place), while the navy from the first moment is everywhere and in its entirety involved.

In *Defense 82* Admiral Thomas B. Hayward spelled out nine major differences between warfare on land and warfare at sea:

—Sea warfare is conducted in three dimensions simultaneously: above, below, and on the surface of the water.

—There are no battle lines at sea, and so rear areas are less secure than on land.

—The Soviet naval threat is worldwide, not just close to Soviet borders.

—Sea control is local and often transitory, shifting from side to side without signifying victory for the side with the advantage.

—All naval warfare involves maneuver.

—Naval warfare must contend with the presence of nonbelligerents.

—During peacetime, naval forces frequently interact with the forces of potential adversaries.

—Naval forces have relatively shorter logistic tails than land forces.

—The magnitude of surveillance at sea exceeds that on land.[2]

The navy recoils from the notion that it might have to operate afloat forces under the direction of other services, which do not fully understand the problems that operations at sea entail. And the history of joint operations proves that "unifying" is an extraordinarily difficult procedure.

In any event, these are the reasons Nimitz pushed so hard for substantial service autonomy. He also fought for the development of nuclear capability for navy weapons and propulsion systems.[3] Nuclear capability would give the service chips in the only game that counted now; it would be incorporated in the earliest possible stages of the technological race, and it would ultimately result in vessels (in this case, submarines) that were relatively invulnerable. As early as 10 January 1947, Nimitz "approved a policy of planning a submarine with nuclear-power plants [and] design studies for nuclear-powered submarines carrying atomic missiles. . . ."[4]

Admiral Louis E. Denfeld, the man who replaced Nimitz on 15 December 1947, was CNO when the unification struggle reached its zenith. Denfeld had to contend with an air force drive for seventy air groups (a total of 6,869 planes, 988 of them heavy bombers).[5] If he could build a supercarrier, one big enough for navy planes capable of carrying the bomb, he would break the air force monopoly on atomic delivery systems. But the supercarrier was canceled by the new secretary of defense, Louis A. Johnson (Forrestal's successor), on 23 April 1949. Johnson shifted funds to the air force, thereby setting off the so-called revolt of the admirals, congressional hearings over the B-36, and Denfeld's dismissal. Denfeld did win one victory: in March 1948, at the Key West conference of the Joint Chiefs of Staff on service missions, held while Forrestal was still secretary, he obtained agreement that strategic bombing would be a "collateral" function of the navy. That meant that the navy's quest for supercarriers and its program for atomic weapons would not be divorced from its roles and missions.[6]

The outbreak and conduct of the Korean War in June 1950 changed public opinion substantially. Air force bombers played no real role, but navy tactical air power, based on carriers, did. And it was the U.S. Seventh Fleet that stood between Communist China and an invasion of Taiwan. The "limited war" seemed to indicate that not all warfare would fit the World War II superpower scenario, that, especially in a nuclear age, fighting might be done by proxy, and that in such wars conventional armies and navies still had important roles to play. These circumstances, plus Admiral Forrest Sherman's undoubted abilities as CNO, shifted the old arguments to new ground. The navy could now rest one foot on its growing nuclear potential and another on its existing conventional capability. What was lacking, however, was a total maritime strategy. How did all the pieces fit together? And did any of them justify expensive supercarriers?

Dwight Eisenhower ran for office under the slogan "security with solvency."[7] He was much concerned with what he called the great equation—balancing military needs against the risks of national bankruptcy.[8] He directed the Joint Chiefs to plan a program of their own to achieve that balance. Out of their discussion came the "new look." As Paul Schratz points out, while the new look "placed its major emphasis on a strategy of using nuclear weapons as a deterrent to war" (Secretary of State John Foster Dulles's strategy of "massive retaliation"), it carried with it a number of qualifications.[9] The reason for the emphasis on nuclear retaliation was not simply budgetary, however; it reflected public impatience with the stalemated Korean War. Thinking had now shifted to the idea that retaliation should be directed at the brain center behind North Korean aggression, namely, the Soviets. As Admiral Robert Carney, CNO from 1953 to 1955, put it, "The policy was a single, unified plan to counter a centralized communist strategy rather than a succession of minor strategies to cope with brush fires."[10] No matter how the policy was described, it implied and brought about reductions in funding for the conventional forces of both the army and the navy. The navy still had no effective argument to justify a greater allotment of funds, and expensive carriers were hard to accommodate in Eisenhower's environment of thrift.

What was changing, meanwhile (although it was not yet appreciated by the public or Congress), was the naval capability of the major threat, the Soviet Union. As Soviet Admiral Sergio G. Gorshkov was to reveal in 1967, the USSR decided in 1954 to build a blue-water navy. Addressing the Naval War College on 16 February 1954, Admiral Carney noted Soviet merchant fleet growth and went on to say, prophetically, that "we cannot exclude that [Russia] will in time build carriers. The Russian Navy is the one Soviet service which is more heavily manned than in World War II."[11]

Admiral Arleigh Burke, CNO from 1955 to 1961, had an enormous effect on the U.S. Navy, partly because of his unprecedented term in office—nearly six years— and partly because of his desire to pursue long-range goals. Burke, even before he took office, was skeptical of navy arguments that in a war with the USSR carrier task forces would launch strategic nuclear attacks on Soviet industrial targets.[12] As CNO he began the policy that all new submarines would be nuclear-powered. He also went ahead with the development of the Polaris fleet ballistic missile. Nevertheless, beginning in fiscal year (FY) 55 Eisenhower's budget gave precedence to the air force, which consistently received 47 percent of the funds, while the navy got 29 percent and the army 22 percent.[13] Before a committee of Congress in June 1956, Burke argued that the navy was a highly flexible resource and could be effective in many cold-war scenarios where strategic air power would be useless. Burke preferred to stake out a unique role for the navy rather than to prove that it, too, like the air force, could drop the bomb.

He also calculated that he needed budgets of $16 to $17 billion annually to replace World War II hulls and modernize the fleet. What he got was $10.9 billion in FY 58, $11.7 billion in FY 59, $11.6 billion in FY 60, and $12.7 billion in FY 61.[14] Restricted funding at a time when the expensive Polaris program was under way forced economies elsewhere. During Burke's six-year tour, only three nuclear-powered surface ships were authorized: the missile cruiser *Long Beach,* the carrier *Enterprise,* and the missile frigate *Bainbridge.*[15] In March 1961 he told the House Armed Services Committee that by adding only 22 new ships a year—the average since 1948—the navy would decline from its active fleet of 817 ships to 440 within twenty years. His prediction did not miss by much.

The advent of Secretary of Defense Robert S. McNamara did not help the navy's situation. Indeed, Burke's successor as CNO, Admiral George Whalen Anderson (1961 to 1963), was in effect fired by McNamara after the famous flag plot altercation during the height of the Cuban missile crisis.[16] The two had already clashed over McNamara's all-purpose TFX or F-111, as it eventually became known. David Lamar McDonald, CNO from 1963 to 1967, was more diplomatic but no more successful in getting McNamara to appreciate the navy's point of view. The thinking of the defense secretary, who believed his young civilian aides knew more than his stodgy admirals, was about as far removed from the navy's as it could be. Whereas years at sea and sudden changes of orders or circumstances encourage the seasoned mariner to "play it loose," McNamara wanted to quantify everything, to know precisely what each weapon and platform was designed to do. He also wanted to judge potential performance against alternatives, especially to determine "marginal utility"—that is, the point at which one began to gain less for adding more.

The navy's admirals and the senior officers could hardly have been less intellectually prepared for McNamara's approach. They did not think in number terms like McNamara—they operated multi-purpose weapon systems that did not fit his mold—and they had not agreed on a formal maritime strategy to explain why the navy had to be configured in a particular way. Throughout the post–World War II era the navy had clung to the goal of fifteen or more attack carriers while searching for a good argument to justify them.

We have seen that initially the problem was more fundamental—to justify a navy at all. Next, saved by the Korean War and by determined progress to develop nuclear delivery systems (thereby remaining competitive in the service-budget ball game), the navy ran afoul of Eisenhower's determined budget trimming. It was when the number of fleet units was declining that the navy had to contend with McNamara. The situation deteriorated further with the Vietnam War. What that war meant to the

U.S. Navy was accelerated operational commitments with aging ships and increasingly tired crews on very long deployments. Budget money went not to new ships but to operations, where it was wasted from the point of view of modernization.

Long-term prospects for the U.S. Navy—especially for its large carriers—were now dimmer than ever. McNamara, testifying before the House Appropriations Committee for FY 63, commented:

> The principal use of the attack carriers in the years ahead will be in the limited war role. As we acquire larger forces of strategic missiles and Polaris submarines, the need for the attack carrier in the general war role will diminish. However, they will still maintain a significant nuclear strike capability which could augment our Strategic Retaliatory Forces. But in the Limited-War and Cold-War roles, the attack carrier force provides a most important and unique capability.[17]

This can be read two ways: as praise (carriers have unique and important capabilities), or as damnation (since they have little use in general war, they are not worth $1 or $2 billion apiece).

In the light of McNamara's statement, CNO Admiral McDonald's own statement eighteen months later could be interpreted as a fallback to a new defensive rationale for carriers. McDonald said that "the primary role of the carrier is, as always, in something less than all-out war. . . ."[18] He was perhaps trying to shift the argument for carriers by conceding McNamara's point (McNamara had also removed them from the Single Integrated [Nuclear Attack] Operations Plan). The CNO went on to say that even if nuclear weapons were effectively banned through arms control and the carrier were deprived of its role in nuclear deterrence, that would "not have any large impact on the need for the carrier."[19]

Even so, using expensive large carriers to sit off a coast and launch expensive jet planes against trucks in the Vietnamese jungle was not a role calculated to modernize and sustain a fleet.

THE VIETNAM WAR

We arrive at the most controversial and least satisfactory of all America's armed conflicts. Conventionally called a war, in a technical and legal sense it was anything but, causing in the end many more practical problems than if Congress and the president had faced the issue squarely.

Lyndon B. Johnson, who had been majority leader in the Senate before being elected president, was not well versed in world affairs. When he led the United States into the Vietnam War he soon encountered complex problems he was not ready to handle. Convinced that America had been challenged, he was quick to respond. But the identity of the enemy remained elusive. Was it the Viet Cong? The North Vietnamese?

Communist China? The whole Communist bloc led by the Soviet Union? Certainly the Soviets were furnishing the munitions. Where should the war be fought? Johnson decided to fight it both on the ground in South Vietnam and in the air (on a restricted basis) over North Vietnam. He did not want to broaden the conflict and take on China and Russia, too. That would have meant a real war, World War III, probably with nuclear weapons used by both sides. And so he proceeded with no clear strategy.

When the conflict dragged on, public support began to wane. The American military, doing their best, found a growing psychological gap between their sense of duty and public appreciation of their performance. Nothing symbolized the separation better than the reaction to the Tet offensive of January–March 1968. To the military it was a victory because the enemy had been killed in large numbers; to the public it was a sign that Viet Cong would fight on to the end, whatever the sacrifice.

After Tet President Johnson, discredited, retired from the political scene. Over the next few years, President Nixon repeatedly lowered the terms on which the United States would end the conflict, seeking an elusive peace with honor. In diplomacy, Nixon turned to detente—which many military men interpreted as appeasement, for U.S. military strength was rapidly declining.

"No more Vietnams!" the popular slogan went. It made a definite point, albeit unintentionally. To many Americans, it meant stay out of other people's problems, or let the Vietnamese kill themselves off if they want. To many strategic analysts, it meant choosing involvements more selectively, more "cost effectively." To many military men, it meant no more fighting with one hand tied behind the back. Why have a reserve, they wondered, if it can't be used when the chips are down?

These were varied responses to a common conviction that the use of force had been poorly applied under circumstances far from ideal.

Admiral Thomas Hinman Moorer, CNO from 1967 to 1970 (after which he became head of the Joint Chiefs of Staff) encountered all the problems of the later stages of the Vietnam War. In January 1969, he told Congress that 58 percent of the ships were at least twenty years old (compared with a Soviet figure of less than 1 percent).[20] The FY 69 shipbuilding budget was the smallest since 1956. When Congress passed the FY 70 budget, it made the biggest reduction in any defense request since the Korean War. The navy received the smallest outlays and only $2.49 billion went for ship construction and conversions. Under Moorer, despite his engaging personality and persistent efforts, the fleet declined to about 760 active fleet ships.[21] Shrinking numbers and smaller budgets, moreover, affected enlisted retention and operational readiness.

After Vietnam neither Congress nor the administration was prepared to choose between substantial cutbacks in U.S. commitments and adequate defense funding. True, President Nixon enunciated his doctrine that allies would have to use their local forces to carry more of their own defense burden, resorting to the United States as back-up. And his overture toward China reduced the enormous implied commitment of fighting the whole Communist bloc. But since the United States had never had the military capability to confront Russia and China simultaneously, the elimination of China as a meaningful enemy did not produce any surplus of American power.

Instead, this overture ("the China Card") and its companion move toward detente with Russia had the effect of giving the administration and the Congress a rationale for less defense spending. The public, emerging from the Vietnam trauma, was unenthusiastic about defense spending; the Congress could argue on the more sophisticated level (as, for example, Senator Jacob Javits of New York did)[22] that the success of the China Card had increased Russia's problems so substantially that the United States could afford to cut back spending. What Javits and the rest of the Congress overlooked or judged to be insignificant was an alternative Soviet reaction: to make great military strides quickly to repair the damage caused by their breach with China and by closer U.S.-Chinese relations.

U.S. defense spending thus declined while Soviet spending increased, as figure 1 indicates.

U.S. outlays had actually decreased before Henry Kissinger's first secret trip to Beijing in July 1971. Defense appropriations for FY 67 were 0.7 percent above the president's original request. For FY 68 they were 2.3 percent below that request, and in the next four years were 6.8, 7.5, 3.1, and 4.1 below it.[23] The China Card simply allowed a better explanation for congressional cuts.

In its report *The Military Balance, 1971–1972*, the respected International Institute for Strategic Studies cited the gross armed-force strength of the United States for that year as 2,487,000, compared with 3,025,000 for the Soviets. The same publication five years later (1976–77) put U.S. strength at 2,086,700, Soviet at 3,650,000. By the time of the 1979–80 report, the figures had become U.S. 2,022,000, Soviet 3,658,000. Thus, from 1971 to 1979, American strength declined by 465,000 while the Soviet strength increased by 633,000, for a net difference of 1,098,000.

The situation with naval forces is more difficult to represent, since in the 1970s the United States still had many World War II ships in commission while the Soviet fleet was new, and U.S. ships tended to be larger. What was perfectly clear, however, was that the Soviets were

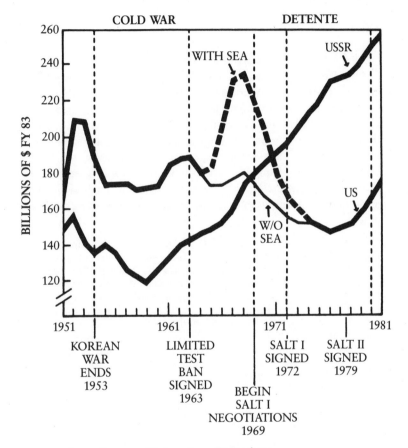

Source: Secretary of Defense Caspar W. Weinberger,
  Annual Report to the Congress, Fiscal Year 1983, p. I-20.

Fig. 1. U.S. and Soviet Defense Outlays during the Cold War and Detente Periods

building a larger, more effective fleet, both surface and submerged, and that their ability to sustain coordinated blue-water exercises was growing, along with a determination to keep substantial forces deployed abroad. Their use of Cam Rahn Bay as a forward-deployed naval base was an insult and a provocation to its U.S. Navy builders; their successful effort to control important choke points such as Aden indicated the magnitude of the new challenge.

ZUMWALT AND A SHRINKING FLEET

Elmo Russell Zumwalt, CNO from 1970 to 1974, tried radical surgery on all of these and other problems. Norman Friedman relates how Zumwalt sponsored a new long-range review of U.S. naval policy called Project 2000.[24] He began to retire older ships at an accelerated pace in order to consolidate his funds and reestablish balance in the fleet, emphasizing the low end of the "high-low mix" of ships.

In his memoirs Zumwalt correctly points out a little-noticed effect the Korean and, especially, the Vietnam involvements had on defense budgets—uneven funding among the services for replacing operational equipment:

> Not only did the Navy's share of the budget shrink during those wars because the Army and the Air Force underwent greater attrition of equipment, but under the circumstances the Navy had to put a disproportionate share of the money it did receive into maintaining its capability for projection—its carriers and attack planes, its amphibious vessels, its ships with the weapons for bombardment. . . . [S]ea control forces—anti-submarine planes and their carriers and ships suitable for patrol and escort duty—were allowed to obsolesce and, finally, retire without replacement. More damaging yet, work on future sea-control requirements—new types of ships . . . [and] new kinds of weapons with which to fight on the surface—was postponed for many years.[25]

Zumwalt went on: "I am not the person to evaluate my own bias, but I think it fair to point out that following three air CNOs in a row, as I did, I was bound to have some redressing to do." As he saw it, his predecessors had tried to keep the air fleet intact and Rickover had used his congressional clout to take care of submarines. The surface fleet had suffered as a result of hard funding choices. Zumwalt also pointed out that certain areas of warfare tended to be ignored by all three "unions": "No union has a vested interest in mines [or] in the increasingly great variety of electronic surveillance instruments that operate independently of ships or planes [or] in secure, high-speed communications. . . ."[26] The consequence was that the Soviets moved ahead in satellites and computers. Zumwalt determined to try to do something about this, too.

The key to solving most of the navy's problems was the budget. But Zumwalt, for all his energy, could do little to reverse the budget problem and its impact on the U.S. Navy's ability to execute its missions. He recounts having heard Moorer say that the view of the Joint Chiefs at the time of the *Pueblo* incident was that the Vietnam "half war" ruled out a simultaneous "half war" with North Korea.[27] Zumwalt's own estimate was "that as of 1 July 1970 the United States had a 55 percent chance of winning a major conventional war at sea, was heading toward a 45 percent chance as of 1 July 1971, and a considerably smaller one by 1 July 1972 if the budget levels under discussion were maintained. . . ."[28]

In a later estimate of 5 March 1971 sent to Secretary Chafee, Zumwalt was even more pessimistic about the FY 73 situation. He gave U.S. naval forces a 35 percent chance against the Soviets and added that he would reduce that to 20 percent unless the "tentative fiscal guidance" he had been given was changed. The United States was headed for a one-ocean navy.

The numbers bore this out. Before Zumwalt took over, active fleet construction from 1966 to 1970 was 88 units, compared with 209 for the Soviets (although most Soviet units were minor combatants). A chart in Zumwalt's book shows the total size of the Soviet navy exceeding that of the U.S. Navy in 1971, and he indicates that between 1970 and 1974 the total active fleet units in the U.S. Navy declined from 769 to 512.

Zumwalt testified in closed session to the Senate Appropriations Committee in March 1971. According to the record,

> Senator Case then asked what would happen if we had a bilateral conventional naval war with the USSR in 1972. Admiral Zumwalt replied that in his judgment we would lose.
> Senator Case stated that this was a devastating reply. He went on to state that if this was an accurate assessment, the Committee was wasting its time on this budget.
> Senator Young inquired of General Chapman as to whether he agreed with Admiral Zumwalt.
> General Chapman stated that he generally agreed. He said he believed that the U.S. had only a marginal capability of keeping the seas open in the event of a bilateral confrontation.[29]

Recalling this session in an interview with the author in 1987, Zumwalt put it equally bluntly: the United States would have lost a war with the Soviets during his watch, and Holloway's, and Hayward's. He remembered the response of Secretary of Defense Laird to this observation: "You've got to at least say, 'or else we escalate to nuclear weapons.' " Zumwalt had readily agreed. In the interview he also spoke of the corroding effects of the Watergate affair on national defense problems.

The whole government was in disarray, and coordination and trust were hard to come by.[30]

By the time Zumwalt turned over the watch to his vice chief of naval operations (VCNO), Admiral James L. Holloway III, the active-fleet figures had fallen further. By the time of the navy's February 1976 request for a five-year, $55 billion shipbuilding program, numbers had fallen to the lowest point since 1939—477 ships (compared with 976 ships at the height of the Vietnam War). And, despite Zumwalt's attempts to put a strategy together, it was still nonexistent.

PERSONNEL PROBLEMS AND THE CLIMATE OF THE TIMES

Elmo Zumwalt's tour as CNO is remembered best today, though, for an entirely different reason. The middle of it coincided with the "Vietnamization" of the Vietnam conflict—another way of saying that, one way or the other, the venture was being phased out. The end, 29 June 1974, almost coincided with the termination of the draft: in November of that year the last draftees in the U.S. Army were discharged. Zumwalt was therefore the first CNO to deal with the psychological aftermath of the war and the need to attract volunteers in a changed recruiting climate. He also had to contend with another spin-off of Vietnam: the war had accentuated racial tensions because blacks had been sent in disproportionate numbers to war. To racial issues could be added an increasing restlessness among an American youth no longer tied to traditional values and in a sometimes frantic search for what they called a more satisfying life-style. The navy did not produce this situation, but it had to do something about it.

Admiral Zumwalt devotes one-fifth of his memoirs specifically to personnel problems. He had no doubt, he writes, why he was chosen over thirty-three more senior candidates to be CNO. All of them had some plan for dealing with the Soviet maritime threat. What made Zumwalt stand out was his insistence that the navy's treatment of people was an even greater threat to its capability than its obsolescent physical plant. Rapid and drastic changes were needed. Where for years normal reenlistments after a first tour ran about 35 percent, the figure Zumwalt gives for 1970 was less than a third of that, 9½ percent. And the end of the draft, whose effect was to send those who did not want to serve in the army to the other services instead, "looked [then] to be no more than a year or two away. . . ."[31]

Right or wrong about what needed to be changed, Zumwalt plunged ahead. He put his emphasis primarily on doing away with the things youth considered "Mickey Mouse"—unnecessary, trivial regulations designed by an unthinking and unfeeling bureaucracy to complicate life. Why couldn't enlisted men go ashore in civilian clothes? Why were they forced to wear old-fashioned "sea scout" uniforms (bell-bottoms)?[32] Why couldn't they have long hair and mustaches and beards?

To overcome administrative inertia and produce change more quickly, Zumwalt chose a highly unorthodox method, the Z-Gram. These were policy or guidance NAVOPS (headquarters memoranda) emanating directly from the CNO and were numbered sequentially.[33] Z-5, for example, set up the pilot program allowing first-class petty officers the privilege of keeping civilian clothes on ship for shore liberty or leave, something hitherto restricted to chiefs and officers. This privilege was progressively extended until Z-92 of 29 July 1971 allowed it to non-rated men. Z-Grams arrived in a heavy stream in the first months of Zumwalt's tenure: 69 in the first six months, 120 in four years. They unquestionably cleared away time-encrusted deposits, as some of their titles indicate: Z-40, Cash/Check Option at Payday; Z-58, Acceptance of Checks in Ships' Stores. They also dealt with controversial subjects; Z-70 covered the grooming and uniform policy. And many, such as Z-84, Copies of Fitness Reports, and Z-21, Compensatory Time Off, seemed rather remote from the proper job of a CNO.

Even today, senior naval officers disagree about the changes introduced by Admiral Zumwalt. Some feel that changes were overdue, given the changing temperament and outlook of American youth; others believe that he produced an intolerable mess for his successor; all agree that he bypassed the traditional chain-of-command with his Z-Grams and special advisory groups for racial problems and the like. In an interview in April 1986, Admiral James Watkins expressed his opinion succinctly: "We lost it in the chiefs' quarters."[34]

Zumwalt supporters say his approach was necessary because otherwise bureaucratic stonewalling would have nullified his policies. His detractors point especially to the pernicious effects of undermining petty officer (and junior officer) authority in bypassing of the chain of command. Some straddle the fence: it was necessary to proceed as Zumwalt did, and it created a mess. Vice Admiral William H. Rowden recalled holding mast in those years and being told by the accused sailor that the CNO's Z-Grams said he could not be tried![35] Vice Admiral Staser Holcomb, a definite supporter of Zumwalt, thought the CNO was right to tackle the problem but wrong in his method. "I think the Navy came into the Twentieth Century under Zumwalt, and would not have otherwise. The *way* he did it left a lot to be desired. You came to work in the morning not knowing what new right had been granted overnight."[36]

Looking back on these events in the interview in 1987, Admiral

Zumwalt said that he should have spent more time briefing the middle and senior grades about why he was doing what he was. He called it a shock approach:

> We were in a catastrophic situation, with the antiwar mood and the antimilitary bias in the country and with the tremendous sacrifices our people were having to make with very long deployments. Our reenlistment rate was at an historic low—$9\frac{1}{2}$ percent. This meant that over 90,000 of every 100,000 sailors coming in were leaving at the end of their four years . We had to turn that around. From the standpoint of management alone, we had to shock the system.
>
> Those were moves we would never make in today's [healthy] navy.[37]

Zumwalt had a second major reason for his approach. He was convinced that he understood the sailors in Vietnam with whom he had spent twenty months in almost daily contact. They were not complaining about an unpopular war, he felt, but rather were fed up with the establishment. Changes were needed to reward them for their heroic efforts.

The draft begun on the eve of World War II had been continued in peacetime, and its administration, even during the Korean War, had aroused little controversy. Partly, this was because there were extensive recalls of World War II veterans and their reserve units. Also, American troop numbers were quite different. In early 1951 in Korea, there were some 250,000 U.S. troops; by early 1969 in Vietnam, American strength was 543,400. So it was in Vietnam that the draft became a sore issue; the war was longer (by four years) and required larger numbers throughout. Moreover, the draft deferred college students but took in poorer minority groups in disproportionate numbers.

The reenlistment problem and the minorities problem overlapped. Zumwalt wanted to make progress with both. In his memoirs he gives *first*-term reenlistment rates, showing a growth from 12 percent in FY 70 to perhaps 37 percent in FY 75.[38] (The petty-officer problem was not improving.) As regards blacks, Zumwalt found himself soon caught in a dilemma. Poorly educated black youths, recruited in large numbers, did not score high on tests and ended up in the worst jobs. In response to accusations of discrimination, Zumwalt had to find some solution. He came up with the notion of parity. That meant if 15 percent of the whites recruited were in "mental group 1," 15 percent of the blacks should be in the same mental group. In this way advancement opportunity would be roughly equal. Zumwalt explained his policy to the NCAAP and other black groups, who gave their tacit support.[39] The formula created equal opportunity in one sense, but necessarily restricted black enlistments in lower categories.

Whatever these initial problems, there is general consensus that Zumwalt laid the foundation for the navy's subsequent progress in this area. Minor but annoying problems, such as navy exchanges not being stocked with black hair-grooming products, have disappeared. More significant, the number of black officers had grown by mid-1985 to more than 2,200, although too few were flag officers. According to Admiral Watkins: "Minority enlisted composition of our force has grown significantly over the past five years [as of 1985], and reenlistment rates for blacks are almost a full 10 percent higher than the Navy-wide average. Retention rates for minority officers also exceed our Navy-wide average." Only a few years earlier, minority personnel had been "clustered within a handful of ratings and billets. This is no longer the case."[40] Zumwalt had set such progress in motion; his successors had no intention of reversing it.

One notable aspect of Zumwalt's approach: for better or worse, there was little said about the need for sacrifice, about tighter discipline, about sailors being an elite group self-confident enough to defy the path so many other young Americans were taking. Zumwalt's sharpest critics compared his program to the cartoon of the officer hurrying after his men saying, "Wait for me. I'm your leader." The comparison is not entirely unfair. It was inevitable that a program focusing more on first-term enlistee grievances than on restoring traditional discipline would create serious repercussions, especially for petty officers. Zumwalt's successors, Admirals Holloway and Hayward, would later have to try and restore a sense of professionalism to a depleted and discouraged petty officer cadre confronting problems in readiness and sustainability.

To give a fair assessment of the Zumwalt era and its aftermath is more than ordinarily difficult. The military services, for no real fault of their own, were in disrepute. The Vietnam draft experience was so bad it led to the end of the draft. Many ROTC units across the country were abolished. Anti-military demonstrations broke out in front of uniformed senior officers addressing public forums. The American flag was burned on campuses. And precisely at this point, an unprepared military became dependent on volunteers. The post-Vietnam environment was clearly not business as usual.

The abolishment of the draft was one more reason behind the decline in American strength, for it was inconceivable, given the climate of the times, that a force as sizable as that maintained in 1971 could have been maintained in 1979 on a volunteer basis even if Congress had funded the Department of Defense more generously. And then there was the question of the quality of volunteers, many of whom used drugs and resented discipline. This was the time when Project 100,000 imposed societal misfits on the military to "square them away." It was a time, like the 1930s, when judges extended an option before sentencing: Go to jail or join the armed forces!

Captain Ash Roach, who as a judge advocate general officer was involved in many of the disciplinary problems, made an acute observation, when asked whether it was Zumwalt's changes that had produced the feeling authority was being undermined (by passing decisions up the chain) or whether it was the way the war was conducted, Zumwalt's changes merely adding to an ongoing tendency. Roach saw the Vietnam conflict as far more significant, particularly because it eroded fundamental navy attitudes about clear goals (what were they in Vietnam?) and authority coupled with responsibility (how did that square with a president in the White House personally selecting the day's tactical bombing targets?).[41]

If we add that the moral issue in Vietnam was obscure or disputed, especially because strategic objectives were uncertain, Roach's point gains credibility. The total result, in any event, was serious disaffection or confusion on the part of American youth. It would be unwise simply to dismiss Roach's view when weighing Zumwalt's actions against Holloway and Hayward's attempts to restore morale.

HOLLOWAY, POLICY STABILITY, AND FLEET REORGANIZATION

By June 1974, when Zumwalt turned over the watch as CNO to Admiral Holloway, the navy was faced with problems everywhere it looked. In interviews in 1986 two senior four-star admirals used the same word to sum up the Holloway program: stability. Whether previous policies had saved the navy or ruined it (both views were strongly held in the officer corps), Zumwalt had certainly made many changes quickly, and a steady hand was required. Holloway provided it.

But he did more than provide stability. Like his predecessors he fought for a larger navy, but he was also, as Vice Admiral Staser Holcomb put it in an interview, a pragmatist. Holcomb, who had had the systems-analysis job under Holloway in 1974–75, was involved in 1976 in the major carrier study directed by Secretary of Defense Donald Rumsfield. Holcomb says that as a member of the study group Holloway took a serious look at the whole range of size options, all the way down to the 20,000-ton CVV (VSTOL, or vertical takeoff and landing, aircraft carrier), and that he was much more objective about the issue than is generally believed.[42] The study justified having conventionally powered carriers, and Holloway's view was that they would be better than none, even if he personally preferred the CVN (the nuclear carrier).

The active fleet numbers had fallen further. When the navy's February 1976 request for a five-year, $55 billion shipbuilding program was ready for submission, they were at their lowest point since 1939. And it was a year and a half later before Secretary Harold Brown authorized a full naval planning study to explain and justify budget requests, a study that became known as Sea Plan 2000. Sea Plan 2000 will be discussed at greater length in chapter 2. In the unclassified executive summary it listed three alternative force levels, options 1, 2, and 3. Option 1 called for 439 ships, option 2, 535, and option 3, 585. Option 1 was where the navy was or soon would be; option 2 was where the Defense Department's plans were heading; option 3 was the navy's real preference—close to the 600-ship navy.

Holloway's drive to reverse the disastrous downward slide in ship numbers was complicated by soaring costs (a belated reflection of President Johnson's attempt to have both "guns and butter") and a shrunken U.S. shipbuilding capacity. In addition, there was a congressional requirement that all new major combatant ships be nuclear-powered, a tribute to Hyman Rickover's persistent lobbying. That requirement added about 50 percent to the cost of a ship. (Not in terms of life-cycle—there costs compared well. But when Congress "buys" a ship it "pays" for it that year.) The conventional version of Aegis-type ships came to $858 million and the nuclear-powered version came to $1.3 billion.[43]

The nuclear provisions inspired by Rickover, whether desirable or not, had undoubtedly placed Holloway in an uncomfortable position. The argument could hardly have come to a head at a worse time. Holloway was dealing with the newly elected Carter administration, which did not favor carriers and which wanted the navy to focus on NATO reinforcement and to operate in third world crisis contingencies. The navy's World War II ships had reached the end of their traditional thirty-year life span. It was an era of inflation. Zumwalt had left the navy divided. And now Holloway was embroiled in an argument with Rickover. That argument became public by June 1976.

Holloway's basic decision, which precipitated the public split, was to go for a few high-performance nuclear-powered ships, combined with a large number of conventionally powered vessels. On 7 June 1976 *U.S. News & World Report,* quoting Admiral Holloway, reported, "With declining carrier-force levels, the reappearance of a strong naval adversary, the same overall global commitments, and no forecast diminution in potential trouble spots, the Navy needs a balanced and effective force of surface combatants."

On 17 February 1977 Defense Secretary Brown told the House Appropriations Subcommittee that the administration was planning to end future construction of large-deck aircraft carriers on the specific grounds of cost: "Continued construction . . . at $2.3 billion a crack would mean fewer of them. Neither I nor [Navy] Secretary Claytor nor Admiral Holloway think that would enhance security."[44] Holloway, speaking on the administration's proposal to drop further funding for a carrier from its fiscal-year budget in favor of two smaller VSTOL carriers, indicated he "would rather see a carrier in this year's budget . . . than two smaller carriers downstream." So Holloway was fighting at least a two-front war, trying to keep any carrier at all, nuclear-powered or conventional.

Secretary Graham Claytor, speaking of the Holloway tenure, said in an interview with the author that "there was never any question of a large carrier." As for supercarriers: "We weren't going to build any more. . . . There were no additional supercarriers going to be contracted for at that time. There was no money. We needed other things worse than carriers, and I thought so, too. We needed airplanes for the carriers we had, for one thing."[45]

Holloway faced serious deficiencies in fleet readiness and made substantial improvements, considering his funding difficulties. C-4 readiness (the minimum level) was reduced by 29 percent between 1974 and 1978, while C-1 improved 44 percent. In an interview Holloway keenly recalled 1975–76. At a session of one of the seapower subcommittees members told him they were thinking of initiating legislation so that COs whose units did not pass inspection would be relieved. Holloway told them he had good COs. "If you take them away I'm going to end up with poorer COs than the worst we've got now." Asked why he couldn't tell them to make improvements, he responded that that would be "like telling a Little League team to go out and beat the Redskins. We didn't have the talent. I didn't have the petty officers needed to supervise, and I didn't have people who were technically trained to do the job. They hadn't been through schools."

It was suggested that the crews be ordered to remain aboard ship until they got their ships in top material condition. Holloway tried to explain the facts of contemporary navy life: his men did not have enough technical skill or experience. There were fewer experienced people every day. And getting tough by canceling leave or liberty would drive the best away.

Shortages of spare parts made everything worse. Even with technical skill and experience, the sailor often had to sit around because he had nothing to work with. Holloway gave an example of F-14s lying unused for two or three months because of one missing part.

Congress did not take in the effect of this on morale or readiness. As late as 1977–78, Holloway said, Senator Culver of Iowa "horsewhipped me publicly" on the issue of readiness at a Senate Armed Services Committee hearing. When Holloway defended himself by saying that he had brought the F-14s up from 38 to 45 percent readiness, Culver was not impressed. Indeed, the problem was severe. Holloway recounted what happened when an amphibious readiness group of five ships deploying to the Sixth Fleet started across the Atlantic: "Only one or two reached Gibraltar. The others all suffered propulsion breakdowns in transit."[46]

Whatever Zumwalt had intended or achieved, Holloway was still dealing with a sick and loosely run navy. At one point, driving through Norfolk Naval Base on the way to look at an alcohol-rehabilitation center, his car was held up by crowds of sailors in the street.

> It was around noon. I was told that these were sailors coming up from their ships on the waterfront to the Enlisted Club for the daily happy hour from 11 to 2 with half-priced drinks and topless go-go girls. Here were these 18-year-old kids abandoning the noon meal aboard ship, drinking as much as they can stash away over the noon hour, and then goofing off the rest of the day. Not much useful ship's work was getting done after 11:00 AM.

After this the CNO established a rule: no hard liquor at on-base clubs until 1700. He also removed beer from the barracks, tightened hair-grooming standards, and changed the enlisted uniform back to sailor hat, jumper, and bell-bottom trousers. But he made the fewest possible changes in this area, for it was a period of stability, not change, that he was after.

Holloway did make one distinct and important set of changes: in fleet organization, and in the fleet's approach to fighting battles under the altered circumstances of modern warfare, where threats are three-dimensional and simultaneous. We shall return to this, the composite-warfare concept, when we look at fleet operations later on. Its essence is not difficult to understand: the battle-group commander uses negative rather than positive control. In three-dimensional warfare, authority has to be subdivided; the commander's job is to see that the whole makes sense rather than to direct the pieces as such.

In other areas, there was little Holloway could do to improve a bad situation. There were simply no funds. It did not seem that things could get worse. But before he was relieved, they did.

Chapter 2

A TIME OF TRANSITION

Vietnam was a watershed. Political pundits made much of the Kennedy administration as a fresh new breeze in American politics; in retrospect it and the Johnson administration that followed seem more like the last of the Mohicans. Who after Kennedy and Johnson and the Vietnam conflict would talk of "paying any price" just to "support any friend" or "oppose any foe"? The climate of the 1960s was one of doubt and widespread disagreement about the proper role the nation should play in world affairs. Military men frequently questioned what had happened to the national will. The Vietnam War, whatever else it did, ended America's era of open-ended commitments. We must be careful here; the United States still played a large role—there was no retreat to isolationism—but there was certainly a new caution, a sense that priorities must be established among competing demands.

THE CARTER ADMINISTRATION

The Carter administration felt that need strongly. When Jimmy Carter became president in 1977, he commissioned a presidential review memorandum, PRM-10. It was designed to show how limited resources could be funneled to maximum effect. In theater terms, that meant emphasis on NATO; in strategic terms, a "swing strategy" for the navy by which Pacific forces would move to support the NATO reinforcement effort; in platform terms, a further downgrading of carriers. Carter would go on to veto congressional appropriations for a supercarrier.

In FY 74 the defense budget had been 28.8 percent of the federal budget. In FY 79 it was down to 23.3, in FY 80 to 22.9.[1] President Carter's early budgets downplayed military needs generally and navy needs in particular. Zumwalt commented in 1987, "I met with Carter

24

early in his four years and he was literally contemptuous of the military point of view." Some three years later, Zumwalt "was one of 5–6 people of the Committee on the Present Danger who met with him to try to persuade him that he really had to get cracking. And then he called a group of us in from the Committee for a Democratic Majority . . . toward the end of his watch and almost beseeched us to support him, that he was doing right by the military. So he did a remarkable conversion after the Afghanistan invasion."[2]

The Soviets invaded Afghanistan in December 1979. In January 1980, President Carter declared that any attempt by an outside power "to gain control of the Persian Gulf region" would be repelled "by use of any means necessary, including military force." The important point about Afghanistan was that the USSR, for the first time since World War II, sent its troops beyond what the United States thought of as the line of containment. Hungary and Poland and Czechoslovakia were all in the Soviet orbit, and the presence of Soviet troops in those countries did not alter the balance. Afghanistan did, especially after the break between Iran and the United States. On 16 January 1979 the shah left Iran for a life of exile; on 1 February the Ayatollah Ruhollah Khomeini entered Tehran; on 4 November four hundred Iranian students seized the American embassy and took its occupants hostage, a situation that was to continue a frustrating total of 444 days.

These events had a pronounced effect on Carter's views and on American public opinion. The shah's Iran and Israel had been the moderate anchor points for American Middle East policy, and under Anwar Sadat Egypt had recently moderated its stance. Now that stability had disappeared, arousing visions of a Soviet march to the warm-water Indian Ocean. This translated into a quite different set of budget figures, with the president asking for more and the Congress outbidding him. For FY 80 Carter requested $135.5 billion (obligational authority); this was increased 6 percent by Congress to $141.5 billion. For FY 81 he requested $158.7 billion, increased a whopping 18.3 percent by Congress to $177.0 billion.

THE CARRIER QUESTION AND THE NAVY'S ROLE

When Admiral Hayward relieved Holloway as CNO in July 1978, Carter's initial approach to the defense budget had not yet altered. The argument about little carriers, middle-sized carriers, and supercarriers was at its height. VSTOL planes seemed to many critics of large carriers to be an obvious alternative. Holloway himself, as we have seen, ordered a study made of the merits of different-sized carriers. His conclusion was expressed most succinctly in an article he wrote years later: "The most telling disadvantage of the small carrier is that it is less cost effective than the big deck. Although the CVLX-45 [a design study for a carrier of about 44,000 tons] costs more than half as much as the CVN-72 ($2.08 billion compared to $3.0 billion) it has less than half as many aircraft."[3]

The argument over the big-deck carrier could be looked at on its own merits, as Holloway did here. But he and others grappling with this complicated political-strategic problem knew that the carrier had become in many minds a symbol for U.S. Navy. Opponents who zeroed in on the large carrier really wanted fewer navy ships; they were arguing about the shape of the navy ten years down the road. There was more at stake than just the supercarrier. Certainly, legitimate arguments can be brought to bear on the issue of small versus large carriers. And it is not necessary to believe in large carriers as the best solution to the navy's platform choices to understand that the argument was about roles and missions, though it was expressed in terms of numbers and platforms. That is why Secretary Claytor commissioned Sea Plan 2000, though he was unwilling to back additional carriers.

Take the point one step further. If the argument about the carrier was really about the size the navy should be if it were to properly carry out its roles and mission, then ultimately it was about strategy—about how a future war would be fought and what role the navy would play in it. The argument, at its most basic, was indeed about PRM-10.

According to Francis ("Bing") West, who became the Sea Plan 2000 director, Secretary Claytor and Undersecretary James Woolsey were having serious problems with the administration because PRM-10 said the United States "needed only 10 carrier battle groups, that you'd have a defensive barrier [along the Atlantic SLOC], that . . . you did not have to worry about the Pacific, that you did not have to go into the Norwegian Sea, that you'd fight along the G.I.-U.K. gap."[4] Vice Admiral Jack Baldwin, who had successive upper-level Pentagon jobs, saw the origins of Sea Plan 2000 in much the same terms but considered its thrust even more basic:

> When the Carter Administration came in they did a sort of zero-based review of the use of military power for national purposes. The output was called PRM-10. By and large it focused on a Europe-centered war. The assumptions were that it would be a short war, and because of the time it took to move the carriers from A to B or to get the sealift going in the Atlantic, naval forces didn't really come into play. Therefore, you didn't really need naval forces.

It would only be logical, Baldwin added, to put money into land forces instead; the navy was in a bad position—its carriers especially threatened—if this remained national policy.[5]

So PRM-10 was a war scenario; and by sketching in certain questionable assumptions, it reached certain questionable conclusions. But no one knew what a future war would be like—whether it would be long or short, conventional or nuclear, "small" or "big." Would nuclear weapons prevent wars between nuclear powers altogether? Or merely cause them to be fought conventionally? Or restrict encounters to indirect or third-party confrontations? This was the kind of academic debate that lay behind the carrier argument. The debate had begun after World War II and it continued unabated until after the Vietnam War. (We touched on some of its political fallout in chapter 1.) And even in the 1980s many defense analysts—Edward Luttwak comes to mind—were dismissing the likelihood of a third world war. The prolonged debate made it much more difficult for the U.S. Navy to argue any case, especially that of the large carrier, before Congress. It was especially difficult in the earlier decades because the navy itself had no internal agreement on strategic issues. The maritime strategy lay in the future.

In Zumwalt's time this fundamental problem was not given high priority, primarily because other issues crowded it out: how to maintain a high-quality all-volunteer force once the draft expired, and "how to maintain sufficient capability during the modernization process . . . to perform . . . assigned missions."[6] This is not to say that Zumwalt's lack of focus on maritime strategy was a mistake. The problems he mentioned were real: just keeping a minimum fleet in operational condition was a difficult task. To the extent that he did address maritime strategy, it was in terms of missions like power projection, presence, and sea control. But these are not missions so much as means to an end. The questions that should have been asked of these means were yes, but why? How? In what sequence? With what?

SEA STRIKE

While Holloway was still CNO but before Sea Plan 2000 was commissioned, an important planning and analysis project, Sea Strike, was under way in the Pacific. It was set in motion by Admiral Hayward, the CINCPACFLT (commander in chief of the Pacific Fleet). Hayward had been distressed about U.S. Pacific strategy when he took command of the Seventh Fleet. When he moved up a notch and became CINCPACFLT he saw that all the basic war plans had the same defect—they were oriented to strategic nuclear war. A conventional war with the Soviets had not been carefully thought out. In Hayward's view, the Vietnam War "had completely absorbed our time and attention" and war plans had suffered.[7] The SIOP included the carriers as back-up forces and not much else; but that was far from being the only role carriers or the navy could perform in the Pacific. Then there was the question of the priority assigned to the Pacific theater in the event of war. Hayward decided on a major overhaul of strategic thinking and enlisted the help of Captain Bill Cockell, nearing completion of a destroyer-group tour, and Captain James Patton, who had spent three years under Kissinger on the State Department's policy-planning staff.

In an interview with the author, Patton, ticking off a list of what was wrong in the Pacific in 1977, began with U.S.–Japanese relations. Most importantly, the Japanese had heard that U.S. forces would be withdrawn to the Atlantic once a major war began. They were worried, as were the Chinese: this "swing strategy" of PRM-10 would leave the Aleutians undefended, ripe for Soviet invasion. The army and air force were already concentrated in Europe or postured for quick movement there. Less than two light infantry divisions were spread through the whole Pacific area, together with fourteen air force squadrons (not wings). The navy was more equally distributed between theaters, with six carrier battle groups plus two marine regiments and planes in the Pacific. "The weakness of the Pacific-based forces of the Army and Air Force," Patton noted, "was the direct by-product of the NATO-first strategy, which assumed that if the mass of Soviet forces encountered would be [in the Atlantic theater], it made good sense to mass U.S. forces there, too." Similarly, because plans called for navy and marine forces to move from the Pacific early in any superpower crisis, the logistics experts had calculated that it would not make good sense to keep ammunition reserves and spare parts there: "so all of that was stored east of the Mississippi River—all of PacFlt's war reserves. That left a Pacific Fleet that would have been unresponsive to almost any contingency, let alone a war with the Soviet Union."[8]

Meanwhile, the Soviets had been steadily building up a large Pacific force. They had made great improvements in east-west transportation, including double-tracking and electrification for the trans-Siberian railroad. Every 150 versts (about 99 miles) they had established major repair facilities. The new Lake Baikal and Amur River line had alone increased transportation capacity by 50 percent. The United States had no way to attack these critical interior lines short of using nuclear ballistic missiles.

Admiral Robert L. J. Long, who served as VCNO from the end of the Holloway tour into the middle of Hayward's, and who then served as USCINCPAC (U.S. commander in chief in the Pacific), spelled the problem out. The Pacific area was being ignored in Carter's time and it was reflected in poor readiness. "For example," he said, "we had less than a week's supply of jet fuel in Korea for U.S. planes." Critical munitions shortages existed—in some categories there was less than a week's supply. And often as many as thirty ships "were considered unfit to carry out their primary mission."[9]

Something had to be done. Admiral Hayward's instructions, said Patton, were to plan to use Pacific forces in the Pacific, ignoring the idea that they would swing. To send a strong message of support to Tokyo and Beijing, and a message of deterrence to the Soviet Union, the CNO's strategic team decided to incorporate in their plans the idea of "prompt offensive action" in the Pacific.

It was not an easy plan to formulate. The navy, for example, had not carried out multi-carrier operations in the Pacific for a long time, and plans would need to emphasize hit-and-run tactics, mobility. Potential damage and loss had to be considered. The yardstick adopted was based on World War II experience: committed four times, carrier forces suffered at least a 25 percent loss in ships and a 50 percent loss in engaged planes. The maximum threshold for the new plans would be the same.

With this stipulation the team reconsidered many other aspects of their plans. As the Sea Strike scenario developed, it became clear for instance that airplanes up to that time had been loaded with ammunition in a haphazard fashion, with no regard to how it might be used; that multi-carrier operations called for a composite-warfare-commander system; that marines up to then "had no place [in the plans] for serious war against the Soviet Union" in the Pacific, at least in the colder climates (marine cold-weather gear was then stored in Georgia); and that the marines did not have any improved Hawks in the Pacific.

In 1976 Vice Admiral Julien LeBourgeois, president of the Naval War College, knowing of Hayward's interest, asked faculty member Francis West to do a separate study of Pacific strategy. It dovetailed with the work of Hayward's Pacific Fleet team. As West said, "Our study at the Naval War College stipulated that you would have to fight in the Pacific as well as the Atlantic in the event of a NATO war."[10] When Hayward endorsed the study, Secretary Claytor went to Defense Secretary Harold Brown for permission to expand it; that granted, West was made director and given a budget of $800,000 as well as authority to nominate the staff of officers (most of them Naval Postgraduate School graduates or operations-research specialists). This was how Sea Plan 2000, which took a year to complete, began.

Patton recounts how West came out to Pearl Harbor to compare notes. West's thinking at that point had Pacific carriers sitting far too close to the Soviet coast to meet Hayward's damage limits, which "created the requirement for 500-mile strikes." Veterans of 100-mile strikes raised their eyebrows, but soon they accepted the idea. Patton, noting West's forward-deployment approach in the Atlantic, at first argued against it on the grounds that Oslo and Bonn, unlike Tokyo, were going to fight anyway. Later, he understood "that the real value of a new strategy was in its deterrent arrangement and in its support for a new fleet, a new Navy."

Looking back on Sea Strike Admiral Hayward modestly commented that "it got too much visibility." This is another way of saying that he had set in motion events that were soon to have wider ramifications in Washington as Sea Plan 2000, its first cousin, took final shape. The product was two thick volumes, of which the second was statistical.

SEA PLAN 2000

Sea Plan 2000 was in fact only one of three navy plans, the other two of which dealt with missiles and sea-based air. But it was by far the main vehicle in the 1970s for responding to navy critics and advancing navy arguments.

The study begins with trends in the environment and the threat, moves on to an examination of the primary uses of naval forces and of the links between policy, force structure, and strategy, and ends with an analysis of engagements and naval capabilities in the future.[11] The analysis of capabilities, based on war gaming and other studies, is relied on to justify a fleet of about six hundred ships.

The critical argument in Sea Plan 2000 is cast around force structures in three options, as table 1 indicates. These options are weighed as follows:

—Option 1 is judged to be a high-risk option with a low degree of flexibility, with minimal capability across the range of naval tasks.
—Option 2 hovers at the threshold of naval capability across the spectrum of possible uses, given the risks associated with technical and tactical uncertainties.
—Option 3 provides a high degree of versatility in the form of a wider range of military and political actions at a moderate increase in cost over option 2.[12]

Another of Sea Plan's tables (not included here) looks at these options specifically in terms of risk. Option 1 has a high risk, option 2 a minimum acceptable risk (a bigger fleet), and option 3 a lower risk (a still bigger fleet). But neither the table nor the text explain how or why. Presumably, fourteen or fifteen CVs and ninety-eight SSNs (option 3 figures) considerably reduce risk, compared with twelve or thirteen CVs and ninety-four SSNs (option 2 figures). But why? Or, to approach the point another way, why stop with fourteen or fifteen CVs and ninety-eight SSNs? For a strategic reason? Or cost?

Sea Plan 2000 contains a great deal of useful information but it

Table 1. SEA PLAN 2000 ILLUSTRATIVE ALTERNATIVE FORCE LEVELS

Type	Option 1 1%	Option 2 3%	Option 3 4%
CV*	10	12	14
Aegis Ship	10	24	28
Cruiser/Destroyer	74	100	114
Frigate	136	152	158
SSN	80	94	98
SSBN	25	25	25
Amphibious Ships	52	66	78
Unrep Ships	38	46	55
Support Ships	49	60	61
Total Ships	474	579	631
MSC/NRF	−35	−44	−46
Total Active Ships	439	535	585

Source: Department of the Navy, Sea Plan 2000, March 1978, vol. 1, p. 18, table D.

*CV levels do not include a carrier in SLEP (service lift extension program). Thus, total carriers would be 11, 13, and 15 in the three options.

suffers from a lack of careful editing. It is difficult for anyone with limited time to digest. It is not surprising, then, that the U.S. comptroller general's analysis of navy studies, based on different assumptions, faulted the document severely: "We believe the Sea Plan 2000 study failed to achieve its objective of providing decision makers with a framework to make force size and structure decisions with more confidence and surety. For example, it presented three force level and funding options . . . based on known unrealistic funding assumptions."[13] This point is neither accurate nor fair. Every planning assumption about funding is arbitrary and probably in some important way unrealistic. The study itself shows, for example, the seesaw history of FY 79 and 80 budget proposals for shipbuilding. There were seven FY 79 proposals, with the final one proposing just over a third the number of starts envisaged in the most optimistic phase of the seven-step budget sequence. The seven FY 80 proposals shifted from an extreme of forty-five units to, again, about a third as many.[14] But the irony of these projections by the comptroller general is that the navy was in fact funded at levels higher than these "unrealistic" figures after 1980.

His analysis concluded:

> We believe Sea Plan 2000, especially its executive summary, is overly optimistic and shortsighted compared to present day and

future Soviet threats. . . . Also, many of the study's analyses rest on
unrealistic and/or questionable assumptions. Consequently, the results of battle analyses are more favorable to the United States and
allied forces than the Soviet threat would indicate.

Office of Management and Budget (OMB) officials said that Sea
Plan 2000 lacks innovative thought. It does not compare alternative
[that is, cheaper] ways of accomplishing Navy missions, but rather
took the traditional approach of adding more carriers to do additional tasks.

After all of this, the report recommends that the secretary of defense
"require the Navy to develop a sound force position that would include
recognizing funding constraints and realistically assessing the future
threat." The first of these two requirements is meaningless; the second
merely says that the comptroller general does not agree with the analysis.
This is admitted in the same paragraph: "Rather than assuming the
carrier to be the centerpiece of future forces . . . we believe the Navy's
mission should be prioritized and analyses of alternative ways to fulfill its
missions be made. Alternatives such as land-based aircraft (including
those of the Air Force) and surface ships carrying cruise missiles should
be considered."[15]

The navy's view, of course, is that it needs a balanced fleet to be
prepared to undertake *any* legitimate mission. To say that there should be
priorities established for missions is all right as long as one means that,
for a given type of war, choices about the sequence of operations must be
made. But the report seems to say that the navy should list contingencies
in probable order of likelihood and budget accordingly; in that case, the
nation would be left unprepared for certain, albeit unlikely, contingencies.

Sea Plan 2000 did briefly lay out basic notions critical to the
development of the maritime strategy, such as the need for forward
deployment and offensive action. It also looked at war in global terms. It
said that the North Atlantic barrier concept made no sense and that U.S.
submarines should take the offensive against Soviet submarines. But the
study's thrust was still toward justifying particular fleet configurations
from the standpoint of capabilities rather than strategy. This is apparent
from West's own statement in an interview in 1987: "The hypothesis that
the carrier battle groups could somehow refuse engagement was a silly
hypothesis. The key to doing this [engaging] with our carrier battle
groups—[remember] this was written in 1977–78—lay in the introduction of the phased-array radar and the acquisition of many targets
simultaneously. As a result, our first priority for the surface fleet was the
procurement of the Aegis cruiser."[16] Building a capabilities-based case
was worthwhile in any event. One study was not going to overcome

congressional inertia or sketch out a strategy around which what Zumwalt called the navy's "unions" could close ranks and concert planning. It was in this significant latter respect, as we shall see, that the maritime strategy of the 1980s went far beyond Sea Plan 2000. Though that strategy could be thought of only as the plan's logical extension, it would also provide a public stance calculated to deter Soviet initiatives.

Above all, Sea Plan 2000, issued in March 1978, provided a crucial year and a half of delay before the budget implications of PRM-10 would further weaken the navy's ability to fight. By then, the Iranian hostage crisis and the Soviet invasion of Afghanistan were taking their political and budgetary toll. That, Vice Admiral Baldwin commented, made the plan a bureaucratic (and, we could add, political) success indeed.[17] Furthermore, as West pointed out, it stirred up the dust in the Pentagon, setting off a heated argument over what size the navy needed to be to fight a global war. Another look was taken at how various NATO wars would be fought, particularly since charges circulated that the United States was not planning to defend Norway in Norway. The Carter administration, as a result, made a major effort to shut Sea Plan 2000 down.

Sea Plan 2000 also made a radical assumption, which Defense Secretary Brown suspected to be a ploy, by arguing that surface ships were becoming less vulnerable because of phased-array radar and that any war, rather than being quick and decisive, was likely to be both conventional and protracted. Until then, the assumption had been that in war the United States would initiate the nuclear phase because of NATO's conventional inferiority. In the study, said West, "we were [unable to envisage] any advantage for the United States in initiating nuclear war."

West was to join Hugh Nott and one or two others at the Naval War College in suggesting a global war game to test these ideas. After three or four games people were beginning to agree that the notion of "*un*global war," as West put it, was preposterous.

HAYWARD BECOMES CNO

On 30 June 1978, with this controversy in full swing, Admiral Thomas B. Hayward returned to Washington as CNO hoping to put the navy's tactical and strategic house in order. He found the same lack of standardized tactics in the Atlantic as in the Pacific Fleet. He was also very much concerned about the rules of engagement, which were too nebulous, certainly now that the United States had a blue-water Soviet navy to contend with. Closely connected to that tactical problem was a political-strategic question: How was the navy to portray its real capabilities and make understood its preferred wartime operational mode to an administration rather narrowly focused on the major theme of NATO reinforcement and the minor theme of Middle East presence? There were, after all, a good many ocean areas around the world, areas where the Soviet fleet could not be allowed to roam at will.

Hayward was a straightforward naval officer, not the person for devious schemes. As an aviator and former test pilot he was convinced of the merits of the large carrier, which was central also to Sea Strike's focus on offensive capability. He entered the CNO's office well aware that one defense secretary after another—including the incumbent, Harold Brown—had rejected this platform as too costly, too vulnerable, and not very useful in the event of a NATO war.

Hayward, who had served under both Zumwalt and Holloway, was director of navy program planning from 1973 to 1975. No stranger to the Washington bureaucracy, he knew he could not fight on every front and survive with enough clout to do the navy good. Rather than be a dead duck, and convinced that he had major, interlocking problems on his hands, he decided to dramatize the plight of the navy in a way Congress would understand.

The problems were much the same as Holloway's. The list began with personnel and morale and went on to include the material condition of an overused and undermaintained fleet, the resulting inability of the fleet physically to carry out its mission, a shortage of ships and planes and shells, officers unprepared to fight the war they might face, and an administration whose notion of war appeared downright naive. Quite a list.

As regards personnel, Hayward thought Zumwalt had been right to move in on the racial problem: "He led the nation, literally, in overcoming some very severe biases that we would have denied existed. . . . [I]n retrospect it is clear that they were there and they had to be addressed and the only way you could get us to move fast was to knock heads together." But as for

> the relaxation of what we would call traditional military standards—that caused the old professionals so much difficulty—I think that history will record that he was wrong. . . . [Holloway] certainly tried to start moving in the other direction, [and] I was in great disagreement with the erosion of the chain of command, with the denigration of the professional—the chief petty officer, first class, the captains, commanders and the lieutenant-commanders who were given little credit for having a dram of wisdom! This situation had to be reversed.[18]

Rear Admiral Bill Cockell, then Hayward's executive assistant, vividly recalled the tours the CNO embarked on to see for himself how things were. It was on a second trip to the Great Lakes, in the wake of a riot, that Hayward, Cockell, and two other flag officers decided to visit a disciplinary barracks that housed a number of deserters. They found the "inmates" for the most part wearing civilian clothes. Nobody yelled attention. About forty blacks were watching television on one side of a big barrier they had put up to have their own private area. The heads had no mirrors and most of the windows were broken. "Literally, the inmates were in charge," Cockell said. "We talked to a second-class petty officer who had the watch in there, and he was sitting inside a wire cage near the entrance. He said the watch always stayed inside the cage."[19] Flying back to Washington, Hayward put together a message for Admiral Malone establishing an 0500 reveille for prisoners, physical fitness drills, drastically restricted television access, and so forth. And he renamed correctional facilities "brigs," the old term.

The problem at Great Lakes was not just prisoners. The naval station there had thirty thousand military personnel and was run, like the recruit stations at Orlando and San Diego, by a four-striper. Hayward put flag officers in command at each. Where recruits had been going from boot camp to class A schools, which had no military structure, Hayward had battalions and regiments set up so that things would be run like a military outfit.

DRUGS AND PRIDE AND PROFESSIONALISM

If Hayward, unlike Zumwalt, did not have to face the pressure of near mutinies, he did have to contend with drugs on a large scale. According to Cockell, many if not most desertion and disciplinary cases turned out to be drug-related. The problem was severe—consider what drug users could do on a busy flight deck, hazardous enough with everyone cold sober and fully alert.

The submarine force had already started an anti-drug program. It came in response to the experiences of officers like Rear Admiral Robert C. Austin, later superintendent of the Naval Postgraduate School, who remembered how the problem of drugs had suddenly ballooned:

> I had been in 1976 to 1978 the commanding officer of the New London Submarine School. I had come out of a squadron command and I was aware of drug usage in the country, that there was a lot of marijuana smoking. But I wasn't aware of it [in a personal sense]. It just wasn't my world. When I went to Submarine School I was given very strict instructions. And I supported those. . . . Zero tolerance for drug usage. . . .

How to do that? I didn't know how. My first inkling came about when I made a barracks inspection and I found some evidence that there might have been some drug paraphernalia there. And I was naive. I didn't know how to recognize it. The senior chief laughed when I said, "What's this alligator clip doing here?" He said, "Captain, that's a roach clip. Don't you know what a roach clip is? It's a holder for the butt end of a marijuana cigarette."[20]

The days of innocence were ending for the navy's officer corps. Vice Admiral William P. Lawrence, who spent almost seven years as a POW and was superintendent of the Naval Academy for much of Admiral Hayward's tenure as CNO, said that the navy's response to the drug problem came just in time: "We erred in the early '70s. We took the attitude that drug use was inevitable. So we developed a rehabilitation program instead of a real tough prevention program. And, because of this, we had a real problem."[21] When the Office of the Secretary of Defense announced how many navy people used drugs, it was time to change. The 1980 drug-survey statistics from the Department of Defense showed not only that the navy use of marijuana and hashish was at 47 percent (tied with the marines), but also that the army figure was 40 percent and the air force figure 20 percent. The navy was worse than the others for all drugs. The air force cocaine figure was 2 percent, the army's 6 percent, the navy's 11 percent.[22]

Cockell recalled how the San Diego *Union* had done a report on drug use by naval personnel in the area and how Hayward at first did not believe it, writing it off as sensational. Cockell had a separate survey done to confirm it. Hayward reversed his position. Convinced by the figures that half measures would not do, the CNO tackled the problem head-on. In a videotape released in December 1981 and shown to every man and woman in the navy, he announced his "pride and professionalism" program and delivered a message to drug users: "We're out to help you or hammer you—take your choice." He mentioned the "get tough" directive he had issued: "That . . . policy is going to be transmitted down through the chain of command until every one of you feels it in your bones." He also had a message for the non-drug users, especially officers and petty officers: ". . . a drug-using serviceman is a wounded man or woman. If he, or she, cannot save themselves, then others must." The navy needed a 180-degree turn from "indifference, passivity, and non-responsibility" to "commitment, activity and accepting that responsibility which clearly is ours." It was in this video that the CNO coined the slogan, "Not here, not on my watch, not in my division, not on my ship or in my squadron, not in my Navy."[23] Zero tolerance.

By the time this video was released, Defense Department authorization to use urinalysis for disciplinary purposes had been given (December 1980) and new technology for wide-scale testing for marijuana had been developed. Before long, the navy would become the leader in random urinalysis testing. A March 1987 briefing sheet on the war against drugs commented that urinalysis was the most valuable detection and deterrence tool used by the navy. Recruits were tested within forty-eight hours of starting basic training. Those testing positive for any drug except marijuana were immediately discharged, while those testing positive for marijuana were cited with a first drug offense. If retests in the next six months showed positive, they were discharged. Retesting occurred when recruits reported to their first technical school and then three times a year throughout their naval service.[24]

The change brought about by this policy was remarkable in view of the pervasiveness of drug use outside the navy. Defense Department surveys document a reduction in nonmedical drug abuse from the initial high of 26 percent to 16.2 percent in 1982 and 10.3 percent in 1985. Productivity loss from drug use for enlisted ranks from E-1 to E-5 declined from 28 percent in 1980 to 15.1 percent in 1982 and 5.8 percent in 1985.

Simultaneously, the navy took extraordinary steps to ensure the validity of testing. For example, over six thousand blind negative urine samples per year were mixed with positive samples. Not one of the negatives was called positive between 1982 and 1987.[25] In FY 86, the navy tested almost two million urine samples three times by alternate procedures. Navy-wide results for drug use of any kind within the preceding thirty days declined from 33 percent in 1980 to 16 percent in 1982 to 10 percent in 1985. And, beginning in 1984, an extensive alcohol-abuse program was instituted.[26]

Pride and professionalism did turn the navy around on the score of drugs and alcohol. It aimed at prevention and (on a limited scale for careerists) rehabilitation. Eventually it would aim squarely at complete elimination of drug abusers, regardless of their rank or time in the navy.

TACTICAL COMPETENCE, PAY, AND READINESS

Dealing with drugs did not improve fleet readiness; it simply kept things from getting worse. There were positive problems that needed addressing as well. One was to improve the tactical thinking of COs, especially those who had flag potential—before they got their promotions to admiral. Hayward wanted every CO to know "when he walked on his ship that he was smarter than anyone aboard. Not when he walked off; when he walked on." To help change the situation for potential flag officers, Hayward created the Strategic Studies Group, to which we shall come back in chapter 9. But the problem of inadequate education for career naval officers went well beyond what one small group could cure. "Look at the Naval War College," Hayward said. "At no time when I addressed the Naval War College in four years was 50 percent [of the student body] wearing dark blue uniforms." Even those who attended followed a curriculum with the wrong emphasis: "War went out [of the curriculum] and management went in. Today [1987] we've reversed that. Not that management isn't important. But if you have to make a choice, I want the guy who comes out to be a tactical operational commander, able to fight a war."[27]

As critical, the students sent to the Naval War College were both fewer and less capable. Not only had the best officers naturally sought active service in Vietnam rather than duty under instruction. There was also the lure of the growing Washington bureaucracy and being "where the action was." The U.S. Naval War College, nominally the finishing school for future admirals, a place for intellectual growth and the encouragement of a vision for the future, was thus receiving few officers from command and sending far too few to command after graduation. The navy was being deprived of its seed corn. The result was a noticeable lack of cohesion and shared purpose in the U.S. Navy officer corps.

Training for the enlisted was in equally bad shape. Hayward went to every boot camp, every A-school, to get a feel for the situation.

> There was no commonality between one A-School and another. Take basic tools, for example: They were coming from salvage obtained by virtue of the initiative of the instructor—not the command, not the Navy. . . . Budget support wasn't there. Boot camps were pretty good. Then as graduates the new sailors would walk across the street for advanced schooling to a fourth-rate institution. Thirty percent of the acoustic tiles were out of the ceiling. There's a crack in the window. Unbelievable! That was the result of years of not enough money by the Congress of the United States.
>
> At the same time we were pushing the hell out of the fleet. There was no decline in fleet responsibilities; they were constantly going up. . . . The operator is going to take care of his primary responsibility, using his scarce O and M money for fuel. There's no money left to repair the curbs that are cracking or the lighting. We had to change that. And we did. It took a couple of years. . . .

Of all the problems Hayward faced the hardest to solve was money. Yet lack of money was the key to much that was wrong with the navy. Midway through his term, on 24 July 1980, he gave an interview to the American Enterprise Institute in which he said he would focus on three concerns: the inability of the navy to meet peacetime commitments, the Soviet navy's increasing global presence, and the lack of trained U.S.

personnel.[28] Money was the common thread: "My basic concern is that the Navy cannot meet its *peacetime* commitments today. No prior Chief of Naval Operations has made that statement, or has had to make it. . . ." Naval assets were not sufficient to defend the nation's global interests: in the Mediterranean the U.S. Navy was half the size it had been a few years before, and in the Pacific there were more Soviet ships operating out of Cam Ranh Bay and Da Nang than there were U.S. ships operating in the South China Sea. Hayward had no easy solution to suggest; ships took time to build and the United States was showing no disposition at the moment to put up the needed funds.

As the Soviets built submarines and VSTOL carriers, the United States had not even determined whether vertical lift was a sensible option: "While the Soviets proceed, we debate." A comparison of the Soviet and American efforts with air-cushion vehicles led to the same disappointing conclusion. Slow momentum was often attributed to paralysis by analysis, but Hayward thought "arrogance of analysis" would be a more accurate description; arrogance deflected badly needed professional military advice.

The weakest area and most critical issue was readiness. Almost every unit the United States deployed was only marginally ready because of the shortage of trained, competent personnel. The key here was either a draft or adequate pay.[29]

Again and again Hayward made the point to Congress that pay must be increased. At the Senate Appropriations Committee hearings for FY 81 he got a boost from Senator Eagleton, who submitted copies of newspaper and magazine articles on the pay issue, then asked the CNO to comment.[30] The 31 March 1980 *Newsweek* ran an article with a representative headline: "GI Joe Can't Make Ends Meet." Other articles mentioned petty officers with families who were eligible for food stamps, seamen working in their off hours at gas stations, and families living in rickety vans. Hayward kept pushing, despite the conviction of the other Joint Chiefs that there was little point, and succeeded in almost single-handedly getting Congress to raise the pay.[31]

Hayward could not turn everything around. The aging vessels of the American fleet were a continual headache for the shrinking number of careerists who had remained in the service awaiting a better day. Command opportunities grew more restricted each time another U.S. ship was decommissioned. To add the final twist, operational demands put upon the naval service by successive presidents had increased. From this point of view, the Iranian revolution had a drastic impact on the navy, requiring it to stretch its Indian Ocean commitment even further. As Hayward later commented, "the readiness of the fleet was at an all-time low. I had to literally create a new readiness-reporting category—'safe to steam' or 'safe to fly.' Safe. Not related to combat readiness or degree of combat effectiveness. Simply, can you get the ship or squadron underway and go out and do what you're being asked to do without having some significant casualty?"[32] To prove his point he cited an incident with the *Kitty Hawk* that had occurred during his tenure as CINCPACFLT: "The ship was steaming—just steaming—on its way to the Far East. Only three engine rooms and fireroom spaces were manned because the Fleet was undermanned so badly. We had to shut one main propulsion space down and trail a screw. Now here was a major offensive ship of the fleet with one screw out! We had E-3s or E-4s doing E-6 jobs. That's stretching it." As the men tried to deal with the problem, a fireroom was flooded and the *Kitty Hawk* was laid up for weeks at Subic Bay, unable to carry out her mission.

Who was to blame? Not the crew or the captain. It was a policy issue—the ships were undermanned—and the trail led back to Washington and Congress. As CNO, then, Hayward determined that Washington was going to be a part of the solution. He set up new readiness categories. Navy Secretary Edward Hidalgo and Defense Secretary Brown were "very uneasy about it. They all thought I was pulling a big stunt. 'Hayward's at it again'. . . . But I told all the commanding officers, 'If you're in such a state, don't get under way. Stop flying.' " The CO of the *Conestoga* did just that, sending out a message that it was unsafe to get under way. This was a gold mine for the media; soon press reports hit the White House. President Carter told the secretary of defense to order the navy to tone it down, but it was too late. Pressures mounted in Congress.

To internal pressures such as this, external pressures were added as the Middle East situation continued to deteriorate. Both Congress and the president did a turnaround which the Reagan administration, when it came in, would amplify. The navy's FY 78 appropriation was $38.6 billion; in FY 82, it was $67.5 billion.

Chapter 3

THE NAVAL ESTABLISHMENT

It has been convenient so far to look at the U.S. Navy as a monolithic institution; now it is necessary to turn our attention inside the institution, to understand how it is managed and how it functions, to comprehend how complex it is and, in the process, to lay the groundwork for an analysis of the major initiatives and issues that arose from 1982 to 1987.

Although it is designed to be a fighting force, the navy is also a large bureaucratic organization. In 1985 the number of civilian navy personnel stood at 342,400, while the uniformed side consisted of 500,000 enlisted and 70,700 officers. Marines were another 198,000 (including 20,200 officers). Add the reserve of 412,700 and the total naval establishment exceeds one and a half million people.[1]

Then there are the facilities. In 1985 these included 542 ships, 6,113 aircraft, and 193 major shore activities. In addition, there were 17 medical centers and hospitals, 27 air stations and facilities, 13 naval stations and bases, 10 ordnance activities, 8 shipyards, 6 naval air rework centers—the administrative picture is growing. And with 10 test centers plus 7 laboratories, we see that the navy is also a major research center. Finally, there is a broad range of training and educational facilities that offer everything up to doctoral degrees and include highly sophisticated war-gaming facilities.

The governing of such a navy is far from simple. The secretary of the navy presides over it. At the apex of the uniformed side sit the CNO and the commandant of the Marine Corps, each a four-star officer. The relationship between the navy's civilian head and its uniformed heads is a difficult one, in both organizational and administrative terms. That

41

would be true even if they did not have personalities—which, of course, they do.

THE SECRETARY OF THE NAVY

The secretary's position goes back much farther than the CNO's. On 30 April 1798 the Navy Department was created.[2] Benjamin Stoddart became its first secretary. By Truman's time and the end of World War II, forty-eight men had held that office for an average of just over three years. If we did not count Teddy Roosevelt's five secretaries the average would be higher. By contrast, if we take only the years between Frank Knox's confirmation, 11 July 1940, and John Lehman's, 23 January 1981, the average tenure would be nearer two years. Lehman, who did not resign until 10 April 1987, served more than six years, or triple the average since 1945. It is interesting that some of the navy's most traumatic periods coincide with the short-tenure secretaries, and that its most successful recent period coincides with Lehman's long tenure. The Lehman tenure came during an even longer tenure in office by Secretary of Defense Caspar Weinberger and President Ronald Reagan. An extraordinary stability prevailed in the top leadership.

The size of the naval establishment ensures that the secretary's first function is to administer. His second function is public relations: dealing with Congress, the press, and the public. For upon the public image of the navy its continued financial and moral support depend. Few secretaries in the time between Nimitz and Hayward considered it a major duty to probe into operational affairs.

The budget is a continual preoccupation—to be planned, fought for, spent, and monitored. Navy contracts represent enormous spending and improper procedures or carelessness here quickly evokes congressional wrath. So, in addition to being front man and administrator, the secretary is by law and necessarily the chief acquisitions authority.

J. William Middendorf II, who was John Warner's undersecretary, became secretary of the navy in the spring of 1974, at the end of the Nixon administration. He expended much energy trying to increase public awareness of the decline in navy numbers and of the simultaneous Soviet buildup and acquisition of bases adjacent to choke points around the world.[3] Middendorf also took a conservative view of the question of the secretary and flag promotion boards. His tour was the reverse of Lehman's in the sense that during it, musical chairs was being played for the top slots in the Defense Department. Although William Clement remained as deputy, Eliott Richardson, James Schlesinger, and Donald Rumsfeld all rotated through the secretary of defense job.

Asked about secretary-CNO relations, former Secretary John Warner, whom Middendorf relieved, said, "The relationship is never the same on any one day. . . . You must remember that the Chief of Naval Operations is in an advocacy role. He is always fighting for his branch of service. The civilian head of the Navy is unique in that he must accede to the directions of the President and the Secretary of Defense with respect to the allocation of resources among the three services." Warner mentioned also the competition between the navy proper and the Marine Corps for resources—an interesting observation in light of the fact that most commentators emphasize the "fair shares" formula that creates navy-marine harmony.[4] Whereas Middendorf fought primarily for the navy program, Warner saw himself more as the implementor of the defense secretary's directives.

Secretary Graham Claytor, who succeeded Middendorf and served under Carter, is the man who set Sea Plan 2000 in motion. He may not have seen its purpose through exactly the same lenses as those in uniform—he said that "it had been some time since we'd had a long-range look at where the Navy was going in the next 15 years or so [but] OMB didn't like it and we had trouble on the Hill. It never got anywhere, but most of these studies don't. They're a basis for further action"—but he was well regarded by the senior naval officers who served under him. Asked about his interpretation of the secretary's office, he commented that the secretary was not the chief executive officer of the navy but rather the chief administrative officer, who had to work closely with the CNO. As for division of labor, he was "the point man" in dealing with Congress and the rest of the government, as well as the one who ultimately decided most issues outside of strategy and tactics. And Claytor drew a careful line in regard to promotion boards. He felt it was not his business to interfere with either flag promotions or assignments, though he looked carefully at who sat on selection boards and thought hard about writing the precepts or rules governing selections.[5]

Other secretaries have intervened more, and more directly. Admiral Thomas Moorer, former CNO and chairman of the Joint Chiefs, recalled Secretary John Chafee saying to him:

> "I just met the most wonderful young officer. I want you to arrange for him to get three stars."
>
> "Who is he?"
>
> He told me and I said, "He won't be in the Navy six months from now."
>
> "Why not?"
>
> "Because he won't get selected for retention. . . . I just know his service reputation and when he comes up before the selection board, they won't retain him."
>
> He thinks to this day that I went to the selection board and said,

"Hey, I don't want [so and so]." I never did that. He's still shaking
his head about that and thinks I engineered it!

Admiral Moorer, at his last morning meeting as chairman of the Joint
Chiefs, in the presence of the secretary of defense and senior Defense
Department officials, made the following deadpan comment:

"You gentlemen have a qualification that I have never been able to
develop which I envy."
"What's that?"
"Well, when you make a trip overseas to one of the commands
and either have a short briefing or eat lunch with one of our
commanders, you always come back with one or two observations—
either he should be rushed to Washington and be made chief of the
service, or we should drum him out of the Corps."[6]

Moorer had seen many of these people in battle—he knew how many
children they had, how many divorces, when they got promoted, and
what commands they had had. But still he was uncertain about them and
wondered how a person's qualifications could be assessed in thirty
minutes.

Moorer considered the proper role of the secretary to be management and dealing with Congress and the media. The CNO was not a chief
of staff; his role as a professional military man was to know what
equipment was needed to meet requirements.[7] Moorer's point needs
qualification because of the National Security Act of 1947 and its 1958
amendments, not to mention the Goldwater-Nichols Act of 1986, which
we shall look at in a later chapter. Nonetheless, he located the crux of an
important question: whether military requirements can be successfully
separated from "contractual guidance," which is a secretarial function.
The issue was to come to a head in the Lehman years.

John Lehman had a view of his duties and powers that went well
beyond that of most other secretaries. On 2 November 1983 he testified
before the Senate Armed Services Committee that the division of labor
according to which civilian secretaries handle administrative and management functions and uniformed military handle strategy planning and
operations was not intended by the Constitution or sanctioned by
existing law. The secretary of defense and the service secretaries "must
worry as much about the soundness of military strategy, military
operations, military weapons and military leadership as they do about
the soundness of contract procedures and spare parts procurement."[8]

Lehman had a point in that, logically, all these functions are
connected. A secretary convinced that the navy's strategy is unsound can
hardly argue effectively for the navy's program before Congress or to the
media. Strategy governs the shape of the navy—or it should. It is either

implicit in requests to Congress or derives explicitly from them. Yet most secretaries are not equipped to make strategic judgments and few have attempted to. By and large they are chosen for their administrative and business know-how or their public relations skills, which is why most CNOs since 1945 have regarded the division of responsibility as Admiral Moorer or Secretary Claytor did. In this respect, John Lehman was unusual. He was an active naval reservist, author of a book about carriers, a Ph.D. in international relations, a man with both business and public relations experience, energetic, ambitious, the ideal secretary to lead the fight for a 600-ship navy. He was also destined to clash with CNOs accustomed to thinking like Moorer.

Vice Admiral Staser Holcomb, remarking that McNamara had stimulated the services into developing their own systems-analysis shops, said that the resulting program-development process ushered in a period in which "the service secretariats, because of the way *they* were organized, were largely rubber stamps." That lasted until the time of Lehman who, "for a whole host of reasons, decided to take charge of that process himself" and thereby produced tension between the civilian and blue-suit sectors. Nevertheless, "he drove a program with an embracing strategy through the Congressional process and made it stick."[9]

The usual navy drill when a new secretary takes over, of course, is to give him a series of briefings so that he "is brought up to speed" on programs, issues, and problems. As Admiral Holloway said in his first speech as CNO, no prudent captain alters the setting of the sails during the first fifteen minutes of his watch. Lehman had no patience for these elaborate briefings. After the first few he allegedly commented, "This is not doing me any good. I don't want all that stuff. I know what we're going to do and I'm going to *do* it. So let's not have any more of these. I'm going to tell you what I want."[10]

Not surprisingly, then, Lehman's tenure highlighted the question of whether we have what Admiral Moorer called "a bilateral system" with distinct functions for each incumbent, or a CNO who, in effect, is only the secretary's senior military assistant. Should the secretary leave certain areas open to the direction of the CNO, or should he provide detailed guidance for everything CNO does?

THE CNO

These would have seemed strange questions to those running the navy immediately after World War I. For many years the CNO had to bow to the secretary's authority for any decision of consequence. When the position was first established, just before the United States entered

World War I (and in anticipation of it), the powers of the office were distinctly limited.

It was created by a rider to the naval appropriations bill passed by Congress on 3 March 1915, and was intended by navy advocates as the rough equivalent to the army's chief of staff.[11] The bill provided for a CNO "who shall, under the direction of the Secretary of the Navy, be charged with the operations of the fleet, and with the preparation and readiness of plans for its use in war."

The CNO's term was originally four years. Admiral William S. Benson, the first incumbent, actually served four and a half years, from 1915 to 1919. By the end of World War II it had become two years; Admiral Chester Nimitz served from 1945 to 1947. The next four CNOs also had two-year terms. Arleigh Burke served from 1955 to 1961—an unprecedented six years. Admiral Anderson served two years. Finally Congress settled on a four-year term. Admiral McDonald served for four years, as have all CNOs since.

The 1915 act creating the billet reflected a controversy between the uniformed navy and the strong-minded Josephus Daniels, forty-first secretary. The navy was concerned that Daniels was not taking vigorous enough action to prepare the fleet for the possibility of involvement in World War I. And because Daniels was opposed to the new billet, the CNO had few assistants and little power.[12] The old bureau system continued to function and undercut his authority.

The bureaus represented separate clusters of power within the old navy—a condition Congress tolerated and at times directly encouraged. Designed to be the main functional components of the shore establishment, they were established on 31 August 1842, when Congress created five of them: the Bureau of Yards and Docks; the Bureau of Construction, Equipment, and Repair; the Bureau of Provisions and Clothing; the Bureau of Ordnance and Hydrography; and the Bureau of Medicine and Surgery.

Over the years bureaus were added and some underwent name changes. The Bureau of Aeronautics was created on 12 July 1921. By that time there was also a Bureau of Naval Personnel, the Bureau of Construction had become the Bureau of Ships, and Provisions had become the Bureau of Supplies and Accounts. The seven bureaus were still intact when World War II broke out and for years after it ended. Headed by senior admirals, they were resistant to central control and tended to treat the CNO as a prime minister rather than a president. From time to time, they even resisted the secretary's less ambiguous powers over them. Given the short average tenure of the secretary of the navy and the CNO's preoccupation with operational affairs, the bureaus often went their own way.

With hostility or indifference from both flanks, the bureaus and the secretary, the position of CNO needed bolstering. In August 1916 Congress mandated that "all orders issued by the Chief of Naval Operations . . . shall be considered as emanating from the Secretary, and shall have full force and effect as such." This did not lead to any dramatic change, and it was not until the 1920s that the office gradually grew in significance. In 1924 Congress gave the CNO control over "all repairs and alterations to vessels and the supply of personnel and material thereto."[13] Now all shipbuilding proposals were tested against war plans for which CNO was also responsible.

In 1930 Congress provided for an assistant chief, today's VCNO. But as late as 2 March 1934, President Franklin D. Roosevelt rebuffed CNO William H. Standley's request for authority over the still fairly autonomous bureaus by requiring that "the orders to the bureaus and offices should come from the Secretary."[14] Traditional American concerns over civilian control of the military were still very much alive. Not until March 1942, when the United States was already at war, did the president assent to requests for more authority for the CNO. In May CNO Ernest J. King used the president's directive, which gave him responsibility for the "direction of . . . the bureaus and offices of the Navy Department," to consolidate his control.

Admiral King considered his other hat as commander in chief of the U.S. Fleet (CINCUS) as more important.[15] The "wiring diagram" for his period as CNO carries the CINCUS title first, the CNO title second.[16] Robert Love comments that King "retained real control over logistics and procurement through his membership on the Joint Chiefs of Staff (JCS), created in 1942 by Roosevelt."[17] The Joint Chiefs exercised command authority in World War II. For King, being CNO was a third hat.

In September 1945, the CNO was finally and formally established as the senior uniformed officer of the U.S. Navy (when a naval officer chairs the Joint Chiefs of Staff, the CNO ranks as number two).[18] During Nimitz's short two-year period as CNO (1945–47), he not only had firm official control over the various parts of the shore establishment but also wielded more unquestioned power than his successors. Until the passage of the National Security Act of 1947, he could actually command the operating fleets. (He also had a second hat as a member of the Joint Chiefs.) The trend the 1947 act began continued with the amendments of 1958, which further restricted the CNO's direct operational authority. In the 1960s, however, the CNO increased control over the shore establishment; the old bureaus were finally abolished, replaced by "systems commands" firmly under the control of the CNO and the navy secretary.

Today, the CNO's relationship to the fleet is direct and clear in one sense: he must equip, train, and administer. This gives him a direct line to the commanders in chief of the Pacific Fleet (CINCPACFLT), of the Atlantic Fleet (CINCLANTFLT), and of U.S. naval forces in Europe (CINCUSNAVEUR). These commanders, though, are commanded by the regional joint commander (USCINCPAC, USCINCLANT, or CINCEUR). But then the CNO, wearing his other hat as a member of the Joint Chiefs, helps formulate and, through recommendations, actually shape the orders of the secretary of defense to regional commanders.

The law speaks of orders as being promulgated by the secretary of defense through the chiefs, but as Admiral Moorer has pointed out, "The Secretary of Defense practically never gives a direct order to a unified commander because he doesn't know how to write a message that would do that. He doesn't know which information addressees should be added."[19] Thus, although neither the secretary nor the CNO is technically in the chain of command, military decisions go through the Joint Chiefs for formulation and implementation. The secretary has no part in this. For a Claytor or a Middendorf, this is no problem; for a Lehman, it is.

As the uniformed chief administrator of a service, the CNO is under the authority of the secretary of the navy, who in turn takes his orders from the secretary of defense. This service hat involves the CNO in the budget process; he directs procurement and recruitment to meet military needs, appoints (or recommends appointments), and convenes conferences for commanders in chief. But as a member of the Joint Chiefs, the CNO does not report to his civilian secretary. He may even be explicitly directed not to tell the secretary anything. Admiral Moorer observed that "the service secretaries, when you get into classified operations, only know what the Secretary of Defense wants to tell them. . . . The CNO is not required to do it unless the Secretary authorizes it."[20]

In his book on the Joint Chiefs, Larry Korb illustrates what can easily happen as a result of such a setup: "Air Force Chief of Staff John McConnell and the other members of the JCS knew that Air Force planes began bombing Cambodia secretly in 1969 . . . , but Air Force Secretary Robert Seamans did not. . . ." When Secretary Seamans actually denied the bombings, embarrassment was inevitable.[21] In Moorer's view, since the secretary of the air force is not in the operational chain he would have been better off declining comment.[22] Lehman would not have accepted this view; it is telling that he titled his memoirs *Command of the Seas.*

Secretaries come and go with the electoral success of their parties.

Table 2. CNO Career Sequence

	1972–73	1974–75	1976–77	1978–79	1980–81	1982–83	1984–85	1986–87
Holloway	CINCLANTFLT COM7THFLT VCNO	VCNO CNO	CNO					
Hayward	SECNAV OFFICE OF PROGRAM APPRAISAL	OP-090* COM7THFLT	COM7THFLT CINCPACFLT	CNO	CNO			
Watkins	ASST CNP	COMCRUDES GRP1	CNP	CNP COM6THFLT	VCNO CINCPACFLT	CINCPACFLT CNO	CNO	
Trost	EA & NAVAL AIDE TO SECNAV	COMSUBGRP5 – ASST CNP OP-096	OP-096 (SYSTEMS ANALYSIS)	DEP/C OF S CINCPACFLT	COM7THFLT OP-090*	OP-090*	OP-090* CINCLANTFLT	CNO

*As of the end of 1989 OP-090 had become OP-08 and OP-095 had become OP-07.

Sometimes they have prior experience in undersecretary or assistant-secretary slots. But the civilian side lacks the cohesiveness of the uniformed side. Table 2, CNO Career Sequence, illustrates the point. Take 1974–75, for example. Holloway was VCNO, then CNO. Down the hall was Hayward, 090, and Trost, 096. Watkins was away but would be back soon as chief of naval personnel. They had all worked together and known each other for years; they were what Nelson called a band of brothers. He did not mean they were personally affectionate, but that they knew each other's minds and trusted each other. During any CNO's tour there are half a dozen or so CNOs-to-be who work to ensure success for the navy's program. The CNO makes the decisions and provides the goals, but he relies on a senior group to understand his mind and realize those goals.

Such cohesiveness does not exist automatically. Admiral Moorer, commenting on two four-star officers, said that in 1974 neither one had support within the navy and therefore neither one would have achieved much as CNO. (Both had become four-stars because a secretary of defense had been impressed with them.) But if a CNO does have the proper service reputation, as is almost always the case, he can normally count on loyal or sufficient support in a navy where professional behavior is the norm and whose senior officers have almost all been tried over the course of an extended career. The CNO knows that his senior subordinates will carry out his program, provided he makes it clear what he wants, does not allow bureaucratic red tape to interfere, and has a system for following up.

Only if the officer corps has a strong conviction that what a CNO does is not for the good of the service will there be trouble—as Zumwalt eventually found out. Impediments to success come from other sources. The program can be misunderstood by the public and by Congress. It can receive bad press. Above all, it can become bogged down. The day's agenda is full; it is time for the next conference, or a deadline has arrived. Problems are continually "bucked up" by the staff ladder for CNO decision. Or there is so much decentralization of authority that the major directors at OPNAV (Office of the Chief of Naval Operations) take off in their own program direction.

This being so, there are two prerequisites for the efficient operation of the navy. First, the CNO must have a good staff organization. We shall see later how Watkins, as CNO in 1982, attempted to deal with the centralization-decentralization issue by creating and strengthening "horizontal integration." By appointing the best talent to horizontal and vertical slots, he hoped to have the issues fairly and forcefully formulated and effectively argued below the level of CNO, thus conserving his time for fully informed decisions.

Second, as mentioned, the CNO must give the navy a sense of direction with major program emphases. This is critical to esprit de corps. As we shall see, early in his tour Watkins laid out goals in his "ninety-day message," which raised a number of the navy's most serious concerns, such as a revitalization of tactics. Many other initiatives, like the full evolution of a maritime strategy, would come later. But in this message the CNO was doing what the chief four-star admiral should do: he was telling his subordinates from the beginning what problems to attack.

THE CNO AT WORK

Today's CNO has a suite of offices on the fourth deck of the E-ring in the Pentagon, just up the passageway from the offices of the secretary of the navy. The suite is flanked at one end by a protocol officer, referred to as "the social side." Here distinguished visitors, foreign and domestic, are received. At the other end, toward the secretary's area, is a suite of working spaces. Next to that is the domain of the indispensable executive assistant and the CNO's main support staff. Behind the assistant's desk is an elaborate switchboard connecting major commands around the world to the CNO. The day's schedule is busy, and an efficient assistant is a must, for it is he who parcels out the CNO's time. The CNO's principal policy staff is also close by.

Beyond the office of the VCNO the Pentagon's corridors get narrower and fast-delivery messengers on bicycles and electric carts jingle their warning bells, posing a hazard to anyone lost in thought. The atmosphere is one of bustling alertness, of men and women operating at the brain center of the uniformed navy.[23] Richard Halloran, defense correspondent of *The New York Times*, published an account that captures the pace well:

> By the time the Chief of Naval Operations, Adm. James D. Watkins, rolls into his unpretentious office in the Pentagon at 0700 every morning, he has started to build a head of steam. Having read the Pentagon's packet of press articles on the 10-minute ride from his quarters in the Washington Navy Yard, the admiral flips through a sheaf of messages from the fleet and listens to aides brief him on the day's activities.
>
> At 0730, the Vice Chief of Naval Operations, Adm. R. J. Hays, and three other senior officers troop in to give the admiral the latest on Navy programs before Congress, advise him on breaking news and bring him up to date on such topics as aviation, submarine and surface ship programs, problems in research or medical or personnel matters.

> At 0830, Admiral Watkins ... strides 100 steps to the Navy Command Center, where briefing officers flash maps and charts on a screen to advise on the Russians' submarine movements or progress in building their first aircraft carrier. An operations officer points out to the 20 senior officers in the cramped room the location of American warships near Lebanon and operating tempos of ships in the Arabian Sea.
>
> At 0900 Admiral Watkins sets sail on the rest of his day, devoting about half his time to his duties as the senior officer charged with recruiting, training, arming and equipping the Navy, and spending the other half, as a member of the Joint Chiefs of Staff, on preparing military advice for the President and the Secretary of Defense, on debating and approving war preparedness plans and on overseeing military operations.[24]

Because CNOs have daily schedules it is possible to track with precision how a CNO spent his day. During his four years of tenure Admiral Watkins arrived every day, Monday through Friday, a few minutes past seven and departed about twelve hours later, putting in a half day on Saturday. Every normal working day the CNO must handle anywhere from fourteen to twenty separate items. (Appendix B shows a typical day, except for a relatively long working lunch.) Official trips also take time. In 1985, for example, the CNO made eleven trips abroad and twenty-nine trips within the United States, for an approximate total of eighty-nine work days.

During these trips it is the VCNO who doubles up his work load. That load normally involves directing the internal navy organization, the systems commands and major officers, as well as preparing the budget. If, as Watkins did, the CNO puts special emphasis on his role as a Joint Chief, both the VCNO and the executive assistant must take up the slack. When Watkins was in Washington he almost always went to meetings of the Joint Chiefs, and as a result his VCNO, Admiral James B. Busey, had to ease Watkins' administrative burden.

But a simple face examination of the almost 1,500 daily schedules between mid-1982 and 1986 is misleading. One reason, as Mike Boorda pointed out, is that they do not show what the CNO is actually thinking about during meetings. Where and when an important decision is made may never be recorded.[25] And time spent with Congress in particular is not accurately reflected for calender year 1985 by the sixteen recorded phone calls or the twenty-two other recorded occasions when the CNO met with members of Congress or their staffs. Phone calls aside, he spent a total of just over thirty-seven work hours in direct communication with Congress. This does not indicate, however, the countless hours he spent thinking about what to say to Congress or how to respond to its questions. Drafts of preparation for testimony may go through a dozen revisions each.[26] Nor does it include the hearings his senior assistants attend.

As for hearings, congressional committees hold them regularly to listen to the posture statement and discuss plans and budgets. When organizational reform is under discussion or a crisis occurs such as the bombing of U.S. marines in Lebanon, special hearings are held.[27] During hearings members of Congress raise many questions. In the navy files a computer printout marked 82 Mar 3 HAC shows no less than 242 issues being prepared for possible presentation before the House Appropriations Committee.[28] These range from single items such as personnel payment recommendations by Admiral Rickover to more complex issues such as petty officer shortages or the F/A-18's operational support costs.[29]

Staffing must be thorough to minimize the number of occasions when the CNO or the navy secretary, in response to questions on the various issues, says lamely, "I don't know." The CNO's files bulge with folders containing drafts and final copies of replies to written questions posed by Congress. The staffing this requires is elaborate, as Admiral Watkins's testimony before the Senate Armed Services Committee on 9 November 1983 indicates: in that year his staff "prepared and submitted to Congress more than 2900 responses to requests for information, provided 245 briefings, and submitted in excess of 4500 responses to questions for the record that emanated out of 110 hearings."[30] They also provided thirty-seven formal reports for the authorizations committees.

OPNAV ORGANIZATION AND REORGANIZATION

The CNO's administrative office, OPNAV, has changed enormously over the years, reflecting changing approaches to navy problems. This is borne out in a comparison of appendix C, OPNAV in 1942, and appendix D, OPNAV in 1985. What is striking is the change from an organization predominantly running units—such as communications, a hydrographic office, and a naval observatory, with a few functions like aviation thrown in—to an organization highly functional in terms of war fighting. Communications, for example, is no longer a separate unit; it is an integral part of command and control.

As the two appendices indicate, OPNAV underwent a slow evolution. In 1948 there was a general planning group, OP-001. In 1958 this group was called OP-90, and there was an additional, long-range-objectives group, OP-93, plus a research and development group, OP-91. By 1968 OP-90 was called navy program planning, and there was an OP-97 for strategic offensive and defensive systems. By 1971 the organization was closer to what we know today: 090 sat on the same diagrammatic line as the assistant vice chief, and there was an 093 for tactical electromagnetic programs, a 094 for command support programs, and a 097 and 098 for research, development, and evaluation. In 1974, 093 was gone but the 095 of 1968, antisubmarine programs, had become antisubmarine warfare and ocean surveillance programs. By May 1977, 094 had blossomed into command and control and communications (C^3) programs. By 1985, 094 was space, command, and control and 098 had dropped evaluation and added acquisition.

The OPNAV platform "sponsors" for air, surface, and submarines (the main "vertical" functions), although not yet on the 1962 diagram, were there by 1968 and from then on. But the effort to create a "horizontal" level for platforms and sponsors was less immediately successful. First there were strategic offensive and defensive systems, then tactical electromagnetic programs, and then antisubmarine warfare and ocean surveillance programs. The right formula proved difficult to find. Even so, by the time of the 9 October 1985 diagram, there was a significant expansion in the horizontal direction.[31]

As of 1985–87, the search for the correct balance had produced an OPNAV organization with DCNOs and directors of major staff offices (DMSOs). The DCNOs, "the barons," ruled over manpower (01), logistics (04), air warfare (05), and plans, policy, and operations (06). Of the eleven DMSOs, some had specific areas of responsibility, like the chief of chaplains (09G), director of naval reserve (09R), director of naval medicine (093), or oceanographer (006), and others had broad areas, like the naval inspector general (008) or the director of naval intelligence (009).[32] But four DMSOs had quite different functions. These were the four "horizontal integrators": 090, navy program planning (and the key man for the budget); 094, space, command, and control; 095, naval warfare; and 098, research, development, and acquisition. Here lay the real difference between OPNAV in 1987 and OPNAV during World War II. If there were barons and war lords (OP-02, -03, and -05), then these four were superbarons. Whether it worked that way is another question.

Most observers credited 090 with a great deal of clout, for he held the purse strings. Vice Admiral Daniel Cooper, a veteran of this job, described his role as "making sure [proposed programs] are presented to the CNO in their embryo stage so he can choose the direction he wants to go." Also, 090 oversaw execution and coordinated with the secretary. Here Lehman made a great change, said Cooper:

> In prior years, someone would go running by the Secretary's office and yell, "We're sending the POM down." And the Secretary would say, "That's ok." And that was it. Now we sit down with the

Secretary for 3–4 hours at a clip about 5–6 times, with several members of the Secretariat as well as the CNO or VCNO and specific flag officers of OPNAV present, and go painstakingly through each and every line.[33]

OP-094 was still new and his function was evolving. Vice Admiral R. E. Kirksey said that when "space" was added to his title it seemed "a little cosmetic at first." Nonetheless, he saw his role as "number-one integrator" because his area of responsibility was so great. "I tie the sensor to the shooter," he commented. As Rear Admiral Larry Layman (941) added, a main thrust of 094's role was to ensure "interoperability" between the navy's equipment and that of other services and allies. Kirksey described himself as the information warfare commander and coordinator in OPNAV.[34]

OP-095 was the "composite warfare commander" who integrated operational concerns. Vice Admiral James Hogg interpreted his role as looking across platforms at alternative ways of solving warfare problems,[35] which is what Admiral Hayward had intended in his FY 81 posture statement to Congress: 095 would "coordinate planning in the area of tactical warfare."[36] And 095 was to be the man who would, under the CNO and VCNO, establish priorities among war-fighting options. He therefore had large powers in one sense, but no money. The position as it was established represented a compromise; 095 would have as much responsibility as the war lords would accept.

Much depends here on the personality of 095 and the attitude of the CNO, for 095's reach extends only as far as CNO will allow. No one wants to shut off the views of the war lords, who, after all, represent traditional and ingrained lines of authority. They represent naval surface, air, and submarine communities that develop great confidence in their own respective ways of preparing for and waging war. Members of each community wear special identifying symbols such as the submariner's dolphins or the flyer's jacket. They have high regard for what their platforms and systems can do. That makes it difficult for them to appreciate what the other groups do or to accept the fact that money and resources should flow to them. This is where 095 comes in; he must determine whether enemy submarines, for example, are best fought by submarines, planes, or surface ships. Or, if all three are viable, whether they are equally cost effective. As John Lehman has observed, a multi-million-dollar airplane flown off a billion-dollar carrier to bomb a ten thousand dollar truck is not a good idea if there is any real chance of the plane's being shot down.

Watkins, who heartily supported Hayward's innovation, OP-095, said it began "to break the old bonds of parochialism inside the OPNAV staff." As VCNO he had helped Hayward establish the 095 position, and he was himself the sponsor of the new OPNAV slot 094, which accelerated and coordinated the navy's growing role in space. He saw 090 and 095 as coequals, each arguing from his special viewpoint: 095 would next sit down with 090 (the dollars man) and tell him the warfare priorities for spending the money. Watkins explained the process: "If 095 doesn't say that they need that to win the war at sea, we don't buy it," regardless of what the platform sponsors said.[37]

Rear Admiral Mike Boorda, although not downgrading 090's importance as the money man, described him as more concerned with whether the numbers added up and whether proposals differed from those of the previous year, and by how much—a straightforward and essential role. His role of setting priorities was crucial. Budget still ran the show, true; but now that budget was looked at from a different perspective. The scrutiny started out from strategic and warfighting considerations—095's very focus. The question then asked was what could *not* be done if the money were spent a certain way. Where were the "strategy stoppers"? This was where 095 played his crucial role.[38]

The three war lords did not disagree as to how the decision process actually worked out. Asked who resolved a disagreement between 02 or 05 and 095, Vice Admiral Bruce DeMars (02) and Vice Admiral Edward H. Martin (05) gave identical answers.[39] If it involved money, 090, otherwise the VCNO. A disagreement would have to be of Olympian proportions to bring in the CNO. In any case, decisions within this group were usually made by consensus. Vice Admiral Joseph Metcalf III (03) pointed out that differences usually stemmed from the priorities various branches of the service would attach to problems. Speaking of destroyers, he said, "I accept a leaky valve if to cure it means redesigning the engine room or quadrupling the price of that valve. It's not valves that count, it's ordnance on target." But a submariner cannot tolerate the idea of a leaky valve, for obvious reasons.[40]

The last step in the process 095 sparked was to "war-game the POM"—that is, once priorities had been set, to test the decisions on the game floor and see if in fact active or passive electronic warfare with hard-kill weapons gave the best payoff.

OP-098, last but not least of the four horizontal integrators, called himself, "the acquisition disciplinarian." Vice Admiral Albert A. Baciocco, Jr., saw 095 as looking at the emerging threat in terms of what the U.S. Navy did *not* have to counter it. There are never enough resources to do everything in the first place; just as important, not all technical solutions are equal. So 098, the "DCNO for decrements"—Baciocco's term—sees his job as keeping the system honest, not spending money for programs that are not proven, and eliminating anything marginal. So 098 worked in parallel with 095, looking at alternative technical options: "Do I populate the ocean's bottom with hydrophones across the world, or do I go and mine his ports?"[41]

The horizontal integrators in OPNAV represent not just wiring diagram changes; they reflect changed relationships in the fleet, which in their turn reflect the changed nature of modern warfare. OP-094 deals with the far-flung contemporary deployment patterns of battle groups linked over the horizon by satellite communications. OP-095 deals with the reality of modern warfare, far more complex than in the old days when a single platform or commander in active charge played such a central role. OP-098 represents Admiral Watkins's and Trost's view that the United States has to rely on its technological edge to deal with superior numbers. The positions of 094, 095, and 098 reflect the navy's thinking since the Holloway-Hayward days that the United States is facing simultaneous, three-dimensional warfare; that future battles will be fought over huge ocean areas and be much more complex; and that the role of the battle-group commander will be one of negation rather than initiation—the composite-warfare concept mentioned at the end of chapter 1.

OPNAV, THE SECRETARY, AND THE SYSTEMS COMMANDS

The relationship between OPNAV and the systems commands looks different to different people, as we shall see in chapter 6. OPNAV is in the Pentagon. In 1987 the systems commands were located in Crystal City, a mile or so away. Although the navy at this time had many commands, such as the Naval Intelligence Command and the Military Sealift Command, only four on the October 1985 locator chart had "systems" in their title: the Naval Air Systems Command, Naval Sea Systems Command, Space and Naval Warfare Systems Command, and Naval Supply Systems Command. There was also a Naval Facilities Engineering Command and a Naval Nuclear Propulsion Program. Sometimes all six of these were and are still loosely referred to as systems commands but the supply and facilities engineering commands and, to some extent, the Nuclear Propulsion Program, have somewhat different responsibilities and/or relationships.

Admiral J. B. Busey, who served as VCNO in 1986 and earlier as an air systems commander, described the OPNAV-systems command relationship and the acquisition process in the following way:

58

TOPPING OFF

The OPNAV staff establishes requirements. The CNO then represents those requirements to the Secretary of the Navy through a very formal process. A TOR [tentative operational requirement] is established formally. "We need a widget to do such and such." The Secretary having agreed with the operational requirement, it is passed by the CNO, by the OPNAV staff, to the appropriate systems command and they then respond by saying, "The state of the art can satisfy this requirement with this kind of vehicle and here is a range of alternatives for you and a range of prices." Then an iterative process goes on between the systems command, the OPNAV staff, and the Secretariat, working in tandem. They narrow down the options until all agree, "O.K., this is going to be [say] the SSN-21." When this is done, the TOR become an OR. The systems command is told to go and acquire it and the systems to support it. Oversight is provided by both the sponsor (in the SSN-21 case, OP-02), the Secretariat staff, and the systems command which acquires it. It goes through milestone reviews and ultimately out the end pops the new submarine and its life-cycle support systems.[42]

Since acquiring a submarine has budget implications, the new system must be fitted into the annual budget reviews by which the navy's POM is produced and survive the competition for funds. Equally important, once the decision to buy is made, the acquisition process must be managed efficiently. It is here that we come to controversial issues.

The navy, and the systems commands that acquire new ships and weapons, are used to the idea of the responsibility of those commands to both the civilian and the military sides of the house. The question is how best provide guidance from the top down, to the officers supervising the acquisition.

The systems commands used to be under their own four-star admiral known as the chief of naval material. He had an enormous staff whose function was to coordinate the systems commands, the systems commands with the secretary, and the systems commands with the CNO. In a joint move, Secretary Lehman and Admiral Watkins abolished this billet and the whole Naval Material Command. This raises a question: How well does the navy work without it? Admiral Tom Hayward, who dealt a lot with industry, commented that industry did not know who had responsibility for decisions. But he added that people eventually make changes work.[43] Most senior officers took the move in stride, and the chief of naval personnel at the time said he hardly noticed a ripple the day after it was made.[44]

One of Watkins' motives in doing away with the Naval Material Command was to sharpen the dialogue between OPNAV and the systems commands: "There needs to be more give and take between the technical people and the policy people in my office. So that we don't do dumb things. We don't over-spec. So we don't demand more than we should for the expected cost of the product." In the way had been "a huge bureaucracy . . . and we got rid of it. Now the door is open. . . ."[45]

But with the Naval Material Command went the coordinator of the systems commands. What about that? Watkins' answer was to emphasize the role of the newly created Space and Warfare Systems Command, popularly referred to as SPAWARS. SPAWARS' job was to look across weapons systems and platforms, whether sea or air or undersea, and think conceptually about three-dimensional warfare. The command was then to translate its ideas into advice for the Sea Systems Command, the Air Systems Command, and so forth to encourage broader thinking. SPAWARS would link up evolving operational concepts with long-range technological research and development. Its role in the systems commands was like the horizontal integrators' role in OPNAV, combining the functions of all four by focusing on space use and electronics.

But SPAWARS has no organizational mandate to coordinate the systems commands, and its head is the same rank as other systems commanders. This begins to explain why the perspective from the systems commands is a little different as they struggle to produce.

The loss of the Naval Material Command did not alter the dual responsibility of the systems commanders in reporting to the secretary for guidance on policy and acquisitions, and to the CNO for guidance on military requirements. It did alter how they reported, and it removed a four-star buffer from the process if and when the secretary and the CNO gave conflicting guidance. For it is perfectly clear that when the secretary prescribes an "acquisition strategy" (that is, the type of contract), he may easily run athwart military considerations coming from OPNAV. Who takes care of that?

We shall, again, return to such problems. The point here is to introduce the kinds of problems that exist and to suggest that they may be viewed differently from different ends of the telescope. The emphasis here has been on process. We shall see further on what happens with its products.

QUALIFIED FOR COMMAND

So far we have been concerned primarily with organization and administrative relationships. In closing this chapter, it is appropriate to consider what kind of person held the CNO post in the years from 1982 to 1987 when rising budgets allowed the careful planning and patient waiting of the lean years to be crowned with success. The CNO for most of this time was James D. Watkins.

The choice of Watkins was no surprise to the navy. He was a

contender merely by virtue of his being a four-star major fleet commander, CINCPACFLT. He had good professional tickets and a reputation for soundness of judgment.

Watkins had come up the nuclear submarine route, commanding the nuclear attack submarine USS *Snook* in 1964. He had served in the naval reactors organization, been executive officer of a nuclear surface ship, the *Long Beach*, and gone to BUPERS to direct the nuclear-trained personnel branch. Vice Admiral Chuck Griffiths, whom he relieved, called Watkins a superb detailer who "was so damned talented" that the chief of naval personnel had tagged him to recommend a major reorganization of the bureau. Watkins's recommendations were "almost revolutionary but very much needed."[46] They centered on the handling of enlisted rates. In 1971 Watkins, selected for rear admiral, became the first flag officer to be assistant bureau chief for enlisted detailing (1972–73). He developed a control system to forecast potential rating shortages. In 1973 he returned to sea and became vice admiral in December 1974. Then he was ordered back to BUPERS, where he served as its chief between 1975 and 1978.

Watkins took a radically new view of the job, using it as a lever to improve many parts of the navy. His attitude was simple and direct: I won't send you people if I think you are not using them well. At this time he demonstrated many of the professional traits that would become his hallmark.

First, his conception of his duties was broad. Second, he always asked what the key element or problem or question was. (In the case of BUPERS, as we have seen, the answer was the enlisted.) Having established a focus he would, third, consider what remedies to apply—a process he once called "looking for the parameters or margins"—and he would consider them in detail. Focus in conjunction with detail—this was what characterized his working method as CNO. He didn't have time for "sound and light." A present-day four-striper who used to attend meetings at BUPERS reports an early one in which Watkins listened for a while to the briefing of several junior rankers, then got up abruptly and said he would be ready to listen to their briefing once they had had time to prepare one.

From the time Watkins left the top job at BUPERS to the time he was sworn in as CNO was less than four years. In that period he served as commander of the Sixth Fleet, as VCNO with four stars, and as CINCPACFLT. During each tour his style of approaching problems became more pronounced: isolating the principle, considering the alternatives, mastering the detail, and setting up monitoring procedures to ensure results.

Although the circumstances Watkins confronted were favorable and he was the first CNO in years to enjoy the luxury of making up his mind about directions the navy would take, smooth sailing was not guaranteed. The budgets Reagan sponsored were contingent on congressional willingness to appropriate them. That, in turn, depended on the public's continuing conviction that the dollars were well spent.

Here Admiral Watkins had an invaluable ally in the form of Navy Secretary John Lehman. Although Lehman was relatively young for his position, he was also well prepared for it, both professionally and academically. Lehman was to lead a successful fight in areas such as ship-construction funding where Watkins could not legally or practically function. And Lehman's liberal interpretation of his duties and responsibilities, while creating internal frictions, also had the merit of forcing problems to the surface. As Rear Admiral David Jeremiah, who as executive assistant to the CNO dealt with both him and the navy secretary regularly, said, "In my judgment that combination of individuals may have been the best thing that could have happened to the United States Navy. . . . There were a whole host of things which the Secretary forced us and the Washington system to do."[47]

There is near unanimity about Watkins's personal approach among those who worked closest with him: Vice Admirals Jim Hogg and Scot McCauley, who were with Watkins when he was chief of naval personnel, and Rear Admirals Jeremiah and Boorda, already quoted, who were executive assistants when Watkins was CNO. Vice Admiral McCauley, like many people who have had a close professional association with Jim Watkins, was at pains to dismiss what he considers wrong ideas about him. Many think him austere. "You have to get to know Admiral Watkins," McCauley countered. "You have to break through that armor plate that he's got around him, that intimidates a lot of people. And about the only way you can do that is on an intellectual basis. But once you break through that, you find that he's a warm, compassionate guy with a great sense of humor."[48] Rear Admiral Jeremiah contrasted the public and private images of Watkins. Most people saw him

> when he was the Vice Chief and certainly when he was Chief of Naval Personnel as the guy who listened when you sat down and played his cards close to his chest, having very little to say. A very austere and reserved kind of guy, introspective. That's simply not the way he is. He's a very personable, outgoing sort of individual, with a lot of energy. He is a presence when he comes into the room.[49]

None of the officers who work closely with a CNO on delicate problems has the same objectivity by virtue of his calling than the chief chaplain. John Cardinal O'Connor, archbishop of New York, was chief of chaplains when Watkins was chief of naval personnel. O'Connor found him "incisive," a man "with a steel-trap mind." But because of his scientific background O'Connor felt that in those days Watkins did not give enough weight to the human side. Like most naval officers of his day, "he had not really been accustomed to thinking through how you make the human, the personal—and along with this the moral and the ethical—how you integrate all of this into a decision-making process." Watkins did not begin with the assumption

> that every major decision must include, as it were, philosophically, the moral dimension. And he was to a degree, a "What's the bottom line?" man and, many times, I would point this out to him and at times he'd be resistant. But, eventually, he would agree. And the point that I would make with him was that you can deal with numbers of ships and numbers of airplanes, and budgets, and strategies and plans—you can deal with all of these in that mathematical fashion and you can ask the bottom line when you're looking at an endless row of numerical figures. But this is not the way human beings work. You simply can't look at someone and say "What's the bottom line?" You have to listen through even though you think you know the answer. . . . He would always take this very well.[50]

Eventually Watkins's viewpoint became more humanistic, and according to Rear Admiral John McNamara, chief of chaplains at the end of Watkins's tour, his efforts in combination with Hayward's established a milieu in which the chaplain corps could function with greater effectiveness. McNamara illustrated this with a story. Watkins was holding a flag officer conference on AIDS.

> There was a thorough discussion of the medical aspects of the whole thing, including Navy policy, which permits the individual with antibodies who is otherwise healthy to remain in the Navy. One of the senior officers who was present, with a considerable amount of emotion, said, "And we all know that 90 percent of those people are either homosexuals or drug addicts. They don't belong in our Navy. We should get rid of them." And Admiral Watkins said, very calmly, "What about the tenth one? What about the innocent?"[51]

To get back to Watkins's work methods, in his first months as CNO he announced that he intended to make the Naval War College "the [navy's] crucible for strategic and tactical thinking" by sending "selected post-command COs through the senior course (or a portion of it) enroute to subsequent assignments. . . ." Such golden words (from Newport's viewpoint) were by no means unprecedented; CNOs in the past have often praised the college. But Watkins had an idea about how to use it, and his idea was precise. Instead of issuing a general blessing, something to the effect that "only the best should be sent," he selected the best, said when they were to go, and determined how it should be done—by collapsing the navy's various training pipelines so many weeks each and using the saved man-weeks to produce billets for people at Newport. Vice Admiral McCauley called this "a typical nuc approach. That's the way he does everything. He doesn't skip from A to Z. He goes A, B, and C. Each step identified. Milestones. He expects people to execute them."[52]

Watkins summed up his administrative philosophy in somewhat different terms: "It's a mistake to just come in and reorganize." Never "try to work the organizational problems first." Don't let the staff loose with an incomplete idea of what is wanted, for they'll spend a month going in the wrong direction. The CNO believed in gathering a small group to work up a concept paper, critiquing it, revising it until it was right, and then having it staffed.

The people Watkins drew for this kind of job had differing formal responsibilities. What the CNO sought were bright people who could argue issues and who represented various points of view so that through them he could find the center of gravity of a problem, the right "formula," the solution.[53] He wanted the controversy to crystallize and the perspective to be clear before going into detail.

In the next three chapters we shall see how that worked out as Watkins tackled personnel, command, and management problems, almost any one of which inadequately dealt with would have soon resulted in less congressional funding.

PART II

SETTING
THE WATCH

Chapter 4

CULTURAL AND PERSONNEL PROBLEMS

On the simplest level, what Secretary Lehman and CNO Watkins confronted in mid-1982 was a situation in which much needed to be done immediately. The navy was too small; it was divided and unhappy. It also faced daunting personnel, command, and management problems. Where to begin?

The single most complicated issue did not relate to the navy in a direct sense, but it had tremendous potential to harm the navy: the growing worldwide antinuclear movement. By the mid-1980s questions were being raised about U.S. nuclear-powered (or nuclear-weapons-capable) warships entering Japanese ports. The movement led to the rupture of an alliance with New Zealand and to a call for nuclear-free zones such as the Indian Ocean. At home, it lobbied against nuclear plants and weapons, with only limited success. But in a military dependent on popular support for funds and voluntary enlistments, it was no negligible issue.

THE CHURCHES AND THE NUCLEAR ISSUE

After the nuclear genie popped out of the bottle in 1945, military thought held that there was no defense, that the only way to avoid war was to deter the enemy from attacking. This deterrence would be achieved by maintaining a formidable nuclear arsenal of sufficient size and survivability to permit a devastating counterattack if the Soviets began a nuclear war.

As the decades wore on, these propositions came under more and more scrutiny, especially ethical.

American churches spearheaded the ethical debate over nuclear weapons and Christian conscience. Although some of the churchmen who took part in the debate were expressing optimistic, perhaps naive, assumptions about Soviet behavior and willingness to cooperate, their basic question was very much to the point. For they asked whether the American people, in response to a Soviet attack, could in good conscience retaliate with a force that might kill more than one hundred million Soviets. Many senior U.S. officials were dubious, too.

During the 1970s, as the Soviets were moving steadily ahead to increase their nuclear arsenals and the United States remained officially committed to deterrence, a significant portion of the American people were questioning the utility and the morality of continuing to build a nuclear deterrent. Some religious leaders were even questioning whether Christians should continue to serve in the armed forces. The criticism reached a crescendo in 1981, when, for example, a coalition of Protestant "peace churches" issued the New Abolitionist Covenant proclaiming that "Christian acceptance of nuclear weapons has brought us to a crisis of faith. The nuclear threat is not just a political issue. . . . It is a question that challenges our worship of God and our commitment to Jesus Christ." That same year at the annual meeting of the National Conference of Catholic Bishops in Washington, D.C., the conference president, Archbishop John Roach, denounced nuclear war. Two weeks earlier his predecessor, Archbishop John Quinn, had said that traditional Catholic concepts of "just war" were outmoded by nuclear weapons.[1] In 1982 the World Council of Churches issued a pamplet that said "the time has come when the churches must unequivocally declare that the *production* and *deployment*, as well as the use, of nuclear weapons are a crime against humanity."[2] In the same year the committee on war and peace of the National Conference of Catholic Bishops issued a draft pastoral letter that stimulated 700 pages of comments and recommended changes.[3] The revised document, 155 pages long, was adopted in May 1983 by a strong vote. It called for "immediate, bilateral, verifiable agreements to halt the testing, production and deployment of new nuclear weapons" and condemned all nuclear attacks on cities. The "deliberate initiation of nuclear war would be an unjustifiable moral risk."[4]

By the time Watkins, himself a Roman Catholic, became CNO, bishops of his church in some cases were publicly proclaiming that military service was incompatible with Roman Catholic teachings. It was to stave off an exodus that Watkins made his first important (and most reprinted) policy speech, "Moral Man, Modern Dilemma," in August 1982 at Marymount College in Arlington, Virginia. Later the text was expanded into an article for *Seapower*. Responding to portrayals of American military leaders as unfeeling automatons, Watkins said, "Let me begin with a fundamental statement . . . *I am a moral man*, I am constantly making choices, every day of my life—choices between good and evil." Sometimes the choice is more ambiguous,

> even, perhaps, between two apparent evils. But that . . . is a part of life. . . . What separates the moral person from the rest is that the moral person makes those decisions based on his or her conscience. [In the end choices] are mine alone [and] I must . . . live with the consequences of my choices and not be afraid of them. It is at this point that I, as Chief of Naval Operations, as a human being, but most of all as a moral man, put myself humbly before God. Then, having done so, I simply do the best I can with the choices at hand.[5]

With the choices at hand. But Watkins knew as well as the most troubled churchman or petty officer or first-team enlistee that those were not sufficient. He was ultimately to play an important role in broadening the choices at hand. In a later chapter we shall see that the navy's role in SDI and Watkins's assessment of the nation's moral concerns were closely connected.

THE MARITIME STRATEGY ISSUE

The second issue Watkins confronted was also complex. Although the Reagan budgets allowed much to be accomplished, it was vital for several reasons to capitalize on them by creating a maritime strategy.

In an interview four months from the end of his tour as CNO Watkins spoke of May of 1982, just before he took over, as a significant turning point. The ninety-page national security decision directive issued then laid out "our entire strategic policy," one "in sync with military thought," unlike the prior administration's policy. PRM-10 had been "a one-and-a-half war strategy; it was a fourteen-day war. It was centered on Europe as the only . . . area in the world we had to worry about. It ignored the Pacific. . . . It was a terrible strategy. It had nothing to do with the real world."[6]

The new national strategy, on the other hand, closely reflected navy views. Watkins hoped to develop a maritime strategy keyed to it and thereby ensure that the White House understood the relevance of the navy. A maritime strategy would bring the added advantage of restoring unity to a divided service. Handled poorly, of course, the attempt to formulate a coherent strategy could divide rather than unite.

There was, of course, a set of strategic maritime concepts existing when Watkins became CNO. Sea Strike and Sea Plan 2000 are examples. But, as Watkins said, the concepts lacked service-wide validity and tended to vary in content as senior naval leaders came and went. He couldn't refer to a document that had any real standing or was generally accepted, that was consistent with the national strategy. Moreover, with morale down, there wasn't any sense of common purpose.[7]

Watkins quickly found the way to change things. He called the maritime strategy his first priority and a key to the navy's success during his tour as CNO: "Once we all felt good about it, as we do today, the organization flowed from that. Because the people in the organization see themselves very clearly in the strategy. They know that a [proposed] reorganization supports the strategy" and therefore no longer see "specters behind every tree, trying to do them in."[8] Thus with one stone he could kill three birds: national strategy, internal unity, and organization.

Watkins tackled both issues, nuclear and strategy, turning potential failures into achievements. The true test of leadership is not whether adverse trends can be halted but whether they can be turned around and made to work for the good.

THE NINETY-DAY MESSAGE

Watkins once commented, "I know how to grease the skids, how to take the lead on implementation, and that's what I pride myself on."[9] He felt that the first step in any implementation strategy was to explain to the navy, in simple terms, what he expected of it. His first formal step in that direction came three months into his tour as CNO when the ninety-day message (see appendix) was distributed to major navy commands on 7 October 1982.[10] Staff responses were requested. Later the essentials of the message were published in newpapers.

All in all, the ninety-day message was an accurate indication of major problem areas Watkins would address during his tenure. Watkins singled out two areas of emphasis: readiness and navy management.

As to war-fighting readiness, the United States had to start by having modernized forces in adequate numbers to prevail. Building on that foundation, it had to revise and improve both strategic and tactical thinking, coupling that with timely utilization of a technological lead. That in turn meant acquiring "high leverage" systems that could be brought to bear on identified Soviet weaknesses. The result would be force multiplication.

The phrase "force multipliers" was to become common navy jargon in the years that followed. Force multipliers would give "immediate dividends" at affordable costs and were preferable to exorbitant capital investments in hardware.

Readiness was divided into five specific areas that required attention: technology, strategy and tactics, the officer training pipeline, the naval reserve, and interservice cooperation. The main point about technology—one Watkins would revert to many times in public speeches—was that the United States had only a small advantage over the Soviets and that Soviet use of America's informative open literature made lead time in exploiting that technology short, a mere three years. To exploit the lead the U.S. Navy had to move more rapidly to introduce "high-payoff-technology tools" into the fighting forces.

Watkins also announced a major innovation in strategy and tactics. This included his plan, mentioned previously, to make the Naval War College into "the crucible for strategic and tactical thinking" by rotating "selected post-command COs through the senior course (or a portion of it) enroute to subsequent assignments." Convening his first Newport conference for commanders in chief in the fall of 1982, he specified that by post-command COs he meant the top half of officers completing a command assignment.[11] Since the senior class at the Naval War College in 1982 included only about half a dozen such commanders, this was a radical change indeed. Watkins knew what he wanted:

> This immediate infusion of high quality, operationally proven professionals into the student body, coupled with war gaming emphasis, an operationally motivated faculty, and superb resident continuity provided by our new Strategic Studies Group there, can provide impetus to the longer-term objective of providing many more opportunities to test and harmonize tactical thinking in a wide variety of strategic applications.

The emphasis was clear: "operationally proven" career officers would join "an operationally motivated faculty" in gaming and as part of the new Strategic Studies Group "to test and harmonize" tactical thinking in a strategic content.

This was not the first time Watkins had thought of more effectively tapping the Naval War College's potential. As chief of naval personnel he had promoted the operational orientation of the curriculum and increased war gaming.[12]

To return to the ninety-day message, the third readiness concern was the officer training pipeline, which was "excessively inflated at the experienced officer levels." By cuts here, the additional billets for the expanded Naval War College class could be filled. Watkins subsequently ordered such cuts.

The fourth area was the naval reserve. The navy could no longer afford to think of reserve units simply as add-ons. They had to become integrated parts of the total war-fighting capability and thought of as such. Watkins wanted horizontal integration for the naval air reserve, significantly expanded surface reserve training, and fully integrated reserve-regular repair capability. The aim was to jump up readiness on call-up.

Watkins was commenting on a longstanding problem. The navy had not fully utilized its excellent reserves for years, and though it had begun to address the problem, Congress was turning up the heat. It was a time when the "total force" concept had taken hold. According to this, the nation in peacetime would not maintain sufficient forces to fight in wartime and, moreover, the reserves of each service would form an integral and vital part of its total fighting force. In short, the reserves were to be used.

The fifth readiness concern was interservice cooperation. Global wars would be fought jointly, and so the U.S. military would have to plan and train accordingly.[13] As General John Vessey, former chairman of the Joint Chiefs of Staff, put it: ". . . traditionally the Navy was often off in its own corner, saying, 'We've got our job to do. And it's a unique job. And it doesn't require a great deal of cooperation and support from the other services. And we don't have much to contribute to what they do. . . . Our job is different . . . and there isn't a great contribution for us to make in the area of [joint] operations' "[14] Vessey claimed Watkins changed that, a point we shall come back to later.

The other main area besides readiness that Watkins addressed in his message was management. He called for a more cost-conscious navy that would find innovative ways of trimming bills, particularly in the purchase and maintenance of hardware.

Management was divided into two areas: cost reduction and "individual responsibility to defeat waste." Cost reduction was further divided into cost discipline and cost technology. Cost discipline required "weapon system configuration control, independent cost estimating, hard-nosed contracting and competition in a variety of forms, e.g., second sourcing, contracting out and utilization of a man-day/dollar productivity competition among public yards and NARFs [naval air rework facilities] performing similar types of work, etc." Secretary Lehman's example was cited here in forcing F/A-18 costs down for FY 82.

Cost technology was described as "a mind set" that used price as a criteria in the design and operation of hardware and in the provision of spare parts for weapon systems. The aim was systems that operated with the utmost reliability but that were not designed to perform at the leading edge of technology for an indefinite period.

As for waste, again, Watkins said it could be fought with mind-set. Waste was not deliberate so much as unthinking: "Waste can easily and unwittingly flow from business management ineptness" and from "lack of personal involvement in and commitment to conservation of resources. . . ." The navy needed a tough, look-under-the-rug approach.

The CNO had much more to say along these lines. He did not think he was indulging in rhetoric.

Admiral Watkins concluded his message by inviting the thoughts and assistance of addressees and asking them to "readdress this message as you deem appropriate"—a navy way of saying don't put this on the back burner. As later chapters will bear out, every bit of this message was to affect the U.S. Navy between the years 1982 and 1986.

THE DIVINING ROD

Laying out a course is one thing. Getting there is another. Admiral Watkins had known in March 1982 that he would be the next CNO. Asked if he had had a fully formulated program in mind by June, he replied that he, like every senior admiral at the time, was too busy dealing with day-to-day problems. What he did put his mind to immediately was selecting key personnel.

One of those was then–Rear Admiral Henry C. Mustin, who in September 1982 became OP-008, navy inspector general. In an institution with serious problems, the inspector general can be the divining rod that points them out. Called into the CNO's office, Mustin was told to abandon the former formal schedule, which brought the inspector's team to installations at fairly predictable times, and to visit installations where the need was greatest. He was to stay away from minutiae, concentrate on policy-connected issues, and set his priorities by using the indicators of potential trouble that the CNO assumed he would find.[15] Mustin "found" those indicators rapidly enough.

The Office of Inspector General of the Navy was established in the early 1940s, by law in 1948. In March 1981, when President Reagan created the President's Council on Integrity and Efficiency, this office began a parallel consideration of how to improve the navy's campaign against fraud, waste, and abuse. It was still studying the problem when Watkins and Mustin took over.

In a briefing room at their spaces in the Washington Navy Yard, Captain Charles H. Kinney, Captain Kathy Laughton, and Pat Talbot explained what happened next.[16] A conference of senior personnel from the inspector general's office, held in October 1983, led to the creation of a plans and analysis division. This division centered around ITAC, the integrated trend analysis capability, which altered two things: the set schedule of inspections gave way, and automated support equipment was used to exhibit trends, including "a special projects list which changes daily as new issues arise."[17] A flexible inspection schedule, displacing the every-three-years sequence, made it possible to schedule visits where troubles were most likely to be developing. And those places were indicated by ITAC computer graphs. The whole operational style of scheduling and data-keeping shifted, and a new focus, on specific major problems that could be traced through different levels of the chain of command, was established. Pat Talbot dated this from 1982, following the talk between Admiral Mustin and Admiral Watkins. Then, as he said, "we went where the action was." The office performed training inspections soon thereafter, between late 1982 and April 1983, going sequentially to the Naval Military Personnel Command, CNET (Naval Education and Training Command), and the reserves. During those three inspections major problems were identified and presented to the CNO and the secretary of the navy for action.

What the office had done in addition to setting up a special projects list was to establish procedures for tracking cases from navy hotline calls. Complementing this was a system called TRACKER. It monitored "individual cases of potential misconduct by senior military and civilian personnel," in close association with the Naval Investigative Service.[18] Of 3,241 cases from hotline calls and congressional queries, 431 had been substantiated as of February 1986. In cases of contracting and procurement oversight or fraud, there were 1,206 open cases and 905 closed cases; 118 cases involving firms had been confirmed, 332 cases involving individuals.

Formal inspections were now followed up by computer monitoring to resolve discrepancies.[19] Inspection reports could go to any command level and portable computers accompanied teams to the field, minimizing delays in the dissemination of recommendations. By 31 January 1986 there had been 422 recommendations; of these, 33 had gone to the navy comptroller, 55 to the Naval Sea Systems Command, 24 to the Naval Supply Systems Command, 13 to the Naval Military Personnel Command, 29 to the Medical Command, 70 to the CNO, and 197 to various other places.[20]

The inspecting system was not just for detecting faults but also for correcting them. The source of more than half the problems lay at higher levels. In the CNET inspection, for example, at least half the adverse "marks" against the command were actually the fault of OP-01; these were relayed up the ladder for correction. Being "proactive" paid off in another sense. Kinney commented that "we're lucky if we have six hours' notice over the Washington *Post*." The earlier a developing problem was spotted, the less adverse publicity was likely to follow.[21]

The new methods used by the Office of the Inspector General were effective. In the medical area, for example, a credentials-verification program successfully eliminated a kickback scheme between navy surgeons and civilian physicians.

In all of this the Watkins method was obvious. There was the effort to break routine, isolate problems, implement solutions, and apply follow-up procedures. As Captain Kinney said, "The key thing is the direction from above."

THE TRAINING PROBLEM

Despite Admiral Hayward's strenuous efforts, nowhere in the U.S. Navy in 1982 was the problem caused by budget shortfalls more apparent than in the training area, which is why the inspector general began his investigations there. Technically, training is only a part, although the largest, of the charter of CNET, located in Pensacola. Established to give focus to a variety of courses held at many different locations, CNET has had a checkered career. Its first commander, Vice Admiral Malcolm Cagle, was given a two-star Washington deputy to represent him "nearer the throne." But the problem of a small flag community that dated back to Zumwalt's time convinced the navy to downgrade the CNET billet to two stars. In the view of Vice Admiral James A. Sagerholm, another past CNET commander, this was a mistake, for a two-star could not deal effectively with the three-stars he had to work with. Compounding the problem, OP-099 (the Washington Office of CNET) was disestablished, removing CNET from the daily action. OP-01 became DCNO for personnel and training. The fact that T for training was added to OP-01's title meant little. As Sagerholm commented, "The T got lost in the shuffle."[22] This was not surprising; OP-01's main business, personnel, was demanding.

In any event, by the time Admiral Watkins became CNO evidence was accumulating that systems reform was overdue. Symptomatic was the withdrawal, first of the Naval Academy, then of the Naval War College, from CNET's chain of command—testimony to the belief of both that their needs were not being served. In these institutions the complaint could be heard that education money was going to the larger activity of training. Actually, as we shall see, the problem was more severe than that; training itself was being shortchanged.

In 1982 Admiral Watkins told Sagerholm he wanted him as CNET. The navy secretary agreed. Sagerholm took the job reluctantly, knowing it would not enhance his career.

At the time, CNET owned seven billion dollars' worth of training facilities in ramshackle condition. Before relieving his successor at CNET Sagerholm toured several. In December 1982, at the Great Lakes Naval Training Center, he visited the headquarters of the flag officer in a beautiful old clock tower that dated back to 1912. It was raining hard when he was taken to an office at the top. Inside, the floor and desks were covered with rubber surgical sheets, duty personnel were in raincoats, and buckets were strategically dispersed to catch the worst of the leaks. Training stations everywhere suffered related problems. These were the places navy recruits received their first impressions of what life in the navy was like.

Rear Admiral Ken Shugart, the man Sagerholm was about to replace, explained with frustration that CNET's budget came from program sponsors, so that the command itself had little discretion in the use of funds. All the money was in O&MN (operation and maintenance, navy), which is where cuts were always made. The only discretionary funds were placed in an MRP (maintenance of real property) account. When the navy budget was cut back, CINCPACFLT would simply cut steaming a few days and air would cut flying; at CNET, maintenance would fall apart.

Money or its lack did not explain everything. Watkins, for example, discovered that "computer systems in our ships [used for tactical gaming and training at sea] had different values in them. I had my OP-095 send the ship's data to the War College and compare it. It was totally different."[23]

By April 1983 Inspector General Mustin's teams had made its visits to the Naval Military Personnel Command, CNET, and the reserve training establishment. Quickly thereafter Watkins zeroed in on the problem and directed the sponsors of these commands see that they were funded correctly. OP-01, under Admiral Lando Zech, was challenged to come back with a plan to make the T in his title stand for something. This led to a new two-star billet, OP-11, dedicated to training. From then on semiannual CNO executive board meetings on training were held and young two-stars were given various training billets. To be effective, however, these officers needed to feel that they were not being dead-ended; those responsible in BUPERS for training billet selections also had to be convinced.

By the time Sagerholm was relieved by Vice Admiral Ron Thunman on 31 October 1985, there had been a major turnaround. Morale had improved as paint was applied and flowerbeds were planted, grass was cut. Whether at Great Lakes or Pensacola or elsewhere, the difference was impressive.[24] It took a little longer to standardize the tactical data.

OFFICER CAREER PROBLEMS

For many years the Naval Academy was virtually the sole source of commissioned officers for the U.S. Navy. That has long since changed, along with the monopoly academy alumni once had on the most senior active-duty billets. But the Naval Academy remains the single most important source of officers, and it is the model on which NROTC and ROC (reserve officer courses) are formed. So what happens to the academy's curriculum is ultimately of widespread significance.

Since World War II a number of changes to it have been made, including the institution of the 80–20 rule (80 percent of the midshipmen must pursue hard-science majors, 20 percent, other majors). The rule answered a concern that the navy was not producing enough technically oriented officers during an age when the nuclear navy was expanding.[25]

There was no unanimity on this point. Watkins himself felt strongly that the navy needed a sound technical foundation; but, beyond that, he felt that all work at the academy, not just sciences, should be demanding and that a central body of naval knowledge be taught. That, for him, was the real issue—a basic core of hard courses for all, so that "any graduate of the Academy should have the *potential* to go into any field in the Navy."[26] Secretary Lehman, for his part, felt that the academy was turning away young people with broad interests. Ultimately he outlined an approach which the superintendent of the academy acted on; it added more humanities courses to the core curriculum and arranged electives in groups to replace a program of free choice that lacked focus. An honors program in humanities was also established. The 80–20 rule was taken off the books.[27]

Admissions criteria also changed. About seven criteria were used to evaluate candidates; now less weight was given to math scores and more to verbal. A humanities-oriented Strong-Campbell test was added to supplement the engineering test, and the higher score of the two was incorporated in the "candidate multiple." The 1986 results broke accepted candidates into an engineering-humanities ratio of approximately 70–30.[28]

The argument over the undergraduate curriculum at Annapolis (and in NROTCs) had even broader implications on the graduate level. The army and air force, not hampered by long tours at sea, could muster a far greater percentage of Ph.D.s for joint-staff positions where such a degree was often an automatic qualification. To acquire a doctoral degree took a big bite out of a thirty-year career. As a result, for many years if not still, Ph.D.s, even those who received their degrees with navy funds, seemed to be passed over for captain and flag rank far too many times.

Vice Admiral Lando Zech, chief of naval personnel from 1980 to 1983 made the point strongly that the navy has to be constantly ready for war and must therefore regularly send its best people to sea. It is too simple to equate academic degrees and professional ability. Zech told a story about a submarine skipper he nominated for the Joint Staff. The nominee was rejected; he had lots of sea duty but no Ph.D. So he was sent instead to command a nuclear submarine. The secretary of defense went out on that submarine and was impressed with the commander, so much so that he turned to his aide and asked, "Why can't I get this kind of officer on the Joint Staff?"[29]

Unquestionably, this problem was not solved in the period covered by this book. At its close, with the passage of the Goldwater-Nichols Defense Reorganization Act, pressures actually increased. The navy, which had never put joint duty as high on its list of priorities as other services, and which had lagged behind in filling the job of quotas for billets with the Joint Chiefs, was now confronted by legislation that effectively barred the door to advancement to the most senior billets for those without fairly extensive joint-duty experience. Since the navy has been commissioning more ships but receiving less manpower than it has requested, this problem can only grow more critical.

There is another factor to consider in relation to this issue of broad-mindedness, about which the submarine community tends to have a somewhat different point of view. Rickover's successor, Admiral Kinnaird McKee, observed that for submarines

> you really do want to groom a guy who is absolutely confident, so he can do whatever he has to do alone, unsupported and outnumbered. That mentality is part of a submarine crew's makeup. The day we lose that, because of people saying everyone has to be theologically balanced, is the day the submarine force loses its effectiveness. A lot of submarine officers have proved their ability to broaden themselves at the appropriate time. The fact of the matter is you don't want to bother them with that until they've gone as far as they can in the submarine force. Because the day a submarine skipper gets worried about broadening his horizons is the day he stops being a good submarine skipper.[30]

McKee had been part of the submarine navy in the 1960s and early 1970s when it was forming as many as twenty-five to thirty new crews a year, two for each submarine. Officers could not be spared for "nice" duty when they were desperately needed operationally.

Yet, as an officer progresses through the career ranks, he becomes less the technician and more the organizer, the manager, the decision maker. The higher he rises the more he must grasp "the big picture"—at first how his specialty relates to other specialties, and later how his service relates to other services. That need does not square well with McKee's proposition, correct as it may be in one sense, that "the whole idea of submarine warfare is to send one boat into an area where it's alone. . . . You don't want to grow a submarine officer who feels like he has to be ecumenical."[31] The submarine officer, McKee is saying, is needed in submarines, he is wanted there, he needs to be there all the time to stay current, and his career opportunity is there. McKee readily admits, though, that his own career did not follow that simple formula once he was a senior commander.[32]

What about those whose careers are unorthodox? This was a question that concerned Watkins, specifically when it was applied to navy mavericks like the later chairman of the Joint Chiefs, William J. Crowe, Jr., a Princeton Ph.D. How did the navy ensure that the Crowes, who rarely passed through all the required promotion wickets and who remained in Washington year after year because they were so good at their jobs, were not lost to the navy? The promotion system had become rigid, with communities, such as air, surface, and subsurface creating well-defined paths for advancement that left little room for mavericks.

So BUPERS went to work to produce a list of, and a tracking system for, unique officers. There were actually two reasons for the tracking system, because there was an assignment as well as a selection hurdle: officers who had not taken "all the ticket steps" might not get assigned to career-enhancing jobs. What was needed was a safety net, and this was provided. To produce the list the chief of naval personnel enlisted the help of the warlords at OPNAV, who proved sympathetic to the cause. Completed, it contained approximately three hundred names.

Although the warfare-specialty assignment sequence was becoming rigid, the tracking of subspecialty assignments was loose. As Vice Admiral William P. Lawrence, chief of naval personnel from 1983 to 1986, pointed out, an officer would go to a postgraduate school and take an oceanographic degree and never once be assigned to such a billet. (This was no secret to Congress.) The remedy was to enlist subspeciality sponsors in the tracking process, which meant that sponsors had to establish personnel billets for this purpose.

It was not just a question of correcting inefficiency to satisfy Congress, though. Both Lehman and Watkins were convinced that the failure to use these officers correctly cost dearly in terms of fighting effectiveness. Watkins's view was that a commander needs his oceanographer just as much as he needs his intelligence officer. Lawrence described how Lehman pressed to put oceanographers on battle group staffs and fleet staffs instead of just in shore-based billets.[33] As a result of these pressures, oceanography's budget doubled in real dollar terms between 1977 and 1987, and by 1984 there were about 20 percent more oceanographers, most new ones out with the fleet. "Mobile environment teams" were stationed at major fleet centers so that small ships could get proper support to make their sonars more effective, sometimes doubling the detection ranges with the same equipment. The oceanographic effort was also linked to space, satellites being used to measure many war-pertinent phenomena.

Rear Admiral John Seesholtz, océanographer of the navy, gave a number of examples of the change in consciousness in the fleet because of the war-bearing implications of oceanographic expertise. To the surface sailor, the sea has always been currents and waves that vary radically. But with data now available from GEOSAT (geophysical satellite) he can "see" underwater mountains where water "piles up." With the SMQ 11 satellite receiver and the desk-top TESS (tactical environmental support system) computer, he has automated data on the environment and can calculate what happens to radar and sonar signals under various air and sea conditions.[34]

On programs such as this, which apply specialist education to war-fighting capability, both the secretary and the CNO were in full accord.

RETIREMENT, WOMEN, UNIFORMS

Three unrelated personnel issues—but every one of them potentially explosive—emerged during Admiral Lawrence's tenure as chief of naval personnel.[35]

First came the change in the retirement system, which after World War II had settled into a formula increasingly more difficult for the Congress to accept: 50 percent of basic pay after twenty years, 75 percent after thirty. The first serious storm cloud to appear followed the fifth quadrennial review of military compensation (QRMC) in 1983. The QRMC report focuses on certain aspects of compensation, and this time it was retirement and special pay. The special pay arrangements on the whole were approved.[36] The report also recommended changing the retirement formula to 40 percent at twenty years and building up to the thirty-year mark with a lump-sum bonus at retirement, using the saved money. The Joint Chiefs decided to fight it, as did the Defense Department. As it turned out, in FY 85 Representative Les Aspin led Congress to adopt a less favorable formula to the pained acquiescence of the services. Instead of final pay as a determining factor, an average of the final years' highest pay was introduced. The 40 percent concept was used for retirement after twenty years, while the bonus feature was eliminated.

The reason the services yielded was that Aspin had earlier made another change requiring the services to fund retirements when new recruits arrived rather than funding for a current year's retirees. With these "fenced" funds, capping the total amount and giving the services a choice between formulas, Aspin had a lever by which he could force service acceptance.

Vice Admiral Lawrence remarked that Congress did not seem impressed with the military argument: If a twenty-year, 50 percent formula was so generous, why did only 15 percent or fewer stay in military service twenty years? (That figure includes first-term recruits, making it less impressive.)[37] Congress was also not much impressed with the navy's argument that a large percentage of experienced personnel was needed. With congressional caps on manpower totals forcing the navy to restrict enlistments, retirement formulas became even more critical.

The problem of women in the navy was an equally emotional issue. The American people were not prepared to see women in combat; most Congressmen were unwilling to contemplate the idea of women shipped home in body bags from combat zones. But women kept asking congressmen why their assignments were so curtailed, pressing for billets with combat potential. Ship-shore rotation raised another problem, one the army and air force did not have to deal with. Ratings like boilertender and sonar technician, essential at sea, have no equivalent billet ashore. When they were rotated, therefore, women usually got general rating assignments such as security. This raised the question of what would happen if women began to take up all the general rating billets ashore. The Defense Advisory Committee on Women in the Service, according to Lawrence, recognized the problem in principle but not so readily in practice.

Nonetheless, a number of improvements were made. One allowed women to be used more in the forward-deployed fleets. Where, for example, women helicopter pilots had been confined to the home fleets (Second and Third), they were now assigned to the Sixth and Seventh Fleets. A second important change was made in career paths for women, who like male unrestricted line officers had often progressed to executive officer, followed by a tour as commanding officer. This routine frequently took able women officers from important assignments in, say, the Navy Department, and put them in command of a relatively insignificant unit so they could qualify. This was changed to allow the option of continuing career specialization. Women could now become program managers.

Finally, there was the issue of uniforms. Under Admiral Hayward, a certified navy twill uniform had been approved that was wrinkle free but flammable; the navy was moving from cotton to synthetics when the Falklands War highlighted the danger of fire aboard ships, which could devastate engine spaces and personnel assigned to them. So the question was which type of material to use in the future. Strong feelings were expressed on each side. Finally it was decided to keep the twill for shore billets and adopt fire-retardant work uniforms on board.

Admiral Watkins' decision to abolish beards was accepted more easily than might have been expected. The main problem was with the reserves; why should their few duty hours a month control their personal appearance? But there was the negative psychological effect that two standards for personnel in identical uniforms was bound to produce. In a total force of which the reserves were regarded as an essential part, one standard, it was decided, must prevail.[38]

WATKINS TAKES AIM AT THE CULTURAL MALAISE

Money and sensible personnel policies were critical if the ranks were to be filled with quality personnel. But the legacy of the past and the problems looming ahead required solutions that went well beyond these changes, however useful. Zumwalt had handled the racial issue and Holloway had tightened discipline, but in a culture far too enamored of alcohol, drugs, and sexual permissiveness, problems were multiplying faster than solutions. Illiteracy and low health standards made it all worse. Hayward had confronted what, in a famous phrase, he called the navy's "hemorrhage of talent." Vice Admiral Lando Zech, a former chief of naval personnel, pointed out that it took six years to make a competent petty officer. The problem was still very real, then, in Watkins' time as CNO. And Watkins, as he looked at this and various other phenomena, did not see them as unrelated.

First, in a flag message in May 1985 he urged commands to get rid of repeated unauthorized absentees. They made up only three-tenths of one percent of the personnel but were responsible for 31 percent of unauthorized absences. This was the damage-limiting side of the problem.

Second, Watkins had to overcome the manpower shortage with a plentiful supply of career-oriented men and women, intelligent, well motivated, hard-working. In an all-volunteer milieu, the navy would have to live with those who wanted to live with it. But an increase in manpower would coincide with a decrease in the size of the military-age portion of the U.S. population. Add to that America's prevailing anti-military attitude, drug abuse, declining educational standards, and poor physical fitness in the manpower pool and the full extent of the problem begins to emerge. In addition, more navy wives were working. Where were the navy's family support programs? The old idea that the wives of the captain and of the other officers of a ship or unit would take care of the problems of enlisted families was no longer valid. They were working too.[39]

This is a formidable list; in Watkins' view it had implications that went far beyond the navy. In a speech delivered to the Baltimore Council on Foreign Affairs on 28 March 1984, he suggested that these problems had their effect on national affairs by contrasting the ability of the United States to act promptly and effectively in the Cuban missile crisis with its dismal record during the Iranian hostage crisis. To Watkins, the Vietnam War epitomized this change; there was a "creeping national malaise [that had begun] to infect this nation's spirit, drive, and determination." If the problem went well beyond the navy, its solution would have to as well. That is why Watkins named the program that emerged Personal Excellence and National Security. From the first, the navy would take the lead, set an example. But the success of the effort would depend on whether that example took fire.

Watkins began to publicize just how bad things were. In a speech at Dowling College on 4 June 1983 he cited a presidential report on education showing that even a decade earlier, American students taking nineteen academic tests never scored first or second in comparison with other industrialized nations and on seven tests came in last.[40] Some 23 million adults were functionally illiterate , as were about 13 percent of seventeen-year-olds. Navy data indicated that a quarter of recent recruits could not read at the ninth-grade level, though most had high-school diplomas. "The competitive spirit," he lamented, "which is a part of our way of life in the United States, is disappearing, and with it the call for excellence." An example was cited. One young man's family was so proud he was in the navy that they went to recruit camp in San Diego to see him train. Instead they found him being discharged after a few weeks because he could not read well enough to understand signs like "Beware of Jet Blast."

Bit by bit, Watkins came to the conclusion that this was a major problem needing "a full court press."

One Zumwalt reform already mentioned was the establishment of the executive panel of civilian specialists to advise the CNO on major problems. Watkins used the panel in plenary session and also established task forces for particular studies, one on personal excellence and national security. In November 1985 the half-dozen members of this task force submitted a forty-five-page report.[41]

The report included statistical detail and careful analysis. It provided many of the facts Watkins was to use in a series of subsequent speeches. It laid out the challenge as it affected navy manpower needs, suggested a three-pronged program addressing education, health promotion, and ethics, and called for a nationwide solution of the problem based on the navy's example.

There was no doubt about the seriousness of the manpower problem: "From a record high in 1980, the number of 18- to 21-year-old males has already decreased by 9 percent. By 1995, this pool will decrease a total of 23 percent from the 1980 high and will not reach today's levels until 2001. . . . If present-quality standards are maintained, the military will have to recruit over fifty percent of available and qualified 18-year-old males by 1995."[42] Elaborating on this point, the report said that the 600-ship navy would require about 625,000 men and women by 1989 (compared with 525,000 in 1980 and 575,000 in 1985). Retention had so far been the principal tool in realizing growth, and as a result the need for new recruits dropped from 99,350 in 1980 to 82,900 in 1984.[43] But congressional manpower caps, in place since 1982, a leveling off of retention rates, and an improving economy had a severe impact on the goal of 625,000 personnel. Furthermore, the segment of youth with the most serious educational problems—minorities—would grow from 16.3 percent to 19.4 percent of the eighteen to twenty-one group by 1995.[44] The heart of the issue was how to "expand the quantity of qualified youth."[45]

On 20 February 1986, on the basis of this task force report, Watkins formally established a major new program under Vice Admiral James A. Sagerholm, recently retired, as OP-00D.[46] The reason Watkins chose Sagerholm is worth mentioning.[47] As noted earlier, Sagerholm had been sent down to Pensacola in January 1983 to take over as CNET. In a meeting with him, Governor Bob Graham remarked that he was trying hard to improve Florida's schools, which suffered from a shortage of math and science teachers. He wondered if Sagerholm had any ideas on what might be done. Sagerholm queried his educational advisor, Dr. Bill Maloy, who also served on the Florida Board of Regents, and thereafter Maloy came up with the "math/science volunteer initiative," a pilot program in Pensacola that would use navy volunteers to teach technical subjects in the Florida school system. Sagerholm also threw his weight behind the Saturday Scholars Program in Chicago, which was particularly valuable in encouraging third- and fourth-grade black youngsters to set higher goals for themselves.

In an enthusiastic letter to Watkins filling him in on both programs, Sagerholm suggested that the whole navy become involved with such after-hours and Saturday programs. When OP-01 foresaw problems, Watkins decided to leave the issue at the CNET level for the time being. Later, when Sagerholm retired, Watkins met with him and said, "If I turn this task force report [on the personal excellence program] over to OP-01, it's just going to get swallowed up in the bureaucracy, and if it ever gets implemented, it's not going to be the same animal. . . . So I want you to head up a small group and push it forward." As Admiral Sagerholm concluded, it was "just a relatively few dollars. And what a leverage on a problem!"[48]

Watkins wrote in his policy memo that the task force recommendations had been the key to his program, which would embrace a "whole person approach" to education, health, and ethics. Enclosure 1 set forth the philosophy that was to guide Sagerholm's efforts.[49] It cited the dismal statistics on education that had appeared in the Dowling College speech. It added equally dismal statistics on physical fitness. Some 50 percent of American youth took no regular physical exercise. In 1984, 37 percent of Naval Academy plebes failed their initial fitness tests. A National Institutes of Health panel had estimated that 34 million Americans were obese.[50] Smoking in the navy was at "an epidemic level"—among active-duty navy it was 60 percent higher than among comparable civilian groups.

Ethical problems had been too long ignored. Adults, by "pretending to Olympian detachment" and having students make judgments themselves, were "affirming the shallowest kind of ethical relativism" in which "ethics and morals were reduced to a matter of personal taste."[51]

These trends had direct relevance to national security. Health and fitness problems degraded overall military readiness, while illiterate recruits could not operate complicated weapons systems. Eroding moral standards threatened the very fabric of the navy's historic tradition of excellence. All of this was of prime military concern at a time when the Soviets had achieved a secondary-school graduation rate of 98 percent and their hard science and mathematics curriculums far outstripped those of the United States.

To these various problems Watkins announced that the navy would respond with a three-pronged approach: it would establish an "Internal Agenda for Personal Excellence" and "partnerships with private- and public-sector institutions," and it would help get a national dialogue going.[52] Dependents and retirees would be encouraged to volunteer for the various parts of the program.

The CNO next sent out a memorandum detailing the first steps:[53] expanding the Saturday Scholars Program, the math/science initiative, the Adopt-a-School Program,[54] and NJROTC; establishing a physical fitness program, a comprehensive weight control and nutrition education program, and a basic skills and continuing-education program; and drafting a navy code of ethics. A number of other issues still needed study before programs were implemented to solve them. These included smoking, stress, and sexually transmitted diseases. Funds would be made available from FY 86 to FY 92 for navy initiatives and partnership programs.

Watkins issued a revised memo on 25 March 1986 clarifying his objectives while pressing for quick progress.[55] By 2 June 1986 he had issued still another memo, which made changes to OPNAV and set up a personal excellence board of directors, with OP-01 (as chairman). Sagerholm would be relieved by an 0-7 or an 0-8 who would combine the OP-00D billet with the new OP-10.[56]

And, three weeks before the end of his tour as CNO, Watkins issued his fourth and final memo on the subject of personal excellence, approving a proposal to promote it by diverting savings from the termination of drug rehabilitation programs. These savings had become possible because drug users were being eliminated from navy ranks. A draft "sailor's creed" was appended to the memo requesting each major navy community to add an agenda of its own. A number of steps to be taken in the health field were outlined.[57]

A comprehensive program such as this one developed so late in a CNO's tour stands a slim chance of surviving unless the new CNO is committed to it. Significantly, Admiral Carlisle A. H. Trost, even before assuming office as CNO, attended a flag officer conference in Pensacola to show his support. Navy Times quoted him as saying that he had come because he was convinced the program was critical.[58]

A navy by itself cannot reform a society. But in this case and to its credit, the U.S. Navy led the way, not only in identifying the problem and its implications but in suggesting some practical solutions. Many of those solutions would take years to achieve results.

Chapter 5

COMMAND ISSUES

Two quite different sets of command problems called ever more insistently for solutions by the time Tom Hayward entered his final year as CNO. One set was organizational and vital to the navy's future: the Rickover succession. The "father of the nuclear navy" was not immortal; one day he would have to retire. The other set was functional: command responsibilities.

THE RICKOVER TRANSITION PROBLEM

The Rickover transition question was highly important and very delicate. It was important because handling it improperly could cause a rupture in the useful and workable relationship between the Department of Energy and the Department of the Navy, which Rickover had improvised. There was the danger of a flight of talent from Rickover's "shop," talent held together in part over the years because Rickover was the boss. Loss of control over the laboratories could initiate a bureaucratic free-for-all that would not only dismantle Rickover's empire but also make it far more difficult (and expensive) for the navy to continue its highly cost-effective nuclear-reactor program. Standards, so essential to the safe operation of nuclear-powered ships, ran the danger of dropping. Neither the navy nor the nation could stand another Three-Mile-Island.

The transition was delicate because Rickover himself had enjoyed considerable political influence with Congress and many of its key members there might easily take offense if he were abruptly dismissed. Delicate also because Rickover, as he aged, became abrasive and forgetful and suspicious of people who might be pushing for his relief. Rickover himself refused categorically to address the issue. He also suspected that there was an organized shipbuilding industry effort to overthrow him.

Delicate, finally, because when President Reagan assumed his office the new secretary of the navy, John Lehman, had a distinctly negative view of Rickover.

Of all the questions analyzed in these pages, this is probably that which most easily arouses emotions. It is one of two on which opinion remains most divided. At one end of the spectrum there is the attitude represented by Admiral Watkins, who worked under Rickover and delivered the eulogy at his memorial service at Washington's National Cathedral. At the other end is the attitude represented by Secretary Lehman, who told Admiral Hayward, then CNO, the first day they got together, "I'm going to fire Rickover. I'm not going to renew him." Lehman was incensed that Rickover had used trinkets such as ship models "to grease Congressional palms."[1] Between these two extremes is the appraisal from William Wegner, formerly a naval engineering duty officer and Rickover's civilian deputy. The two worked closely together over the years.

Rickover developed his congressional clout in self-defense, having predicted that the navy would pass him over for promotion. Rickover was not only promoted by Congress to flag rank but as time went on he was also given two, three, and ultimately four stars.[2] In 1962, when Rickover reached the age of sixty-two, normal mandatory retirement age, President Kennedy extended his tenure. Though no extension beyond age sixty-four is allowed, under law a retired officer may be recalled for a specific task. Rickover was granted two-year recalls for almost two decades.[3] Admiral Watkins explained how this had happened:

> Generally, the process went like this: about six months before the issue had to be resolved (because there has to be an official action taken by the Secretary to continue the recall), Rickover would jostle his contacts over on Capital Hill, saying, "The Department of Defense should be coming in with the request. Why aren't they? It takes time to plan and we should be getting on with it. It's typical of the Department of Defense over all these years to hold back and it's worrisome to me and I've got to know. . . ."[4]

According to Bill Wegner Rickover did not want to push for the recalls himself; he preferred that the navy secretary initiate action. But it did not work that way. Sometimes an extension came only at the eleventh hour. Wegner said Secretary John Warner was helpful; CNO Zumwalt was not.[5] In President Carter's time there was no problem: Carter admired his old boss. With Reagan's advent, Rickover lost his clout with the White House. That, plus political pressures from contractors and Rickover's increasing age, is what brought the issue to a head in 1981.

Whether outsiders knew the full extent of the problem as it showed up inside Rickover's shop is questionable. Wegner explained that while Rickover's long-term memory remained intact, by the time Wegner resigned Rickover's loss of short-term memory was pronounced. "You could go to him and talk to him about a subject and 15 minutes later he would have no recollection that that subject was even discussed. Difficulties arose."[6]

Shown specific testimony with some odd features, Wegner agreed that the problem was Rickover's age. The testimony was made to Senator Proxmire's committee in January 1982.

> Q. In your opinion are we spending too much on defense?
> A. Too much! For example, in nuclear submarines, there is no reason why we need as many as the Russians—a matter of judgment. We have 121 submarines (33 FBM and 88 SSN). We have enough authorized, but need to replace obsolete subs. Must have sufficiency!
> Q. Is buildup justified?
> A. In the future, naval wars will be decided under the polar ice.
> Q. What about *the two nuclear aircraft carriers* which the Navy wants in 1983 and will cost over $6 billion, not counting the planes? How long will they last in a war?
> A. *Two days.*
> Q. How long will our whole fleet of carriers last?
> A. If in port, they may last longer—may not. . . .
> Q. Is the 600-ship Navy realistic or necessary?
> A. You can't just mention the number of ships. In general, I think we are overarming. . . .[7]

Wegner commented that, first, Rickover would swear he never said this. Second, if the record of the last fifteen to twenty years were reviewed every one of these remarks would show up in context. For example, Rickover said more than once that if it were up to him he would sink all the nuclear ships—they were not safe. But his comment postulated the existence of a perfect world. Wegner added, "He even said once we ought unilaterally to get rid of all our weapons!"[8]

Insiders with the navy's interests at heart were worried about what would happen not only if Rickover was not reappointed but also if he suddenly keeled over dead. Rickover refused to discuss it. "In his mind," Wegner said, "when he went, the program went." When Rickover actually did have a heart attack, what happened was not reassuring. Admiral Ike Kidd, then chief of naval material, assigned a provisional head who lacked credentials for the job and was not a four-star. Secretary John Warner intervened to tell Wegner to carry on; the new appointee told Wegner to take over while he was out of town for a week. This was a preview of a problem that could not safely be ignored.

Wegner and Watkins, shaken, began to discuss the issue of Rickover's successor. Rickover, recovered, would not react one way or the other. Choosing Wegner as his deputy had been a defensive act on Rickover's part; he did not want a serving naval officer appointed who would have full powers to act if he became incapacitated. Rickover, legally, had to have a deputy for such things as signing fitness reports. Wegner was his deputy for that, but clearly was not Rickover's relief. When the author probed further—surely Rickover had to be concerned about the future of the nuclear program—Wegner answered, "No, I don't think so."[9]

Rickover's argument was that although there is a vice president to take over if a president is incapacitated, he is not groomed for the job ahead of time. Why was his situation any different? Wegner conjectured that this was either a defense mechanism to avoid the issue, or a ploy to stifle any discussion of the problem because his enemies would use the opening to his disadvantage. Rickover would admit that there were plenty of capable people around to succeed him, but he would not give his enemies a chance to name a successor.[10]

After Rickover's heart attack, Wegner and Watkins, then chief of naval personnel, drafted a set of letters that clearly identified Wegner as successor until someone was appointed by the CNO and the navy secretary. For this they obtained the concurrence of the Atomic Energy Commission. Rickover signed the letters without comment, refusing to get involved. He trusted Watkins.[11] So now the future was covered against the possibility of another heart attack. There remained the question of what would happen if Rickover were not reappointed.

Rickover almost did not get an extension the year that Watkins left for the Pacific. In 1979, Wegner himself retired. What would 1981 bring? In May 1981, Energy Secretary Edwards wrote the secretary of defense recommending another two-year extension. The letter had to be answered, and Admiral Hayward asked Watkins to prepare a memo on account of his close association with navy nuclear programs over the years.[12] In his response Watkins recommended that the CNO not get involved with the issue of whether Rickover's tenure should or should not be extended, but rather that he comply with Edwards's request to provide background information, giving pros and cons.

Soon thereafter Watkins departed to become CINCPACFLT. Navy Secretary Lehman, Defense Secretary Casper Weinberger, and Deputy Defense Secretary Frank Carlucci were left to consult on the issue. A few months later, in September 1981, Hayward called Watkins up to tell him that it looked as if there would be a transition to new leadership in the naval reactor program. Because Watkins was probably the only person in the navy entirely familiar with the succession problem and what had to be done to preserve the program, could he come back to Washington and help?[13]

Watkins returned quietly on 24 November to begin confidential talks with key people on Capitol Hill and in Rickover's office. He and Wegner sat down to think through how they would prepare for the transition. Wegner commented that

> the effort was not directed at protecting Rickover. It was to preserve what was so essential, once Rickover was gone. If we left it up to nature, things would atrophy in a very short period. . . . You knew, underneath, that the day he left it would be, "Let's go back to the old way of doing business." [Rickover's successor] would walk in the door and they would say, "We only did that because of Rickover. We aren't going to do that any more. We're not afraid of *you*."[14]

There were still no documentary or legislative provisions that said, for example, that the naval reactor program had to be run by a four-star admiral. The choice before them was to push either for a presidential directive or for the enactment of a law. Senators Henry Jackson and Warner were consulted, along with Samuel Stratton, William Nichols, and Melvin Price in the House. At the meeting Watkins stressed that the navy had to have continuity in the program and could not afford to lose technical talent or the laboratory: there might be "some social chinks" in Rickover's armor, but "there was far more substance."[15]

Watkins got the clear message that the time had come for Rickover to go. The latter still retained much support in Congress but it was diminishing. Since 1979, when his closest advisors had left him, the new group had been less effective in keeping Rickover from making mistakes in judgment. There were no decisions taken at this meeting, and on 3 December Watkins met with government officials in the Navy Department, among them the assistant secretary for logistics and shipbuilding, the assistant secretary of the Department of Energy, and the deputy to the director of naval reactors. This time a definite program was put together to ensure continuity and to give the new director of naval reactors the same tasks, responsibilities, and accountability that Rickover had. Because these had not been clearly defined by law—for that matter, at all—a legislative package was put together along with a letter to the president.

The package consisted of five items. First, there was a memo from the defense secretary to the president asking him to "set the tone" by signing an enclosed memo of guidance to the defense secretary and the energy secretary. The enclosure referred to "measures . . . to assure the continuity of this program and its present functions."[16] Second, there was a proposed executive order or legislative amendment. This further specified the job of the director of naval nuclear propulsion programs in the Energy Department ("He shall serve jointly in the Department of the Navy in the same capacity . . .") and made other changes to standardize what Rickover had been doing.[17] It placed the director at level 4 of the executive schedule if he were a civilian, and at the grade of admiral if he were a naval officer, and set his term of office at not less than eight years. He would report directly to the CNO. (In the final version, this was changed to the secretary of the navy and the secretary of energy.) Third, there was a "memorandum of understanding" for the energy and navy secretaries stating that "the basic structure, policies, and practices which have been developed over the years . . . shall continue to govern. . . ." Fourth, there was a letter from the navy secretary to the appropriate congressional chairmen. Fifth, there was a memo for Admiral Rickover, which expressed the hope that as he ended "a truly legendary Navy career," he would agree to the president's request that he "begin a new career as . . . nuclear science advisor." Wegner and Watkins knew full well that this would be viewed by Rickover as a "phony gold watch" and would be rejected by him.

Rickover expressed basic approval of the new legislation to codify his position. But that was only the technical obstacle. Despite the implication of the "new career as . . . nuclear science advisor," Rickover had to be told flat out that his tenure was not being extended. He was, according to Watkins, informed personally by the secretary of the navy. Unfortunately, his wife had heard the news on television the night before. There had been a leak.[18] A conference was held in the White House on 8 January 1982 with him, the president, the defense secretary, and the navy secretary among others, present. Again, it did not go very well. Rickover asked for a private session with the president, "about ten minutes. That didn't go any better and there was a huge group of reporters outside and we knew at that point that the story wasn't going to remain quiet much longer. . . ." After that interview President Reagan had no incentive to reconsider an extension for Rickover.[19]

THE RICKOVER LEGACY

Watkins, asked what he thought of the argument advanced by critics to the effect that Rickover invented his own navy so he could outwit the traditional one, responded that there was some truth to that. But since Rickover was dealing with radioactive material controlled by the Atomic Energy Act, it was quite logical for him to be appointed to a position in the Energy Department. This gave the leverage to work around the navy's bureaucracy once he found it standing in the way of the standards he wanted to put in place. The navy initially told Rickover, in effect, to go off and build his *Nautilus*. But he could not do that the way he wanted to in view of the navy's bad maintenance and defective training. As Watkins said, "He felt this new program had to have a whole new set of standards than what we had before, and all that had to be more disciplined, it all had to be derived from a better-educated officer base, enlisted base. He didn't see any of that going on in the rest of the Navy." Zumwalt, who clashed with Rickover, still saw the merit of the nuclear-power discipline system, said Watkins. About 1973 Zumwalt put into effect what subsequently evolved into the operational propulsion plan examination for conventionally powered ships. "My feeling," said Watkins,

> is that what we have done in the past ten—really now close to fifteen years—is put emphasis on engineering again. That is the guts of going to war in a ship at sea.
> It's the source of the energy for your weapon systems, that's everything. Your lifeblood flows from down there—your damage control—everything. So if you lose any of those energy sources in combat, you count on the engineer to get you back on line. All those sources of power, temporary cables, all of that kind of stuff is too often forgotten between wars. We began to build a white collar group of officers who liked to sit on the bridge and watch their guns go "boom."[20]

The Vietnam War showed what could happen at the worst—brand new ensigns with no engineering experience operating plants. Holloway had Watkins as BUPERS chief set up a tough operations and maintenance course in Idaho for all senior officers going to command at sea. That brought a change. As for Rickover, his leadership techniques were unusual, but the product was first rate. The navy had learned a lot from his insistence on quality and responsibility. His emphasis on high standards, full documentation, and disciplined organization had been wholly beneficial. Without that, concluded Watkins, "you ain't going to make it."[21]

Admiral Kinnaird McKee, Rickover's successor, took issue with the proposition that the submarine navy and the nuclear submarine navy in particular had become a separate navy. It had merely "adhered to a significantly higher standard. . . ." McKee himself had not been directly involved in the transition. "I didn't want to be since they expected me to take the job," he explained. It would have complicated relations with the staff. McKee added that the civilian staff had made the transition to the post-Rickover era without serious strain or loss of key personnel. The new organization was working as planned, continuing the dual-hatting arrangement.[22]

That arrangement brought tangible benefits to the navy. Rickover, writing to Hayward, mentioned that it amounted to $400 million in research and development funds from the Department of Energy. By comparison, the funding from the Navy Department itself was more like $100 million. Energy was also paying for the eight operating prototypes used for training navy crews.[23]

Probably the most eloquent testimony to Rickover's achievement is in the safety record for nuclear submarines that he left behind. It is well to remember that, for Rickover's last years were marred by a controversy over gratuities he had received from shipbuilders. While few, even of his enemies, felt that these had influenced Rickover's judgment, many of the gifts apparently amounted to more than mementos. Admiral Watkins wrote Congressman Charles E. Bennett on 15 February 1985, "I am concerned that the nation may overlook his lifetime devotion to public service . . . because of possible misperceptions of influence which simply have never been seen to exist by those who know him. ."[24] Attached to the letter was a statement Bennett inserted into the *Congressional Record*:

> I have never met a man who worked harder or evidenced less interest in material possessions than Admiral Rickover. His life was devoted to his job. . . .
> Admiral Rickover could have retired in 1952 at three-quarters pay and made a fortune in the private sector. But he stayed on serving his country for another 30 years. That's when he designed and built the nuclear propulsion plant for *Nautilus* and for all the ships that today comprise forty percent of our major combatants. . . .
> . . . In Admiral Rickover, the American public got a great bargain![25]

Admiral Watkins, delivering the eulogy for Rickover, said among many other things that "it was easy to miss the compassion of a man who cared so much . . . that he penned personal notes to each and every family who lost a loved one aboard *Thresher* after she was lost. . . . While others looked for short cuts, Admiral Rickover always insisted upon establishing rigorous standards of performance that matched technology to human potential." It was no small achievement.[26]

COMMAND PROBLEMS: THE *BELKNAP-KENNEDY* COLLISION

Ned Beach, in his history of the U.S. Navy, shows clearly that command problems and collisions at sea are as old as the navy itself.[27] Less than ten years after the tragic collision of the USS *Evans* and the HMAS *Melbourne* on 18 August 1969, which cost seventy-four lives, there was another collision between the USS *Belknap* (CG 26) and the

USS *Kennedy* (CV 67). This one brought less loss of life but stirred up far more controversy, not only within the navy but also in the press.

A CNO memo to all flag officers and officers in command, issued by Admiral Holloway on 2 October 1976, summarized the events.[28] Just after 2130 on 22 November 1975, when the *Belknap* was on a relative bearing of 200° about four thousand yards from the *Kennedy*, the latter illuminated the flight deck and prepared to turn into the wind for flight operations. The *Belknap*'s skipper was not on the bridge but below having coffee. The *Kennedy* signaled her intent to turn from her course to port, the *Belknap* acknowledged it, and the *Kennedy*'s execute signal followed soon after.[29] At orders from her officer of the deck, a lieutenant junior grade, the *Belknap* slowed speed "and came left toward the new course of 025T."[30] The officer had previously discussed a Corpen J *starboard* maneuver with his commanding officer. Now he reacted with the same tactic to the *Kennedy*'s port signal, slowing and intending to follow the carrier around. The *Belknap* began to ease to port. The officer, beginning to doubt this maneuver, summoned the CO to the bridge and ordered left full rudder just before he arrived. The CO was in time to mitigate the effect of what followed, but not to prevent a collision that left eight dead and forty-eight injured.

The *Navy Times* reported that five minor collisions came in the next weeks. This brought to six the number of such accidents within a month.[31]

The *Belknap* case was tried under the Uniform Code of Military Justice and resulted in an acquittal for the CO and a verdict of guilty with no penalty for the officer of the deck. This angered many retired naval officers.

Newspaper coverage of the court-martial was extensive. Many of the articles misrepresented the way the navy would have described the problem. There was, even in the *Navy Times*, a highly misleading account that began, "The acquittal of Capt. Walter R. Shafer was a triumph of principles of common law over traditions of the Navy," for his lawyers had "managed to convince a military judge that the naval tradition of the absolute responsibility of a captain for his ship is only a tradition in the eyes of the law."[32] The San Diego *Union*'s headline was "Judge's Ruling Scuttles Accountability Law of the Navy."[33] The Washington *Post* account said the navy judge had "ruled that a Navy regulation giving a commanding officer absolute responsibility is unenforceable unless the Navy proves the officer was 'criminally negligent' in performing his duties."[34] And so forth.

The CNO, Admiral Holloway, attempted to put the whole affair in perspective in the flag-officer memo of 2 October 1976, but it was marked for official use only. A further distribution of the memo to the judge advocate general community on 12 October carried that same restriction.[35] This gave rise to a lot of confusion among outside groups.

The memo was designed to assure the addressees that resolution of the *Belknap* case did not jeopardize the concept of command responsibility. When criminal charges were brought, as here, a guilty verdict required legally admissible evidence beyond a reasonable doubt that the accused violated the Uniform Code of Military Justice. That was proper. But "the acquittal of a commanding officer by a duly constituted court-martial absolves him [only] of criminal responsibility. . . . It does not . . . absolve him of his responsibility as a commanding officer as delineated in U.S. Navy Regulations."[36]

Mail pouring in to Holloway's office had expressed misconceptions about the role of military justice in the navy. After the collision, a navy investigation had concluded that both officers were personally responsible for it, a finding approved by CINCUSNAVEUR and, on review, by the CNO. By that finding both officers were accountable. What sanctions were to be applied? The incident would be noted in fitness reports and eventually affect promotion and command opportunity.[37] As Holloway's memo concluded,

> Every day in command tests the strength of character, judgment and professional abilities of those in command. In some cases, commanders will . . . answer for their conduct in a court of law. In all cases, they will be professionally judged by seagoing officers—a far more stringent accountability in the eyes of those who follow the sea.[38]

Ultimately the officer of the deck and the CO resigned from the navy. The CO's request that his record be cleared of the letter of reprimand was denied. The decision reiterated strongly everything that Holloway had argued.[39]

MILITARY JUSTICE

Admiral Hayward was fortunate not to have to deal with the issue of major collisions at sea, but he was nonetheless concerned about the effects of the military justice system on the navy's approach to discipline problems. The advent of the Uniform Code of Military Justice brought a system of military courts that operated by federal judicial rules. In the decade of the sixties the trend in federal court procedure favored the rights of prisoners. The results were evident in a series of reports submitted by Captain R. J. Grunawalt, OP-00F, to CNO Hayward. Grunawalt had traveled to Norfolk, San Diego, and Pearl, interviewing a number of flag officers, dozens of COs, and a spread of judge advocate general corps personnel.[40] The consensus among these people was that the military justice system was too technical and cumbersome, the court-martial process too lengthy. Some of the people interviewed said that as a result, cases that should have gone to a court-martial were being settled at mast instead.[41] Additionally, there was a grave lack of pretrial detention of the accused, many of whom did not even show up on the day of their trial. This happened in five to seven cases a week at Norfolk. Those who were sentenced and punished had an easy life. One consequence of the system was that COs often entered into pretrial agreements with the accused to avoid the time and expense of prosecution.[42]

In San Diego, one vice admiral in a representative comment said he was disillusioned with the military justice system and "the erosion of discipline in the navy." The navy needed to "tighten down the screws." Another vice admiral called court-martial results "inadequate" and "a waste of time."[43]

A significant problem with the trials stemmed from decisions by the U.S. Court of Military Appeals, which, for example, had interpreted right to individual counsel to mean compliance with any request by the accused regardless "of the delay, distance, and expense involved." Witnesses for the accused were being treated the same way.[44] Admiral Hayward brought up most of these issues for discussion at his 20 July 1979 conference of commanders in chief. But many of the problems were beyond simple navy solution. We can see here, however, one reason for Admiral Hayward's emphasis on pride and professionalism.

THE *RANGER* FIRE AND THE F-4 LOSS

In January 1983, a short article by Admiral Watkins appeared in the *Proceedings* of the U.S. Naval Institute.[45] It focused on command responsibility, repeating "the old adage . . . that 'authority can be delegated—responsibility cannot.'" He cited article 0702.1 of Navy Regulations, which said that a CO's responsibility was absolute, and article 1102, that all "in authority in the naval service are required to [set] a good example of virtue, honor, and subordination. . . ." His ideas were similar to those expressed by CNO Holloway in relation to the *Belknap* case.

But by May 1983, Watkins found it necessary to speak out again, as evidence accumulated on his desk of departures from his strict standards. In a speech to the U.S. Court of Military Appeals (reprinted also in *Naval Affairs* the following year), "Hobson's Choice: A Call to Accountability!" he repeated his theme of the links between responsibility, authority, and accountability. The phrase Hobson's choice came from the rule at Hobson's eighteenth-century English riding stables that patrons would ride "the next horse out of the barn no matter what their preferences. . . ." Watkins was alluding to a *Wall Street Journal* editorial of 1952 that used Hobson's choice to illuminate the notion that a CO "is given honor and privileges and trust beyond other men" but that he must answer for any disaster. In his speech Watkins gave illustrations of why it was imperative to "raise our level of sensitivity to the inseparable principle of responsibility and accountability":

> It's an injustice when a former aviator knowingly defrauds the government by continuing to draw flight pay for years, and it is decided to take no action—punitive or nonpunitive—after the officer agreed to repay the funds.
> It's an injustice when a general court-martial ordered for a staff officer who used drugs in the presence of enlisted subordinates is deliberately downgraded to a special court-martial, just to prevent revocation of a professional license.
> It's an injustice when a chief petty officer caught trafficking in drugs is awarded only a summary court-martial by his commanding officer out of deference to the chief petty officer's position of authority, while lower rated personnel similarly involved receive the maximum judicial sanction.[46]

Despite such prodding, disasters resulting from lack of accountability were only weeks or months away. On 23 October 1983, 241 marines were lost in Beirut after a truck loaded with explosives crashed into their barracks. This incident brought into question the long chain of command and the notion of diffused responsibility.[47] On 1 November 1983, a fuel leak and resulting fire aboard the USS *Ranger* (CV 61) in the Arabian Sea cost the lives of six sailors. The inquiry established that the leak was "specifically attributable" to negligence by two enlisted men, one of them a third-class petty officer. But it also "revealed deterioration in the training capabilities of personnel in the Engineering Department as a result of the culpably inefficient performance of . . . the previous Engineer Officer, who detached from USS *Ranger* on 17 October 1983."[48] The inquiry findings concluded that, although initially no disciplinary action had been recommended against the previous engineering officer, he should be charged with a violation of article 92 of the Uniform Code of Military Justice, dereliction of duty. No other persons in the chain of command were charged.[49]

The question is this: Where does responsibility and accountability end? How far up the chain?

Admiral S. R. Foley, Jr., CINCPACFLT, "declined to refer to a court-martial" the above charge because the engineer's responsibility for the tragedy was "too subtle for effective resolution in a criminal forum where the standard of proof is guilt beyond a reasonable doubt." Instead, appropriate fitness report supplements would be put in the officer's file.[50]

The CNO disagreed: "Accountability for the derelictions . . . demands more than documentation in . . . fitness reports." Since CINCPACFLT was not prosecuting charges, Watkins cautioned the engineer about his performance of duty. And because "the two officers in command of the *Ranger* during the year prior to the fuel oil fire failed to bring the full authority of their office to bear to resolve the serious engineering deficiencies," and the executive officer had "failed to ensure the establishment of an adequate training program," these three officers were also cautioned under article 0702.[51]

The inquiry findings also revealed deficiencies in the navy's relieving process. The *Ranger*'s relief-of-command report for July 1983, when the second captain took over, failed to mention the ship's unsat OPREP (unsatisfactory operation report) and the engineering department's training problems. Watkins directed an immediate and thorough review of relieving procedures with a view to reviving the more precise and time-tested procedures set out in Navy Regulations until 1973.

Watkins directed that, the petty officer having been acquitted, the remainder of the other enlisted man's sentence be remitted. In other words, blame had been unfairly focused on the lower ranks.

In a message to flag officers in December 1984, Watkins addressed principles of command.[52] Glowing fitness reports "for a commanding officer whose documented performance is lacking undermines the very principle [of accountability]." Detaching COs were immediately "to identify specifically unsatisfactory conditions within the command which have the potential to adversely affect safety, well-being or readiness— officers succeeding to command should comment on the condition by endorsement." He ordered the officers to pass his "news gram" down the chain of command for compliance.[53]

Such intense pressure, plus improvements in the material condition of the navy, began to restore traditional standards. After the USS *Coral Sea* collided with an Ecuadoran tanker early in 1985, the captain and four other officers were given letters of reprimand and relieved. In another incident around the same time, on 17 March 1985, two F-14s lightly collided and lost a missile. The pilots lied about the incident and even conspired to destroy the taped evidence. They were given general discharges under honorable conditions. In the aftermath Vice Admiral James E. Service, commander, Naval Air Force, U.S. Pacific Fleet, was extensively quoted in the newspapers for saying, "If [a pilot] will lie to you in peacetime, certainly he'll lie to you in war and you can't depend on him. If you don't have that integrity in warfare, you're in a world of trouble."[54]

In changing Navy Regulations, Watkins was addressing the need for procedural change in the system to ensure the accountability of COs. But in another incident, this one involving an F-4S, there was also a problem with the system itself. On 2 April 1984, while operating in the Arabian Sea, an F-4S and its pilot were lost when the catapult tow hook or its supporting structure failed. The exact nature of the difficulty was uncertain ; apparently it involved "the premature separation of the bridle from the aircraft during catapult launch."[55]

Tow hook fittings have a service life of 850 launches, and F-4S airframes have a service life of 1,200 launches. The aircraft in question had been launched 1,393 times "without any service-life-extending modifications." Service life information had been developed by NAVAIRSYSCOM (Naval Air Systems Command) between 1960 and 1970 but had not been made available to fleet units.[56] Pacific Fleet units were given such information only after the USS *Midway* requested it on 5 April—after the incident.

NAVAIRSYSCOM conceded responsibility for compiling and publishing structural and fatigue data but claimed that the appropriate instruction for its dissemination had not been received. Because CINCPACFLT did not control NAVAIRSYSCOM, the CNO's intervention was requested. The CNO, although he recognized that in addition the plane's port engine had failed (how was not known) and that the exact cause of the pilot's death could not be determined, concluded that the accident was the result of serious institutional shortcomings. Not only was NAVAIRSYSCOM at fault. In OPNAV, OP-05 should have ordered fleet-wide dissemination of its critical service-life information— which NAVAIRSYSCOM itself had recommended numerous times. Personnel at the naval air rework facility at North Island were also to blame for not seeking clear engineering instructions for F-4Ss exceeding the 1,200-catapult limit. "In these circumstances," Watkins wrote, "NAVAIRSYSCOM, NARF NI and OP-05 ran aground just as surely as any ship at sea, and those responsible must be held to the same measure of accountability. . . . I have administratively admonished the officers at these commands who remain on active duty and were directly involved . . . during this critical period. I have similarly held their supervisors accountable. . . ."[57]

The CNO's decision came a year after CINCPACFLT's assessment of the incident—a sufficient indication of its complexity.

MEDICAL COMMAND PROBLEMS

In the early and mid-1980s the navy was in deep trouble in the medical area. An illustration was the death in Naples of Clarence Harvey Lenhart, USN (Ret.), in 1981. By the time Admiral Watkins's tour as

CNO was about to begin, the investigation into this affair had worked its way through a lengthy chain of command, but the seventeenth endorsement (that is, command comment on the investigation) still left much of the affair obscure. That endorsement, dated 14 June 1982, directed that all remaining questions be answered.[58] It was Admiral Watkins's introduction to the question of command responsibility.

The investigative report describes conditions at the hospital at which Lenhart, in great distress, was treated: "numerous items of equipment, including but not limited to the blood gas machine, the suction machine, the laryngoscope and the hospital elevators, were inoperative or not properly functioning and . . . the duty personnel responsible for providing support to the attending physician were unfamiliar with emergency room equipment and procedures."[59] The staff tried to give him oxygen but the device would not work; they tried to move him to other equipment on another floor but the elevator would not answer the button. Lenhart's condition worsened and presently, with his wife watching, he died.

As each level in the chain of command made its written comments, the sixteen evaluations piled up. In calling for still another investigation, the CNO commented if this were a case of poor command, as it appeared to be, "the responsibilities for these inadequacies should be fixed. Corrective actions such as those taken after the fact in this case, while necessary, do not resolve the question of responsibility/accountability for identified deficiencies in a command."[60]

Well known within the navy was the fact that the CO of the Naples hospital had prior to this new investigation been selected for flag rank. To leave the situation as it was would have been to invite the collapse of discipline in the navy. The blame was fixed—properly—at the command level.

The Lenhart case, having taken place in Naples, made a relatively small impression on the American public. The Billig case at Bethesda became notorious. With all the elements of drama, and culminating in a court-martial, it was thoroughly aired in the press. The charges against Commander Donal M. Billig, chief of cardiothoracic surgery at Bethesda Naval Hospital, involved two dozen counts, stemming especially from deaths during or after operations he performed. On 3 March 1986 he was found guilty of two counts involving manslaughter, one count of criminally negligent homicide, and eighteen counts of dereliction of duty related to three patient deaths in 1983–84. In one case, Billig was accused of bungling a heart operation and vanishing from the hospital, leaving nurses and residents to save the patient. It turned out that Billig was nearly blind in one eye as the result of an accident in 1978. He was sentenced to four years in prison, and the officer who recruited him was convicted of five counts of misconduct connected with falsifying statements about Billig's record.

Concerning the case the CNO wrote to the navy secretary:

> Multiple opportunities existed to act to ensure the integrity of the patient care system, but at each opportunity, responsible individuals failed to respond correctly. No single individual is considered responsible alone for the consequences of Commander Billig's professional incompetence. Rather, a number of officers, when confronted with adverse information, elected not to make difficult decisions. . . .[61]

The secretary's proposed administrative letter of censure to the director of surgical services at Bethesda, Captain John R. Fletcher, MC, USN (Ret.), stated that the director "knew of an improper, unwritten arrangement concerning the supervision of Commander Billig which existed outside his written privileges, and . . . [was] advised by three other cardiothoracic surgeons that Dr. Billig was deficient in his surgical skills." Without any justification, the director had gone so far as to recommend full privileges for Dr. Billig.[62]

Following this crisis Bethesda's credentials system underwent radical reform, but the navy's public image had been tarnished.

Two cases illuminated the navy's medical problems at sea. Both involved independent duty corpsmen (IDC) cases and both took place in the Indian Ocean, a year apart. The Michael P. Smith case was in 1984, the Mark Mercier case in 1985. The two cases were quite similar.

Smith, an electrician's mate fireman on the USS *Davidson* (FF 1045), reported to sick bay with cold-like symptoms. The IDC diagnosed this as bronchitis and prescribed Tylenol and bed rest.[63] Smith got progressively worse. On the fifth day he was moved to sick bay at the direction of the department head, the diagnosis was changed (but not the medication), and two days later he was transferred to a carrier. After two days there he was transported to a shore-based hospital, where he died within fifteen hours of "adult respiratory distress syndrome, complicated by pneumonia and pneumothorax."[64]

The investigating officer concluded that the IDC was derelict in the performance of duty but did not report any "shortcomings in officer performance." The report traveled up the chain of command, at each level deferred to the level above until it reached the administrative group commander. When it became apparent that the latter intended nonpunitive action, the type commander intervened. A flag mast was held by the commander of the Naval Surface Force, Pacific Fleet, at Pearl Harbor on 5 February 1985. When still nothing happened, CINCPACFLT ordered a second investigation whose results he described as follows:

> The facts of the investigation revealed a division officer who failed to carry out his responsibilities. . . . Not once during [the deceased's] illness did the division officer visit the man nor did he take affirmative steps to resolve the conflicting reports as to the sailor's condition and adequacy of care he was being provided. These impressions were confirmed at Flag Mast.[65]

The executive officer was characterized as one "who at no time during the illness checked up on the deceased. He relied entirely on erroneous reports . . . and several casual personal" visits. The *Davidson*'s CO requested a court-martial. One was subsequently held before a panel of post-command surface-warfare-qualified O-6s. The executive officer was found guilty of dereliction of duty on two counts.[66]

The Mercier case began on 17 June 1985 after his ship, the USS *Worden*, made an African port call. A message from one of the battle group medical officers alerted the ship to the danger of malaria. The message was read by the CO, the executive officer, and the IDC. When Sonar Technician Mercier reported to sick bay with malaria symptoms he was misdiagnosed as having tonsillitis. Mercier's condition worsened, but the division officer informed the executive officer who later informed the CO that Mercier was greatly improved. This information was based on an "erroneous report from the IDC." That evening the CO, who had meanwhile ascertained the truth, directed the executive officer to prepare a message to the carrier requesting a medevac for the next day. Two hours later, Mercier choked on his own vomit. The executive officer had not yet drafted the CO's message.[67]

This time the investigating officer said that the IDC and the executive officer were at fault but that the CO, who "knew too little, too late," was not.[68] Commander, Seventh Fleet, ordered a further investigation. A flag mast was held for both the executive officer and the CO, while the IDC was convicted by general court-martial of dereliction of duty.

Captain G. B. Powell, Jr., in an article in the Naval Institute *Proceedings*, later drew the moral from these cases about the urgent need for a greater sense of command responsibility. In the first case, the CO stated at his court-martial that he had no obligation or duty to visit a sick sailor. In the second case, the CO said he had never visited the sick crew member, thinking he could rely on the executive officer's judgments.

Among the systemic reforms triggered by these two cases was to assign each IDC to a medical officer, when at home or deployed, who would oversee his work. And in the future, battle group medical officers were to visit each IDC in company at least monthly.[69]

These command problems were not easy to handle, and every one of them could have ruined the navy's long-deferred chance to turn things around after the Vietnam years. It was hard to turn the clock back and recapture a stringent regard for personal responsibility and command accountability—for the traditional navy way. That the fight was finally won would be too easy an assumption, for men are always also fallible. But it was with a sense of pride that the CNO in the spring of 1986 published a flag officers' news gram that included an excerpt from a message from the former skipper of the *Enterprise*. That ship had gone aground on 2 November 1985, and the captain, at admiral's mast on 3 January 1986, was held accountable. Here is what he said to his crew:

> We are held accountable for our actions in this Navy of ours, and it must be so. . . . Accountability prevents carelessness—it's that simple. . . . [I]t is therefore right and proper that I be held accountable. I would not have it any other way. . . . I will be relieved because of my negligence. . . .
>
> I am proud to be part of an organization that preaches and practices *accountability*, even when I am the object of it. If our nation's civilian society would practice accountability more scrupulously, there would be far less negligence, crime and corruption in our country. . . .[70]

The force judge advocate, COMNAVAIRPAC, forwarded these words to his peers with the comment, "The attached letter . . . says it all."[71]

Chapter 6

MANAGEMENT ISSUES

The personnel problems of the navy, discussed in chapter 4, were connected to the command issues discussed in chapter 5. Some of those command issues were also related to management problems, as in the F-4S case. Now we turn to issues that stemmed principally from management problems.

It was enormously difficult to bring efficiency to defense management. Some of the reasons for this lay outside the Navy Department and had to do, for example, with the complex nature of the law and of the congressional appropriation process. Add to that the relatively short time in office of navy secretaries before Lehman. Inside the navy, the lack of a clear advancement path to senior command via management billets and of sufficient higher command attention to waste and fraud, especially in the handling of spare parts, compounded the problem. There was also a significant internal management problem in the Naval Material Command.

PRICE COMPETITION

Admiral Rickover, in a personal statement to the House Committee on Armed Services, 16 June 1981, clearly outlined much of the shipbuilding cost problem and the associated competition issue that would absorb navy attention in the following years:

> Competition in defense procurement is often more illusory than real. While 35 percent of the Defense procurement budget is spent under contracts the Defense Department considers competitive, only about 8 percent is spent on formally advertised procurements—that is, where any company may submit a bid and the contract must be awarded to the lowest responsive and responsible bidder. In some competitive procurements only two or three firms are asked to bid.

105

> In other so-called competitive procurements the competition is not
> based on price, but on design or other technical factors. Sixty-five
> percent of the Defense procurement budget is awarded in contracts
> which the Defense Department itself labels as non-competitive.[1]

He went on to document some of the results. One sole-source contractor "typically negotiate[d] a target profit equal to 10 percent of the estimated cost," did the work for a "risk-free, cost-plus-incentive fee," and ended up making, on the average, a 17.5 percent profit on his actual incurred costs. Another contractor averaged a 21 percent profit on contracts where his risk was negligible. And a company that manufactured high-pressure air flasks for Trident submarines insisted on netting between 27 and 38 percent of estimated cost.[2]

In personal testimony the previous month, Rickover had told Congress that "over the past decade, the Navy has not been effective in dealing with shipbuilders that are not performing efficiently, that deliberately underbid, or that harass the Government with frivolous or inflated claims."[3] Rickover pointed to the existing backlog of $2.7 billion in unsettled claims.

He cited the comparative performance of Electric Boat (twenty submarines) and Newport News (thirteen submarines) in building the SSN 688. Electric Boat spent $148 million on each of the first five, compared with $98 million per unit at Newport News; on projections for the following five, it appeared likely that Electric Boat would use 30 percent more man hours than Newport News and charge more than $25 million per submarine more. Where Electric Boat delivered its sixth SSN 688 four years after due date, Newport News delivered its sixth submarine only eight months late.

Why, then, had Electric Boat won more contracts? Despite this record Electric Boat continued to be the low bidder, and navy lawyers advised that the company be awarded the contract.[4] Until Lehman, this practice continued.

Not that Newport News was without sin. In the 1970s it submitted bills amounting to nearly $900 million in sixty-four thick volumes. Claimants know that omnibus claims like this take a decade or more to sort out and that "as time passes, Government officials come and go, memories fade, witnesses get harder to find, and the pressures on Government officials to reach a compromise settlement grows."[5]

Rickover argued for improvements, which were soon to come. In the spring of 1984, less than three years later, Secretary of the Navy Lehman commented to the Senate Armed Services Committee that fixed-price incentive contracts were the best answer for "shipbuilding in particular and especially for those systems that require design changes."

Even here, there had to be a safety valve. In prior years, when this type of contract was used, the government's share for the almost inevitable extra costs had run at about 85 percent; Lehman now made it 50-50. The AV-8B was being procured with a firm fixed-price contract.[6]

As large-ticket items were being shifted to fixed contracts, another and more prosaic type of hardware was the focus of the nation's headlines: spare parts.

SPARE PARTS

In mid-July 1983, Secretary of Defense Weinberger wrote to forty-five prominent American newspaper editors about cases of over-charging for military spare parts and what the services intended to do about the problem.[7] It was complex, for the Defense Department purchased $15 billion worth of spare parts each year. He referred to a new arrangement in each service for "competition advocates."

Even while the Defense Department was gearing up to handle the problem, its dimensions were increasing. A congressional committee report of 9 November 1983, cited inspector general audits that "showed that expectations of cost reductions between 27 and 76 percent" were "not unreasonable" if the Defense Department purchased spare parts through competitive contracts or by direct purchase from the actual manufacturer.[8] What ran costs up in particular was contracting with one company for a lifetime supply of parts. In July 1983, testimony by the Office of the Secretary of Defense cited a navy installation in Florida that was ordering spare parts from a contractor although the same part was listed in the Federal Supply System at a fraction of the cost. Although an audit half a year earlier had detected such problems, they were still uncorrected by the time of the second audit. Whether this was attribut-able to inefficiency, problems with the Federal Supply System, or lack of computers and personnel was not determined.[9]

Congressional testimony on 4 August 1983 by a senior official in the Defense Department indicated that its "best assessment" for spare parts competition was "close to 30 percent and . . . rising." Over 3.6 million spares were "in the active inventory with about one million purchased annually."[10] The same day Joseph H. Sherick, the depart-ment's inspector general, testified on recent adverse publicity about exorbitant prices for spare parts: "You are all aware of the horror stories, the diode that should have cost 4 cents and we paid $110 and the hammer that should have cost about $10 and we paid over $400." The media reports, he indicated, should make it more obvious that it was Defense Department audits themselves that had been uncovering such cases. He cited six sources of the spare parts problem, including lack of cost-consciousness on the part of inventory personnel and the fact that it was "faster, easier, and safer to buy sole source." He spelled out safer: If a critical part failed, the manufacturer would be at fault, but if a procurement official had decided to obtain the part from some other contractor and it failed, his judgment might be called into question.[11]

When the navy's posture statement for FY 85 was presented in the spring of 1984, the issue was still being given extensive press coverage, so much so that Admiral Watkins tackled the question. He, like Sherick, emphasized that the inefficiencies had been revealed first by internal navy audit procedures. The navy was now seeking to buy directly from the original manufacturer or by competitive means "instead of buying sole source from prime contractors," who added their fee on. From this time forward the navy would stimulate spare parts competition in procurement. This would assure that navy purchasers knew their job and knew costs, and would provide warning when prices appeared unreasonable.[12] The new system was called BOSS ("Buy Our Spares Smart").

To illustrate the results of this approach, changing from a sole-source contract on two special gimbals saved $300,000. A "price fighter" team identified twenty-eight items significantly overpriced, which brought a potential savings of $1.4 million. Sole-source contracts converted into competitive bidding saved almost $2 million. After a flag officer had been appointed as "competition advocate general," there was an increase in competitive awards from FY 82 to FY 83 of 40 percent. The savings on eleven FY 84 contracts amounted to over $480 million. The navy was being far more vigorous in acquiring "asserted proprietary data" from defense contractors without charge. This permitted it to increase the number of parts farmed out to competition.[13]

But the issue did not die. On 10 December 1985, in a presentation to the president's commission on defense management, the Packard Commission, Secretary Lehman listed two items that had been way overpriced (five acquisitions had been correctly priced). The navy had bought a 4-cent diode for $110 and a $15 hammer for $436.[14]

Watkins, speaking to the House seapower subcommittee in April 1985, pointed out that "in the diodes case, we bought two. We were given a refund and that closed the deal. We found the overcharge, we exposed it, we hammered the contractor, he cleaned it up. What the [news]paper didn't say is we bought another 22,000 from the same contractor, for 4 cents each." Regarding the $600 toilet seat that had gained notoriety in the press, he made the following argument:

> There are even people on the Hill with miniature toilet seats around their neck. I don't think such action is appropriate when *we* are the ones ... who exposed ... the whole issue in the first

place. . . . We expose abuses. Then somebody . . . pulls out a toilet seat, hangs it round his neck, and the next thing you know we lose $1 billion in defense.[15]

Secretary Lehman, sounding a favorite theme, told the same group that the $600 toilet seat showed what could happen after forty years of taking procurement out of the hands of the managers: "That toilet seat was not bought by the Navy, it was bought by a collection of bureaucracies created in the name of reform. The Defense Logistics Agency and its subgroups along with various bureaus in the Navy bought that. . . . It's like Alice in Wonderland. . . ."[16]

In August 1984, one year after the flag-level competition advocate general billet had been established, a report was issued. It noted that for the current fiscal year, 86 percent of the navy's ships would be bought competitively. Competition was also being introduced into the procurement of shipboard weapon systems such as the MK-48 ADCAP (advanced capability torpedo) and for propellers for DDG 51–class destroyers. Aircraft, missile, and electronic systems would be obtained through increased competition. A second production source was being established for the Phoenix, rolling airframe, and Standard missile programs. Competition for Aegis cruisers had already saved $228 million, and for the SSN 688s, $108 million. The chief of naval material had established project BOSS, which generated over one hundred cost-saving initiatives. Rights in technical data were being monitored to prevent restrictions that raised prices or gave benefits to some companies exclusively. All activities with procurement authority exceeding the $25,000 level now had competition advocates.[17]

In short, the report of the competition advocate general recorded much progress. It warned that careful command attention would have to be paid to the problem. But, as it turned out, harmful publicity still lay ahead for the navy. In June 1985 the *Kitty Hawk* affair broke, some two weeks after the related Miramar affair. As one senior Judge Advocate General Corps officer put it (in this case the one handling both of the affairs), the CNO disseminated regular advice and warnings to the navy but the amount of paper flowing over a CO's desk was formidable. Every memo demanded attention. Which was the most important? Could the spare parts problem, having been addressed, be put on the back burner? As it turned out, the answer was a resounding no.[18]

SPARE PARTS, THE *KITTY HAWK*, AND MIRAMAR

The *Kitty Hawk* affair started on 11 June 1985 when a petty officer charged that fraud, mismanagement, and improper supply procedures plagued operations aboard CV 63. The charges were brought to Congress, which resulted in a mountain of navy paperwork. The problem soon boiled down to one issue, supply procedures. Fraud and abuse played very minor roles, despite Robert W. Jackson's charges.

Supplying a modern carrier like the *Kitty Hawk* involves staggering amounts of money. At the time of the incident, she had an annual operating budget of $10 to $12 million, plus $4 to $5 million to support eighty onboard aircraft and additional funds to cover the needs of a six-thousand-person crew. An inventory of 116,000 line items was located in fifty storerooms and had a value of $233 million. Of these, some 108,000 were consumable items valued at $37 million.[19] To reverse the point, some eight thousand key supplies were worth $196 million. (This ratio was about the same in 1987. The *Carl Vinson* [CVN 70] had a key inventory of some seven to eight thousand items. These, the "repairables," added up to 80 percent of the total value of the inventory.)[20]

Repairable items were (and are) "traded" at the intermediate level repair facility that specialized in stocking parts for a given airplane. One depot was at Whidbey Island, one at Miramar. Trading was carried out on a bad-for-good basis, which required only inventory (but not financial accounting) data.[21] It was a straight one-for-one trade. But if a shore facility was not able to fill the order, an "open purchase" was authorized. Open purchasing was not unusual since maintaining readiness was the prime criterion for spending money.

Readiness and cost-effective procurement are not easy to coordinate. The CO's first concern has traditionally been readiness. The *Kitty Hawk* report pointed out that the shipboard uniform automated data-processing system (SUADPS) was created "to set operating stock levels based on demand patterns, and to reorder material mechanically for stock." If one part was used, one part was needed. The system was designed to keep bins full. The investigative report commented that "the SUADPS system was not designed for inventory management of repairables," which is where Jackson's charges were leveled, but rather "for the financial management of repairables [that is, paying for them] and for interfacing with shore accounting and billing systems."[22] In other words, SUADPS orders parts and keeps track of the *process* of paying bills.

The CO's second concern was not costs or cost-effectiveness but rather maintaining the quality of life aboard ship and compensating in some measure for the rigorous operating schedules imposed on crews.[23]

Moreover, the shore supply establishment had not been overly responsive to carrier procurement needs. The supply depot at Miramar, for example, was filling only 55 percent of its orders, each of which on average required four to five man hours.[24] (By 1987 this had changed to 94 percent of orders filled at an average rate of thirty-seven minutes.) Thus carrier supply officers and their departments, with their "make it happen mentality," had no real sensitivity to costs.[25]

Miramar–*Kitty Hawk* changed that. The new standard became readiness with accountability, that is, cost-effective accountability. Whereas before, open purchasing by carriers was frequent, now it became increasingly rare.[26] A second change had even more interesting results. A one-time amnesty on hoarded spare parts was declared. Supply officers estimated that bases like Moffett Field turned in about $12 million worth of such parts; bases like Miramar, maybe $100 million.[27]

Where did these parts come from? A good repairman instinctively keeps a few spares for emergencies—especially if the accounting system permits it. When the U.S. Navy emerged from the Vietnam conflict it had acquired a number of wartime habits, including the placement of readiness before cost. The principle that "one out requires one in," while critical to readiness and still the rule for repairables, encouraged blind ordering. Also, those who operated the supply system assumed a normal erosion or wastage in transit alone of 10 to 15 percent. This allowed the accumulation of extra parts, while shortages in the late 1970s simultaneously encouraged hoarding.

There was an additional problem in the data system itself. In 1987 data still had to be entered on floppy disks from a keyboard and then transferred to the computer memory. These steps slowed down recording and left room open for error. As Commander Dave Gibbs of the Supply Corps explained in 1987, "I could go to the shelf now and see that I have two things there. But then I go to the SUADPS record and I may have five of them. . . ."[28] Moreover, much record-keeping was still done by hand.

The system's time lag created equal problems when it came to cost. As the *Kitty Hawk* investigation showed, bills were "continually processed . . . through the full thirty-six-month life of a congressional appropriation [with] over 20 percent of the expenditures . . . received two years after the obligation was incurred" and involving "back logs of up to $100M in unreconciled billings. . . ."[29] Whose fault was it? Line's? Staff's? System's?

The situation was highly flammable from a public-relations point of view; the signals being sent down the chain by the secretary and the CNO were not producing quick remedies, and the authority for remedies was fragmented. To make matters worse, problems with supplies purchasing at Miramar Naval Air Station were already making headlines when the *Kitty Hawk* affair broke. Miramar highlighted an additional difficulty, one about as old as the U.S. Navy: the appropriate division between line and staff corps functions. The systems commands of the navy, like naval supply (NAVSUP), deal with specialized problems outside the career interests of general line officers. Supply officers are technical experts who administer according to complex regulations that few line officers normally take the time to master. CINCPACFLT's preliminary findings into the Miramar affair emphasized this very point: that supplies and services were under the direct authority of the navy secretary and "not delegated through the usual chain of command but . . . [through] the supply officer of an installation" via NAVSUP. It was also NAVSUP that conducted inspections, called contract management reviews (CMRs).[30]

At Miramar a CMR, the only detailed inspection of purchasing, was usually conducted every two years by the Navy Regional Contracting Center, which understood the complicated federal acquisition regulations. But the line command chain was not routinely informed of its results. A supply management inspection in September 1983 "incorporated a review of 'Buy Our Spares Smart' implementation," but since a command inspection took place in the same month and did not include BOSS initiatives, line and staff were not looking at the same problem, this despite a 1984 CMR indicating deficiencies.[31]

The dimensions of the supply problem at Miramar were huge. The facility supported 23 squadrons, 248 aircraft. Its supply department employed 554 military and civilian personnel, 290 of them in supply support, 13 of them in open purchasing. Stocks at Miramar included 62,000 items worth $210 million. In FY 84 Miramar processed 226,713 requisitions, with 9.6 percent of these from the private sector. Between October 1982 and May 1985, 27,013 open purchases were made. Of those bought between August 1984 and May 1985, only 29 were, upon review, "considered to have been purchased at unreasonable prices."[32] The problem items at Miramar might have amounted to less than three dozen, but that was enough to draw media attention, especially to items such as ashtrays and ejection-seat wrenches, whose costs the man in the street could judge.[33]

CINCPACFLT's report pointed out that the admiral in charge of the fighter airborne early-warning wing of the U.S. Pacific Fleet (who had been summarily relieved by Secretary Lehman) "was not aware of the results" of the inspection at the time it was made and added that "neither the investigation nor this review identified any failures by him to perform his duty."[34]

But in the CNO's judgment, the BOSS guidelines on spare parts purchasing promulgated in NAVOP 086/83 were clear. He sent numerous personal messages to the flag community, including the line rear admiral commanding the Pacific Fleet's fighter airborne early-warning wing, and under whose authority Miramar came, reminding all flags "that their personal interest in the procurement functions performed by subordinate activities was essential to the success of the BOSS initiative." But the rear admiral concerned, T. J. Cassidy, Jr., "failed to take aggressive personal actions [and] is accountable for this failing."[35] Watkins went on to say that a CO could never use the excuse that he had been unaware of problems.[36] He noted revisions in the system for CMR routings so that major claimants and type commanders, as well as the VCNO and the inspector general and assistant secretary for supply and logistics, could now get "copies of any unsatisfactory CMRs"[37]

Captain Roach summed the Miramar affair up by saying that at that facility different people had different information and the command style of the admiral discouraged negative reporting. When all was said and done, "the detailed instructions bypassed Cassidy but he still knew from CNO that he should look at it all."

Both the *Kitty Hawk* affair and the Miramar affair resulted in adverse publicity for the navy, focused on costly spare parts. Each highlighted the need for reform of the system. *Kitty Hawk* ultimately represented a case of inadequate data processing combined with a procurement system that ignored cost to maximize readiness. Miramar was ultimately a lesson on the danger of separating line and staff functions.

Vice Admiral Robert F. Dunn, then commander, Naval Air Force, U.S. Atlantic Fleet, wrote an interesting letter on this point to VCNO Admiral Busey on 10 October 1985, while Miramar was still fresh news. He cited "the rampant growth of special interest communities" on shore stations, which made "station commanding officers . . . responsible for only a small cross-section of what goes on at their stations." Things like "PSD, Navy Exchange, Commissary, medical and dental, EOD, and frequently public works and supply, have their own chains of command separate from the station CO." In a similar letter to Admiral Busey, Vice Admiral James Service, Dunn's counterpart in the Pacific, wrote that "these stove pipe organizations demonstrate a tendency to serve them-selves. . . . [Instead,] the officers in charge . . . should all be department heads." One skipper apparently remarked to him "that the only thing he commanded was the head and coat racks and the only ground he had was a 50-foot circle around the flagpole."[38]

As the history of the navy shows, no decision on one side or the other of this command question is likely to be permanent.

SUPPLY-SIDE ADMIRALS AND ABOLITION
OF THE NAVAL MATERIAL COMMAND

BOSS and the institution of a competition advocate for systems procurement were not the only Washington initiatives to improve the management side of the navy. The 1 April 1985 *Pittsburgh Press*, in an article titled "Supply-Side Admirals," announced the navy secretary's new policy of reserving "100 of the 253 admiral appointments for 'material professionals' who previously will have been trained as managers in such places as Harvard Business School, Wharton School of Business at the University of Pennsylvania, and the Naval Postgraduate School. . . ." The paper came down in favor of the change: "Weapons procurement now is so scandal-ridden that support for the defense budget is threatened. . . ." (This was written before the *Kitty Hawk* and Miramar cases.)

In March 1985, Admiral Watkins, responding to questions after addressing an air force brigadier general conference, explained the rationale for the move. The navy had "been the poorest of the services in developing a flag community that is business conscious." It had always put the unrestricted line "in the warfighting mode, when in fact only small numbers of the flag level move back and forth to sea." It had been doubly unfortunate, then, to equate three stars or four stars predominately with sea duty at the very time managerial talent was needed. For this reason the navy had created "a new career field which has at its apex a four star" for those who, say, at the sixteen-year point, opted and were selected for it.

Watkins pointed to the priorities the navy itself had attached to sea duty, where an officer who touched ground with his ship would be tossed out even where the damage was slight. But a naval officer who misspent several billion dollars because of naive business practice—"we usually give him," said Watkins tongue in cheek, "a Legion of Merit!" The navy was through calling people in and saying, "This is the third time you have fallen off the gangway when you walked aboard ship. You really ought to be a material manager."

The speech was humorous, the action dead sober and overdue. Of the 100 flag billets, 38 would be from the unrestricted line, with a follow-on stream of 200 captains—10 percent of the navy's 0-6s.[39]

As fundamental as this change was the announcement, made on 9 April 1985 by Secretary Lehman and Admiral Watkins, of the forthcoming abolition of a whole layer of the navy's Washington command structure. As of 9 May, said Lehman, the Naval Material Command and its four-star billet would disappear, taking with it 450 billets.[40]

Under the old setup, the Naval Material Command had authority over the five systems commands: Naval Air, Naval Sea, Naval Supply, Naval Facilities, and Naval Electronics. The chief of naval material reported, dual-hatted, to the CNO and the secretary. In (pre-Lehman) practice, the guidance or orders he received from the secretary could be minimal and confined to rather general acquisition-policy considerations.

Now this setup would be replaced. Under the new arrangement, Naval Electronics would disappear, to be replaced by a new systems command for space and warfare systems. All five systems would report directly to the CNO for execution of their missions and to the secretary for policy.[41]

Lehman blamed the Naval Material Command for second-guessing programs and delaying them.[42] He ordered the systems commands to cut their staffs by 10 percent. On this organizational change he and Watkins were in complete accord. The total reduction would amount to approximately one thousand Washington billets.

The CNO and the secretary also agreed that the Naval Material Command should be abolished. But their reasons, or those they emphasized, were different. Watkins's preliminary memo of 20 March 1985 on warfare systems organization began as follows:

> We will fight the next war with Battle Groups and Battle Forces on a global scale, not with individual platforms or in a single theater. The Battle Group requires information from intelligence sources, non-organic sensors, and organic sensors, and the capability to control and coordinate multiple platforms and weapon systems in order to detect, engage, and destroy the enemy. Today we express operational requirements and then conceive and acquire warfare systems on an individual platform basis. We need to go a step further and establish procedures and a structure that will produce an effective warfighting force through the engineered integration of all constituents that are requisite to Battle Group effectiveness.[43]

In a follow-up memo of 5 April 1985, the CNO forwarded a proposed restructuring plan developed by a group headed by the undersecretary of the navy. Old and new diagrams indicated the abolition of Naval Electronics and the establishment of the Space and Warfare Command (SPAWARS). The aim was to eliminate layers (including 450 positions) and provide a systems command focused on integrated use of ships and aircraft within the battle group. SPAWARS would also integrate space technology into warfare strategy.[44]

It was fairly apparent that the CNO's interest lay equally divided between decreasing layering and advancing the composite warfare/battle group point of view. He viewed the whole arrangement of the material command as inefficient. The tendency for the chief of naval material was to insist that all decisions pass through him.

The secretary's problem with the old arrangement grew mainly out of the fact that the chief of naval material had four-star rank. Vice Admiral William H. Rowden, commander of the Naval Sea Systems Command in 1987, thought the navy's rationale for the change glossed over the subtle but demanding issue of seniority: "A major reason why the Chief of Naval Material was disestablished was one of seniority among admirals and civilian secretaries. The Chief of Naval Material as a four-star officer was senior to the Assistant Secretaries and could make decisions on acquisitions."[45] This meant that the secretary had to get the chief of naval material to agree to any acquisition strategy or policy, and then he had to implement it through his assistant secretaries, which was awkward.

If the secretary was having trouble, what about the VCNO? From a strict chain-of-command point of view, of course, the chief of naval material was no different from any four-star field commander such as CINCPACFLT, with whom the VCNO had to deal. But the proximity in Washington of OPNAV and the systems commands, and their need to interact, increased the possibility of friction between the VCNO and the chief of naval material. Admiral William N. Small, VCNO from 1981 to 1983, before the change, commented that he and Admiral John G. Williams, Jr., chief of naval material from 1981 to mid-1983, were promoted on the same day and were on the same level of the chain of command. Small said that as VCNO he "never had a major role to play in the dealings between the Chief of Naval Operations and the Chief of Naval Material; the CNM felt himself to be an equal to the Vice Chief, with the same access to the CNO. . . . Tom Hayward's view was that we both worked for him and administrative things for OPNAV were under VCNO but the Deputy Chiefs had direct access to the systems commanders, which was the way [Hayward thought] it ought to be."[46]

So the setup, said Admiral Small, did not as such create friction within the uniformed side of the navy. Admiral Ronald J. Hays, who succeeded Small and was VCNO when the chief of naval material billet was abolished (he chaired the study that led to this), commented that the position had become a bottleneck. He cited the example of Chief of Naval Material Admiral Steve White disconnecting the Air Systems Command's hotline to OP-05 (DCNO, air) so that all communications would go through him. This despite OP-05's comment that he had no business to conduct with the chief of naval material.[47]

In any dual control system, with guidance partly from the CNO, partly from the secretary, everyone must work hard to see that communications do not break down and that coordination is achieved. That had at one time been the chief of naval material's job. It is possible that, in time, the Space and Naval Warfare Systems Command (SPAWARS) will assume this coordinating role. But SPAWARS has a full plate now. In many ways, especially conceptually, it has the toughest job of any systems command. Its CO, Vice Admiral Glen Clark, said that OP-094 is SPAWAR's principal sponsor because SPAWAR's only product line is C^{3}I (command, control, communications, intelligence) equipment; but 095 is its principal customer or sponsor for the choosing of warfare systems "architecture." So SPAWARS is both a procuring agency with a life-cycle responsibility for C^{3}I and for spacecraft, and a conceptual agency for warfare systems architecture and engineering—a new function in the navy. SPAWARS develops systems concepts under OPNAV direction and then builds the systems.

Clark commented that until recent years "we have been largely a black box Navy. That is to say, we have developed operational requirements on the basis of black boxes or small systems. And every time we have put one together it has been, relatively speaking, independent of all the other systems and components that are going to work around it."[48] He categorized the earlier approach as stovepipe, each part being chosen without much thought of how it would fit into the system. This was still going on at a time when technology required a much more integrated battle force, one that could operate as a single entity. Clark illustrated his point by considering the Tomahawk missile, which could be launched from well outside a ship's on-board sensors; there had to be additional sensors from other platforms to defend against it.

Clark's view was that platform sponsors, the war lords, were still dominant in OPNAV, that 095 had not yet developed real clout, and that 095's "warfare appraisal system" had produced only modest changes. That would not change unless the OPNAV process was reversed and it was 095 who put the program together, the platform sponsors merely suggesting alternatives.

The efficient coordination of the systems commands with each other and with OPNAV, the CNO, and the secretary is no easy matter. First, a link between OPNAV and the systems commands is required to ensure that military requirements continue to be looked after properly. (But OPNAV should not design or get into the technical end, while systems commands should not get into policy.) Second, since more than one systems command is involved in any final platform/weapon system, proper communication and coordination must be set up between them. Third, the secretary and the CNO must avoid contradictory guidance. Fourth, for the secretary to make proper decisions, the CNO must regularly apprise him of the thinking of the chief OPNAV personnel.

It is apparent from this list alone why a chief of naval material was established in the first place, even if the setup did not always work to everyone's satisfaction. It is also apparent why a line of responsibility from the secretary through the CNO and on to OPNAV and the systems commands would ensure communications and clear-cut authority lines. What the single line of control would not do, however, was allow the secretary to exercise direct authority without layers between. For Secretary Lehman, this was the rub. To control costs, he felt he needed much more direct contact with program offices within a systems command.

Lehman followed his April 1985 abolition of the chief of naval material with a new navy acquisition policy on 20 November 1985.[49] In his presentation to the Packard Commission on Defense Management on 10 December 1985, Lehman explained that policy, explaining how the chain of accountability had been shortened.[50] In April 1986 the commission forwarded a report on acquisition to the president in which it urged that Congress move in the same direction by creating a new position, undersecretary of defense, acquisition, and that the secretary of defense designate service acquisition executives within each military department who would, in turn, have direct control over program managers. Three levels.[51] In 1986 Congress created the new position and specified that the "Office of the Secretary of the Navy shall have sole responsibility" for acquisition and a number of other functions.[52] The secretary was also solely responsible for research and development, although he could assign that part of it having to do with military requirements and test and evaluation to the CNO (or marine headquarters), and CNO's office could provide advice or assistance.

Events were moving along the path Secretary Lehman preferred. The question remains, how well was the setup working in terms of communication and coordination?

In his final press interview before leaving office, Lehman pointed to a phone on his desk that directly linked him to one of the systems commands. He picked it up and was immediately conversing with the CO of that command. Or so it was reported. Vice Admiral Rowden, asked in an interview about this point, pointed to his own direct phone link to the secretary. Rowden commented succinctly: "That phone has been out of order for about nine months." No calls came through it, nor did Rowden expect any. Liaison between his command and the secretary's office was left to the assistant secretaries—in Rowden's case, shipbuilding and logistics daily, and research and engineering once a week. There was a regular Thursday lunch with the first of these two assistant secretaries and with all the systems commanders. As for links to the VCNO and the CNO, Rowden was in contact with the VCNO as needed, but the CNO he had not visited within the nine months that had passed since Admiral

Trost had taken over. He could see the CNO if he wanted, but if each of the five systems commanders took thirty minutes of the CNO's time, they would eat up two and a half hours of a busy schedule. At the same time, Rowden felt that the CNO had "a diffused view" of the systems commands and that coordination now depended on the three-star level. No one in OPNAV had the responsibility, commensurate with authority, to put the organization together: "There is no [OPNAV] sounding board for that now. I believe that is a great deficiency, and I believe the CNO does, too."[53]

We saw in chapter 3 that it is the CNO's horizontal barons who are supposed to integrate acquisition and programs in OPNAV. But their direct links to the systems commands, except for SPAWARS, are not great. For the Sea Systems or Air Systems Command, it is "their" warlord who counts most in OPNAV. According to Admiral Rowden, OPNAV coordination under any organizational arrangement tends to focus on budget, on line items, rather than on policy and military requirements.

But with the secretary and his principal assistants dealing directly and in detail with systems commanders (and even program managers within systems commands), how does this procedure ensure that everyone knows what they should? The Navy Department's Program Strategy Board, which meets at the level of secretary-CNO, may be highly useful for initiating programs, but for tracking them? Vice Admiral Rowden, again, thought that the CNO's military requirements could gradually get buried, especially under contractual and budgetary pressures.[54] This was possible particularly because the difficulties that interfered with a military requirement showed up only gradually. A seemingly trivial event occurred in the contractual process and only later, when it was too late, did its significance become apparent. The CNO often learned about it only after the fact.

Under the old system, with a chief of naval material, a single officer and his staff were responsible for coordination. That involved a lot of billets, a lot of overhead, and often a lot of delay. That the old system could frustrate a secretary, responsible for contracting, is clear. But without a chief of naval material how are the military and business requirements to be coordinated? The CNO is responsible for the first, the secretary for the second. Both are busy men. Who, under them, can deal with the whole problem?

DIVIDED OPINIONS ON THE SYSTEMS COMMANDS

There was no issue, no question, in the Watkins years that divided opinion more in the navy than this one.

Lehman's view was that the abolition of Naval Material not only trimmed the bureaucracy but also consolidated the business side of the systems commands in the secretariat. No longer could a command argue, for example, that the CNO said the F/A-18 had to fly x fleet per second and therefore cost did not matter, it was a military requirement.[55] The change also broke OPNAV domination of the systems commanders. Under the new streamlined procedure, the secretary reviewed three elements of a program—specifications schedule, and budget—then turned it over to the program officer for implementation. Any further change to those elements required CNO/secretary approval. That ended a pattern of constant changes from OPNAV.[56]

In short, in Lehman's view the purpose of the reform was to free program managers from excessive control.[57] Obviously, the idea of cutting OPNAV out of the picture did not appeal to Watkins, though he believed OPNAV should avoid the technical sphere. According to him, there should be connections between the systems commands and the secretary for contracting, and between the systems commands and the CNO for military requirements. Lehman wanted to set military requirements himself, particularly for air warfare systems. "I felt that was wrong," Watkins commented.

> It had the potential to mix the politics of procurement in time of peace too heavily with the warfighting needs of the sailors who had to fight and win with these systems in time of war. . . . [Lehman] put himself into a position where he thought he had to run the Navy all by himself. And he couldn't! One Secretary, no matter how talented, can't do it. You have to rely on the CNO and all the officers under him.[58]

Watkins did however think that the abolition of the chief of naval material had improved control:

> We have an organizational change that has an OPNAV program coordinator sitting in the same office with the Program Manager. This means there is less time wasted by the PM in briefing OPNAV sponsors on what their programs are doing over there. . . . Before, the PM didn't have time and he was muzzled on money. He was told to shut up and do the best he could with the reduced budgets provided.[59]

Admiral Robert L. J. Long, former VCNO, gave his view succinctly: "I do not support having major Navy programs controlled directly by the Secretary of the Navy and his assistant secretaries." The CNO should be intimately involved in setting up requirements and seeing that programs are established to meet those requirements. The secretary should establish policy, the CNO execute it.[60] This was also the view of former Navy Secretary Claytor.

Vice Admiral Richard A. Miller, number two at Naval Material under Admiral John Williams, Jr., and then Admiral Steve White, felt there was legitimacy to the argument that the assistant secretaries had been exercising prerogatives not rightfully theirs by bypassing the chief of naval material and dealing directly with the systems commands. In the secretary/CNO division of responsibility, development was the gray area and the question of who would be program manager to superintend development was key. Assistant Secretary Paisley had put people forward for the job himself, but White had drawn the line. The chain of command was being undermined by assistant secretaries dealing directly with captains and commanders and ignoring their four-star boss.[61] Miller concluded that with all the problems attending the Naval Material Command, it still served the vital function of coordination.

Admiral Williams, the next to last chief of naval material, pointed out another facet of the problem. Since the navy would "always put the best operational people into the best operational jobs, it was the operational people one cut below" who would end up working in the systems commands. The new management career path was a step forward in this respect. Also, OPNAV had been overbearing: "You could not get OPNAV to quit, once they told you what they wanted. They wanted to manage *how* you [went] about obtaining it."[62] In Williams' view, there had to be some type of organization to oversee those elements common to the systems commands. The secretary could not provide overall guidance because there was a constant succession of politically minded people filling that position; some would understand contracting, others would not. A system that put the secretary in direct charge would work well sometimes and at other times not at all.[63] Williams, concluding, added that the officers in charge of systems commands should be specialists, not unrestricted line officers.

Vice Admiral Robert R. Monroe favored the abolition of Naval Material on the principle that both Defense Department and navy management organizations needed thinning. He told with approval a story attributed to Rickover, who supposedly said that the way to deal with the Washington bureaucracy was to line them up and have them count off 1, 2, 3. All 1s would go back to work, all 2s would be put in sealed rooms able to communicate only with other 2s, and all 3s would be sent packing. Monroe went on:

> If you want money you go to work in industry. If you want academic fame you go to a university. If you want power you go to Washington. Everybody in Washington wants power, so everybody wants to do everything. The people in OPNAV want to do the systems commands' "how we buy it" jobs as well as their own. And the

systems commands want to decide *what* we buy, as well as managing the acquisition. NavMat tried to do both OPNAV and SysCom jobs. They had to go.[64]

An ideal arrangement for the systems commands, in Monroe's view, would be to limit NAVSEA to hulls, machinery, electrical systems, sea-keeping, and ship-keeping. A combat systems command would design all shipboard combat systems and work with NAVSEA to develop interfaces between the combat systems and the ship, and to develop modular spaces for combat systems within the ship. The objectives would be systems uniformity between ships, and ships designed for ease of update. Naval Air would be left alone, since it has functioned well.[65] Monroe's concept takes Hayward's and Watkins's one step further.

John Lehman, during his long tenure and with his driving personality and business sense, took personal charge of navy contracting and rearranged the department to respond efficiently to that personal direction. But the usual navy secretary is not a John Lehman. How well will his management concept work without him?

CONTRACTING IN THE LEHMAN ERA

Secretary Lehman often pointed the finger at government itself as a major source of inflated defense costs. The bureaucracy was excessive, and there were too many rules, too many decisions year by year, too many special-interest riders on defense bills. On 22 April 1985 Lehman said to *Navy Times*:

> My personal staff answered 125,000 phone calls from Congress and the 32 committees and subcommittees of oversight we have grown to. We have responded to 25,700 written queries for data and information.
> This is just one year's tally. Official notifications and reports to Congress totalled 1,500. This is by my staff and CNO's staff. Hearings, just in 1984, . . . and large-scale committee briefings totalled 1,250. This is just the Navy Department.[66]

Fourteen months later, in June 1986, at the current strategy forum at the Naval War College, he reported "some good news. After five years of often unsung work, the changes promoted by Secretary of Defense Weinberger have begun to break through the GOSPLAN [Soviet national planning] mentality." He cited new discipline and accountability through management by service secretaries, reform in procurement, and "a quickening response by industry."[67]

Specifically, the navy had made several fundamental changes in the way it did business. First, it had sought to become competitive by avoiding single-source selection wherever possible.[68] In shipbuilding, competition had increased from 15.7 percent in 1980 to 86.6 percent in 1986. Lehman pointed to a resulting cost underrun averaging $1 billion for each of the previous four years, 1981–85. Similarly, $1.2 billion was saved through competition in the aircraft account. Other reforms included emphasizing fixed-price contracts, controlling gold-plating, and "curbing our tendency to chase R&D rainbows." Such changes were revolutionary. Compare the "Congressional-executive bureaucratic octopus that favors the status quo regardless of how absurd and costly the consequences." In a favorite thrust, he mentioned the "1,152 feet of library shelf space for acquisition laws and regulations, 3,183 House and Senate subcommittee staff members, 7,600 Congressional lobbyists, 17,963 Congressional staffers, 45,000 MilSpecs. . . ."[69] By contrast, the navy had wiped out 450 billets from Naval Material and another 600 from the systems commands.[70]

The whole Lehman approach involved much more than these highlights, of course. On 21 February 1986, in FY 87 testimony before the Senate Appropriations Committee, Lehman explained it in much more detail. For example, the navy had adopted what was known as phased maintenance for a whole class of ships—routine servicing and repair at stated intervals. Such overhauls had always encountered problems, some foreseeable, some unanticipated. The earlier approach had encouraged contractors to bid at an unrealistically low initial price. Then they would "get well on the open-and-inspect work," the part which could be anticipated to have unanticipated problems.[71] Naturally, the overall cost would soar. Now the approach was to divide the two sets of problems. A base package for a given ship class was awarded competitively; the open-and-inspect work was handled separately. Until "you open up a pump and turbine," Lehman said, "you do not know how much work you have and there is no way to fix-price that in advance." That cost would have to be extra.

Later, Lehman cited the new acquisition policy for ships and aircraft. He characterized the V-22 tilt rotor aircraft purchase as a case study of proper acquisition because it coupled fixed-price development with clear milestones as the program moved from concept to development to production.[72] It was not a multi-year buy. The navy had built-in competition from the start. When the program passed from pilot to full-scale production both Bell and Boeing would have production lines, but the two companies would have to compete each year for their share of the units produced. This procedure would ensure not only two sources of supply but "real competition every year for the life of the program. . . ."[73]

Answering a question about the F/A-18, Lehman said the navy would acquire it from a single company ("sole source") but on a multi-year contract. The savings there would come from an efficient production run extending over more than a year. It made a lot of sense to make sole-source contracts multi-year contracts.

In almost simultaneous testimony to the House Armed Services Committee, Lehman explained other parts of his business strategy. Asked about discontinuing payments for upfront tooling and test equipment, Lehman clarified the point. It was not a question of refusing such support where there was some clear risk that the program under development might be canceled. But once the milestone decision to go into full production was reached, the contractors would have "to invest capital to sell us products," not often the case before. He cited the example of the Pratt and Whitney 404, initially developed by GE. Pratt and Whitney had become involved as a second source and bought the necessary tools. Returning to the V-22, Lehman commented that the navy would buy initial pilot-production tooling because the program was still high risk. When, however, the V-22 was put into full production, two-thirds of the tooling would be purchased by contractors, saving $600 million.[74]

Lehman, in response to a question about whether all new construction would be competitively bid, said he wanted "fixed-price 50/50 share lines," but that there were limitations. For example, Trident would if necessary continue as cost-plus simply because of the president's specific priorities, although the navy hoped to get Newport News to compete on it. Another example was aircraft carriers, which were not built in sufficient numbers for fixed-price competition.[75] The fifty-fifty share line meant that the navy established a contract price and then added a ceiling of 25 percent, the cost of which the navy would share. Above that the contractor absorbed all costs. The navy also offered an incentive of fifty-fifty sharing under the contract price.[76]

Lehman contrasted this to the situation in the 1970s, when ships were typically "only five-percent designed when lead ship contracts were awarded," making it impossible for a contractor to estimate his time and materials accurately. With the Arleigh Burke DDG 51 program, that had changed; now all competing contractors participated in the completion of a design and shared data so that no single one was guaranteed the lead contract.[77] It was a formula very different from total-package procurement: "This summer we will be picking a final design [for the DDG 51], one of the two competing designs. The loser will then move over and participate in the completion of the [winning] detailed design. . . . Both companies would then compete for DDG 51 production.[78]

Quite a set of changes.

PART III

CAST OFF
ALL LINES!

Chapter 7

MODERNIZING THE FLEET

Solving the personnel, command, and management problems of the navy was necessary to avoid moving backwards. To move forward, the fleet had to be modernized. This required a three-faceted approach: technical, political, and strategic.

Technical, because ships (as well as the planes and systems that went with them) had to be designed to meet needs for many years to come in an era of rapid technological change. Because they were expensive, and expected to engage in strenuous operations far from U.S. waters, they had to be rugged and highly capable. And because they might engage the Soviet fleet, they had to incorporate the latest technological designs and anticipate future ones.

Political, because Congress would approve funds and because repeated appropriations over the course of a decade were necessary if a proper fleet were to be built. Thus it was imperative that scandals and mismanagement not destroy public confidence in the integrity and efficiency of the U.S. Navy.

Strategic, because modern ships funded by Congress would still have to be used effectively in battle. Where to deploy and how to conduct battles were critical questions.

While in some ways strategy was the foundation stone of the whole process of modernization (how you will fight determines what you need), in fact it unfolded in the sequence just listed: technical, political, strategic. Platforms and systems are developed over a period of many years, and planning begins long before funding. And whether funds are forthcoming or not, the U.S. Navy knows that it always needs large, technologically advanced, rugged ships, regardless of the specific strategic scenario. The time-consuming part of modernization is design and

127

development; the most delicate part is selling the program to Congress; the most difficult part, intellectually, is the strategic question.

THE ACQUISITION PROCESS

Before winning political support from the administration and financial support from Congress, major programs for systems and platforms must first survive the Defense Department's acquisition process. To understand the arguments over some of the navy's prime modernization programs, it is necessary to look at that process, especially testing and evaluation.

Over the last fifty years acquisition has become more complex. As Admiral Ike Kidd pointed out, in the 1930s when President Roosevelt wanted to enlarge and modernize the fleet, the procedure was to go to Congress and request the amount to be spent that fiscal year. The U.S. Navy "bought ships in those days by the yard—literally"—forty feet one year, fifty feet the next. Finally, Congress decided it wanted to know the total cost. Funds would then be metered out as the navy needed them.[1] But World War II set aside considerations of cost. Congress appropriated funds in the amount requested.

By the time the World War II fleet was being phased out under Zumwalt, the Department of Defense had become a tremendous bureaucracy with an elaborate process for justifying requests for new systems or platforms.

With McNamara in charge at the Pentagon, systems analysis, with its attempt to define marginal utility, was the accepted approach for determining what systems and platforms were worth buying. By the early 1970s the navy was learning the new approach—that is to say, it was becoming good at systems analysis; it did not in fact acquire in any numbers the ships and systems it needed. To get a system approved without a platform, or a platform without a system, was difficult. The forerunner to the Aegis system is an example. Vice Admiral Robert Monroe explained:

> You couldn't go ahead with a missile program until its ship program was proceeding in parallel. The years in which the Washington environment was favorable to a ship program, the missile wasn't ready, so the ship was ultimately cancelled. The years in which you could move ahead with a development program for the missile and the radar, you got stopped because you didn't have a ship. . . . [This] was (and continues to be) one of the cardinal abuses committed in the name of systems analysis. Good systems analysis would recognize that a ship's life cycle is 30–40 years, a combat system's life is 5–10, [and plan accordingly].[2]

In the mid-1970s this problem merely supplemented the reluctance of Congress to support a modernized navy. By the late 1970s, the Carter administration's strategic concepts, which downplayed the need for that navy, was an additional negative factor.

McNamara's system for acquisition was modeled after his commercial experience. He developed total-package procurement, in which research and development were included with production in the same contract. The C5-A is an example.[3] According to Vice Admiral Monroe, the Defense Department told industry what it wanted in general terms, then industry took over and delivered the final product. It was a one-sided process in which government abdicated responsibility to industry. In 1969 Deputy Secretary of Defense David Packard discarded total-package procurement and in its place established the Defense Systems Acquisition Review Council (DSARC). The new approach at this stage involved participatory management by the services, with the Defense Department setting basic objectives, strategy, policy, and dollar limits and the services seeing that their weapons systems and force levels conformed with those broad guidelines. Monroe, who spent much of his career in testing, evaluation, and acquisition, called the Packard approach the best in three decades for combining participatory management and a specific weapons-acquisition process that emphasized "fly before buy"—working the bugs out of the pilot model before beginning full production. The new procedure involved a milestone approach in which the development steps were clearly laid out, from the time of establishing need to ultimate full-scale production.[4]

Deputy Secretary of Defense Packard also changed testing procedures. He distinguished between two kinds of testing: traditional development testing, which involved technical performance, and operational testing, newly instituted for the Defense Department. With the latter, said Monroe, "you don't care whether the plane can fly exactly Mach 1.5 or not. What you care about is whether the plane is effective in its combat mission." Development testing was carried out under controlled conditions, with the company that produced a product frequently doing the main testing. Operational tests were different:

> First, operational tests are performed against a real or simulated enemy who is doing his best to defeat the system. (Up to this time, enemies haven't even appeared in the process.)
> Second, operational tests are conducted under realistic operational conditions. When the developer tests, it's sunny and warm, with calm seas and little wind. Operational testing will be conducted at night, in heavy weather, icing temperatures, etc.
> Third, the crew will be a typical cross-section of fleet personnel—

not only for operating the systems, but for maintaining it. The developer will not be present.[5]

Operational testing and evaluation is important in the acquisition process because it is primarily conducted at the watershed point between development and production. In DSARC terminology, this is milestone 3. Milestone 1 is marked principally by paper studies. During milestone 2, a decision-coordinating paper establishes the readiness of a system to move from advanced development to full-scale engineering development. So the acquisitions process proceeds from need to concept to full-scale engineering development to production.[6] In 1986 DSARC was renamed the Joint Requirements and Management Board (JRMB) and given an expanded membership.

Operational test and evaluation, the linchpin of the JRMB process, terminates inefficient programs before they become too expensive and burden the fleet with unusable equipment.

Consider this point in terms of bureaucratic pressure. The head of the navy's Operational Test and Evaluation Force (OPTEVFOR) reports directly to the CNO and the secretary of the navy. He is the honest broker at the table when OPNAV and the systems commands, although willing to concede that a system still has bugs in it, want to press ahead. Overeager program managers often try to fool the CNO with technical jargon. Vice Admiral Monroe said that when he headed OPTEVFOR (1974–77) and attended milestone 3 meetings, there would frequently "be a conference table lined with about twelve three- and four-star admirals, and the only support I had in the room came from the CNO. On numerous occasions I'd be the only advisor recommending that the system not go into production."[7]

If we translate milestones into money and jobs at stake, we can see that pressures build up not only in the navy but also in industry and in Congress as a program moves along. Monroe gave an example of a typical milestone 2. At this point you must have decided whether the power source will be a Klystron or a traveling wave tube, you must have proved that you can get a given level of sensitivity in the receiver, and you must have shown that the composites to be used can survive at mach 7:

> You say, "We think we will be ready at the end of 1976. So, up until then, we'll spend $10 million a year. For '74, and '75, and '76 we'll put that much in the program. Then we'll pass Milestone 2 and go into full-scale engineering development. So for '77, '78, and '79, we put $50 million each in the program." All right. You put it into the POM and Congress enacts each early-year's budget. You come up to January of '76 and the President submits the $50 million budget for this system for '77, and by summer, the Congress enacts it. So by

summer '76 you have $50 million for '77. Now, in the fall of '76 you test the composite durability at Mach 7, and it doesn't work. And your power source development has been delayed, so you don't know whether either the Klystron or the traveling wave tube will produce the power levels needed. What you *should* do is simply delay the program a year, saying, "We haven't made it boys. We'll spend only $10 million in '77 also. Give up the excess $40 million, and we'll plan to ramp up in '78."[8]

One can easily see how pressures, industrial and political alike, mount. Jobs hang in the balance for industry, which also donates generously to congressmen, whose letters to the navy get instant attention. The service for its part is thinking, If we delay the milestone we may lose the program, and we've got to meet the threat. Although the program is not ready, there is tacit agreement between part of the navy, part of industry (those with the contract), and part of Congress (those from states who do the contracting and subcontracting) to pass milestone 2.

If we keep in mind that such pressures attend the development of every major weapon system, we shall understand better Congress's insistent and detailed questioning of programs. For Congress understands well that there is a built-in contradiction between annual appropriations and a cost-effective progression from one milestone to the next. But Congress has not been willing to do away with yearly allotments of funds. As for the navy program officer, he knows the system he is developing will have bugs. So long as he is confident they will be overcome, he wants to push ahead. And the CNO is aware that he may lose the program if he openly admits that it still has problems. Finally, the navy's operational testing and evaluation is designed to expose bugs. In the Aegis case, to which we shall turn shortly, this last point was critical.

AN OVERVIEW: BEHIND THE POWER CURVE

Two intersecting problems confronted navy design personnel in the 1970s as they looked ahead to the 1980s. First was the problem of ship numbers. In almost any category—frigates, carriers, submarines—inventory was far too low and undergoing bloc obsolescence. Replacements would need to be procured in large numbers in a relatively short time. The question of unit costs and total costs was therefore critical. Second was the rapid progress of the Soviet navy toward blue-water status. The Soviet effort was translating into improved ship types in uncomfortably large numbers. Now the United States was engaged in a large-scale and expensive arms race from a handicapped position.

In 1974, Secretary of the Navy J. William Middendorf II addressed the issue of ship numbers:

... just six years ago we had an active fleet of nearly 1,000 ships. Because most of these were constructed during World War II, and because of budget restraints, we have cut our Navy in half so that today we are about to go below 500 ships.

The service life expectancy for warships is 25 to 30 years. In 1968 the average age of the active fleet had increased to 18 years. It therefore became unmistakably clear that we had to reduce the numbers of our older ships in order to build the new ships we need[ed].

Between 1963 and 1967 the Navy planned nearly 50 new ships per year. Then came the fiscal demands of the Vietnam war with its requirements for operating funds at the expense of shipbuilding.

We also undertook the costly conversion of 31 Polaris submarines to carry the Poseidon missile, which substantially upgraded the nation's strategic deterrence capabilities.

In the last six years although we were forced to reduce the numbers of aging ships in the active fleet, the Navy received authority to build 13 ships per year. This rate of shipbuilding—13 ships per year—means that the U.S. Navy will never recover the strength of 900 ships but also will not even be able to sustain a fleet of 500 ships unless increases are made in the number of ships being built each year.

We have, in effect, undertaken a course of action which if allowed to go uncorrected would amount to an unilateral navel disarmament.[9]

The effort was going to take a lot of money and much determination, the latter of which a two-term Reagan administration and the steadying effect of a single secretary of defense would provide. The Reagan budget did not simply throw larger and larger amounts of money into defense, with each service getting a certain percentage increase. The true picture can be seen in table 3, taken from Secretary Weinberger's FY 87 annual report. Note that the army in current dollars nearly doubled from FY 81 to FY 87, growing more proportionately than the navy. The air force, starting with fewer constant dollars, almost reached parity with the navy.

For the navy in particular, FY 84 and 85 were watershed years. In FY 85 the Aegis missile-defense system came under severe attack, the advanced 688-class submarine was being pushed along with the new SSNX or 21 class, and the *Arleigh Burke*–class destroyers (DDG 51) were in the critical design phase. Congressional hearings were voluminous and sustained, and the navy was criticized for the alleged failures of the Aegis system as well as its refusal to procure diesel submarines or to allow allied nations to build them in U.S. shipyards. FY 85 was not the largest shipbuilding or ship-conversion year in the plan, but it was the year that would make or break the 600-ship plan.

Table 3. DEPARTMENT OF DEFENSE BUDGET AUTHORITY BY COMPONENT, FY 87

(dollars in millions)

	FY 1981	FY 1982	FY 1983	FY 1984	FY 1985	FY 1986†	FY 1987
Current Dollars							
Department of the Army	43,252	52,254	57,529	68,664*	74,270*	74,862*	81,528*
Department of the Navy	58,011	69,569	81,854	87,365*	99,015*	98,481*	104,503*
Department of the Air Force	53,144	64,821	74,074	90,851*	99,420*	98,330*	105,192*
Defense Agencies/OSD/JCS	7,483	9,222	9,256	10,746	13,126	15,850	19,486
Defense-wide	16,475	17,885	16,761	524	970	1,867	891
Total—Direct Program (B/A)	178,365	213,751	239,474	258,150	286,802	289,391	311,600
Constant FY 1987 Dollars							
Department of the Army	56,630	62,119	65,871	76,270*	79,439*	77,540*	81,528*
Department of the Navy	72,749	83,416	92,848	96,456*	105,572*	101,831*	103,633*
Department of the Air Force	65,963	73,478	83,457	100,081*	105,910*	101,627*	103,311*
Defense Agencies/OSD/JCS	9,464	10,997	10,594	11,889	13,977	16,417	19,486
Defense-wide	21,332	21,795	19,363	583	1,043	1,906	891
Total—Direct Program (B/A)	226,138	251,807	273,133	285,279	305,941	299,321	308,849‡

Source: Secretary of Defense Caspar W. Weinberger, *Annual Report to the Congress, Fiscal Year 1987* (GPO, 1986), 314.

*Includes retired pay accrual.
†Lower budget authority in the military personnel accounts in FY 1986 reflects the congressional direction to finance $4.5 billion for the military pay raise and retirement accrual costs by transfers from prior year unobligated balances.
‡Original table has incorrect total of 311,600.

THE ISSUE OF UNIT SIZE

The clearest path into these complicated issues is the question of unit size. The U.S. Navy preferred bigger ships. (Academic critics of U.S.-Soviet ship-number comparisons invariably pointed out that the United States had more tonnage if fewer units.) Both the Congress and the public tended to regard size and cost as direct variables. Few admirals testifying to Congress were able to explain the point well, and even relatively informed discussions in journals left the point obscure.

Most understood the beginning of the analysis: The U.S. Navy had to operate in high or rough seas, forward deployed, for substantial periods of time. What was lacking was informed receptivity to two points: that it is not hull size but rather shipboard systems that determine most of the cost (they become obsolete faster than hulls), and that hull size is critical to flexibility in updating and (in the case of submarines) to quieter operation.

With the expected service life of a ship calculated even at the usual minimum of twenty-five years (some have gone thirty or forty-five years), the hull long outlasts the systems inside it. Consider, for example, that a ship at the end of its twenty-five-year service in 1990 entered service in 1965, and that a ship retired in 1965 began service in 1940. Think of the revolutionary changes in technology each of these periods saw: in the first, nuclear warheads and missiles and jet planes; in the second, the advent of computer-controlled battle-group-wide defenses and space-related communications.

There are two ways one can approach the design of a ship: assemble current systems, distribute them for weight and survivability, and enclose them in a hull; or design a hull so that systems can be pulled out and replaced as necessary. The navy made progress toward the second approach in hull design with the 963-class destroyer built by Litton. In this case, modular hull pieces moved down an "assembly line" and were welded into a single unit. The *Trident* design for Electric Boat at Groton worked on the same principle.

For the modular idea to work, wires and power lines running throughout the length of the ship must be kept to a minimum. The ideal is a system of plug-in, plug out by section. In the *Burke* class, a series of data buses serves as a shipboard multiplexing system. Only five coaxial cables run the length of the ship, allowing in excess of four thousand noncombat signals (such as propulsion and damage control) to tap into five data buses. They replace the usual five thousand cables running all over the ship. Modular components have been used in the *Burke*'s weapon system, too, and the vertical launching system is modular.[10]

This setup, combined with systems that can be used in various ship types, permits the economies inherent in larger production runs. (Additionally, the Aegis hull was derived from the *Spruance* destroyer and, modified, was used in the *Burke* design.) *Burke* systems improvements will eventually be funneled into Aegis cruisers.

Extra space built into ships to allow such changes is like clothing one size too large bought for a growing child. When asked in congressional hearings why the new SSN 21–class submarines could not be delayed and the navy simply improve the 688s, Vice Admiral Ron Thunman answered, "But we have no further space and weight in the 688 class to do the things we think are absolutely necessary to counter the Soviet submarines that we expect to see in the 1990's."[11] And in the FY 84 hearings the year before, Vice Admiral Walters, then DCNO for surface warfare, made a similar comment to the Senate Committee on Armed Services in reference to the *Spruance* destroyer. Originally, it "had a lot of margin in it for growth. From that ship we built [another] four that were originally built for the Iranians and are all in active service in our Navy. . . . In that process we used up some of the margin that was left. . . . [With the Aegis hull we] have used most of the margin in the ship. . . ."[12]

The fact is that cost considerations frequently convince navy designers to cut space which they cannot say with conviction will definitely be needed by the time of a ship's midlife upgrade. Vice Admiral Fowler, head of the Naval Sea Systems Command, responded to a question in congressional hearings by saying that "if I am going to realize these potential savings by [putting] in power and air-conditioning [I don't need] at this point, I can't do it on speculation alone. I have to have some idea of what will be needed. Do I need more today? Am I going to carry extra power from now until the year 2000 just because I might need it at that point? The answer is clearly no."[13] To cite another example, Vice Admiral Thunman's Group Tango, which designed the SSN 21, actually worked on three versions, A, B, and C. The final proposal was essentially B, since C, while larger and faster, was also judged too expensive within the navy community.[14]

So there are tradeoffs. But extra space and weight do translate into extra flexibility.

As for hull size versus systems in relation to total cost, the Aegis cruisers are a pertinent illustration. The total cost of three such ships in the FY 85 program, including advance procurement, was given as $3,150.0 million (follow-on units for FY 88 were estimated as two for $2500.3 million).[15] But navy figures show the entire ordnance package for the cruiser came to $654 million, with $190 million of it specifically for the Aegis system.[16] Non-ordnance costs amount to less than a half of the total, perhaps less in follow-on ships.

As we turn now for the first time to congressional hearings, we should keep in mind that they do not follow a logical path but tend to jump from one subject to another, particularly when it comes to the questioning that follows statements. And rarely in the course of hearings do congressional committees come to grips with the issues. Rather, committee members express the concerns of Congress. Their questions are markers on a potential political minefield.

THE ISSUE OF TESTING

Let us begin our discussion of testing with Admiral Walter's point in the FY 84 hearings about the Aegis cruiser. The platform "has a stable center of gravity and buoyancy reserve and, albeit *the margins are not there* that we would design in a new ship [a completely new hull design] . . . , it does have all the margins . . . to be perfectly safe under the worst conditions, which includes an 80-foot hole in the ship, flooding, 15-degree list in heavy seas with a 35-knot beam wind."[17] Any sailor would understand what this meant, that the margin used up had not decreased the platform's essential seaworthiness. But what the senators heard was the phrase "the margins are not there." Senator Hart asked what the highest sea state had been that the CG 47 had encountered in sea trials. The offhand answer: close to sea state 4, mostly. Had any icing been encountered in the sea trials? No. What would happen with a combination of high sea state and heavy icing?[18] The ship would be stable; the navy fully anticipated that it would perform under any conditions in the North Atlantic or any other sea. Hart responded, "Even though you haven't done any sea trials under those conditions?"

The questions and answers went on in this vein, Admiral Walters adding further information about testing with models at the David Taylor model basin.[19] There the navy could test under simulated conditions. Walters also indicated that weapons and other systems were tested to full capacity early on new ships, but that the hull itself was not immediately tested because new ships were often cruised for the first time in more tranquil waters.

The transcript is clear evidence that the senators misunderstood the word margin, which was used in two different senses: margin for growth in capability, and margin of stability. Nor did they get a clear picture of the testing process and what it was designed to do. Assistant Secretary George A. Sawyer did say that "the CG limit, the margins we are talking about with regard to this ship, is not based on an intact stability, but damaged stability. It considers a ship that has two compartments flooded and up to 15 per cent of her length essentially breached. . . . She then is subjected to a high-wind condition, above 30 knots, and must be able, after a permanent list of 20 degrees, to right herself."[20] No senator asked in what ocean this had been done. (The model basin was mentioned only later.)

The House and Senate FY 85 seapower subcommittee hearings took place almost simultaneously in the spring of 1984. Because the final Senate session was held last, however, we shall first look at the issue in the House.

Admiral Walters told the House subcommittee that despite comments in the press, the Aegis ship and missile system had been tested more than any new ship he could remember. Admittedly, operational tests had revealed some problems. But these tests had been severe. Their purpose was to expose kinks, not to prove how good the Aegis was. The failures fell into three categories: human error, systems breakdowns, and missile failures. Congressman Sisisky asked Walters what other kinds of failures there could be.[21]

Note that, although Admiral Walters gave a coherent statement, he mistakenly assumed two things. First, that Congress really knew what the navy was trying to determine through testing. Second, that it understood the notion of failure and success with reference to the navy's test objectives. To be fair, Walters had one arm tied behind his back, for classification of test results limited what could be said. That the spotting and firing capability was superior to the shot used was left unclear.

Obviously unsatisfied, Congressman Sisisky pressed for more details, asking whether the problems had been corrected. Walters answered yes on most points, but added that the navy was unsure about the cause of the missile failures since there had not been complete telemetry coverage.[22] His statement further increased the committee's doubts. It failed to underline the difference between trouble with the system and trouble merely with the missile.

More congressional discussion followed to clear up the muddle on 5 March 1984. In a briefing, Captain Al Carney summarized the operational evaluation report. This time the navy assumed less and began with the basics: "Operational testing is measured with one of two criteria. They are called operational effectiveness and operational suitability. In the area of operational effectiveness, we are talking about warfare mission areas such as antiair warfare, antisubmarine warfare, antisurface, and so forth."[23] In operational effectiveness, the Aegis cruiser Ticonderoga had met or surpassed all twelve objectives, and there was a shock test pending. In operational suitability, all twelve test objectives had been met.

The goal of operational testing was to evaluate new systems by putting them under maximum stress.[24] Carney gave details of firing results for twenty-one "opportunities" and eighteen missiles fired. (The record makes hard reading because of deletions, but apparently the committee was told that one-third of the shots hit their target.)

Vice Admiral Albert Baciocco alluded to another primary part of the testing problem, aerial targets. This entailed designing an offensive weapon such as the Soviets were assumed to have in future production by a certain date and then using it against a future U.S. defensive system. For example, an old navy missile, the Talos, now served as a low-altitude target called the Vandal.[25] The availability of proper targets was, as further hearings indicated, a complication in the testing program.

The navy was now heading for real trouble. On 3 April 1984, Representative Charles E. Bennett began House subcommittee hearings with the remark that Congress was not going to support the large increases being proposed for FY 85; he wanted to hear from the navy where cuts could best be made.[26] Lehman admitted that a ship program might have to be cut, but the DDG 51 program was the worst candidate for elimination, especially since the present outlays on it were small.[27] Attention shifted to the controversy over the Aegis system.

Representative Duncan Hunter, referring to the least successful of the Aegis tests, against low-flying supersonic missiles in their terminal phase, said he understood that the navy had no supersonic missile it could match against the Soviet's latest anti-ship missile.[28] It was true, Lehman responded, that the problem of the inner-zone defense area was difficult. The British had found the same problem in missile fuzing to destroy the low supersonic Sea Skimmer.[29] But the Aegis system was not designed for terminal defense. It was designed to add a particular type of area capability to the fleet's multi-layered defense. When Hunter remarked that funding for the Aegis system might be in trouble in the full committee, Representative Sisisky agreed.[30]

Admiral Watkins said there would be further tests, that the problem was apparently with the missile and that the navy now thought it knew what to do about it. Incoming missiles normally traveled through a high trajectory before descending low. The goal was to shoot them down before they could skim the sea.[31]

The navy made some of the most critical points late in the House proceedings: that the function of the Aegis was not terminal defense; that it was the most marginal Aegis requirement that produced the poorest test results, and that those results were not really the fault of the Aegis system but only of the missile used.

Now there was a danger of losing the program or having it severely curtailed. The navy had failed to explain in detail at the outset that good test results did not mean no failures. Walters had explained at one point that tests were made to determine what was wrong, but he had not stressed the point. It was widely reported that the Aegis tests had been only one-third successful, by which they meant that five of sixteen missiles had been shot down. The real issue was whether the tests pinpointed what needed to be corrected and whether the system could be corrected. If such was the case, failures would actually be successes. Much of the failure was simply due to faulty computer programming and poor crew training. There had also been some problem with tailoring attack missiles to the desired specifications.

What made the situation worse for the navy was the determined and effective campaign mounted against the Aegis in Congress by Representative Denny Smith, Republican, Oregon. This is not to say that Congress should not make sure it is spending its monies properly. If Smith is to be faulted, it is on the grounds that he emphasized only one aspect of the problem, the Sea Skimmer (about which more in a moment). The real fault lay with the navy's presentation.

The Senate subcommittee hearings were held on 14, 28, and 29 March, 5 and 11 April, and 1 May 1984. By no means did they put the Aegis issue to bed.[32] The high point came on 5 April. Congressman Smith, who had been invited to the Senate hearing, indicated his belief that the more successful Aegis results had come from intercepting anticipated shots; surprise shots accounted for the high degree of failures. He argued that the test capability had not been fully utilized and that the navy should take the testing as far as it would go—"max the system."[33] Smith did admit that arranging simulation for an attack with, say, eighteen missiles simultaneously might never be possible. (He was referring to the inherent technical limits of simulated tests. Arranging a coordinated attack from different levels simultaneously is an extremely difficult operation.)

Norman Friedman, called as the next witness, made a helpful distinction between developmental testing and operational testing. In the former, technicians test; in the latter, the crew. In developmental testing you look for things to fix and question whether you want to buy the system in the first place. In operational testing, when most of the design problems should have been solved, you look for relatively small glitches. With a computer-oriented system like Aegis most of the late changes will be in the computer programming, in the instructions that run the ship.[34] The public figure given for the designed firing capability of the Aegis system, Friedman said, was eighteen targets simultaneously. Next to that six sounded inadequate. However, compared to previous systems designed to handle three targets simultaneously (and in reality able to handle only one or two), six was good.[35]

Vice Admiral Walters tried again, along with Captain Donegan, to straighten out some of the misconceptions. Senator Cohen bored in on specific "failures." The captain of the ship, against the advice of his computer, had fired and thereby raised the failure score. But Donegan responded that the captain had made a correct decision, that he would have been graded down if he had not done so. Cohen summarized what he had heard: the computer was right, but so was the captain; two correct judgments added up to one mistaken result, "rather Orwellian." It showed the complexity of this kind of test, Walters interjected.[36] Donegan added that the failure rate was misleadingly high for the missile firings, because when the computer was disregarded and three targets were missed, the same wrong answer was produced three times in a row. That made "the box score" go down.[37]

Admiral Watkins, convinced that the Aegis program was in jeopardy, ordered the *Ticonderoga* home early for additional tests costing $30 million. On 2 May 1984 he met with the Defense Department news corps to announce the results of this latest series of tests. He said there had been much misinformation abroad but that the furor was legitimate. Still, the system was fundamentally sound. It could handle a hundred or more targets simultaneously, and could use more than ten and less than twenty-four missiles at one time. Where, in the early tests, five out of sixteen targets were hit, this time, it was ten out of eleven. (Actually, sixteen missiles were fired in salvoes to achieve the ten hits, but in each case the lead missile worked.)[38]

Watkins gave the history of the system—twenty years from concept to deployment. By January 1983 when the *Norton Sound* was commissioned as an afloat testing platform, some ninety thousand hours of testing had already been done. One of the problems the two sets of operational tests for the *Ticonderoga* had encountered was that the Atlantic Fleet Range could accommodate a maximum of only four targets simultaneously.

Predictably, even though the target missed on the second set of tests was from a high-altitude attack, the news corps' questions focused predominantly on the terminal phase. At that point the target would be low over the water, somewhere between 15 and 35 feet above the surface—the Sea Skimmer problem. And the Sea Skimmer target had been subsonic. Wouldn't a Soviet missile be supersonic? What had caused the one failure this time?

Watkins carefully explained the difficulties of developing a supersonic, low-level target and emphasized that a subsonic target made no real difference in testing the effectiveness of the Aegis system because the two were not organically connected; it was a missile problem. As for the failure, not all the data was in yet. Near the end of the conference Watkins announced that the main reason for the briefing was to head off the possibility of the *Burke* class being jeopardized by bad publicity. (Because the *Burke* used the Aegis radar-control system, it could be tarred by the same brush.)

Even with handouts, the reporters varied somewhat in what they heard and printed. There was however near unanimity on their main point—that in the first set of tests five out of thirteen (another said six out of eighteen) targets had been shot down, and this time it was ten out of eleven. The success rate had risen from 33 percent to about 90 percent.[39]

Two of the four major stories cited Congressman Smith on the issue of the navy not testing Aegis against four Sea Skimmers simultaneously—the way the Soviets would attack. A *Washington Times* article quoted navy officials as saying that the Exocet missile was a "piece of cake" for the Aegis system.[40]

Notwithstanding Smith and the various misunderstandings about operational testing, from this point on the controversy receded. Neither the Aegis system nor the *Burke* follow-on was lost. In retrospect, it can be said that the Aegis was rescued by the second set of tests (which cost a lot of money and were not really needed from a strictly technical point of view). It had been a close call for the U.S. Navy.

THE NEW-DESIGN SUBMARINE

The navy adapted the *Spruance* hull design to the *Ticonderoga* class and the Aegis system, and also used the Aegis in the new class of *Burke* destroyers. New submarines were designed along the lines of existing classes up to a point—the original 688 *Los Angeles* class, for instance, was followed by the improved 688s. These were much better submarines. Major improvements included a vertical launch system, modifications for mining and for the Arctic, sensor and combat-system upgrades, and increased quietness.[41] Even so, there came a time when a new design was inevitable. Congress wanted to know why the 688s could not be further improved. To Vice Admiral Ron Thunman, DCNO for submarine warfare, fell the burden of preparing the design and defending it before Congress.

Thunman, briefing the Senate Armed Services Committee on 29 March 1984, showed the anticipated nineteen-year gap between the advent of the 688s in 1976 and the appearance of the new-design SSN in 1995.[42] The *Los Angeles* class had originally been designed primarily as a battle-group escort. What had inspired work on a new concept was the increased quietness of Soviet submarines.[43]

Thunman's problem in explaining navy policy was complicated by the fact that four 688s were in the FY 85 budget while funds were being requested for the new design precisely because these 688s were not good enough for the developing threat. The number of U.S. subs had to be increased on account of the Soviet's three to one numerical superiority. Improved 688s would have double the capability of older 688s.[44] In particular, they would be equipped with SUBACS (the advanced submarine combat system) and quieter propellers, electrical systems, and reactor coolant pumps. They would be able to operate under the Arctic icepack and would have a vertical launch system, which provided more firepower.[45] Thunman made it clear that the new-design submarine was designed to answer an anticipated Soviet threat in the mid-1990s. In response to a question about size, he commented that it was an asset rather than a liability because it enhanced quietness and allowed for the installation of larger and more sophisticated acoustic sensors, increasing the chance of first detection of the enemy.[46]

The FY 85 hearings before Congressman Bennett's subcommittee yielded the name for Thunman's "new design" submarine. If it was designed for the twenty-first century, why not give it that name? And so the submarine became the SSN 21, later known also as the Seawolf.[47]

Vice Admiral Thunman's testimony on 29 March 1984 had followed that of two civilian witnesses, Norman Friedman and Norman Polmar. Polmar, although supporting a goal of one hundred submarines, raised questions about the new design. Friedman, for his part, gave it support. Submarines got better when they grew bigger.[48] Growth permitted enlarged salvoes, a higher computer capacity, an improved ability to deal with multiple targets simultaneously. But the main improvement that came with size was quietness. The only way to improve a quieter sub was through better signal processing (which required a larger computer) or by using an active sonar (which had to be low frequency and therefore big). So large size led to further size. The offsetting factor was that the size of the ship was not really what drove cost up. It was the electronic and the combat systems inside. Squeezing down size did not bring commensurate savings.[49]

Behind all this discussion was another more fundamental point: the submarine is, of course, noisier at higher speeds. A good submarine is one that can sustain higher speeds without seriously risking detection. A larger submarine can yield, as its greatest dividend, a higher tactical cruising speed. It also has the tactical advantage of closing on (or breaking from) a noisier enemy while still being able to hear.

Admiral McKee, a year later at the FY 86 hearings, spoke in greater detail about submarine speeds. There were several: safe transit speed, search speed, tactical speed. The highest possible tactical speed was the greatest need during an attack, but in every case speed had to be considered against quietness.[50]

DIESEL VS. NUCLEAR

Part of the congressional discussions concerned the recurring question of the diesel submarine. In 1983 Watkins had said before the House seapower subcommittee that all the studies run to date had proved the diesel submarine neither cost effective nor militarily effective until the navy had enough nuclear attack submarines to handle the Soviet threat.[51] Pressure for diesels continued, though, coming to a head in the FY 85 hearings as the result of two separate but eventually intersecting pressures. First there was the question of cost. With nuclear submarines at a billion or so apiece, Congress wanted to substitute much cheaper diesels. Second, several of America's smaller allies were pressing to build diesel submarines in U.S. shipyards, to American designs. This suggestion appealed to congressmen from areas with underemployed shipyards. The question persistently put to the navy was, If you won't take them yourselves, why not build them for allies?

Since the navy had concluded that the improved 688s represented the end of the road and a new nuclear attack submarine design was essential, the diesel issue was delicate. Unlike the Aegis issue, this one was handled well. Vice Admiral Thunman took the lead role in the hearings, effectively aided by Admiral Kinny McKee.

One of the most problematic aspects of the navy's argument was how to explain simultaneously that diesel submarines were useless for U.S. purposes but valued additions to total NATO strength. Here the testimony of Norman Friedman before the Senate Armed Services Committee in spring 1984 helped. "A nuclear submarine differs from a diesel submarine in a fundamental way," he explained. "In a nuclear sub, whenever that reactor is running, machinery has to run. There are pumps that run the water through it. There are generators that run the pumps. There are all kinds of things that are a source of noise."[52] By contrast the diesel sub, which ran on batteries, was quiet. However, it was not very mobile; it might go 20 knots, but only for an hour. When forced to go at high speed for extended periods, it had to expose itself and snorkel.[53] The diesel was effective close to shore, in coastal waters where it was hard to detect, or in a strait where the enemy's surface ships would have to pass. But these were not the missions of the U.S. Navy.[54]

Norman Polmar, following Friedman, argued that U.S. shipbuilders should construct diesels: "Today, there are three countries—Australia, Israel, and South Korea—that wish to buy diesel submarines here in the United States. To do so would improve our naval shipbuilding base, help our relations with those countries, provide them with improved military capability and the U.S. style of training. . . . "[55] Vice Admiral Baciocco skirted the issue, arguing somewhat vaguely that building diesels would have a negative effect on U.S. submarine design and shipbuilding capability. Senator Nunn was openly skeptical, and Senator Cohen expressed incredulity that the United States could be so short on design people that diesels and nuclear submarines could not be built simultaneously.[56] Not mentioned was the ever-present navy concern over security. It would have been impolitic for any navy official to make that point for the public record and gratuitously offend U.S. allies. Thunman contented himself with saying that the navy had no mission for diesel submarines: they lacked covertness, endurance, mobility, firepower, and the sensors to do the job of U.S. attack submarines.[57] With U.S allies it was different. Their submarine mission was barrier operations, close to the homeland, where they were not opposed by ASW aircraft. Diesels could attack Soviet surface ships, but they would not be very useful against Soviet nuclear-attack submarines. With transits of three to six thousand miles necessary for U.S. submarines to arrive on station, the increased vulnerability of diesels to detection and their slower speeds made them an unwise investment.[58]

Although congressional pressures concerning the diesel issue were great, the navy's argument made a good deal of sense. In the end, Congress accepted the navy's position.

STRATEGIC HOMEPORTING

During the Zumwalt and post-Zumwalt era the fleet was concentrated at a relatively few bases. Newport, Rhode Island, for example, once the home of a cruiser-destroyer force, now based only a few older destroyers assigned to the reserves. Quonset Point, farther up Narragansett Bay, had at one time been the frequent destination of U.S. carriers; now it was converted into a shipyard. Conversely, other bases like Norfolk became overcrowded. Although such shifts could be interpreted politically (Rhode Island was one of the few states to vote against Nixon's reelection), short funds could be more easily stretched with fewer bases.

Once the fleet began to expand again, overcrowding worsened. From a strategic point of view the concentration of many ships in just a few ports, with Soviet missile accuracy increasing, was dangerous. Moreover, there were serious problems with existing homeporting assignments. The West Coast and Gulf Coast were underrepresented and at the same time in need of forces. The ships they had were not well integrated into battle groups. For example, the submarines assigned to the new Trident base at Bangor, Washington, had no defensive forces to protect them. (The very advent of the Trident program and the continuing expansion of the submarine fleet required that the problem of strategic dispersal be rethought.)

To create a viable plan for dispersal was one of Admiral Watkins's early priorities. Vice Admiral Tom Hughes, DCNO, logistics, was tasked to flesh out and implement the broad concept.[59] Hughes began with the idea that the ports he chose would have to want the navy as part of their community. He considered five additional criteria. The first was to create battle groups rather than simply scattering ships around. The second was to improve unit integrity so that the ships could leave port as an effective fighting force and also train usefully. Third, the industrial base of the United States would be considered. How would ship assignments affect it and, particularly, strengthen it? Fourth, it was necessary that bases have logistic support structures already in place—the navy could not underwrite new roads and railroads. Fifth, dispersal should take advantage of the natural features of U.S. geography so that deployment needs were met.

The importance of these five criteria differed depending on the base under consideration. The choice of New York had a great deal to do with its being an industrial base point; Northwest assignments pivoted on an increased Soviet operating tempo in the Pacific; and Gulf-Coast assignments were determined by the NATO reinforcement problem.

A version of the strategic homeporting concept was promulgated as early as 5 October 1982. The chairman of the House Committee on Appropriations' subcommittee on defense was informed of the early plan in a letter from Admiral Watkins dated 24 November 1982. The careful procedural steps followed in each homeporting case were summarized by Admiral Hughes in a memo of 27 December 1983.[60] The overall plan was updated and revised on 7 July 1984.[61] Individual changes were also made—for example, on 29 July 1983 Secretary Lehman designated New York City as a SAG (surface action [battleship] group) homeport and announced plans for two naval reserve frigates to go to Boston. On 24 October 1983, a revised plan for all the reserve frigates was sent to the secretary.[62] For example, in the case of Staten Island, the estimated cost to the navy was to be $100 million, but New York and New Jersey would contribute $15 million in constructed support facilities and the army would transfer Fort Wadsworth to the navy.[63]

Of course, to many congressmen the homeporting issue was

primarily political—sharing out the patronage. The navy's problem was to convince Congress that it had a solid strategic-dispersal plan that yielded balanced battle forces along with pork-barrel fallouts. The navy, which had to be careful at the same time that Congress would not balk at the expense of adding infrastructure to a number of new bases, sought state and city contributions.

There was one further complication. The navy's expansion to six hundred ships underlined how dependent the U.S. shipbuilding industry had become on navy orders. (At one point during the expansion, Secretary Lehman remarked that not a single American merchant ship was under construction in the States.) Members of Congress were compelled to press the navy for bases and new construction, and the navy's plans to overhaul ships (overhauling was closely tied to home-porting) developed amid intense political pressure.

From the navy's point of view, a critical variable in ship overhaul, at times almost more important than cost, was the effect of dislocation on navy families. Temporary lodgings had to be obtained for hundreds over a period of six or nine months; children were suddenly thrust into new schools. Or, alternately, families were separated for periods that extended long deployments at sea. Such stresses discouraged reenlistment where it counted most, among mid-career petty officers.

All the problems implicit in fleet modernization surfaced repeatedly in the FY 86 hearings, particularly because there were not the high-visibility programs of previous years—the DDG 51, battleship reactivation, and the carrier-service-life extension program. Meanwhile, pressure to cut the defense budget was enormous.[64]

Sure enough, the discussion soon included proposed cutbacks at shipyards. One of Secretary Lehman's remarks put the whole issue in useful perspective:

> Four years ago we were building naval ships in only nine yards, and 75 percent of all naval ship construction was done in only three of those yards, Electric Boat, Newport News, and Pascagoula. Since that time we have expanded that base by raising competition from 15 to nearly 85 per cent. We have moved from only 9 yards to 21 yards, building new construction ships.[65]

Earlier Lehman had said that the number of overhauls set in FY 85 was fifty-five, excluding the service-life extension program. He did not expect the total work load to decline. It would shift from year to year, and the long-term trend would be in the direction of fewer and very large overhauls.[66]

The homeporting issue was still alive in FY 86 and discussed before the House seapower subcommittee in September 1985. Chairman

Charles Bennett and his group heard Frank C. Conahan of the General Accounting Office say that the navy homeporting plan would cost over $1 billion in new construction. Bennett, though he "was not trying to throw any cold water on the idea of dispersal," said that costs were a central consideration.[67]

On 10 September, at the wrap-up session of these special hearings on the 600-ship navy, Secretary Lehman pointed out the vulnerability that resulted from homeporting 122 ships at Norfolk. While the navy had no intention of reducing the number of ships in San Diego, Long Beach, Norfolk, and Charleston, another 130 new ships could hardly be added, either. These homeports, from a military point of view, were already dangerously packed. Would it be cheaper to go ahead anyway? In some cases, yes; in other cases, no. Some ports were so saturated that entire new facilities would have to be built.[68] With the cooperation of states and cities where new bases were to be located, the costs were much more modest than anticipated. Everett, Washington, would cost $272 million, while the alternatives, San Francisco or San Diego, would need new piers and a new infrastructure. For all six homeports on the Gulf Coast the cost was only $171 million, because state and local governments would contribute $50 million in offsets as well as substantial infrastructures. That $171 million would not be enough to cover the cost of redoing any existing homeport to take on the added ships.[69]

The common sense behind the navy's strategic dispersal plan ultimately convinced Congress, although cuts were to come here, too.

Chapter 8

CONGRESS AND THE 600-SHIP NAVY

We can see from chapter 7 that Congress in the Reagan years was not prepared to accept the navy's program without serious questioning. Given the need to build a new and modern fleet, were the navy's specific proposals about unit types and sizes well thought out? The navy might have preferred these questions to be resolved on their technical merit, but with the large sums Congress was being asked to appropriate, the decision would inevitably turn on broader political and policy considerations. Congress had to be convinced and remain convinced that the program represented solid professional judgments by navy seniors rather than a simple grab for whatever Congress might be cajoled into offering.

As the Reagan years went by Congressional support fluctuated. By the time of President Reagan's reelection there was growing sentiment to cut back appropriations. The president's insistence on not raising taxes in the face of a growing federal deficit eroded first enthusiasm and then commitment. The navy had an evermore difficult job convincing Congress that 600 ships was not just a figure someone had idly jotted down on the back of an envelope—that it and the projected fifteen carrier battle groups at its core represented a sensible plan.

What happened to the navy in total obligational authority from FY 75 on is shown in table 4. The service was given more than it requested in FY 80 to FY 83. Before and after it was given less.

BACKGROUND

Although the year 1980 marked a low point for the U.S. Navy, the barrage of publicity was on the navy's side and the press was a positive help. Among many others, Richard Halloran of the *New York Times* underlined one of the navy's personnel problems: a shortage of 23,300

148

Table 4. Navy Appropriations

TOA Historical Data (dollars in billions)

	FY 75	FY 76	FY 7T	FY 77	FY 78	FY 79	FY 80*	FY 81*	FY 82*	FY 83	FY 84	FY 85	FY 86	FY 87
DON Request to OSD	29.3	34.6	7.8	40.6	43.9	45.4	43.2	46.4	60.1	79.7	87.6	98.4	106.3	107.0
							45.4	49.5	64.3					
							47.0	54.3	68.1					
Pres. Budget	29.0	33.7	7.4	37.4	39.4	41.0	43.3	49.7	70.8	88.0	86.9	101.3	104.9	103.5
Appropriation	27.6	30.9	7.1	36.5	38.6	39.9	44.8	54.4	67.5	81.9	82.2	95.7	98.0	

Source: U.S. Navy Office of the Comptroller.

*FY 80, 81, and 82 submissions to OSD/OMB reflected minimum, basic, and enhanced levels, in keeping with zero-based budget guidance. No deflators for cross-year adjustments are shown.

petty officers and 1,800 pilots. The *Wall Street Journal* compared navy boiler technicians earning $12,516 after eight years with civilian counterparts making $22,680. Those boiler technicians who did not quit were working 72-hour weeks, and only 39 percent completing second four-year hitches were reenlisting.[1]

Against this background, in testimony before the Senate Appropriations Committee's subcommittee on defense in March 1980, Admiral Hayward applauded President Carter's statement that the United States intended to sustain at least a 550-ship navy in the 1990s. If the projections were not realized, however, the navy would be in serious trouble.[2] The historical record for the outyears in any five-year budget projection was not grounds for optimism and, as pro-navy questioners on the committee brought out, that year's budget fell short of the eighteen new ships needed annually to meet the president's announced goal.

Asked by Senator Jake Garn how many ships were enough, Hayward replied there was no right number, but that America's geopolitical responsibilities required maritime superiority and offensive punch.[3] Current force levels represented absolute minimum strength with twelve carrier battle groups, ninety attack submarines, and lift for little more than one marine amphibious force.[4]

Even the next year, in early 1981, with President Reagan and Secretary Lehman in office, Hayward's formal posture statement prepared for congressional committees was gloomy. Ships took years to build and good petty officers required years of training. Though the U.S. Navy was far better than three years earlier, the Soviet navy had grown faster.[5] Thus the U.S. navy, half the size it had been ten years earlier, had to cover more than twice the ocean area. Forces were seriously overextended, and for the first time in memory the U.S. Navy was unable to meet all its peacetime commitments. Hayward added a final somber note: "It would be misleading to continue speaking of a 'narrow margin' [over the Soviets] when, in fact, we have entered a period in which any reasonable estimate of the balance falls within the range of uncertainty."[6]

On 6 April 1981, in hearings before a subcommittee of the Senate Committee on Appropriations, Secretary Lehman began his remarks in the same vein. The United States had lost the margin of superiority that a maritime power required. Accordingly, the navy was submitting a budget as a first step to achieving six hundred ships by the end of the decade. The new budget would emphasize pay and improved conditions for personnel, a shipbuilding program producing approximately thirty units a year, and weapons of affordable price and timely manufacture.[7]

Lehman's posture statement was equally emphatic:

Maritime superiority means that we must be capable—and be seen to be capable—of keeping our sea lines of commerce and communications secure in those areas of the world where our vital interests depend on them. If we are to survive as a free nation, our access to our allies, our energy sources, and our trading partners cannot be hostage to the offensive power of any combination of adversaries. We must have the naval and Marine Corps power to militarily defeat any martial attempts to interfere with such access.[8]

Lehman's shipbuilding program was simple and clear: to provide a capable fleet of about six hundred ships and fifteen battle groups. It would include the recommissioning of one or more battleships and twenty-seven C-class carriers. The secretary did not however intend to be "wed irrevocably to a fixed number or set of numbers"; for example, he did not mean by six hundred ships—about a third more than the number at the time—that there would be exactly four of everything the navy then had three of. But it would include a minimum of fifteen carrier battle groups.[9] Congressional skepticism about the battleships yielded fairly quickly to the fact that these ships had armored plating, much of it over a foot thick, designed to absorb an 18-inch Japanese shell, that missiles could easily be mounted on them, and that the total cost would equal the construction and outfitting of an FFG 7 with one 3-inch gun.[10]

Lehman told the committee that the 600-ship navy would require seventy to one hundred thousand more personnel.

Although the outlook was brightening, all was not well. Hayward indicated the navy had one less carrier and with only twelve could not meet the demand for two carriers in the Indian Ocean, in the Mediterranean, and in the western Pacific.[11] The new budget request for 283 aircraft came closer than any budget in recent years to meeting the navy's annual requirement. But that requirement, to replace aircraft lost or retired, came to 330.[12]

Lehman's FY 83 posture statement, delivered before the House Armed Services Committee on 8 February 1982, was more optimistic than his earlier ones.[13] On the subject of strategy he remarked: "Unlike land warfare, . . . conflict . . . between the navies of the United States and the Soviet Union . . . will be instantaneously a global conflict. We must, therefore, recognize that the choice is to maintain security of the sea lanes in each [ocean area] or write them off and suffer the consequences."[14] Security would require a forward strategy as opposed to the Carter administration's pull-back strategy, which had been based on the assumption that the Soviet threat was too great for a bold response.[15]

Lehman commented on many of the new initiatives. Two years before enlisted retention had been 44 percent; now it was over 65 percent. At training costs of nearly $100,000 per person, that represented substantial savings.[16] Even better, over 500 pilots ($850,000 each to train) and 125 naval flight officers ($650,000 each to train) who were expected to leave the navy and Marine Corps had reenlisted.[17] Bonuses of $90 million expended over two fiscal years had already, in twelve months' time, brought a training savings of $450 million.[18]

CNO Hayward, in testimony that followed Lehman's, elaborated on the issue of retention. The new emphasis on pride and professionalism, better pay and bonuses, and the leadership and management and education training program had brought total career enlisted retention rates from 67.0 percent in FY 80 to 81.1 percent in FY 82, first quarter. Crucial second-term reenlistments, 50.5 percent in FY 80, were now at 69.0 percent. Although officer retention was still a problem in the mid-grades and the navy was still short some twenty-two thousand petty officers, it was a proud final report for Admiral Hayward.

THE FY 84 HEARINGS

The FY 84 budget hearings were Admiral Watkins's first as CNO. Hayward's last budget appropriation (in 1987 current dollars) had reached $81.9 billion, more than double FY 79's $39.9 billion. Now the problem would be maintaining the momentum and increasing the base as new ships came on line.

Secretary Lehman's formal FY 84 posture statement pointed out that the navy was using more Alaskan than Middle East oil now. The lower forty-eight states met one-third of their oil needs by way of the Alaskan sea lanes. Meanwhile, the Soviet fleet in the Pacific had grown to 765 ships and combatant craft.[19]

The U.S. active fleet now had 514 ships and would have 600 by 1989. Over 110 ships were being built, which had saved at least six shipbuilding yards from going out of business. Impressive contract savings had been achieved through fixed pricing and second sourcing.[20]

The USS Ohio, the first Trident, had deployed to the Pacific in October 1982. Growth was planned for various ship types, including two CVNs, more attack submarines, the first Aegis cruiser, and more amphibious ships. Twenty-five ships had been delivered to the navy in 1982, twenty a total of eleven months ahead of schedule. Nineteen ships were on or below budget.[21] Cost savings had been realized in larger orders as well. The navy had negotiated a two-carrier buy with Newport News, which accepted the risk of Congress not proceeding with both units and signed a contractual obligation for their early delivery.[22] By the end of the year all but two ship programs, the Trident and the LHD, would be awarded competitively—in other words, 94 percent of the five-year shipbuilding and conversion plan.[23]

Admiral Watkins's prepared statement during the FY 84 hearings sounded a theme that would recur throughout his tenure as CNO: "We want to affect enemy strategy and will: in peace to ensure stability and protect our interests without recourse to force; in crisis to contain or to resolve the dispute on our terms before crisis escalates to conflict; and in war to terminate conflict on our terms at the lowest possible level of damage and loss. These concepts are central to maritime strategy. . . ."[24] What was distinctive about this approach was Watkins's unwillingness to define U.S. strategy as simply reactive; he wanted to take the initiative by deterring or inhibiting the enemy from fighting. Watkins was prepared to face the given threat; he also wanted to help shape it. The difference between reaction and initiative in strategy is both subtle and immense.

Early offensive pressure was the key: "By confining and destroying air, surface, and subsurface threats to the transoceanic sea lanes well forward, we control the initiative and capitalize on geographical advantages, thereby maximizing the effectiveness of our forces."[25]

Watkins went to pains to detail how the enlarged budgets had been put to good use. Spare-parts procurement increases of almost 50 percent for FY 81 to FY 83 had already improved ship readiness from 80 up to 90 percent. For 1981 and 1982, readiness in aviation squadrons had moved from 65 to 85 percent.[26] Unspectacular but equally vital was the twofold increase in spending on sealift for FY 81 and FY 82; taking into account the decommissioning of six ships , there was still a net gain of twenty-one.[27]

In his testimony Watkins underlined the improvement in petty officer retention. Hayward's shortage of 22,000 was down to 17,400 in 1982. But the fleet was confronted with an overly vigorous operations tempo.[28] Happily, the Joint Chiefs had now relaxed some of the rigid deployment guidelines of the past and introduced flexible operations.

The questioning in various congressional committees for FY 84 focused on the issue of the 600-ship navy. In the House Armed Services Committee hearings Representative Stratton charged that no one really knew the cost of a 600-ship navy. Lehman responded that that wasn't true; the 600-ship navy was fully funded in the five-year plan that the committee had in hand.[29] At another session Secretary Weinberger had said the navy was really aiming at a 650-ship force for the early 1990s. Was that true? Lehman explained that the excess referred to auxiliaries and sealift ships which, not being battle force ships, did not count in the total.[30] Representative Au Coin wanted to know about replacing ships reaching the end of their service life—wouldn't that affect the totals?

Lehman: "This year is essentially the last of [moving to] the 600-ship Navy. . . . We will get to 600 ships by the end of this decade, barring major [future] cuts, with the 17 new construction ships that are in this year's budget." There were fewer than 20 ships left to be authorized. But didn't the 14 carrier-battle-group goal require 28 Aegis ships, and hadn't only 11 been appropriated? The answer: the navy would get to 600 well before it had 28 Aegis ships, but future Aegis ships would replace some of those 600.[31] Au Coin suspected a juggling of figures; he wanted to know the cost over a thirty-year life cycle. Lehman made him an offer: if Au Coin specified "the inflators you would like me to use in each of the 30 years, we will run it through the computer for you."[32]

Congressman Bill Chappell from Florida wanted to know how the ship inventory was counted. The answer was complicated; the Carter administration had altered the traditional way of counting, and the Reagan administration had subsequently reverted to the old way for counting reserve ships and fleet auxiliaries. But new destroyers in the reserve force, because they were deployable battle force ships, were counted, while old, non-deployable destroyers were not. "The key words are deployable battle force ships," Chappell said.[33]

Even with the building program, the navy would be stretched if it actually came to war with the Soviets. Lehman pointed out that the service could do little about the disastrous shape of the nation's merchant shipping. Hitler had started World War II, when the United States had 6,000 merchant bottoms and 50 submarines. Now it had 600 bottoms against a Soviet submarine fleet of 280 attack submarines.[34]

The second committee-question topic was the cost and effectiveness of the F/A-18 and the related question of whether the navy was pushing for enough planes of all types or trying to buy too many types. Lehman pointed to three considerations. Low production rates and higher unit costs were justified for surge capability during wartime mobilization. Competition was a second factor. If the A-6 had been "bought out" and the line closed, "we would be paying more for F/A-18s." The third factor was political pressure; sometimes procurement was extended when the navy would have preferred to discontinue it.[35]

Lehman emphasized the reliability of the F/A-18. In peacetime training, lower accident rates reduced the cost of ownership and the need for replacements. In wartime, there was "a major force multiplier effect. You can generate more sorties per day from a given airplane." That translated into a cut of fifty technicians, each of whom cost $150,000 to train.[36]

The third area of questioning concerned the vulnerability of the navy's ships—especially carriers, which were expensive—to satellites and missiles. Lehman admitted that, today, the rough geographical area of any surface ship could be located. But reconnaissance was not good enough to exploit a sighting militarily because a force would be moving at 30 knots in "random spreads of advance." In any case, surface ships were hidden tactically, not strategically.[37]

The Falklands experience also came in for review when Watkins was asked for a comparison of British air defense with the American system. Watkins reviewed the multi-layered U.S. defense, beginning at the outer ring with the EC-2 Hawkeye and its radar, and the F-14 and F/A-18 used for interception. If the Argentinian aircraft that launched the Exocet that hit HMS *Sheffield* had come within 200 miles of a U.S. carrier battle group, it would have been intercepted before it had a chance to release missiles. "Our objective is to eliminate the archer rather than concentrate solely on going after the arrows," as Britain had had to do. The British had lacked a long-reach early warning aircraft.[38]

THE FY 85 HEARINGS

As we saw in chapter 7, FY 85 was a crucial year because the Aegis system was under fire and the future of the *Burke*-class destroyer, as well as the new-design submarine, was uncertain. Congress was beginning the long road back to level or reduced budgets. Indeed, it was precisely because defense expenditures were coming in for close scrutiny and the navy program was encountering difficulties that Congressman Charles Bennett decided to give it all a thorough airing in March, with hearings before the House Armed Services Committee's subcommittee on seapower and force projection. That ground was covered in detail in chapter 7, and we shall not repeat it here. If our coverage is brief, it is not because the hearings were insignificant.

The navy's posture statement was tabled with the House Armed Services Committee in February 1984. The first hearing took place on 8 February. Lehman began early on with a mention of the naval maritime strategy. In three years, fleet manning had risen from 91 percent to 100 percent.[39] The navy would take delivery of 37 new ships, there were 118 ships under construction or conversion, and the 600-ship fleet would be a reality in 1989. Watkins, following Lehman, opened his remarks with a strategic analysis, then emphasized that "60 percent of this year's budget goes to readiness and sustainability."[40]

In this hearing questions covered, among other topics, the Aegis system[41] and America's involvement in Lebanon. Hearings before the Senate Armed Services Committee on 7 February 1984 covered other ground.[42] Asked about operations, Watkins gave a report on the three carrier battle groups sent to the northwest Pacific in greater force than any time since World War II. Watkins was upbeat. Because of its technological lead the navy could stand a "three-to-one numerical superiority on their [the Soviets] part and still defeat them at sea. . . ."[43] This conclusion was based on close observation; the navy did routinely steam close to the enemy and observe his operations. Watkins detailed how the five layers of defense protected the U.S. carrier force.

Lehman had said the year before that America's narrow margin of maritime superiority over the Soviets was gone. Did he still think so? Yes; the navy would not achieve superiority until the end of the decade. Watkins, pressed on the same issue, said the navy sought "sea control in those areas where it makes the difference."[44] It was definitely ahead in the areas of ASW, the navy-marine team, tactical air at sea, the Trident, and the D-5 missile. Numerically, how was the navy superior and how inferior? Lehman explained that maritime superiority was measured by whether the navy could perform the task required by the threat—not by stacking up the number of destroyers in one navy and comparing it with the number in the other.[45]

As for the size of the navy, was six hundred ships a "way station" or a "plateau"? Plateau, Lehman said. Did that mean that no new ships would be authorized after this fiscal year? There would be "new starts like the *Burke*-class destroyer," but they would replace ships that were part of the 600-ship navy.[46]

These Senate hearings were followed in March by the hearings of the subcommittee on seapower.[47] What all the discussions revealed was more substantial questioning of navy plans.

THE FY 86 HEARINGS

Like the FY 85 hearings, those in FY 86 were to prove difficult for the navy. The budget squeeze would be much more pronounced.

The navy's formal posture statement was upbeat. It was Lehman's fifth year of presentation. He began with the maritime strategy, stressing its joint aspects. U.S. Air Force AWACs, tankers, and fighters were now an integral part of every significant naval exercise and theater strategy. The strategy, reviewed and refined by the navy's senior operational commanders and tested repeatedly in war games and simulations at the Naval War College, was also the foundation on which the annual budget was built.

Combat readiness had improved, with increased munition stocks and spare parts, and competitive procurement of those spares, at 6.9 percent as recently as 1982, had risen to 25.4 percent. Whereas in 1981, 13 percent of ships and 25 percent of aircraft squadrons were not combat ready because of personnel shortages, that was now down to less than 1 percent for each. The whole personnel situation had been transformed, with the petty officer shortage below six thousand and retention higher than ever.[48] The fleet was 100 percent manned, up from 91 percent four years before, even though the navy had grown meanwhile by 50 ships. New construction, conversion, or reactivation of 103 ships was proceeding at twenty-one different shipyards.[49] There were already 530 battle force ships, compared with 479 when President Reagan took office. Lehman warned against the popular notion that in a period of high interest rates and deficits, the defense budget had to be cut.[50]

Watkins stressed the continued high tempo of navy operations in what he called "an era of violent peace." The administration's frequent first recourse was to move or deploy naval forces in any crisis, resulting in an operating tempo 20 percent above that of the Vietnam War period.

It was understandable why the navy got so much use. It provided credible, capable deterrence at any level of potential conflict worldwide. That deterrence could be precise and graduated; but it also required forward-deployed, sustainable forces.[51] Even with remarkable economies in the use of personnel, the navy would not continue to add ships if there were not the numbers to man them. The *Burke* destroyer, equal in size to a World War II cruiser and far superior to it in firepower, would operate with less than a third of the personnel that cruiser had needed. Manpower costs were only 30 percent of the budget now, compared with 41.6 percent in 1974.[52] Watkins warned of the trend in Congress to cut requested end-strength.

In the hearings before the Senate Armed Services Committee on 5 February, questions focused on America's shrinking manpower pool and looming budget cuts. Admiral Watkins said the real problem lay ahead: by FY 88 one out of every two eligible males would have to join the military if the manpower pool was not enlarged.[53] Lehman was optimistic in pointing out that the pool had been declining for the past four years by nearly 8 percent without interfering with navy recruitment goals.[54]

The discussion about budget and possible cuts began with a favorite FY 86 question: What was the "real growth" needed in navy funding to continue the expansion? The answer was 6 to 8 percent, about the same as before.[55] Suppose the budget was cut? Lehman, referring to the cuts President Reagan had agreed to earlier with Congress in view of the deficit, said that F-14 production as a consequence had already been reduced from twenty-four to eighteen units, raising the price per plane by $3 million.[56]

There were no aircraft carriers in the 1986 budget. Senator Barry Goldwater, noting Lehman's statement that no new carriers would be needed until the early 1990s, commented that that meant replacing seven retiring carriers in ten years at very large cost. Had the navy looked seriously at alternatives? Lehman, although he liked "little carriers," called them "more expensive . . . for the same air capability . . . for the same reason supertankers have put handy-sized tankers out of business." Carriers were now built for a fifty-year life and were very survivable— seven layers of armor, multiple hulls, triple-armored decks.[57]

Senator Sam Nunn said that the budget, when passed, would not likely allow more than 3 percent real growth. How would that rearrange navy priorities? Lehman answered that, if worst came to worst, the navy would ask that its operational tasking be reduced.

Les Aspin was now chairman of the House Armed Services Committee. In his opening statement at the hearings on 5 February, he said that the navy had spent $1 trillion or so on defense and that the committee needed an accounting of what had been accomplished.[58] Thus on 7 February, when Lehman began his inform l summary of the posture, he emphasized the financial side. All of the ships being delivered were ahead of schedule and either on or under budget. This was the third straight year "of net and substantial cost underruns in shipbuilding," which had yielded $2.4 billions in savings. Out of those savings, the navy had financed the entire $430 million cost of the renovation of the battleship *Missouri* and funneled $640 million to the MX program.[59] All aircraft were procured on a fixed-price basis, and aviation spare-parts procurement was now 50 percent competitive. The new F/A-18's safety rate was eight times better than the F-4's, four times better than the F-14's. Yet the F/A-18 required only half the maintenance man-hours required per flight hour.[60]

The high operations tempo and its effect on personnel was the second focus of questioning in the House committee. Admiral Watkins cited a case of a carrier that had spent 155 consecutive days at sea—with Indian Ocean deployments, the normal deployment distances were doubled. Such long cruises affected retention severely, especially in ratings where there were already shortages. He had had to cut off sea duty after five consecutive years, because otherwise boiler technicians would be serving fifteen to sixteen out of twenty years at sea. (Their retention rate was a meager 2 percent.)[61]

By the time of the hearings of the Senate Appropriations Committee's subcommittee on defense in March, budget cut pressures had increased. The Navy Department's total request was $102 billion, an increase of $8.7 billion over appropriations for the current year to date, incorporating as a goal 4.5 to 5.0 percent real growth. Earlier, the Senate Budget Committee had sliced $19.2 billion off defense and stopped any real growth.[62] Senator Ted Stevens, presiding, began the question period

Table 5. Navy Budget By Appropriation Account

Fiscal Years	(figures in thousands of dollars)		
	1984	1985	1986
Military Pay	11,445,908	16,164,107	17,221,400
Operations and Maintenance	22,265,628	25,334,741	25,797,700
Aircraft Procurement	10,157,608	10,903,798	12,062,600
Shipbuilding and Conversion	11,484,848	11,620,826	11,411,600
Research, Development, Testing, Evaluation	7,586,318	9,274,106	11,264,300
5 account totals	62,940,310	73,297,578	77,757,600
19 account totals	82,253,357	96,525,942	104,876,700

by pointing out that the Budget Committee's action would hold real growth for 1986 to zero and limit 1987 and 1988 growth to 3 percent. He expressed extreme skepticism about the 1987 and 1988 growth. What was more important to the navy, modernization or six hundred ships?[63]

Lehman answered that the Navy's program was a balanced one that grew out of the nation's commitments: "Article V of NATO is as much a part of the law as any domestic piece of legislation. We have to swear to protect Norway as if it were Long Island. . . . We have to either face up to the fact that we cannot meet all of these commitments, or we have got to fund them." Since 60 percent of the budget "goes to operate what we have today in peacetime, that leaves 40 percent. To take out the Navy's share of what the Budget Committee passed as a cut would be $6 billion out of 40 percent of our budget." The result would be a slash in procurement, ammunition buys, aircraft programs, and the shipbuilding program.[64]

At the outset, Stevens had requested detailed navy figures on real growth for three years. The information given him covered nineteen categories for FY 84, FY 85, and FY 86. Of these nineteen, only five exceeded $5 billion for any of the fiscal years, and they were the same five (see table 5). It is easy to see, since the five accounts take up such a great percentage of the total budget, that significant cuts were possible only here.

Senator William Proxmire asked whether SDI would not soak up large amounts of money; coupled with a 3 percent growth limit, it could spell trouble. Lehman answered that "the basic principle [was] to start channeling the money . . . that goes to strategic forces [roughly 14 percent of the defense budget] into protecting the American people instead of avenging them."[65] The navy steamed more than 50 percent of the time, compared with 15 percent for the Soviet fleet. That was too much for the United States, too little for the USSR.

The FY 86 hearings before the House Appropriations Committee's subcommittee on defense brought few surprises,[66] but on 4 April 1985 when the House Armed Services Committee's seapower subcommittee held its final hearings for the FY 86 budget, Chairman Bennett led off with the bad news that reductions would have to be made. There was a growing belief that defense dollars were not being spent wisely, and growing alarm about the budget deficit.[67] As it had many times before, the Congress was saying to the navy, "Tell me your priorities so I can cut more efficiently." And as it had many times before, the navy refused to say what it did not need. In the end, Congress had to make up its own mind which way to go and how far to cut. Reductions turned out to be just under 5 percent.

THE FY 87 HEARINGS

The FY 87 hearings were held in the shadow of the Gramm-Rudman Balanced Budget and Emergency Deficit Control Act of 1985. This act provided for set-percentage cuts in the various areas of future federal budgets if the deficit was not reduced below a certain level. Everything that was difficult before now became harder. The House Armed Services Committee met on 5 February 1986, under the chairmanship of Dante B. Fascell. Secretary Lehman, making his sixth presentation, repeated much of what he had said in earlier years. In his judgment, readiness and capability had about doubled over the previous five years.[68] During that period, too, the navy had averaged just under 6 percent real growth. This year it was asking "for a mere one percent real growth compared to the appropriations Congress passed . . . in the 1986 budget." The navy would need a steady 3 percent real growth over the next five years.[69]

Watkins opened by stressing that the maritime strategy was "a sound standard for assessing the validity of budget decisions."[70] He reviewed with pride the navy's operations in 1985, citing the capture of the *Achille Lauro* "shipjackers" five hours from the first alert given to the president. The navy was larger and 75 percent newer and more capable, with 121 new ships, 288 modernized ships, and 45 older ships decommissioned. Similarly, 30 percent of naval aircraft had been replaced or modernized since 1980.[71] Three times as many aircraft squadrons and twice as many surface ships reported high readiness in 1985 as did in 1981. These improvements owed much to shorter deployments outside the continental United States, which were now being limited to six months, with a minimum of twelve months between deployments.[72]

As for the Balanced Budget and Emergency Deficit Control Act of 1985, it added significant uncertainty to budget calculations. Whereas, in FY 86, the navy had been "able to spread the 4.9 percent [cut] in ways that, although they hurt, maintained a balanced approach," if funds were sequestered in FY 87, the navy would not be "able to make logical and balanced reductions." The act did not allow any discretion for FY 87.[73]

The question period began where Watkins left off—on Gramm-Rudman, according to which half of any arbitrary cuts would come from defense. Barring new taxes, the automatic cuts would kick in. This would mean a $30 billion cut in the $320 billion defense budget, "which translates into about $60 to $90 billion in budget authority."[74] If the defense budget was going to amount to $259 billion or $260 billion, wouldn't it make sense to plan ahead? "Whether the defense structure is blown up or burned down," Lehman responded, the result was the same—disastrous.[75] Where would navy cuts be made? Not in "people programs." That meant $5 cuts in hardware for every dollar saved.[76]

The Senate Appropriation's Committee defense subcommittee met on 21 February 1986, with Senator Ted Stevens presiding. Stevens opened the session by announcing that the Navy Department's budget request represented an increase of $5.3 billion over enacted appropriations and "$8.9 billion, approximately six percent real growth, above the Gramm-Rudman-Hollings sequestered baseline."[77]

Lehman submitted his full posture statement for the record and summarized it orally. The navy now got eight times as much oil from the western hemisphere as it got from the entire Middle East.[78] Pacific trade was 30 percent greater than Atlantic trade, and the Soviet Pacific fleet was stronger than ever. The basic reasons for the 600-ship navy, derived from "a simple, logical strategy," had not altered in the six years Lehman had appeared before the committee. Three percent real growth would assure program completion; if "the built-in overhead" in defense could be cut further, an adequate defense could be had for less.[79] He pointed to the record: in shipbuilding, a billion dollars a year in cost underruns, and for F/A-18s, which had cost $22.5 million five years earlier, a price of $18.7 million each.[80]

Watkins said the navy proper was requesting total obligational authority of $94 billion, over half of that for readiness, principally manpower, operations, and support.[81] Ninety percent of the request for increased active manpower (11,400) was for sea and flying duty. Included in the request was money for the fourteenth Ohio-class submarine, four 688s, five Aegis-equipped ships (two cruisers, three

Arleigh Burke–class destroyers), and the lead AOE 6 (fast combat support) ship. A total of 172 planes were being requested, 120 of them F/A-18s.

The discussion turned to unrest in the Philippines and the U.S. facilities at Subic Bay and Clark Airfield. Watkins pointed out that the Soviets had recently moved a regiment of naval infantry to Cam Rahn Bay, the largest forward-deployed base they had anywhere.[82] The best alternative site, if Subic was abandoned, would be at least 500 miles from the South China Sea and the heavily traveled sea routes between the Middle East and Japan.

The issue of homeporting arose, specifically a General Accounting Office draft study recommending triple berthing for some ships in existing ports. Lehman commented that over the next fifteen years it would cost $200 million more "to disperse the fleet than to triple berth. . . . That $200 million is money very well spent."[83] Watkins added that even the worst alternative would cost almost $1 billion.

If "the sequester order goes into effect for fiscal year '87," Senator Proxmire said, "the Department of Defense may have to cut $49 billion in budget authority," of which the navy's share would top $15 billion. What would be cut? Lehman responded that Gramm-Rudman allowed very little discretion, "so we would cut everything, every . . . line would be cut a percentage amount. The result would be utter chaos. It would drive waste and chaos into our contracting to such a degree that it is hard to contemplate." Every fixed-price contract would have to be renegotiated on the losing end since it would be the navy breaking the contractual relationship.[84]

How it all came out in the end, after Congress made its decision, is shown in table 6. Note that, in unadjusted dollars, the navy's budget authority for FY 87 was less than for FY 86. In constant 1988 dollars, the topping-off effect is even more marked: from the high point of FY 85 there is a decline of almost 10 percent by FY 87. Such pressures were to continue as the Reagan defense proposal in 1987 for over $400 billion was reduced to President Bush's 1989 request for just under $300 billion, which represents a steady state budget from FY 88 on. If such budgets are followed by actual reductions, the navy may find itself repeating the dismal cycle described at the outset of this book.

It is therefore useful to maintain a sense of perspective about what really happened in the years when, in Les Aspin's words, a trillion dollars was spent on defense. The defense buildup did not represent a great increase in the percent of net public spending on defense: the 25.5 percent of FY 70 compares with 16.5 percent in FY 75, 15.3 percent in FY 80, 16.7 percent in FY 82, 17.5 percent in FY 84, and 17.8 percent in FY 87.

Table 6. DEPARTMENT OF DEFENSE BUDGET AUTHORITY BY COMPONENT, FY 88*

(dollars in millions)

	FY 1983	FY 1984	FY 1985	FY 1986†	FY 1987	FY 1988	FY 1989
CURRENT DOLLARS							
Department of the Army	57,529	68,664‡	74,270‡	73,128‡	74,525‡	80,102‡	84,747‡
Department of the Navy	81,854	87,365‡	99,015‡	96,113‡	95,345‡	102,343‡	108,693‡
Department of the Air Force	74,074	90,851‡	99,420‡	94,870‡	93,833‡	100,437‡	107,235‡
Defense Agencies/OSD/JCS	9,256	10,746	13,126	15,520	16,641	19,070	20,919
Defense-wide	16,761	524	970	1,759	1,352	1,342	1,696
Total, Direct Program (B/A)	239,474	258,150	286,802	281,390	281,695	303,295	323,290
CONSTANT FY 88 DOLLARS							
Department of the Army	68,293	79,046‡	82,446‡	78,911‡	78,037‡	80,102‡	81,851‡
Department of the Navy	95,341	99,137‡	108,774‡	103,105‡	99,598‡	102,343‡	105,070‡
Department of the Air Force	85,028	102,112‡	108,388‡	101,322‡	97,926‡	100,437‡	103,551‡
Defense Agencies/OSD/JCS	11,141	12,493	14,656	16,876	17,413	19,070	20,260
Defense-wide	19,868	596	1,068	1,880	1,399	1,342	1,640
Total, Direct Program (B/A)	279,671	293,383	315,331	302,094	294,397	303,295	312,372

Source: Caspar Weinberger, *Annual Report to Congress, Fiscal Year 1988* (GPO, 1987), 327.

*Numbers may not add to totals because of rounding.

†Lower budget authority in the military personnel accounts in FY 86 reflects the congressional direction to finance $4.5 billion for the military pay raise and retirement accrual costs by transfers from prior-year unobligated balances.

‡Includes retired pay accrual.

This was not defense spending unrestrained. Nor was defense creating the budget deficit; it merely constituted a portion of total government overspending.

The navy's buildup in these years, contrary to what some critics have alleged, did not proceed at the expense of the other services, as table 3 also shows.

Anyone who reads the record of these years has to be impressed with both the quality of the navy program and the persuasiveness with which it was argued. Undoubtedly, as the 1980s progress, the arguments are pressed with an increasing sense of sureness, particularly because of the effective blending of two strands of navy thinking: capability analysis, which in first instance yielded the 600-ship figure, and the strategy of how the U.S. Navy must fight its forces. That maritime strategy thinking was applied to good political purpose is apparent.

Chapter 9

TAPPING THE NAVY'S INTELLECTUAL RESOURCES

One of the best things the navy did in the 1980s was to tap its intellectual resources. It is much to Admiral Hayward's credit that he made the first major move in this direction by establishing the Strategic Studies Group.

Admiral Watkins went much further. He was quick to see that the best force multiplier of all was the navy's intellectual assets. Earlier, as chief of naval personnel, he had come to the conclusion that the navy was wasting its seed corn by not utilizing the Naval War College adequately. And in his first weeks as CNO he had determined to change that.

Watkins initially wanted to foster an intellectual climate to give the navy a new and clearer sense of tactics and strategy. Later, as ideas sparked ideas, he came to understand that the intellectual ferment thus begun could provide the concerted sense of purpose and direction for the whole navy that had been far too lacking after Vietnam.

ANTI-INTELLECTUAL?

The navy has often been accused of being anti-intellectual. Sometimes quoted in support of that charge is the remark of the chief of the old Bureau of Navigation about Alfred Thayer Mahan: "It is not the business of a naval officer to write books."[1] And it is true that few American naval officers have written books, at least on professional topics like strategy.[2]

There is a good reason for this: Naval officers spend a lot of their time at sea, busy and without source materials or the company of writers. Those who have never sailed in a navy ship may imagine the experience to be as leisured as service recruitment ads suggest. The professional naval officer, standing one watch out of three, conducting drills, and writing reports, knows the reality is much different. War may always be a moment away. As for those posted in Washington, many put in long hours. In either case, the time for reflection is minimal. To use a bureaucratic slogan, There are always fires to put out.

The navy's conservatism is often cited as a reason for its anti-intellectualism, yet over the years it has produced mavericks like William Snowden Sims and John Dahlgren, neither of whom hesitated to challenge accepted wisdom. The navy was the first U.S. service to found a war college—in 1884—and maintain it. There is not a single famous navy leader of World War II who was not a graduate of that institution. And then there is the U.S. Naval Institute, its respected publication *Proceedings*, and the Naval Postgraduate School at Monterey.

Nevertheless, it is true that in the decades after World War II the navy failed to draw on its intellectual capital. Preoccupied with staying alive during the bureaucratic battles noted in chapter 1, then with running operations during the Korean and Vietnam wars, the navy brought little of its brainpower systematically to bear on professional problems. At the height of the Vietnam War, as the number of naval officers attending the Naval War College at Newport steadily fell, the army happily filled the vacated slots. Naval officers became a minority in the Newport student body.

THE CNO'S EXECUTIVE PANEL

One of Admiral Zumwalt's most important innovations was the creation on 28 July 1970, the end of his first month in office, of the CNO's executive panel (CEP). Its objective was to clearly define the navy's mission and purpose in light of American policy. Though in Zumwalt's time it failed to produce an accepted formulation of maritime strategy, CEP was an important step forward. Eventually it would serve as a high-level sounding board and think tank for almost every topic of importance to the navy.[3]

Naturally, CEP meant different things to different CNOs. Originally it was only a plenary group that met quarterly with the CNO. Then standing subpanels were created, sometimes by adding outside experts, to deal with strategy, science and technology, force enhancement, and long-range planning. In Zumwalt's time, CEP considered ways the navy could work around severe budget cuts and foster innovative thinking about naval warfare. Under Holloway, it emphasized more traditional military concerns such as tactical nuclear policy. With Hayward as CNO, it focused more on the Soviet threat and the implications of arms control, and spent much time on the use of sophisticated sensors and weaponry.[4]

Under Watkins the subpanels, now called task forces, assigned small numbers of CEP experts to handle specific problems. In August

1982 six task forces were commissioned, including one for space and one for naval strategy. Each group was asked to conduct an intensive review of its issue and make concrete policy recommendations in a report to CNO. Admiral Watkins insisted that the reports be useful. One led to the establishment of the Navy Space Command. And several CEP members provided advice that would play a role in the creation of SDI.[5]

In 1983 five other task forces were created, including one on Arctic warfare and another on strategic C³I (command-control communications intelligence). ASW (antisubmarine warfare) also received long overdue attention. The seven task forces formed in 1984 included terrorism, technology transfer, SLCM (submarine-launched cruise missile) defense, and personal excellence. In 1985 a final set of five task forces looked at strategic defense, the role of the naval reserve in the maritime strategy, and the Pacific basin, among other topics.

CEP is unique because it gives the CNO frank, direct advice. It would be easy for CEP proceedings to disintegrate into mere intellectual kibitzing. The task force arrangement helps prevent this by requiring specific reports. Moreover, the executive director of CEP is double-hatted as the navy's long-range planner, so there is a direct link between think tanks and planning. Members of a task force serve without pay and meet about twenty-five days a year. By June 1986, twenty-three task forces had held over one hundred meetings.

The official memo describing CEP says that it is purely advisory.[6] That hardly conveys the tone of these task force meetings, which tend to be intellectually explosive.[7]

To give a single striking illustration of CEP's contribution, consider the task force on strategic planning in 1984. This group held meetings in March with six DCNOs/DMSOs and a flag representative from the Naval Material Command. On 10 April they gave their report to the CNO; this was followed on 20 April with a staffing memo to the CNO recommending how to use the report for the forthcoming CINCs conference.[8] The report was presented on April 24 in Annapolis along with the CNO's comments, and then the flags broke into two teams to discuss the issues raised. A large part of that discussion was on the best organization for OPNAV and the relationship between OPNAV and the material command in the future. How could the horizontal and vertical slots be better coordinated?[9]

THE CENTER FOR NAVAL ANALYSES

Another brain center, the Center for Naval Analyses (CNA), was set up during World War II. It is the oldest organization conducting operations research and systems analysis for the navy and Marine Corps.

Its name has changed over the years, as has its location and university or institute sponsor. Its present name was given when the Operations Evaluation Group and the Institute of Naval Studies were united in 1962. In 1987 it was housed in Alexandria. Like most think tanks associated with a single service, it has been accused of neglecting the concerns of its sponsor.[10] Such was rumored to be the issue in the conflict between Secretary Lehman and Rochester University, which administered the CNA contract between 1967 and 1983. That conflict led to the present arrangement with the Hudson Institute as CNA's sponsor.[11]

In 1986 CNA had four divisions: naval warfare operations; naval planning, manpower, and logistics; Marine Corps programs; and field operations. Its seven research departments indicated the thrust of its efforts: air warfare, amphibious and land warfare, information sciences, resource analysis, strategic studies, submarine/antisubmarine warfare, and surface warfare. CNA also had thirty-eight analysts assigned to thirty navy and Marine Corps commands around the world.[12] They evaluated systems performance, tactical development, and fleet effectiveness.[13]

As of 1986, almost half the two hundred members of CNA's research staff (of whom over 90 percent hold advanced degrees) had served as field representatives. Two-thirds specialized in the hard sciences. Some fifteen naval officers were also part of the staff. For management purposes CNA reported to the VCNO via OP-91 and OP-090's scientific officer. Its policy council was chaired by the assistant secretary of the navy for research, engineering, and systems.

The basic philosophy of CNA is derived from a statement by Sir Isaac Newton in 1694: "If, instead of sending the observations of able seamen to able mathematicians on land, the land would send able mathematicians to sea, it would signify much more to the improvement of navigation and to the safety of men's lives and estates on that element." Many CNA's field representatives are not at sea, but all of them, from Yokosuka to Point Mugu, from the Patuxent River to Naples, work in places where they can see firsthand what fleet problems need solutions. The navy on the whole has benefited from CNA and kept it a viable institution even under funding constraints.

THE NAVAL POSTGRADUATE SCHOOL

Someone from another service once remarked enviously on the navy's choice of geographical locations for its educational institutions: Annapolis (the Naval Academy), Newport (the Naval War College), Monterey (the Naval Postgraduate School). All are beautiful seaside sites. The Postgraduate School was actually founded at Annapolis but later was moved to the old Del Monte Hotel grounds at Monterey. Like all the navy's educational institutions, its funding and student numbers have fluctuated over the years.

The Postgraduate School has its own resident programs and also administers the programs of all navy students sent to civilian universities. Why maintain a postgraduate school at all? Congress poses this question at least once a decade. Why not send all the students to Tufts or MIT or Cal Tech? The answer is that the Postgraduate School offers many degree programs tailored specially to navy needs and not easily accommodated at civilian institutions.[14] A number of them also involve sensitive, classified materials.

A criticism for which Congress until recently had grounds was that the navy sometimes failed to utilize Monterey students in subsequent assignments. Because the students often rank as high as lieutenant commander, command or key staff billets and billets requiring technical expertise compete for their services.

The most serious criticism that might be levied against the Post-graduate School is that, like the war college, it has been underutilized. The navy for many years after World War II was trying to stretch a small officer corps to meet a broad range of needs. That was especially true in the late 1970s.[15]

There is a perennial gap between the number of specialists the navy needs in a particular field and the number of students preparing for that specialty at the Postgraduate School. Billet needs are established through a system of consultation with users of graduates, but that does not mean candidates are always available.[16] The oceanographer of the navy, for example, will be asked to estimate future personnel needs for his specialization; filling that quota depends on whether enough officers are recruited or volunteer, and whether the navy has sufficient funds for the program.

Navy billets requiring graduate education increased from 4,987 in FY 75 to 6,503 in FY 85, representing a 5 percent per annum increase in nontechnical areas and a 2 percent increase in technical fields. To meet the 6,503 figure there was a personnel pool of 7,087, but sea-shore rotation, attrition, and command and staff detailing competition made a much larger pool necessary. To fill the billets required more than twice the base figure (14,230 vice 6,503), and the Postgraduate School estimated that it would take an annual input of 1,475 to maintain the requirement, once reached.

The inputs have not reached those levels. Quotas for all fields in 1985 totaled 725, increasing to 750 in 1986 and 800 in 1987. Between 1986 and 1987 additional needs were added, for example, in manpower

Table 7. U.S. Navy Graduate Education

Fiscal Year	Quota	Input	Fiscal Year	Quota	Input
87	800	—	82	600	590
86	750	725	81	611	568
85	725	707	80	522	480
84	700	654	79	471	460
83	700	614	78	820	511

personnel training analysis, intelligence, applied mathematics, ASW systems techniques, operational oceanography, weapons-system science, nuclear physics, and avionics. There was a decreased need for personnel in financial management, educational and training management, and systems-acquisition management.[17]

Data from FY 78 through FY 87 reflect a purging of subspecialty billet quotas between FY 78 and FY 79, then a steady climb in those quotas. Input after FY 78 approximates the quotas fairly well in the later years. The data are given in table 7.

The quality of the student body at the Naval Postgraduate School is high, representing the top half of officers in a given rank. Unrestricted line officers are taken directly from promotion board lists; there is therefore a bank of eight thousand potential candidates for eight hundred navy quotas.[18]

By 1984 the school had awarded a total of 19,271 degrees since 1946. Of these, 6,238 were B.A. and B.S. degrees, almost all awarded prior to 1982, when undergraduate education was phased out. In addition there were some 12,551 master's degrees, 361 engineer's degrees, 116 Ph.D.s, and 6 doctor of engineering degrees. Of the 12,551 master's degrees, programs with more than a thousand students each were electrical engineering, management, and operations research. National security affairs, aeronautical engineering, computer science, computer-systems management, mechanical engineering, meteorology, oceanography, physics, systems technology, and science had between 250 and 999 graduates.

Steering a balance at Monterey (or at Newport) between academically sound courses and courses that serve navy needs is difficult. If the Naval Postgraduate School is just like any other university, why maintain it out of navy funds? On the other hand, if it is not like civilian universities, why pay for it? Rear Admiral Robert Austin, superintendent of the school and himself a graduate of it, explained why it was useful:

I went through an aerospace missiles system curriculum here in the early '60s. I got into a conversation just the other day about ASW. And someone had raised the question, "Why do we have an ASW curriculum at the Naval Postgraduate School?" And I said to him, "Well, it is probably for the same reason that we had the aerospace missile curriculum in the weapons engineering department when I went through here."

It didn't have anything to do with a *missile*. If you had walked me up to a missile I probably wouldn't even have recognized it in 1960 after going through the curriculum. Some people would be alarmed by that.

I've overstated it, but an enormous amount of it had to do with fundamentals. You sort of have to go through the litany of the curriculum of the time [to appreciate what I mean]. . . . It was physics, it was electrical engineering, it was aeronautical engineering, it was meteorology, it was upper-air atmosphere physics, it was computers, it was acoustics, it was chemistry, it was electronics engineering for circuit principles, radar design principles, telemetry, it was information theory, it was operations analysis. . . . It was an enormously valuable underlying set of principles. And it was enormously valuable to me. It was education. Education.[19]

Admiral Austin reported that in a meeting with Admiral Watkins this very point had been made: the objective of the Naval Postgraduate School was education, not training.

THE NAVAL WAR COLLEGE: A TURNAROUND

We noted that the Naval War College was founded in 1884 and that it was the first service war college in the United States. In 1984, the centennial year, it was the oldest war college in continuing existence in the world.

Between 1966 and 1986 the Naval War College had nine presidents, of whom subsequently five retired, one was promoted to three stars, and three to four stars—surely a good showing. By contrast, during many of these years the number of graduates who made flag rank was no higher (and in some years was lower) than for their peers who did not attend. The curriculum, despite much propaganda to the contrary, was challenging in content and became more so. On the other hand, before President Stansfield Turner came in 1972, the civilian faculty was too small and the military faculty often consisted only of staff. And the overall quality of the student body, especially for commander-captain ranks, was not up to par.[20] The students were distinctly inferior to those at sister institutions in Carlisle or Maxwell and much below the caliber of students at the National War College.[21]

Captain Tim Somes, chairman of the operations department in 1987 at Newport, said of his own student days a few years before that about ten of his fellow students in the senior course were post-commanders, that is, had already held a command.[22] By 1987, however, there were sixty to seventy post-commanders in the course. These students now represented the cream of the professional navy crop.

Stansfield Turner made a remarkable number of well-publicized changes at Newport during his brief tenure, convinced that they would bring in a rush of talented post-commanders. As we can see from what Somes said, this did not happen. The creation of a first-rate civilian and military faculty by Turner had little immediate effect. Not until Admiral Hayward's time did the dismal situation begin to change. It was during Admiral Watkins' tenure that the number of post-commanders increased significantly. We have already seen how: The CNO collapsed the training pipeline and transferred the empty slots to Newport for post-commanders.

Watkins, knowing that it would be impossible to free all these people for (or even accommodate them in) a year-long course, arranged to have some of them attend a shorter one. With this and other changes Watkins made certain that, downstream, an impressive number of Naval War College graduates would be selected for flag rank. This way he overcame the geographic advantage enjoyed by the National War College in Washington, which many navy students wanted to attend because they were already in the Pentagon, the Navy Annex, or Crystal City jobs.

What the new students found upon their arrival at Newport had not been produced overnight or by one college president or CNO. It had been built up slowly over a period of one hundred years. Almost closed in its early years, the Naval War College survived to become a sought-after institution in the 1930s (when steaming time was scarce). It fell upon Washington indifference in the 1950s and 1960s, then underwent improvements in the 1970s and 1980s. In his tour as president of the college (1966–1968), Vice Admiral John Hayward had the vision (and the political acumen) to lay out a plan for badly needed modern buildings. Vice Admiral Richard G. Colbert, who succeeded him, saw that program through and established the Naval War College Foundation. Vice Admiral Benedict J. Semmes served as president only a short while before the dynamic and restless Turner was appointed to the office. Vice President Julien LeBourgeois patiently selected those of Turner's changes worth preserving and quietly discarded the rest. After Rear Admiral Huntington Hardisty's six-month term as president, Vice Admiral James B. Stockdale came in convinced of the need to stress professional ethics and instituted a broader electives program.[23] Rear Admiral Edward Welch was able to consolidate these innovations; he also helped CNO Hayward establish the Strategic Studies Group. Rear

Admiral James E. Service, succeeding Welch, presided when Admiral Watkins significantly improved the student body.

THE CURRICULUM AT NEWPORT

Before Turner, the senior course consisted of four parts: fundamentals of strategy, which filled in gaps and then moved rapidly to the graduate level in such subjects as international relations, international law, and military history; national strategy; U.S. military concerns in major geographical areas; and naval operations. The course involved research and war gaming. Students also took electives and had an opportunity to earn a master's degree from George Washington University. The program was inadequately staffed but for the most part pertinent to the navy profession. Its major weakness was the naval operations portion of the curriculum, which was not advanced enough for unrestricted line officers but was too advanced for other naval officers or officers from other services.

Vice Admiral Turner, who believed the program lacked depth, decided to reduce it to three basic courses, eliminating the outside degree program and a good deal of the gaming and electives.[24] The program developed unevenly. The strategy course, with a strong civilian faculty, got off to a good start, although it ended abruptly with World War II. The management course was disappointing at first but eventually transformed into an excellent format. The naval operations was the worst. Originally, Turner wanted it to focus on the tactical implications of technical improvements in naval systems. The course gradually became broader in scope but still lacked coherency. Under retired Vice Admiral Thomas Weschler, who served as course chairman, this changed; he got students to utilize a three-star and four-star vantage point in assessing operations. (On the command and staff level, the viewpoint was two star.)

In an interview, Vice Admiral Weschler said that before teaching the naval operations course he went through all the materials being used in it and found two problems:

> Number one, I didn't find the word *joint* in any of the readings I had. I felt that jointness was the wave of the future, the only way that an armed force, without being abnormally large, could get jobs done that we were very likely to be called on to do. And our diversity of talent [in the armed services] was such that we fit together very nicely.
> . . . [Two,] the course still smacked an awful lot of Naval Academy and ensigns' notebooks. Too much attention to how weapons worked and how equipment worked. . . .
> And my feeling was that anything that was *within* the ship was not

an appropriate discussion item for the College, that we had to start from the inter-ship relationships, force and task group relationships, that anything within the ship had to be accepted as a given and for those people who came here and hadn't that experience, it was up to their moderators and classmates to help them bridge that gap and make sense out of it. . . .

One other thing I began to feel as I began to put together the course material. Command and staff and the senior course were almost identical at that time except in length.[25]

This was a Turner change. Since less than 15 percent of the students at the junior course (actually the intermediate-level course, command and staff) came back for the senior course (naval warfare), Turner had decided to offer only one course. The decision was never fully implemented and was ultimately reversed.[26]

The seniors, in Weschler's view, needed materials not then in the course. In addition, war gaming needed to be reemphasized "to pound home all of the things we had been talking about in the abstract."[27]

Captain Hugh Lynch, who succeeded Weschler, continued the trends toward more operational thinking and war gaming when Watkins was chief of naval personnel and Holloway was CNO. How the navy looked to a student under Captain Lynch, who later himself became chairman of the same department (renamed Operations in 1987), is told by Captain Tim Somes:

Each segment of the Navy—submarine force, carrier battle group, or the various aviation communities—knew tactically how they were going to fight their end of the war. But there was no coherent approach to how we were going to fight as a whole Navy. We were paying lip service to the joint operations idea but we were continuing to focus not only along subspecialty lines but on service-bias lines.[28]

Somes thought the war-gaming methods were defective, a point we shall return to in a later chapter. And, of course, navy commanders of the period were off preparing to fight their own war and competing for the same inadequate resources. When they came to lecture at the war college, it underlined the lack of an overall strategic concept.

Within this context, the war college continued to struggle with the operations curriculum, teaching students who until 1983 were there in minimum numbers and for the most part without the command experience that could bring expertise to the seminar room and help them benefit from their year of study. Creating a meaningful operations curriculum, even without these handicaps, was a formidable job.

How many navy officers in each class had held command varied from trimester to trimester. In August 1981 the number was sixteen, and, counting November and April additions, for 1981–82 it reached twenty-five. In the following academic years, when Watkins was CNO, the numbers rose steadily from twenty-eight to forty-four (1983–84), reaching fifty-six in 1985–86.[29] Added to that number were the interim short-course students who, to overcome the backlog from past neglect, came for eight weeks immediately after being detached from their successful tours in command. By 1987, out of approximately two hundred fifty post-commanders available each year, the short course had fourteen students four times a year.[30]

With quality students in such numbers, much could be accomplished. The seed corn was no longer being wasted.

Simultaneously, there were important developments in research and gaming. In the 1960s, all students had conducted required research. In the early 1970s, after the Center for Advanced Research (CAR) was established, only some students, excused from part of the core curriculum, would do a special project. CAR ultimately became part of a bigger unit, the Center for Naval Warfare Studies, created when Admiral Hayward was CNO. It administered student research and directed the war-gaming program. It also acted as landlord to the new Strategic Studies Group.

A second significant change, already hinted at, was the move toward joint thinking. Well before the Goldwater-Nichols Defense Reorganization Act of 1986, both the curriculum and gaming had taken on that focus. It was aided and spurred on by the fact that the Naval War College student body had a large number of officers from outside services, a much greater percentage of mixing than other service colleges. Thus for the first time since the birth of the navy an oft-quoted remark of Henry L. Stimson lost its relevancy: he had commented on "the peculiar psychology of the Navy Department, which frequently seemed to retire from the realm of logic into a dim religious world in which Neptune was god, Mahan his prophet, and the U.S. Navy the only true church."

THE CREATION OF THE STRATEGIC STUDIES GROUP

In many ways the Strategic Studies Group, established, as we have seen, in 1981, was to be a catalyst at Newport and for the navy as a whole. A special group such as this was not an original idea at Newport; it had been tried at least twice before.[31] What was different this time was, first, that the idea originated with the CNO, and second, that the group had a dynamic director, former Undersecretary of the Navy Robert Murray.

Captain Somes explained how having the group at Newport brought special dividends. First, it increased the number of post-commanders. Senior students and studies group members naturally exchanged views. The atmosphere was one of ferment. For example, as Somes and his studies group opposite number Submariner Bill Owens conversed, each began to understand why the navy was having trouble formulating strategy.[32] Such fruitful interaction was to continue and expand—not just at Newport.

Somes said that the Strategic Studies Group took "the bumblebee approach. They went around the world and pollenated." They took ideas and "spread them throughout the entire senior Navy community." Whether the SSG invented the maritime strategy was, in Somes' opinion, a moot question. People throughout the navy, it turned out, were thinking along similar lines.[33]

Bob Murray, recalling those early days, commented that even before he came to Newport as the group's director he had been

> trying to think through how naval forces fit into national strategy. Most of the discussion at that time was on who was more important, the Atlantic Fleet or the Pacific Fleet. . . . So one of the things I had hoped to accomplish at Newport in working with the SSG and the War College was, could we think through naval strategy from the perspective of naval officers rather than just from an academic or intelligence point of view? What were the blue-suit people actually thinking as they went about their business and how could we help them think more about how to use their forces? It seemed to me that in general as a country we had a fairly cohesive view of what our strategic aims were: nuclear deterrence with the Soviet Union, deterrence in general against the Soviet Union, especially at the points of greatest conflict with the Soviet Union.[34]

But how would the navy fit into that strategy?

We saw in chapter 2 that Admiral Tom Hayward did not have a rigid plan in mind when he set the studies group up. It was a critical part, though, of his overall plan "to upgrade the tactical and strategic competence of naval officers." He explained:

> It seemed to me that not enough flag officers were tactically competent nor did they have the exposure they ought to have to step back and think globally—at any point in their career. It shouldn't be when they get to be a fleet commander or even CNO. If then, it's too late. It's got to be before they're flag officers. So pick them at the captain level, put some commanders in there. . . .
>
> I wanted these predicted superstars to have that special training . . . . It would give them a much better baseline from which to think, to react, to have confidence and that sort of thing. That's what we designed, and we designed it with substance more in mind than structure. There was no unique structure to it. It was conceived for the purpose of providing an opportunity to think, think, think tactics and warfighting.[35]

There is a whole continuum of operations beginning with individual ships, progressing to fleets, and then moving on to a global strategic view. Hayward felt that understanding had to be deepened all along the continuum. Of the Strategic Studies Group he remarked,

> I didn't care what the specific subject of their year's focus was. They could pick a Pacific or Med scenario, or whatever. It didn't matter; it was the exercise I wanted them to go through. But there had to be a core agenda of some few months' duration where they would have to do some very specific background reading to absorb a baseline of naval strategic knowledge on which to base later problem solutions. The problem could be one of their own or they could come down to OPNAV and ask for one, or go to the fleet and ask for one. It didn't make any difference. But they were to travel. . . .[36]

They were to travel to pick up the ideas of others and to bounce their own ideas off fleet staffs. In addition to fleet visits, flag officers who left an operational command were to try and visit the war college for a day or two and exchange ideas with people there.

Murray found that naval officers tended to be technically oriented and did not think through the roles and missions of the navy.[37] Conceptually, they needed to reconcile force structure with training, and training with proposed use of forces. Not just naval forces—total forces. The Strategic Studies Group would work, Murray thought, "somewhere below grand strategy" because the strategic goals were not really in dispute.

It was Murray, then, who began to think of a series of structured reports that might build upon each other. This is what the group ended up doing.

Both Admirals Hayward and Watkins made a point of personally selecting the members of the Strategic Studies Group. This procedure was not only good for morale; it was necessary that the right people be selected so that a limited resource could be put to effective use and so that the flag community (denied these "head-and-shoulders" contenders for flag rank) would not complain. "You had to prove to the fleet that this was a good use of these officers," said Hayward, or the idea would surely wither. He "handpicked every officer that went there . . . with the expectation . . . of seeing every one of them selected for flag. . . . Why waste the time on a guy who wasn't destined to be flag?"[38]

The idea certainly did not wither in the years when Watkins was CNO, nor in the period of the Trost tenure covered in this book. We shall see in later chapters, as we examine the maritime strategy, how with Watkins' enthusiastic encouragement the new group had a profound effect in helping to make it coherent. Successive annual studies groups, building on each other's efforts, honed the rough edges of the strategy, looking at it in a global perspective and testing it through gaming. After detachment from Newport, group members, like post-command students, went to carefully picked assignments where they could directly apply what they had learned.[39]

Chapter 10

FORCE MULTIPLIERS: GAMING, RESERVES, ALLIES

In the early to mid-1980s the phrases war stoppers and force multipliers were frequently heard in navy circles. War stoppers are inhibitors such as the lack of sealift for army divisions ready to embark. Force multipliers are those things that give America's regular mobilized forces additional reach or effect. The greatest force multiplier is brain power, discussed in chapter 9. Here, in chapter 10, we shall look at three additional force multipliers: war gaming, reserves, and allies.

WAR GAMING: ITS EVOLUTION AT NEWPORT

The center for navy war gaming is the Naval War College at Newport. The first war college in the United States, it was also first to realize the utility of gaming. Lieutenant McCarty Little is credited with introducing gaming at the college.[1] He began working with Alfred Thayer Mahan on ship tactics, moving cardboard ships over drawing paper. In 1886 he gave what was apparently the first war-gaming lecture. By 1894 war gaming was seen as a way to apply broad principles to specific issues and became an integral part of instruction. Previously, games had been used for demonstrations and to examine particular problems. Three kinds were used in 1894: a two-ship game, a fleet-action tabletop game, and a strategic game played on charts, with players in separate rooms, representing an entire war.[2]

So by 1894, basic gaming techniques were already in place. What was to change most notably in the next century were gaming facilities and devices. In the 1930s gaming took place in Pringle Hall; in the 1950s it was moved to its present site, Sims Hall.[3] In Pringle, a huge floor space was divided into colored squares like a chessboard, each square representing a specific square distance.[4] At Sims, the same floor concept was used initially. Over the years, gaming progressed from entirely manual exercises to elaborate computer modeling in the 1970s and 1980s.

In the 1960s and early 1970s, the umpire room at Sims Hall had an enormous screen on which the game moves were displayed with various symbols and different colored lights. This was NEWS, the naval warfare simulator. It used analog computers for high-speed simulation and could reenact scenarios such as the Battle of Midway. As new equipment and funding became available, NEWS gave way to four successive modifications, the last of which was ENWGS (enhanced naval war-gaming system), pronounced "en-wags"; analog computers were replaced by digital. Both ENWGS and its predecessor included plans for remote connectivity. In 1978 Newport began plans to hook up the fleets and design further improvements. The remotes became operational in October 1982, permitting the U.S. Navy to play through Newport from major headquarters without physically moving major staffs to Newport.

This change was important in many ways. When Admiral Tom Hayward was CINCPACFLT, because of the expense and time lost coming to Newport, the Pacific Fleet had to use the limited facilities of the Postgraduate School at Monterey. The Atlantic and Pacific fleets did not have the opportunity to play a common game simultaneously. Today, the entire U.S. Navy can play the same game at the same time.

Newport's game floor is much less dramatic looking than the NEWS umpire room with its large lighted screen and many lighted symbols. Nowadays the game floor consists of individual computer consoles at which umpires sit to monitor players' moves. What is impressive and different is the sophisticated modeling that governs many of the results. It permits a hundred or more variables to be taken into account with precision; before, only a few variables were included in the game and their effects were often decided by a roll of the dice.

GAMING: SHORTCOMINGS AND PAYOFFS

Gaming started at Newport as an educational tool. It was used by the faculty and students to test ideas and tactics they had conceived. Only in the most limited sense was gaming thought of as a research device by which extensive and continuing analysis could be made systematically to discover trends. This distinction between education and research is obviously not clearcut. If, as in the 1930s, enough students play the Orange war plan, an appreciation of strategy will grow over the years as successive moves yield the same results. This is what Fleet Admiral Chester W. Nimitz was referring to when, at the end of World War II, he said, "The war with Japan had been reenacted in the game rooms at the Naval War College by so many people, and in so many ways, that nothing that happened during the war was a surprise—absolutely nothing except the kamikaze tactics towards the end of the war; we had not visualized these."[5]

The educational games by the late 1960s were not entirely helpful. There was ample gaming activity, but it lacked realism in major areas, principally in communications intelligence sensitivity, and sometimes scenarios were unrealistic.[6] When Admiral Turner came to Newport he phased out senior student games played at NEWS, although he continued student seminars with tabletop games. NEWS became oriented toward the fleets, especially the Atlantic Fleet, but was much underused. "In the Turner era," Captain D. C. Klinger commented, "gaming nearly petered out. If it had not been for [Admiral] Ike Kidd and his [Atlantic] command readiness series of games, this building [Sims Hall] might have reverted back to the barracks it once was many years ago."[7] It was Admiral Kidd who sustained gaming through the late 1970s. But to professional gamers there was a drawback to Admiral Kidd's method. He moved the games in specific directions rather than allowing them to be played "free" so as to force his staff to make certain decisions. For example, he wanted to determine what he needed to deploy into the Norwegian Sea; his games therefore tended to pound the same logistical lessons home about this area.[8] While the gamers were grateful for Kidd's support, they looked for opportunities to play games with a less restricted purpose.

The educational games played in the 1960s and 1970s were oriented to students. They were not useless, but as Captain Jay Hurlburt said, "There was no *analysis* being done, no sense of what we might be learning, no idea of what the sequence is that would lead you to victory or to disaster."[9] What he meant was that individual students were learning what kinds of game moves produced what kinds of results, but there was a lack of cumulative corporate knowledge. This was to change through a number of separate developments.

One was when Captain Hugh Nott, retiring as college chief of staff and associated with the Center for Advanced Research (CAR), and then-Commander Hurlburt started a tactical elective that fostered research gaming.[10] A little later the problem arose of what to do with the new students arriving at off-times in April and November rather than in August. The college decided they could be usefully employed during the summer break by gaming. This greatly expanded manpower. Meanwhile, the two other talented individuals who then constituted the CAR brain trust, Bud Hay and Francis West (director of the Sea Plan 2000 study and later an assistant secretary of defense), convinced that gaming was not being properly utilized, became involved with the college's program.

Then, in 1981, Hayward established the Strategic Studies Group, which from the first was significantly involved in gaming. Hayward was certain the Carter administration's swing strategy to bring Pacific assets to a war in the Atlantic was unsound. There would no longer be such a thing as an Atlantic war or a Pacific war. As Captain Hurlburt pointed out:

> The students were doing theater games, Ike Kidd was doing Atlantic games. Nobody was doing a global game. So you never got to look at the sequence of things and frequently you found that [in the game] both the good guys and the bad guys were bringing forces from other theaters into the theater that was being played, as a way of aiding their problem. . . . There was no competition for the assets.[11]

When you ran out in the Atlantic, you borrowed from the Pacific. Meanwhile, the Pacific fleet might well be doing gaming using Atlantic assets. The navy's own gaming procedures were helping to disguise just how inadequate U.S. forces were.

The consequences of this growing realization were two, each of great significance to gaming and to the development of an integrated maritime strategy: the global war game and systematic game analysis.

The first global game was played in 1979 and has been annually ever since. Bud Hay, who designed the game and directed it after 1980, said that in order not to lose the sense of political realities and constraints, it was not too futuristic. From the outset, the global game was seen as an analytical tool, using a study-game-study approach. With the Naval War College as sponsor, the general inclination of an outside sponsor to drive the design of the game and get his own version of the issues could be avoided. Equally important, there would be no grading. (Under Kidd, game play had affected fitness reports. One admiral got a whole flotilla sunk once. . . .) The new game would be played on a non-attribution basis, without directly challenging any command's sacred cows and without pitting one theater and its claim on resources against another. It would serve as "a forum in which people can bump against the hard issues. . . ."[12]

As an aid to analysis, Bud Hay developed what he called Intelfusion, a huge spread sheet in the computer representing red, green, and blue views, plus "ground truth." The area being researched was the navy's set of assumptions. Intelfusion was a method of sifting out wrong assumptions for better analysis and better planning later.

Global turned out to be the premier gaming event of the year. Played over a period of three weeks and covering about twenty days of war, it quickly proved to fill a great need. From the outset it drew high-level civilians and active and retired flag officers. By the mid 1980s, especially at the urging of CNO Watkins, representatives from the Joint

Chiefs of Staff and the secretary of defense were at Newport to play the global game.

The new gaming required people who could take an analytical rather than a managerial approach.

In many ways these innovations represented returning to what both Dr. Robert S. Wood, the Strategic Study Group's second director and dean of naval warfare studies, and Captain Hurlburt described as the much more sophisticated games and game reports in the archives from the 1920s and 1930s. By the late 1970s, the habit had become strong, said Wood, of viewing game success from the standpoint of smooth performance:

> The criteria had become, are there any glitches? If things went smoothly and the coffee was there and it was neat and clean and everybody had been forced to think through a problem in an organized way, then they were happy. But if you suddenly begin to think of gaming as research, it gets a lot harder. There are problems with models, data bases. Then you have to allow much freer discussion. The games become much more open-ended. You don't know what the end is going to be. It's a far more fluid process. . . . When an umpire says [in these new games], "You just lost your carrier," he can't simply rely on saying, "That's just for game purposes, just so you think about it." He, in fact, has to defend that decision. Because ideas are now being tested and not simply people. [The transformation of gaming from] primarily a training mechanism for those who gamed, [into] a research tool for thinking through issues and gauging various options . . . began to drive us more and more to thinking in terms of the development of campaigns—much like in the pre–World War II period.[13]

To service the administrative planning of these and other games and their evaluation, Dr. Wood established a strategy and campaign department under Dr. Don C. Daniel. The center now served all gaming and research efforts and acted in addition as landlord to the Strategic Studies Group.[14]

In 1987 gaming took place around the clock, seven days a week. This was the direct result of the increased realization of its payoffs. To illustrate the tempo, from July 1985 through August 1986 the Naval War College gaming department conducted forty-six games or seminars, nine at remote locales. Inter–war college games were also played, with communications and video data links. Thirteen of the games were student curriculum games. There was an inter-American game, and eleven fleet-sponsored games. Special-purpose games were played: OP-095 sponsored a series to investigate programmatic issues, OP-06 sponsored bilateral games, and OP-04 and OP-914 held their own games. The global game involved over eight hundred participants, one-fourth from the army and air force. Navy play of solely navy games was now the exception rather than the rule.[15]

The use of a dedicated intelligence unit to look at things from a Soviet viewpoint made scenarios more realistic and complex. With each game followed by a game report supplemented every six months or so with a summary of significant issues, a systematic archival approach was now in place. There was a formal procedure for sifting significant information from games so that, over time, people could begin to see trends.

In testimony before the Senate Armed Services Committee on 14 January 1987, Captain Hurlburt emphasized that point in describing the new gaming:

> When I hear the phrase "We proved in a war game that . . . ," I wince. War games don't prove anything because they are not reality and cannot be duplicated as can laboratory tests. [Individually] they serve to educate, provide insight, and generate issues for further work. They are best used to investigate processes. . . . War games impose a strict discipline that forces participants to organize separate bits of technical facts into operationally coherent packages and help them explore the feasibility and implications of plan, concepts, or new technologies. . . .
>
> Nimitz [in his oft-quoted remark] wasn't saying that they knew how the war would come out, but that they had looked at all the options. . . . Some of the battles actually fought had been considered unlikely during games, but when they did develop in the real world their importance was understood.[16]

That is gaming's real contribution.

GAMING AND THE STRATEGIC STUDIES GROUP AS CATALYST

The Strategic Studies Group further encouraged this change toward analytical gaming and benefited from the fact that it was already in progress when the group was established.

Admiral Hayward placed the group at Newport primarily to keep it away from the volatile atmosphere of Washington. If he could take a talented group of naval officers and give them most of a year to read and think together, they could stimulate each other and profit from the experience. Each would become a more valuable navy asset. Hayward was not expecting a formal product from their group study. The only real requirement he imposed was that participants read the classics on seapower and make some kind of report at the end.

Robert Murray, the first director of the studies group, decided early on that the report could and should be a group report dealing with a specific problem area. In the course of a few years, with each report building on previous ones, an integrated global strategic view (naval) would emerge.

The reports of the Strategic Studies Group, unavailable to the general public, have had considerable impact on the navy. The first report, in 1981–82, dealt with the most controversial area of all, NATO's northern region. The second report, 1982–83, looked at the Mediterranean, Pacific, and Indian Ocean areas. The effect of each annual report, which digested information from previous ones, was cumulative. Every studies group visited major commands worldwide, briefed the CNO's executive panel, gamed their own product in its different versions, and interacted with students in other games. The CNO personally approved their reports, and the CINCs conferences were consistently briefed on their findings. As a result of all this cross-pollination, the Strategic Studies Group stimulated and synthesized strategic thinking. The method was in effect socratic, but it was not always clear, or even important, who was educating whom.

It was gaming that gave substance to these reports and excited high-level interest. Murray almost immediately found out what generations of naval officers had experienced: how difficult it is to talk about naval strategy in the abstract and how useful it is to put ideas into practice through gaming. "The war games," said Murray, "turned out to be a terrific vehicle for us to argue issues."[17]

What participants did not try to do in gaming was equally important. It could be used for certain types of analysis but, as Dr. Wood commented, could easily, if not watched, also produce a lot of bureaucratic static: "It was clear to both Bob [Murray] and to me that we couldn't get deeply into issues of budget and force structure because we would be directly competitive with OPNAV and, with our particular access to the CNO, that could have created a major bureaucratic battle which you have to assume you are [also] going to lose, just by virtue of [lack of] proximity."[18]

On the other hand, the focus "somewhere below grand strategy" had an enormous potential payoff. For example, Murray, referring to NATO defense, said that games showed

> that if you applied rapid mobilization and deployment of Marine forces and ASW forces to northern Norway in this potential World War III environment, before the Soviets invaded, . . . you erected a very strong defense.
>
> If you erected a very strong defense, it did two things. One, it allowed you to carry out operations, especially ASW operations. It kept [the opponent] on the defensive and made it harder for the

threat to develop to the south. And, secondly, it undermined *his* defense. The Soviet navy's task is to defend Murmansk and that whole northern area . . . if possible, and they've organized their navy to do that and also to protect their SSBNs, which they consider more vulnerable than we consider ours.

If you occupied northern Norway at a time of tension but still during peace, it was not an act of going to war, and they would have far less confidence that they could defend that northern sector. . . .

That would strengthen the NATO central front in two ways. First by not occupying Norway, they [the Soviets] couldn't swing south and cut off NATO. Secondly, the submarine force would be much more on the defensive and therefore the supply lines to NATO would be much less vulnerable.[19]

The success of the Strategic Studies Group and the high-level support it consistently got from the CNO also had an impact on the Naval War College. Resident student research became directly geared to major parts of the group's report. Wood cited in particular the marine amphibious part of the report and some of its logistics work as coming from these students. They were a sort of "cutting edge," because the group was too small to do all the work.[20]

The personal supervision of the Strategic Studies Group by the CNO, begun by Admiral Hayward, continued under Admiral Watkins and into Admiral Trost's tenure.[21] The CNO's personal support also augmented the Naval War College's resources. Wood mentioned as especially important the warfare analysis group, which helped connect gaming to some of the broader kinds of traditional operational analysis so essential to game realism.

The Strategic Studies Group, in Wood's words, "gave a whole new dynamic to what happens here in Newport." Its ideas, traveling from high-level command to high-level command, created a "bumblebee effect"; the intellectual pollen spread in each direction. What Admiral Hayward began, and Watkins and Trost continued and fostered, wrought in Newport something far beyond what had been envisioned. Headquartered at the war college and with access to both a more capable student body and a more effective gaming center, the Strategic Studies Group acted as a catalyst—a force multiplier for the whole navy in the most meaningful way.

THE NAVAL RESERVE: A POLICY TURNAROUND

In the 1950s an officer reservist reporting for on-the-job training would be asked what he wanted to do. Much depended upon his ingenuity if the two weeks of training duty were to produce any result. Far more useful were the two-week courses and seminars, especially those sponsored by small, elite units of the naval reserve such as naval research, naval security, and intelligence. Although naval research had no specific mobilization manning structure for reservists, it had numerous ongoing programs to which these individuals could make a clear contribution. The naval security group, on the other hand, controlled the size of its reserve with the specific goal of using all reservists upon mobilization.

Larger, less specialized units with their great range of ratings presented an organizational challenge to Washington. In the late 1950s there was an effort to use some of the drilling units, if they were at or near a navy port, to man reserve ships. But ship equipment was mostly obsolete and so were airplanes.[22] There were many reasons for this neglect. Senior admirals in the regular navy in the 1960s, even some of the best, had little appreciation for the great asset they had in the naval reserve and how it might be applied to the total force concept. In principle the navy accepted the idea that reservists would augment regular forces in wartime, but in the meantime they were considered a bit of a nuisance by regulars. During Admiral Zumwalt's tenure as CNO the reserve shrank from 129,000 to 38,000—a process only stopped by an alarmed Congress.

What brought about a change was, as always, the conjunction of several things. The All-Volunteer Force instituted under President Nixon reduced the number of personnel in the regular navy. To those looking ahead to the 600-ship navy, it was obvious that the reserves would sooner or later play a greater, more integrated role in the regular navy, whose personnel pool would not expand as much as its mission. Congressional pressure played a critical role, especially from influential congressmen like Charles Bennett of Jacksonville, chairman of the seapower subcommittee of the House Armed Services Committee for many years. Congress insisted not only on larger reserve forces but also on an integrated concept for their utilization.[23] During the Reagan years, increased budgets permitted more flexibility of resources.[24] Finally, in the early 1980s a secretary of the navy came into office who himself was an active reservist and who was determined to promote the new total force concept. He introduced language into regular navy flag promotion board guidelines about knowing the value of the reserve and using it effectively, and he elevated the reserve's head from two stars to three, even though the navy at the time was short of three-star billets. Rear Admiral Cecil Kempf, OP-09R from 1983 to 1987, became Vice Admiral Kempf as of 21 November 1985.[25]

Other organizational changes were made. For some years the chief of naval reserve, as he was called, had been headquartered in New

Orleans and been an aviator. One fallout of the series of inspector general training studies mentioned earlier was a recommendation to reorganize the reserve into two elements, aviation and surface, with a reserve flag officer in charge of each, and to move the commander of the reserve billet to the Pentagon's E-Ring.

By 1983 it was clear that there was going to be a huge growth of the naval reserve. The proposed changes therefore made sense. On 1 October 1983, the senior billet was moved to Washington while the senior flag in the reserve command in New Orleans became deputy. Admiral Kempf now had three titles: chief of naval reserve, a time-honored hat whose principal value was that it was readily identified by Congress; commander, Naval Reserve Force, which established his authority over the New Orleans staff; and within OPNAV, director, Naval Reserve. Two rear admirals, temporary active reservists, both were assigned to him in New Orleans—one as commander, Air Reserve Force, the other as commander, Naval Surface Reserve Force. About 20 percent of reservists were in air.[26]

Vice Admiral Kempf was certain that moving to the Pentagon was a good idea. In New Orleans, distance had denied him a central role in Washington discussions. He was at few or none of the critical meetings when budget decisions were made—still another reason for the reserve's eclipse. Now that situation was reversed. By direction of the secretary and the CNO, Kempf (OP-09R) sat with each of the three internal-navy boards that processed the budget. The lowest-level board consisted of the barons within OPNAV, who worked up sponsor's program proposals. From there different groups handled aviation, surface, logistics, medical, and personnel budget proposals. These were sent to the CNO for CNO/secretary review of the proposed navy program objective memorandum. At each level, OP-09R was free to comment on whether the reserve was getting its fair share, which Admiral Kempf carefully defined as "its fair share of the assets for the role the Reserve is going to play." This procedure represented an enormous change just in itself.[27]

Both the secretary and the CNO favored making OP-09R a DCNO, but that would have required changing the law.

Admiral Kempf managed 400,000 personnel, some on active duty, the rest subject to recall in case of war. The selected reserve numbered about 118,000, the individual ready reserve (for those not associated with a drilling unit) about 70,000 more. There were forty-eight selected-reserve rear admirals. Kempf, despite advances in the navy's appreciation of its reserve, still thought it necessary to devote a considerable portion of his time and energy to promoting his arm. For him running the reserve was like running a navy in miniature—there was a piece of everything in it.

Secretary Lehman insisted that reserve air wings be made more useful in case of mobilization. He equipped the two reserve carrier air wings with the same aircraft used by regular-navy wings, F-14s, F/A 18s, A-7s, and E-2s. Reserve pilots were to be given day and night training in the whole range of air operations, from air defense to deep interdiction (1,000-mile) strikes, air-to-air refueled both ways. In January 1986 at San Diego Admiral Kempf visited the *Ranger* with Carrier Air Wing 30, all reservists, embarked. There was no regular air wing present.

In changes such as this the secretary sometimes took the lead, but he had Admiral Watkins's support. The idea of using still scarce new airplanes for the reserve met with grumbling from other corners of the navy, however, for it had not yet recovered from the Vietnam War attrition. Lehman slowed down the modernization of active-duty forces to bring reserve units up to date.[28] This held for the surface as well as the air reserve; reservists were training in *Oliver Hazard Perry*– and *Knox*-class frigates, whereas previously they had been using old World War II destroyers.[29] The total program outlined by Lehman involved twenty-six frigates by 1990 and the F/A-18s and F-14s already mentioned.[30]

Some areas of warfare were predominantly or even exclusively in reserve hands (e.g., minesweepers [88 percent]). The 1986 concept, later changed, was that the planned MSH *Cardinal* and MCM *Avenger* classes would be operated for the first year by a regular crew to shake out the glitches and then go to the reserve. That did not mean they would be 100 percent reserve manned as in the 1950s; a little over half a ship's crew was to be active or temporary active in order to keep maintenance up.

In 1986 the core of the reserve, 118,000 active, drilling, selected personnel, was to rise to about 140,000. Turnover, once a ruinous 33 percent a year, was already down to less than 19 percent, partly because of the modern equipment. Earlier studies had attributed 50 percent of attrition to boredom in training. The navy was making a strong effort in training to fully integrate the reserve into peacetime and wartime missions.[31]

THE IMPORTANCE OF THE RESERVE ROLE

As of December 1985, the total strength of the naval reserve was 409,700. Of these, 123,147 were retired reservists and 13,425 were standby reservists, leaving 273,128 ready reservists for immediate mobilization. Of the 123,147 retired reservists, almost 100,000 were officers and the rest were aging but experienced petty officers with at least twenty years of service. More important, one-fourth of the ready reserve were officers (57,585) and officer candidates (9,392). The regular navy in 1985 had only 70,657 officers—almost the same number. Enlisted personnel in the regular navy in 1985 amounted to 495,444, compared with 206,251 in the ready reserve.[32] The enlisted selected reserve alone had a sizable group in relation to the regular force.

Secretary Lehman, addressing Congress in 1986, noted that the navy five years earlier had massively reorganized the reserve "from a vertical to a horizontal relationship with the active forces. Essentially, that means that the Reserves must provide immediate augmentation to the active force in time of emergency across the entire spectrum of warfare. It means also that, in peacetime, we rely on Selected Reserves to provide real-time fleet support across their missions areas."[33] That is, the naval reserve was no longer just a supplement filling out regular components, say, by adding a certain percentage of personnel to the wartime crews of ships. In line with the total force concept, some functions were assigned entirely to the naval reserve. These included fleet logistics airlift units (U.S. based), light attack helicopters, fleet composite aircraft (U.S. based), combat search-and-rescue helicopters, and mobile inshore undersea-warfare units. Some of the important activities dominated by reservists were the military sealift command (85 percent), naval mobile construction battalions (68 percent), and special boat forces (66 percent).[34]

These percentages begin to explain Secretary Lehman's emphasis on new equipment for the reserves. Carrier air wing reserve strength is only 13 percent of the total. But just 13 percent here is critical. The same is true for navy surface combatants (frigates), which were to go up to 21 percent by the end of FY 91. So is 34 percent for naval intelligence.

Better equipment and more responsibility in both peacetime and wartime put a greater premium on sensible administrative policy. The ready reserve, as indicated, had two components: the selected reserve (drill pay status) and the individual ready reserve (personnel in areas too remote to drill or to integrate into a unit). Selected reservists plus other reserve personnel were programmed to act in one of three capacities: as commissioned units, reinforcing units, or sustaining units. Commissioned units included forty reserve ships in 1985 (among them fifteen frigates and eighteen minesweepers), twelve cargo-handling battalions, nineteen mobile construction battalions, eighteen mobile inshore undersea warfare units, and fifty-two air squadrons (among them two carrier wings, two patrol air wings, one helicopter air wing, and one fleet logistic support wing). There were 2,500 reinforcing and sustaining units manned by professionals from more than thirty fields who trained in the whole range of shore or special-function activities, for example, the Naval Supply System Command, the Naval Security Group, submarine forces, intelligence, the medical command, the oceanographic command.[35]

COOPERATING WITH THE ALLIES

Working more effectively with the other services, capitalizing on gaming, and using the reserve to good purpose are all force multipliers that help the U.S. Navy protect American interests. Coordinating with U.S. allies, both formal and informal, is another substantial force multiplier, but one not automatically dependable. Allies should rather be considered important variables in a strategic equation.

Allied navies have different priorities depending predominantly on the geographical areas in which they operate or which they represent. Argentine navy leaders stress relationships with Brazil, Chile, and Peru. Chile, on the other hand, is preoccupied with the expansion of Soviet activities in the South Pacific. Canadian leaders have a three-ocean outlook, the third ocean being the Arctic; U.S. insistence on innocent passage of Arctic straits runs counter to the Canadian inclination to extend territorial seas. French attention is directed to the Mediterranean and the Gulf of Oman. The Norwegians, with a navy of one hundred ships, are concerned about their sea approaches and about the proliferation of oil rigs in the Atlantic, which at 750,000 to one million tons are hazards to navigation and also act as hiding places for submarines.

Thus allies do not necessarily share priorities with the United States. Despite much easy rhetoric to the contrary alliances do not stem from common interest, except in the negative sense that they arise out of common fears or concerns about the threat posed to each of them by the same enemy. The sixteen nations of NATO are held together not by common policies and interests, although these can be substantial, but by an agreement that the Soviet Union must be challenged and deterred with effective force. This is the reason Greece and Turkey, who otherwise, in the absence of a threatening Soviet move, are perennially eyeing each other with concern, are part of NATO.

In the post–World War II period the United States made formal alliances with over forty states and military agreements with many others. That large number ensured the occurrence of situations such as the Falklands War, when two U.S. allies, Argentina and Great Britain, fought. The fact that fellow U.S. allies can also be enemies inserts a disturbing element of uncertainty into the American allied network.

Further uncertainty is caused by the divergent values of allied nations. In 1987, as the Iran-Iraq War continued and the pace of attacks on tankers accelerated, the United States felt it necessary to assert the freedom of the seas in the Persian Gulf; nations like Japan, far more dependent on Persian Gulf oil, hung back. In a crisis, U.S. allies may even deny the United States vital overflight rights.

Three factors, however, more than offset the uncertainty. First, the United States and its allies do face a common threat in the Soviet Union's military might. Second, the choice of the United States ultimately comes down to going it alone—which would be unfeasible—or working with allies. Third, abundant resources would be necessary to defeat the Soviet Union in war. The difference between allies and no allies is probably also the difference between victory and defeat. Shipping alone makes the point. U.S. flag shipping is completely inadequate to survive even an optimistically limited assumption regarding Soviet submarine sinkings.

For all these reasons, the United States has a vested interest in fostering allied cooperation. Nowhere is this more critical or more recognized than among navies. Of all U.S. services, the U.S. Navy is the least insular in its thinking. All commanders of U.S. vessels must have a working knowledge of international law. Ships deploy to foreign regions and make port calls in foreign cities. Sailors become aware of foreign sensibilities and pride. They must operate at sea in the shadow of the potential enemy.

Consequently, the navy has long taken the lead among U.S. services in establishing relationships with its counterparts abroad. All navies appreciate the facts of life at sea. This was the starting point for one of the most interesting and unique service-supported initiatives to date: Admiral Arleigh Burke, as CNO, established the naval command course at the Naval War College, with the first class of twenty-three, each student representing a foreign nation, convening in the spring of 1956. Out of this grew the most distinguished naval alumni club in the world; by August 1986 it numbered over nine hundred officers, more than half of whom had been promoted to flag or general officer rank. Seventy-five had become chiefs of their naval or military services, a number of them cabinet officers, and at least one chief of state.[36]

Captain Richard G. Colbert, chosen by Burke to be the first director of the course, returned years later to the Naval War College as president. In that capacity, and aware from his experience with the course of the possibilities for fostering international naval cooperation, he convened the first of a continuing series called the International Seapower Symposium in the late 1960s. The delegates were official representatives of their governments, but they were neither to negotiate issues nor to promote their own national policies. What they would do is confer—meet in plenaries to hear a variety of distinguished colleagues speak on naval topics and in regionally oriented seminars to exchange views on a personal and informal basis. This formula worked—controversial issues were for the most part avoided, common problems addressed and dissected with skill—and the success of the first conference ensured the success of the next.[37]

Such camaraderie spilled over to the biennial conferences of the naval war colleges of the Americas and to the Inter-American Naval Conference series for CNOs. The latter forum and the International Seapower Symposium gave U.S. CNOs an excellent low-pressure opportunity to exchange views with foreign colleagues.

Behind this camaraderie was the basic reality of the naval experience. All seamen are in one sense alike: they know the suddenness of a storm at sea. The sea is their common environment. It makes them, in principle, open to understanding the others' problems. It cannot erase deeply ingrained national antagonisms, but it can lead the Greek and the Turk, the Indian and the Pakistani, the Israeli and the Egyptian to the same room for a look at what they have in common instead of only what divides them.

Common experience at sea is, for the most part, an intangible; but human and therefore international relationships frequently turn on intangibles.

ALLIES: SOME SPECIFICS

On this observation many specific programs have been built. One is a program of major fleet exercises with foreign navies. It has four goals: to strengthen alliance cohesion, enhance what the U.S. Navy calls interoperability, sustain combat effectiveness, and demonstrate capabilities. If one was more important than the others between 1982 and 1987, it was enhancing interoperability.

Interoperability is a blanket term with broad application. Many observers have pointed out the weaknesses in coalitions whose member forces use different equipment, doctrine, weapons, ammunition, operational procedures, and languages.[38] However, operational procedures, for one, can be standardized with good will and recurrent training in annual fleet exercises such as UNITAS, in which U.S. fleet units proceed around the American continent, exercising with Latin American nations' ships as they go. Exercises can provide excellent inter-navy training while avoiding political sensitivities. A single exercise might involve the Koreans and the Japanese separately, or permit the French to participate in a low-profile manner so that they can keep their distance from NATO.

Differences in equipment can be overcome by international agreements for joint design or production of systems. In some cases the United

States has provided systems or variations of systems to other navies. Japanese destroyers, for example, are likely to be equipped with the Aegis system.

Sometimes an enormous amount of good will can be generated by relatively minor joint actions. Consider, for example, the request by the Spanish navy in 1983 for a fuel arrangement that would allow greater Spanish participation in Sixth Fleet exercises. This was of mutual advantage. Admiral Watkins wrote to the Spanish CNO suggesting an agreement for mutual fuel support with reimbursement on an in-kind or cash basis; U.S. ships would be able to refuel more easily at Spanish ports and Spanish ships would not need their own tanker in Sixth Fleet exercises.[39] In another case, a small allied navy found itself without sufficient modern acoustic and magnetic exercise mines. In a letter of 1 September 1983 Admiral Watkins suggested joint training in which the United States would supply the exercise mines. Examples like these could be multiplied a hundred times over. They add up to fruitful cooperation that may well help preserve peace in the world.

Trips abroad by the CNO are another practical way to enhance allied cooperation. They promote personal relationships and pinpoint problems. Typically they involve full schedules, meetings with U.S. embassy officials and foreign officials and hands-on visits to foreign ships or installations. Often agreements are made and questions are raised that require extensive follow up. The host country is almost invariably interested in U.S. technical assistance and military aid, plus less expensive military educational opportunities in the United States. For its part, the United States is usually interested in broadening its ship port-call program and in arranging opportunities for local and perhaps bilateral training.[40] Deployed U.S. carrier pilots must have access to low-level air ranges if they are to maintain a perishable skill; this is a fairly predictable part of the discussion with Israel. In the case of India, a nonaligned nation, discussions remain much less concrete.

Relations between the U.S. Navy and the Japanese Maritime Self-Defense Force are cordial. The emphasis here includes phased steps for improving interoperability, such as the mutual decision to explore the equipping of Japanese ships with the Aegis system.[41] Relations with the Chinese navy in this period were still exploratory.

A significant part of the CNO's dealings with foreign navies is directed toward Latin America. The dampening effect of the Falklands War on U.S.–Latin American naval relations is reflected in a letter of 1982 to Watkins from Admiral Harry D. Train, CINCLANT. Train commented that Venezuela and Peru would not take part in the annual UNITAS exercise, and that Uruguay would permit port visits but no operations.[42] From that low point near the beginning of Watkins's tour as CNO, things improved. All of these nations participated in the twenty-sixth UNITAS exercise in 1985. Of the nine phases of the exercise, five were bilateral, four trilateral.[43]

Restoring relations with Argentina was not easy, however, as the Puerto Madryn incident showed in 1984. In September of that year, owing to a number of errors both American and Argentine, a U.S. ship reprovisioning at Puerto Madryn was mobbed. There were no U.S. casualties, but the incident set back cooperation.

As the U.S. maritime strategy developed, Admiral Watkins undertook an effort to create bilateral maritime strategies with the Latin American naval powers. His visit to Venezuela in January 1984 initiated a serious dialogue that produced a strategy approved by the Venezuelan navy in April of that year.[44] In the spring of 1985 a similar dialogue occurred with Colombia in which interoperability was the focus.[45] By August 1985 talks with Ecuador were under way, and the CNO's schedule called for meetings in the following months with representatives of Brazil, Uruguay, Peru, Chile, and Argentina.[46]

The speech delivered by Admiral Watkins to the 1985 International Seapower Symposium expressed the logic behind all of this. He began with the concept of deterrence. It was not enough for individual nations to be strong. Rather, there had to be a coalition of forces with shared national objectives. The global war game had underscored the importance of bilateral strategies. To develop these, strategic dialogues would have to be initiated with individual navies, identifying common elements of existing strategies. From there, viable regional strategies could be conceived. The next step was to test them. Because of tight budgets, much of the testing would have to be done not at sea but through Newport's war-gaming facilities, which had been proven helpful in supplementing exercises and even supplanting them.

The CNO's invitation to use U.S. gaming facilities and his consistent efforts to find practical solutions to the problems of other navies capitalized on U.S. assets at relatively low cost to yield large results.

PART IV

FULL STEAM AHEAD!

Chapter 11

THE MARITIME STRATEGY

A maritime strategy must be a broad, coherent plan for using naval forces to deal with a projected threat. By the mid-1980s a coherent strategy had been developed by the U.S. Navy. Clearly formulated, the maritime strategy responded to the rapidly expanding Soviet navy. Communicated effectively to Congress, it was well received there and succeeded in convincing Congress to fund the expanding navy. As a result many were willing to claim a share in the formulation of this strategy. The joke at the Pentagon was that it had a hundred fathers. In fact, it did.

WHY IT TOOK SO LONG

Given the navy's problems obtaining support after the aged fleet began to be retired in large numbers, it is reasonable to ask why the maritime strategy was not developed sooner, since it could have been used to argue for more resources. There are three good reasons, the first of which was the Vietnam conflict, which focused navy attention on immediate operational problems. The second was that the formulation of a coherent intellectual plan did not come easily to the U.S. Navy. The navy is operational in peacetime, and so its best want to go to sea. The army and air force, with fewer operational commitments in peacetime, typically send their best to staffs and schools. Consequently, the army has been far better than the navy at producing tactical and strategic plans. Many joint commanders have remarked that navy officers know less about staff planning than officers from other services. On the other hand, almost from the beginning, the navy has led the U.S. armed forces in war gaming. This hands-on conceptualization of problems, however, more readily encourages tactical generalization rather than strategic planning. The navy's lackluster approach to planning also is a result of experience

199

at sea, where anything can happen and very suddenly. Drills for dealing with all possible emergencies are a must; rigid programs can lead to disaster. Thus the navy tends to think in terms of contingencies, which are also the terms of war gaming, and to avoid locked-in approaches to problems.

The third reason concerns the nature of strategic thought in the 1960s and 1970s, especially the question of whether a war between nuclear powers could or would remain conventional. The most basic assumption of the maritime strategy developed in the 1980s was that it would probably be conventional. In the 1980s this idea, or at least a war that did not begin with an initial surprise nuclear attack, was no longer the startling proposition that it had been in the 1950s, the 1960s, and into the 1970s. In earlier days analysts spoke of war beginning the way Admiral Moorer described it tongue in cheek: the president would go to his bathroom and press one button for the steward to bring coffee, the other to start the war. As time went on, difficulties with the nuclear surprise attack scenario began to emerge—such as, if you keep it secret enough, your own people are surprised by the return salvo. In the case of two equally armed opponents, each with a second-strike capability, it began to seem that the net result of a nuclear attack would be mutual destruction. Meanwhile, wars remained strictly conventional, though none was between nuclear-armed superpowers. The advent of satellites added a new complication to the idea of mounting a surprise attack, for the data yielded from them was sufficient now in quality and quantity to rule out the feasibility of surprise. That removed the strongest incentive for using nuclear weapons.

In these decades the military community sat quietly by as civilian pundits explained the new nature of warfare. It did not seem worthwhile to examine the successive stages of a mutual slaughter. What would be the point of thinking about the unthinkable? Neither did they get very far in those years thinking about conventional war, being so often assured it would no longer be fought. Real military thought almost atrophied.

When the navy community seriously reentered the academic debate in the 1970s, one thing at least had changed—the Soviets had created a blue-water navy and there was now an obvious threat to be countered. By that time, too, the idea that the threat could be adequately dealt with through land-based missiles had been abandoned. So in the 1980s it was not *a* navy that had to be justified, but a particular kind of navy, used in particular ways.

These ways were implied by the navy's building program proposals, but they had ultimately to be justified by explicit concepts. Ultimately, then, the argument had to be joined on which set of strategic scenarios were the right ones. It could not simply be assumed that all propositions being debated were equally likely. But since those propositions ranged from all-out nuclear war to superpower conflicts played out indirectly through third parties, it was a tall order to develop a sufficiently focused yet flexible strategic concept for the navy.

CREATING ONE SHEET OF MUSIC

Zumwalt, preoccupied with keeping the navy together, had not done much in the way of strategy.[1] As we have seen, he talked in terms of isolated missions such as power projection, presence, and sea control. The navy's initial serious postwar effort to create a coherent strategy came with Sea Plan 2000, initiated in August 1977 under Bing West and completed and issued in March 1978. It consisted of two thick volumes, of which volume 2 was statistical. The thrust of Sea Plan 2000 was to make a case based on platform and sensor capabilities, comparing U.S. and Soviet assets to justify a fleet of about six hundred ships.

Sea Plan 2000 did little to explain how these ships would be used in a war with the Soviet Union, if one came. It reflected the navy's instinctive bias in favor of playing it loose with a balanced fleet capable of reacting effectively to a range of challenges. Buzz words such as forward strategy were included, but they sounded empty outside the framework of combat logic and operational sequences.

By the last part of Hayward's term something was being done about this, although the parts that finally came together to produce a maritime strategy were not created with that specific goal in mind. There were two main sources of the strategy: the Strategic Studies Group and fleet staffs, who engaged in a Socratic dialogue at fleet headquarters and at Newport's gaming facility, and a branch of OPNAV known as OP-603, which was to produce the briefings.[2] John Lehman said that the Strategic Studies Group's work was really the result "of the tree shaking" that he started.[3]

Professor John Hattendorf has written the definitive account of the bureaucratic origins of the maritime strategy.[4] Most of it is unclassified. He says that the charge of OP-095 to integrate program plans from the point of view of overall warfare led its head, Vice Admiral Kinnaird McKee, in the direction of strategic thinking. Meanwhile CNO Hayward set up a strategic- and theater-nuclear-warfare division in OPNAV (OP-65). The strategic concepts branch (OP-603) soon became the key office in responding to OP-095's need to coordinate navy program planning with future policies. The briefing OP-603 prepared for OP-095 came to be called the maritime strategy. All this work began about the

time the first Strategic Studies Group convened at Newport at the end of
August 1981. (That summer, three global war games had been played.)[5]

Hattendorf traces OP-603's briefing to three memos written by
VCNO Admiral William N. Small, the first in December 1981, the others
in 1982.[6] The second one noted the ongoing interaction between the
studies group, OPNAV, and the fleet. In a follow-up, Rear Admiral John
A. Baldwin, then in systems analysis, wrote a memo for Admiral Small's
signature summing up staff views on the need to tie strategy and force
development and fiscal responsibility into an integrated sequence. By
May 1983, this memo was influencing the annual program objective
memorandum listing appropriations for the next five years. Action on
strategy appraisal went to OP-603, then headed by Captain Elizabeth
Wylie. A series of talented officers in OP-603 turned the paper into an
approved briefing.[7] The first version, the Weeks-Johnson briefing, was
presented to Admiral Watkins's first conference of commanders in chief
at the Naval War College in October 1982. Vice Admiral Arthur Moreau
then gave it to Secretary Lehman on 4 November 1982.[8] By February
1983 the briefing was being given to the House seapower subcommittee.
A later version was produced by Commander Peter Swartz under Captain
Roger Barnett, who now headed 603, with Admiral Moreau's guidance.
It was completed in mid-1983. By now it was standard procedure to use
the insights gained through the articulation of the maritime strategy to
influence the acquisition and program process.[9]

What these briefings did was integrate the newer thinking of the
Strategic Studies Group with the initially more traditional thinking of the
fleet staffs. The amalgam, considered in the light of war-gaming experience, gradually provoked a consensus. To use Admiral Watkins's phrase,
the whole navy was "singing from the same sheet of music" as he directed
the orchestra.

CONTENDING VIEWS
While strategy was being refined inside the navy, the debate
continued in full force outside. By the 1970s and early 1980s the notion
that even a superpower war could remain conventional was accepted.
Some defense analysts, like the much-read Edward Luttwak, dismissed
the possibility of a third world war. (That line of thought quickly led to
the conclusion that large carriers, especially nuclear carriers, were an
expensive luxury.) Others—John Lehman called them armchair Persh-
ings—took issue with the direction of navy thought because they believed
the United States ought to spend less on the navy and more on the army.
Usually this argument started from the implicit or explicit point that only
so much money could be spent on defense. Because the Soviets had (it

was said) overwhelming conventional force on the central front in Europe, U.S. land and air forces there needed strengthening. The absurdity and expense of trying to defend West European soil mainly with troops transported across an ocean did not weigh heavily with this group. The obvious solution was for European nations to raise more troops. The United States could hardly do it for them.

Some opposition to the navy came from those who thought that Europe was the crucial theater and that war could be confined there. A less extreme version of this view was that a war might extend beyond Europe; the United States should remain on the strategic defensive everywhere. According to another view, as indicated, in war the navy would merely convoy army reinforcements to Europe, presumably without neutralizing Soviet satellite support bases like Cuba or Nicaragua. That such reinforcement routes would be extremely vulnerable to attack from these flanks was usually ignored. (This view also tended to write off Norway, at least northern Norway.)

Navy theories about the "big war" began at virtually the opposite extreme. They had developed long before the 1980s and in many ways went back to the writings of Alfred Thayer Mahan. Let us summarize his point of view.

The United States, he held, was an island nation separated by large oceans from the centers of foreign power from which serious threats would originate. Thus the United States was a natural seapower and the navy its first line of defense. In the early or mid-nineteenth century that usually translated into preventing a foreign invasion, as in the War of 1812. By the twentieth century it was generally taken to mean reinforcing such "rimland" powers as Great Britain against expanding and threatening continental nations like Germany. Or, later, Russia. (In Asia, until after World War II, with China weak and Japan expanding, this continental-offshore policy could not follow the same path.) The point was that either the U.S. Navy would control these oceans or some other navy would, and if that other navy were unfriendly U.S. security would be threatened. (This was the sense behind President Reagan's insistence at the recommissioning of the *New Jersey* in December 1982 that "maritime superiority for us is a necessity.")[10]

Sir Julian Corbett, the early-twentieth-century English naval theorist who had the English Channel principally in mind, regarded command of the seas as attainable locally, at the place of need. Mahan thought command of the seas was attained with decisive fleet engagements in vast ocean spaces. The two theories are not necessarily mutually exclusive: their objective is the same, which is to control what you need to, when you need to. (No navy can command all the oceans all the time.) In

World War II, the immediate line of defense could sometimes be measured in thousands of yards, with a whole convoy strung out over a relatively small space. Today, that has utterly changed. Now, with satellite links to deployed ships, "the place of need" a navy may wish to control easily extends far over the horizon. A multiple-carrier battle-group formation can occupy 56,000 square miles.[11] The threat to a convoy can come from hundreds and even thousands of miles away.

If this fact is accepted, there is no choice between an escort navy and an offensive one. The navy will be shaped by tactical consider-ations—hitting the archer before you have to fend off his arrow, to use a favorite Watkins metaphor. Nor does the navy have the luxury of declining battle in certain geographical areas, since U.S. alliances reach over the globe and the Soviet fleet is dispersed worldwide. (The largest Soviet fleet has been deployed in the Pacific for some time now.)

Although the academic theorist and the budget cutter were inclined to reduce contingencies to one likely scenario, the navy had to be prepared to take on any contingency, including the unlikely big one. That meant, to most postwar CNOs, a sufficient number of expensive attack carriers to press a forward strategy against the major foe as well as smaller units to handle brushfires. But with the most expensive units being outlandish for brushfires and the smaller, cheaper units being inadequate for total war, the navy had a problem. How was it to communicate the need for a balanced fleet? How was it to prepare for the total spectrum of conflict? How far should it go in stressing the most likely contingencies?

THE KOMER-WATKINS DEBATE

Robert W. Komer, undersecretary of defense for policy in the Carter administration, was a vehement advocate of a small navy. On 17 February 1983, during the Reagan years, the House Budget Committee called him as a witness. Though the maritime strategy was taking distinct shape within navy circles, though there was a vigorous new CNO, a dynamic young navy secretary, and a new president determined to reinvigorate America's defenses, within the halls of Congress the navy's developing plans still met with resistance. The most articulate critic was Robert Komer.

The chairman of the House Budget Committee, introducing Komer, remarked that there was a general recognition that the navy could not spend the amounts called for in the administration's five-year defense budgets. To decide where cuts should be made was going to take a great deal of wisdom.[12]

Komer referred to a "huge procurement bow wave" that ought to be cut back before cancellation costs got too high.[13] He estimated it would save about $17 billion to cancel the following: a nuclear carrier, its embarked air wing, seven to eight escort ships, two Aegis cruisers, and an underway replenishment force of six to seven ships.

It was not the size of the 600-ship navy so much as the types of ships making it up that he quarreled with.[14] The counting method for arriving at six hundred varied. It had once been six hundred U.S. Navy ships; now it was six hundred combatant ships that could deploy. But then you had to add support ships. These "ship numbers," Komer said, are frequently a "charade."[15] (His implication is wrong. The numbers and types that added to six hundred changed, as we have seen, but only because the navy had not earlier recognized the pitfalls in the system they were using.)

Komer underscored his basic difference with the Reagan administration: its determination to be ready to fight and respond to any challenge, anywhere. That was physically impossible. Priorities had to be established, and there were only three areas in the world vital to the stable balance of power the United States wanted to underwrite: Western Europe, Japan, and the Persian Gulf. If you could not fight in all three, you needed to "finesse at least one" of them.[16] A global war was unlikely. What the United States should go in for was "sequential operations" instead of the approach of the Joint Chiefs. Then there would be no need for a fifteen-carrier navy.[17] One Joint Chief, who wore a dark blue suit, wanted to have more naval forces and so had come up with the "doctrine of simultaneity [to] attack the enemy on all three fronts simultaneously."[18] But that would be like "sticking pins in the hide of an elephant." It would have no critical effect; the adversary would not even be slowed down very much.[19]

That same day Admiral Watkins testified, remarking at the outset that he did not think the chairman had cited the national strategy or the defense strategy properly. Secretary Weinberger understood that with the present force he could not fight on all fronts with equal effort simultaneously. Nor was that the kind of force the navy was trying to build. Komer was a believer in the fourteen-day war in Europe, which implied a small navy and a swing strategy to bring all the forces to the Atlantic theater. That would be the "very worst kind of national strategy we could have," because it would denude the United States of forces in northeast Asia, where the Soviets had one-third of their forces.[20]

In the questioning that followed, Congresswoman Geraldine Ferraro said she would vote to trim the budget. What would happen if, as Komer suggested, a carrier was cut? "The contracts have been executed," Watkins responded. "Twelve thousand tons of steel have been ordered.

We have $560 million that has already been subcontracted for to over 500 contractors nationwide."[21]

Perhaps because this forum was the Budget Committee, the issue was not fully joined about why Komer was wrong. The navy's argument instead emphasized the size of the Soviet Pacific threat, how much the fleet was already doing, and what canceling a carrier would cost. Clearly, the navy still needed to articulate a strategic argument.

Komer was anything but a quitter. In a book published in 1984, *Maritime Strategy or Coalition Defense?*, he wrote: "Two main schools of thought have been reemerging in the conventional arena. One school advocates . . . a maritime-supremacy strategy . . . as the major means of offensive force projection against the Soviet Union," while the other advocates defending "Western Europe, Japan, and Persian Gulf oil," with a "more balanced emphasis on land and air as well as naval forces. . . ." These schools "strongly disagree over what [maritime superiority] means and what kind of navy is essential for the purpose—a sea-control navy or one designed primarily for offensive force projection against the U.S.S.R."[22]

Komer, and those who thought like him, wanted a navy large enough to dominate those areas of the Atlantic Ocean and Persian Gulf where U.S. land forces had to transit by ship. They wanted the navy deployed to protect convoys and to be built of sea-control ships that would be less expensive than carriers. The navy's view, by contrast, was that the Pacific could not be written off, that convoys were best defended by curtailing Soviet submarine deployments, and that carriers provided the offensive capability the nation needed if it was not ultimately to have to defend the United States off its own shores.

So the root argument was how to fight a war: whether to escort with sea-control ships against Soviet submarines circling a convoy or to take the offensive, which would at some point certainly require large carriers.

A subset of the same argument concerned the point at which that would occur. Critics alleged, on the basis of Lehman's supposed views, that the maritime strategy would have U.S. carriers dashing full steam ahead to Soviet shores to attack Kola bases as soon as war broke out—"going in harm's way." The charge continued to be made in part because of a running battle between Senator Sam Nunn and Secretary Lehman sparked by the latter's deliberate ambiguity on this point.[23] But with this additional argument reverberating in the media, it was more necessary than ever to publish an unclassified version of the strategy and give the navy's considered views wide publicity.

PUTTING THE STRATEGY TO WORK

The first full-scale public test of the new strategy came in the halls of Congress in June 1985, when Congressman Charles Bennett, chairman of the seapower and strategic and critical materials subcommittee of the House Committee on Armed Services, began extensive hearings on both the 600-ship navy and maritime strategy.[24]

Congressman Bennett, aware of charges that his committee had been brainwashed by the navy team of Lehman, Watkins, and Kelley, sent an invitation to the hearings to every member of the House and gave a fair and ample hearing to the views of critics.

From the navy point of view these hearings, properly handled, could convince Congress that the service knew what it was doing and knew what it wanted, and that it had a well-managed, efficient program.

The hearings fell into four parts (which produced a 301-page transcript). The first, in June 1985, was a formal presentation of the newly evolved maritime strategy. The second, on 5 September, dealt with the operational implications of the strategy and therefore with ship numbers and kinds. The third, on 6 September, focused on costs and whether the right kind of navy was being built. It was during this hearing that opponents of the strategy, of the kind of navy being built, and of the costs involved, were heard. Finally, on 10 September, at the final session, the navy gave its rebuttal.

The June presentation began with national strategy, moved to the maritime strategy derived from it, and then on to how that strategy determined ship numbers. The number, said Lehman, "was not plucked out of a hat [but was] deduced from the maritime tasks that were handed to the Department of the Navy" as a result of national commitments and national strategy.[25] The first determinant of strategy and of navy size and configuration was the spectrum of tasks the navy had to perform, from peacetime presence through crisis response to actual war. For example, crisis response had sent the *New Jersey* on a 322-day deployment covering 76,000 miles (all this without the ship falling below C-2 for materiel or personnel readiness).[26] The charts accompanying the presentation showed the Soviet peacetime posture and Soviet naval exercises.

The brink-of-war or actual war portions of the spectrum were presented by Admiral Watkins. Three phases were involved, with phase 1, the deterrent or transition phase, focused on controlling escalation.[27] If U.S. forces were deployed correctly at the time of crisis, they could encourage the Soviets not to move closer to war. Conversely, a position easily seized would be a temptation to Soviet forces, especially if significant tactical and strategic advantage would accrue to them. The most obvious illustration was northern Norway, whose occupation by the Soviets could put them astride the Atlantic flank but which, retained by NATO, would seriously inhibit Soviet submarine and naval air use.

Phase 2, "seizing the initiative," reformulated the age-old military advice that the best defense is a good and timely offense, throwing the enemy off balance before he can do the same to you.

Phase 3, "carrying the war to the enemy, winning the battle and bringing the war to termination on terms favorable to the United States," reflected new uncertainties about warfare in a nuclear-armed world plus the old problem of how to end a war once it was begun. The right military pressures had to be chosen so as to influence a Soviet decision to cease fighting on terms not disadvantageous to the United States.

These phases were not confined by timetables.[28]

Watkins also explained the concept of notional battle forces and air wings, how battle forces were dispersed (two battle groups across 56,000 square miles), how navy-air force cooperation worked, and how the navy was linked to the army and to U.S. allies.[29]

Questions at this opening session began with Congressman Duncan Hunter (California) pointing to the large Soviet submarine fleet and shortages in U.S. strategic sealift. That was why the navy had to deploy forward instead of merely escorting shipping, Lehman said—to catch Soviet subs before they could do their damage. Watkins added that the navy's calculations were "all based on the fact that our allies are going to be with us; that we can husband our resources together as a nation with our sister services; that we can fight sequentially [through time, not space]; that we have the political will at decision-making time to move forces early to do the kinds of things that are tough politically. Those decisions are very critical to success and we see it in our war games."[30]

Watkins went on to relate in detail how operational expertise and the use of the navy's gaming resources at the Naval War College had been used to generate successively refined and modified versions of the maritime strategy.

At the next subcommittee hearing, 5 September, the questioning became more tactical and operational, so much of the transcript is classified. The afternoon session featured Admiral Kinnard McKee and Vice Admiral Nils R. Thunman and was devoted to submarine warfare and the development of the new SSN 21. The purpose of this session was to get the subcommittee straight on certain technical details before "hostile" witnesses were heard.

The third day of hearings, 6 September, was given over to the opposition (or the merely skeptical) to present their views. Already, at the 24 June session, Congressman Bennett had asked Lehman to comment on Congressional Budget Office projections that achieving and sustaining the 600-ship navy would only be possible with a 3 to 6 percent real growth through the mid-1990s. The answer was that six hundred ships had already been bought and that about 3 percent real growth would sustain them.[31] Now Dr. Eric Hanushek, deputy director of the Congressional Budget Office, repeated the claim that 3 to 5-plus percent real growth would be needed, a level unprecedented in peacetime. It was not just sustaining six hundred ships but also replacing them with more modern and more expensive versions.[32] At least 5 percent would be needed for shipbuilding and conversion into the mid-1990s.

Dr. Hanushek then presented three less costly strategies and tabled a Budget Office study of alternative projections.[33] As it turned out, these alternatives were merely different spending plans, not war-fighting strategies. Hanushek cited examples of cheaper ships such as diesel submarines as ways of saving money but would not judge their effectiveness: "We do not have a complete way of summing up the effectiveness, ultimately, of our forces in different deployments.[34]

Mr. Frank C. Conahan of the General Accounting Office testified next, pointing out that the analysis done by his organization indicated that the navy would "not achieve its desired 600-ship force mix" until the year 2000, meaning that replacements would continue even after the six hundred ships were built.[35]

Admiral Ike Kidd weighed in to redress the balance: "There is no record of a lightweight [boxer] aspiring to the heavyweight crown and winning, no. We are an international heavyweight . . . and if we are going to compete in that class, we best be prepared to do so."[36] From a logistics standpoint, it was going to take six thousand shiploads every thirty days to keep Europe alive and fighting during a war. The U.S. Navy had to have enough control of the seas to permit this. One million personnel would be flown over in the first few weeks in unarmed air transports that needed air cover en route, and only "bird farms" (aircraft carriers) could provide that protection.[37] The figure six hundred was not too high, particularly when compared with the four hundred ships sunk or damaged at Okinawa.[38] Speaking about ship types, and from his experience as CINCLANT with exercises in the Norwegian Sea, Kidd claimed that small, fast ships could not measure up in sea conditions there.

Retired Admiral Stansfield Turner spoke next, zeroing in on the central point of the objectives the navy hoped to achieve with its particular mix of ships.[39] He gave a formal briefing, with slides, of his own conception of what that strategy ought to be. In contrast to the Lehman-Watkins argument, he saw three military objectives in order of priority: intervention in the third world, nuclear deterrence, and the defense of Europe. The United States's most likely task would be third world intervention, the one for which the navy was least prepared. It was well prepared to deter a nuclear war, and there was not much point in trying to beef up the defense of Europe until NATO allies contributed more.[40] A navy could do four things for its country: sea control, amphibious assault, tactical bombardment, and strategic bombardment.[41] Turner favored first providing more amphibious capability, then adding sufficient sea control to ensure use of the Atlantic sea lanes and support for amphibious operations, and last, enhancing submarine invulnerability.[42] Making explicit his differences with Lehman and the maritime strategy, Turner said he wanted to shift "to small aircraft carriers, more destroyers, more submarines as escorts, more deception devices and more mines . . . . [T]he Secretary wants large carriers so he can go into the Norwegian Sea in the event of general war in Europe." Turner doubted that any SACEUR (supreme allied commander Europe) would divert sizable forces from the central front to defend northern Norway.[43] If it came to war, the job in the Atlantic would be so great that the United States would have to swing forces out of both the Pacific and Indian oceans.[44]

Retired Rear Admiral Eugene J. Carroll, Jr., deputy director of the Center for Defense Information, came next. He tabled a publication put out by his organization[45] which concluded that because the Soviets were still second best they would choose to fight defensively.[46] Rather than breaking out into the open sea, they would withdraw to their own home waters, to their "basins," where they would become a formidable opponent to anyone foolish enough to attack them. The U.S. Navy could defeat them in the open ocean, "but in their own home waters [with] land-based air . . . they [would be] a fearsome defensive force" for which a 600-ship navy and fifteen carrier battle groups would prove far too little.[47] If that assumption proved wrong, the Soviets would almost certainly resort to nuclear defenses rather than accept defeat. The maritime strategy was wrong; the United States should not go into Soviet basins but rather deny the Soviets access to the open sea with mines and submarine barriers. The primary role of the U.S. Navy was to reinforce and resupply allies.[48] As for ships, the navy needed not the SSN 21 but diesel subs, more frigates, more antisubmarine aircraft. This completed Carroll's long list of disagreements with Lehman and Watkins.[49]

Congressman Bennett began the questioning by asking Carroll whether he believed that any war, if it became nuclear, could be confined to land. Getting a negative response, Bennett said it would be a short war in that case. Carroll agreed. Why build any other ships at all then? The answer was confused: If the United States refrained from nuclear war and from threatening Soviet survival, the Soviets would not want to cross the nuclear threshold, but if the United States went after them "in this aggressive forward strike strategy, they may have no choice except to surrender or fight with nuclear weapons."[50] Congressman Floyd Spence of South Carolina intervened: "We can't go in and beat them because . . . they will start a nuclear war. Is that right? How are we supposed to fight them then?" Carroll had no clear answer to that question, either.[51]

THE SEAPOWER SUBCOMMITTEE HEARINGS: THE NAVY WRAP-UP

In the last of the seapower subcommittee hearings, on 10 September 1985, Secretary Lehman responded to the critics. He started by reviewing the analysis from which the size of the navy was derived.[52] Size was determined by three factors: geography (because the world was 73 percent water), the vital interests of the United States, which had forty-odd treaty partners and therefore far-flung security obligations, and the nature of the threat—the element "most often overlooked in the trendy armchair debates" and in congressional staff studies. These were the considerations that set the size of the fleet, not the individual strategies of theater commanders or of military or civilian people in Washington. Strategy played a major part in how the navy trained, in how it designed ships, and in what it put into them. But strategy alone did not drive the size of the fleet.[53] That size, in short, was set by how the navy must fight in wartime; in peacetime, it deployed in almost exactly the same way except at an operational tempo roughly three times lower.[54]

Lehman said fleet size was set by *how* the navy must fight in wartime. If he had said that size reflects *where* the navy must fight, and that where it fights determines also ship *types*, he would have addressed more squarely the arguments of his opponents. We arrive here at a basic problem with the entire congressional discussion of six hundred ships and the maritime strategy, for in reality fleet size depends on a series of connected factors: the size of the threat, where you face it, how you intend to deploy and fight against it, and the ship types needed to do that. Lehman had earlier argued that strategy played a major part in training and ship design but "does not by itself drive the size of the fleet"; that distinction can, in fact, be used effectively against criticism. Here, however, in arguing that the fleet size was a function of how the navy must fight in wartime, he was limiting the issue more to strategy.

Lehman might have been trying to keep size and strategy distinct more for political than logical reasons: if size and strategy are treated as a single concept there is only one target for critics to hit. With a certain amount of separation between size and strategy, if strategy gets shot down size does not automatically fall with it. Also, to weave size and design and strategy too tightly together would arouse misgivings among sizable groups of naval officers skeptical about rigid planning.

Lehman next gave a detailed and highly lucid area-by-area survey of navy deployment needs for carrier battle groups and surface action groups in peacetime and wartime. In the western Pacific, for example, the navy maintained an annual peacetime average of about one and a half carriers; in wartime that would increase (for planning purposes) to 4 carriers plus 1 battleship surface action group and 3 underway replenishment groups. When the numbers for all areas were added, the total came to 15 carrier battle groups, 4 battleship surface action groups, and 10 underway replenishment groups.[55] All in all, the navy would need roughly 105 surface combatants plus 70 underway replenishment ships and 40 escorts. With an additional 7 convoy escort groups (a notional 70 ships and 100 attack submarines) plus a notional 40 SSBNs and 27 material support ships, about 33 fleet support ships, 6 patrol hydrofoils, 31 mine warfare ships, and 75 amphibious ships, the number came to somewhat over 600. "This is a force," Lehman concluded, "which is set in size as I have suggested, not by any one person's strategy, but by the size of the world, the breadth of our commitments, and the size of the Soviet Fleet. . . ."[56] Deliberately or not, he was here still assuming that everyone agreed on the need per ocean area, on the ship types to be built and deployed, and on how such ships would be committed.

Lehman quickly disposed of several principal issues raised by critics. The free world could not win a war without naval superiority, whatever might happen in a land war. Even a continental defense strategy depended on achieving maritime superiority early in a conflict. The maritime strategy explained how the U.S. Navy would do that.[57]

Was it the right strategy? Strategy was understood in different ways in Washington. Some thought it was a "cookbook" on when or where to move ships, or a formula for fighting each ship. Policymakers thought of it as a framework, a constantly evolving "notional concept to enable us to allocate resources" in a way that allowed theater commanders to act effectively.[58]

Was the United States acquiring the right navy and making sound judgments about carrier size? There were no absolute answers. Lehman believed that the *Nimitz* class was the "optimum size and design for putting air capability at sea." The United States could use more submarines and could build more if it were willing to sacrifice capability. But that would be to abandon America's technological edge over the Soviets, who could always otherwise outdo the United States by building "cheaper, smaller, less capable ships in larger numbers." The high-tech solution was the wisest investment.[59]

On the issue of costs, the Congressional Budget Office was correct in estimating the need at 3 percent real growth, but not in its contention that 3 percent could not be sustained.[60] The Vietnam period was an anomaly and not the norm that office assumed it to be. Straight-line projections, furthermore, which ignored the possibility of cost-effective improvements in bureaucracy and elsewhere, were misguided. Growing defense costs were not inevitable: the last Aegis contract had cost $900 million; four years before, the contract had exceeded $1 billion.[61] Lehman concluded that the United States had the right-size fleet under construction, built to the right requirements, and that it could maintain and afford that fleet.

During the question period that followed, dominated by Congressmen Norman Sisisky and Herbert Bateman, both of Virginia, Lehman said Congress would have to stand up to budget pressures if growth were to continue. Seventy billion dollars had been "whacked out of the Navy budget" in the last four years.[62]

In response to arguments about forward deployment and the Norwegian Sea, Lehman said that Soviet war plans included the invasion of Norway and that the United States was obligated under NATO to defend that country. Defense required air and sea superiority in the Norwegian Sea.

> That superiority will not be achieved easily. The submarine threat has got to be dealt with before any aircraft carriers go there, and land-based air cannot provide 24-hour-a-day air superiority over that theater. Sea-based air must play a part. We are pledged to provide reinforcement and Marine amphibious capability. We are not going to leave those forces to the prey of Soviet Backfire bombers and submarines.
> So the idea that the northern flank or the eastern Mediterranean ... cannot be defended is silly.[63]

Those who argue for building "a low-threat navy" ignored the power of modern missiles—witness the use of Exocets in the Falkland islands war. NATO forces deployed on Russia's northern flank, "one of the more ill-defended areas of the Soviet Union," were "certain to be the least vulnerable military capability that NATO has."[64] NATO had "numerous ... bases in northern Norway and they do not move at 31 knots." Nor did they have seven layers of air defense.

"The Navy is in far better shape," Lehman concluded, "and will sustain far better the attacks of the same cruise missile and bombers that will be attacking the land bases. ... Other than that, I agree with everything that Admiral Turner said."[65] And with that the subcommittee brought its hearings to an end, having well achieved Congressman Bennett's stated goal of airing all views. The critics had not been able to mount a successful attack on the navy's maritime strategy, but neither had they been silenced. The fight to win acceptance was far from over.

THE NEXT STEP: PUBLICATION

Those who took the time and trouble to read the published hearings could get a clear enough understanding of the maritime strategy from the navy's briefing. But the strategy needed to be available in easy-to-read form for maximum effect.

Watkins, at his first briefing by the Strategic Studies Group while still CINCPACFLT, had seen that the maritime strategy could be used both to convince Congress and bring conceptual unity to the navy. Now he wanted it for a third purpose: to influence Soviet thinking. All three goals could be advanced by publishing an unclassified version. He would use it "to influence Soviet actions, as a deterrent, telling them something they already knew from their intelligence sources and the recently exposed Walker spy ring, but telling them in public and out loud"—a rationale that met with much opposition within the navy.[66]

To avoid bureaucratic wrangling, he sent his version of the maritime strategy to the *Proceedings* without clearing it with the Joint Chiefs of Staff or Lehman, though he did invite P. X. Kelley to write an article on the marines and he suggested that Secretary Lehman submit an article also. He was willing to run risks, confident he "could build consensus after the fact"[67] by conveying a clear message to the Soviets and to the American public.

The January 1986 issue of the *Proceedings* ran a 48-page supplement that included three articles, one on maritime strategy by Watkins, a second on marine amphibious-warfare strategy, and a third by Secretary Lehman on the 600-ship navy.[68]

This supplement, of which the Soviet Union has a large number of copies, presents the first objective of the maritime strategy as deterring the Soviets from attack by convincing them that the odds are against them.[69] There is an important *if* that goes with that proposition: "Keys to the success of both the initial phase and the strategy as a whole are speed and decisiveness in national decision making," wrote Watkins. "The United States must be in a position to deter the Soviets' 'battle of the first salvo' or deal with that if it comes." It is seven days' steaming time from the East Coast to the northern Atlantic.[70] Defending Norway meant being there when the trouble started, not ten days later. The problem was that too late a reaction would be useless; too early a move could be opposed as provocative. The military implications called for haste; the political implications called for a possible caution that Watkins was warning could unhinge the whole operation.

A critical Soviet navy mission in wartime would be to protect Soviet territory and ballistic missile submarines, their ultimate strategic reserve. The expectation was that initially the bulk of the Soviet navy would deploy in areas near the Soviet Union. But those areas included Japanese, Norwegian, and Turkish waters; the view some U.S. critics advocated, of holding American maritime power near home waters, would inevitably mean abandoning U.S. allies.[71]

Consequently, forward operations would have to be conducted with attack submarines and barriers would have to be erected at global choke points. In phase 1 battle groups would move forward in "an aggressive campaign against all Soviet submarines, including ballistic missile submarines"—that is, nuclear-armed ones.[72] (This proposition has been criticized as unnecessarily provocative, opponents arguing that the Soviets may choose to use these nuclear missiles rather than lose them.) As for carriers, "to apply our immense strike capability, we must move carriers into positions where, combined with the U.S. Air Force and allied forces, they can bring to bear the added strength needed on NATO's Northern or Southern flanks, or in Northeast Asia." This strategy did not entail automatic attacks on specific targets, but the United States would not allow the Soviets to use their naval aviation "to attack the fleet with impunity, from inviolable sanctuaries."[73] In phase 2, the navy would seize the initiative as far forward as possible, destroying Soviet forces, neutralizing Soviet clients if required, and fighting its way toward Soviet home waters. The goal of phase 3, war termination on favorable terms, would be achieved by completing the destruction of the Soviet fleet and threatening its support structure in all theaters with air and amphibious power.[74]

By 1987, something like 120,000 copies of this scenario had been printed.

THE NUCLEAR EQUATION

As we have stressed throughout, the maritime strategy is a conceptual approach to the problem of war with the Soviet Union. Admiral Trost, in his tour as CNO, often stressed that the strategy was not an operational plan with a fixed timetable, that in time of war the theater operational commanders would make decisions; the maritime strategy was rather an evolving tool for organized thinking about problems.[75] Even its fundamental assumption that a future war would likely be conventional has not ruled out alternative propositions.

Admiral Hank Mustin, Trost's OP-06, examined the pluses and minuses of either side resorting to nuclear weapons in a conflict. The result was that neither could gain by doing so. The consensus of the intelligence community was that the Soviets were "moving away from the idea of a theater-nuclear war in Europe because it doesn't advance any of their time lines" and because they believed, given their superior conventional forces, that they did not need it. The Soviets, said Mustin, also "consider a nuclear exchange as an essentially uncontrollable process." The use of nuclear weapons in a theater context would only invite an American nuclear response on targets ashore; it would be self-defeating. If the Soviets did initiate a nuclear attack from ashore, they would not be able to target forces at sea with enough certainty because NATO had more dual-capable (able to fight in either a conventional or nuclear mode), forward-deployed ships. If they initiated a nuclear attack at sea, the same logic would apply. NATO, on the other hand, would not initiate a nuclear attack at sea because it could win at sea conventionally. If NATO were to initiate a nuclear attack from ashore, the Soviets could take NATO out ashore but not at sea. "So," concluded Mustin, "powerful, dual-capable, forward-deployed ships" were even more important in a nuclear context. In short, later thinking confirmed the direction of earlier thinking.[76]

THE STRATEGY'S IMPACT

There is no agreement in the navy about who created the maritime strategy. The ideas go far back, at least to Mahan. Lehman was certainly using the term forward strategy before the maritime strategy took sufficient form to be extensively discussed within the navy. The paper trail, as Hattendorf shows, is reasonably clear. But papers and briefings in themselves count for little. It is what is done with the maritime strategy that counts. Although Lehman tended to discount Hayward's interest in the creation of a strategy, his role in both Sea Strike and setting up the Strategic Studies Group was key to the development of the strategy. What made Lehman impatient was his wish, as Train indicated, to influence congressional judgment and thereby recreate a strong American navy. Watkins was the right man to supplement Lehman's congressional and public relations efforts because he could see even in the early stages of the Strategic Study Group's work that, with what Captain Somes called its bumblebee approach, it could pollenize the navy with strategic thought which Watkins could then parlay into a greater sense of navy community, into an instrument with which to think through war-fighting initiatives and stimulate reactions in the other services, and finally, into a means of influencing Soviet actions. The maritime strategy thus developed and published did indeed explain why a certain type of force in certain numbers was being procured to be fought in a certain way. That strategy did not end all argument against the prevailing navy view. But it did provide a solid, rational, and coherent intellectual basis for the navy's program, which could be and was justified to Congress and which influenced navy procurement, training deployment, and operations.

Reviewed by key officials within the State Department and Department of Defense, the maritime strategy was accepted as being part of presidentially directed national policy. Subsequently, it was officially reviewed and accepted by the House Armed Services seapower subcommittee.

Watkins hoped for one further result: that the Joint Chiefs of Staff might be encouraged to take the next step and produce a coordinated national military strategy with intellectual strength to it.[77] The January 1987 White House publication, "National Security Strategy of the United States,"[78] may fall short of that hope, but it is indeed a giant step forward.

There would seem to be enough credit to go to all the hundred fathers.

Chapter 12

THE CNO
AS JOINT CHIEF

The CNO has not one hat but two. As the chief of his service, Admiral Watkins used the maritime strategy as a force builder, a program guide, and a way of giving the navy a unified sense of direction. But, functionally speaking, his effort to influence Soviet strategy and to help produce an articulated national strategy was made under his second hat, as a member of the Joint Chiefs. It was in that forum that he had a role in actual naval operations, there that the gist of navy thinking about offense versus defense (which led to the strategic defense initiative) became of national consequence.

There is a tendency to think of the CNO as simply the navy's chief uniformed administrator and to downplay his role as a member of the Joint Chiefs. Yet Watkins put more than half his time and effort into the latter and he considered it—correctly—as ultimately more important. The two hats, although they can be distinguished functionally, merge in practice for two reasons: they are worn by one individual, and the training, equipping, and manning of the navy (a CNO function) cannot be considered apart from force employment (a Joint Chiefs' function). Under what hat does something like force interoperability with sister services and with allies fall?[1]

Until 1986 the way the Joint Chiefs functioned had changed relatively little since it was established under the landmark legislation of the National Security Act of 1947.[2] President Eisenhower proposed changes in the direction of more "jointness," which were enacted by Congress in 1958; but they did not alter the Joint Chiefs so much as expand that part of the Department of Defense devoted to joint defense.

What the Joint Chiefs are supposed to do has been the subject of much dispute and thousands of pages of congressional testimony. In

218

World War II there was no question that they gave the orders, under the direction of their commander in chief, President Roosevelt. Once a secretary of defense had been created, a new command layer was established. The secretary transmitted his operational orders through the Joint Chiefs—meaning they were not per se in the chain of command but acted as the conduits, the transmission agents. In theory, they were to give military advice rather than act as executives; in practice, their advice directly affected and altered commands.

This staff-command relationship is not easy to maintain: he who sets an agenda often controls the problem. And it is the Joint Chiefs who, in practice, formulate the defense secretary's instructions to the unified and specified commanders after advising him what needs to be done. Admiral Moorer made the same point more graphically. After retiring, he picked up a newspaper that said President Nixon was about to resign. The headlines said: "Nixon to order 82nd Airborne to Washington to capture Congress." "As if," said Moorer, "Erlichman could pick up a phone and call the general down there" and simply tell him to move. "It takes 25 messages at least to get the 82nd Airborne going—the airplanes are out in Kentucky and some of their forces are out in the field, and so on. So it's ridiculous, you know, because the first thing that general would do is pick up the phone and call the Chairman of the Joint Chiefs of Staff and say, 'What the hell is going on here?' "[3]

Whether the present procedures would do in the case of a new world war is another question. Common sense tells us how the system would really work—much as in World War II. Since decisions would have to be made somewhere, and unified commanders in the field would not be in a position to weigh what was going on outside their geographic area, it would again be the Joint Chiefs. The larger-scale the operations, the more prominent the CNO's role as chief navy decision-maker would be.

A DEMANDING ROLE

Each individual head of service is automatically a member of the Joint Chiefs of Staff. Until reorganization in 1986, these service heads plus the chairman were collectively known as the principal military advisors to the president. The term principal is now given only to the chairman. The Joint Chiefs also advise the secretary of defense, giving him far more advice far more often than they give the president.

Until the 1986 defense reorganization act (whose ultimate effects cannot yet be assessed), the chairman of the Joint Chiefs was required to indicate to both the secretary of defense and the president any differences between his individual advice and the advice of the chiefs as a group.

Defense secretaries vary tremendously in how they treat the Joint Chiefs, some remaining aloof (like McNamara), some actually joining them every Tuesday in session (Weinberger). Secretary McNamara apparently felt he had no real obligation to forward those views of the Joint Chiefs with which he disagreed. But twice in Admiral Watkins' tour, in meetings of the Joint Chiefs with President Reagan, Secretary Weinberger reported to the president that he and they disagreed.

How often the Joint Chiefs meet with the president to discuss substantive issues varies a great deal. Admiral Zumwalt says he and his fellow Joint Chiefs met with President Nixon twice; according to Admiral Watkins, he and his colleagues had thirteen meetings with President Reagan, the most interesting of which was on the Strategic Defense Initiative (SDI).[4] As of early 1986, Joint Chief meetings with President Reagan approximately equaled the combined number of times the Joint Chiefs met with Nixon, Ford, and Carter. It is reported that President Reagan enjoyed and valued these sessions, which however came to a near halt when in 1986 the White House chief of staff and the national security advisor were replaced.

"The Tank," where the Joint Chiefs meet, formally designated the Gold Room, is located on the second floor of the Pentagon. A large table accommodates enough chairs for the chairman, the director, the service chiefs, and their principal operations deputies. Another narrower table seats backup officers and along the wall are seats for action officers who come and go as agenda items require.

Being a member of the Joint Chiefs takes considerable time and energy. This was particularly true between 1982 and 1986, during the Reagan defense buildup. Admiral Watkins spent about two-thirds of his time working as a Joint Chief, either in session (three times a week, three to four hours per meeting) or with his staff preparing for sessions.[5] General P. X. Kelley, former commandant of the Marine Corps, spent about half his time doing the same.

In this period from 1982 to 1986, before the enactment of the Goldwater-Nichols bill, the chiefs had an additional demand on their time because General John Vessey, their chairman, had them take turns (three months each) acting as chairman whenever he was not available. For the quarter during which he was acting chairman, a chief had to stay abreast of the entire agenda. Over his four-year tenure as CNO, Watkins was acting chairman for about 150 days.[6] "That doesn't mean," he said,

> that during those hundred and fifty days, I was ... necessarily heavily involved in JCS matters—routine functioning of the Office of the JCS goes right on and the acting chairman doesn't need to interfere. He's not down there to run the administration of the JCS.

He's down there to handle the day-to-day interface with the Secretary of Defense, to be in attendance for the JCS at the National Security Council meetings and to respond to emergent events or crises.[7]

Watkins represented the Joint Chiefs at National Security Council meetings perhaps thirty times in the four years. He estimated that 90 percent of his time went to the Joint Chiefs when he was acting chairman.

General Kelley called the rotating chairmanship a great benefit and a distinct chore.

It's a demanding [duty] because you're both the service chief and the acting chairman. But, I haven't found it to be overburdening, particularly if you are willing to delegate, as the [1958] law provides that you do, to your assistant commandant. I have attempted to delegate, as has Jim Watkins, the sort of day-to-day running of [the service] to my assistant commandant. I can focus more on the broader, national-level issues.[8]

The point Watkins and Kelley made was the same: the experience broadened their horizons, as General Vessey had intended it to. As acting chairman each needed to have command of broad issues if he was to advise the president of the United States.[9]

REFORMING THE JOINT CHIEFS OF STAFF

In the first half of the 1980s the functioning of the Joint Chiefs and the Department of Defense was under congressional scrutiny, especially as stories of incompetence in weapons procurement or spare parts scandals arose. Congressional testimony by previous defense secretaries, plus the testimony of General David C. (Davy) Jones, former chairman of the Joint Chiefs (1978–82), led to changes in the organization that then-members (and many previous members) thought unnecessary. One of those changes was to create the position of vice chairman of the Joint Chiefs, which eliminated service chief members as acting chairmen.

The discussion in Congress inevitably raised the question of structure versus process. Did the problems of the Joint Chiefs of Staff, if indeed they existed, derive from the way the law was written or from the way particular chairmen and chiefs used their other hat? General Jones, in a *New York Times* magazine article of November 1982, reprinted by Congress, wrote that after serving as chairman of the Joint Chiefs of Staff for two years he had become convinced of the need to overcome defense problems with "a basic restructuring of military responsibility."[10] He proposed structural changes—vesting authority on the operational side in the chairman, and giving the chairman a deputy and control of the Joint

Staff. This was close to what the Goldwater-Nichols reorganization bill eventually ordained.

Opposition to Jones's views came particularly from the navy, though it was certainly not an exclusive navy position. Admiral Moorer, also a former chairman, commented: "General Jones said when he was Chairman, he didn't have enough power. So when I testified—he was sitting next to me—I started out by saying I had to conclude that General Jones and I didn't have the same job. . . ."[11]

General Vessey, as the incumbent chief of the Joint Chiefs, disagreed too. In his view, it was reform in the method of handling their agenda that cried out for change. Vessey, who has been called a soldier's soldier for his direct, commonsense approach to problems, had ten years in the Pentagon E-Ring to observe how the Joint Chiefs of Staff functioned. When he took over, it was after a period marked by friction between the Joint Chiefs and the defense secretary and between the chiefs and their chairman (Jones). Vessey told how it had been when he was army vice chief of staff in the Pentagon: "I would race down the hall with a major and with a great big fat briefing book. He would brief me and I would try to keep from losing the page in the book by the time I got to the meeting." A lot of meetings had to be held before things could get done. That experience convinced him that the way to proceed "was to have the Chiefs address the issue themselves, then give the staffs some guidance on how to go. In the old way of doing it, the staffs provided the guidance to the Chiefs. . . . I think if [we] recognize that the Chiefs are responsible and not the staffs, and that they have to work in that job," that they will function well and effectively. And that is the way it worked in Vessey's time: "The Chiefs found themselves looking at things that they never looked at before. And that was because they were able to turn around the relationships between their staffs and themselves."[12]

That was sound procedure; no law was needed to make it so.

THE CHARGES: POOR ADVICE AND LOG ROLLING

One reason the reorganization act was passed despite testimony that the Joint Chiefs of Staff was already functioning well was the related charge before Congress that the chiefs avoided significant issues, even at the expense of preparedness; they engaged in log rolling, avoiding tough decisions. Former Secretary of Defense James Schlesinger charged that their advice to the secretary and president passed "through a screen designed to protect the institutional interests of each of the separate services. The general rule is that no service ox may be gored."[13] General Jones said that the organization's "hidden agenda is to come up with an agreed position. . . . The tough issues are not addressed." Jones felt that the trouble with U.S. defense planning originated with a national policy commitment much greater than any likely defense budget would support. But, "since requirements exceed resources, the military services invariably allocated resources among their traditional missions, and seek ways to justify a greater share of the budget."[14]

Here again the incumbents in 1982–86 had a drastically different view. (Of course, Schlesinger and Jones are reflecting a different time period, before the Reagan defense budgets. Theirs was a time of austerity, to say the least.) Watkins's comment was forthright: President Carter, unlike President Reagan, had not listened to the military point of view and neither had his secretary of defense, Harold Brown. The effect filtered down.

> I had the impression that the JCS were considered unenlightened thorns in Harold Brown's side. I believe that during that period of time, the Joint Chiefs of Staff under General Jones lost the credibility that subsequently gave birth to all of this brouhaha on Capitol Hill. . . . All this started in the late '70s, at a time when we had reached a new low in developing and executing a meaningful national strategy, one that matched the real world situation, at a time of pressures on the military to keep accepting unacceptably low budgets based on a lousy strategy of 1½ wars and a short duration conflict of 14 days.[15]

With an inadequate budget driving an inadequate strategy, neither the secretary nor the president wanted to hear the dissenting views of chiefs who would not concur with their chairman.

Had the Joint Chiefs failed to give meaningful military advice to the administration? Questioned on this point, they unanimously rejected the claim. It was true, Watkins said, that split decisions on formal documents occurred rarely, perhaps once a year. About one out of ten times the Joint Chiefs took issue with a position "being pushed by the administration or by [the Arms Control and Disarmament Agency] or by State or by Defense. We disagree and go up the line with a strong position that is not all that well received by the administration. We may be 5 to 0 on a position that's totally opposed to the administration . . . It's not a goal of ours to always have harmony."[16]

Obviously, a total negative vote by the Joint Chiefs on an administration idea could be seen as a lack of meaningful advice. General Kelley described the Joint Chiefs under Vessey and Admiral Crowe as a "congenial group of people who are willing to attack very difficult problems, who are very willing to express contrary views, and who, unlike what some criticize us for, do not kick cans down the street. We don't roll logs." Adequate defense budgets promoted harmony, but the chiefs were "not in the nitty-gritty of trying to examine each other's budget. That's a different forum, that's a defense resources forum."[17] The Joint Chiefs got into the budget only "on cross-cutting service issues where a single program could benefit all the commanders in chief but which also cut across all the services.

Asked whether the availability of more generous defense budgets played a hand in the marked camaraderie of his Joint Chiefs, Vessey commented:

> We were on a rising tide of support. The dollars were a lot easier to come by then. . . . On the other hand, the Chiefs would sit down together and look at their own programs and say, "Mr. Secretary, you could cut out six of these RPV [remote piloted vehicle] programs, some of mine and some of his, and consolidate some others, and reduce your expenditures in that field by 7 to 8 billion dollars." The Chiefs would do that. . . .[18]

Watkins described the Joint Chiefs of which he had been a member as always manifesting some degree of service protectionism; its existence was healthy because members depended on the service chief most concerned to speak up and explain the issue from his point of view. There were often heated debates, but a chief straying into someone else's area needed to know what he was talking about to retain credibility.[19]

These views are quite different from the views and charges of General Jones.

HOW THE JOINT CHIEFS OF STAFF FUNCTIONS

In a routine week, the Joint Chiefs have three formally scheduled meetings: Tuesdays, Wednesdays, and Fridays. These sessions normally last from two and a half to four hours. Preparations on the navy side are made in OP-06's office, plans, policy, and operations. During Watkins's tenure OP-65 was, as part of that group, almost solely devoted to work relating to the Joint Chiefs. He was the CNO's trusted agent on all strategic matters, such as the issue of D-5 missile employment or sea-launched missiles.[20]

The chairman makes up the agenda, but the chiefs can add items to it. New items may even be added the morning of a scheduled staff session because the operations deputies meet beforehand and go over a range of topics of special interest to their respective chiefs. Operations deputies meetings handle 90 percent of the items, routine things like logistics lift and the normal movement of carriers. It is the remaining 10 percent or so—the controversial issues—that come up for the chiefs' consideration. These may concern the INF portion of the Geneva talks on arms control or mutually balanced force reduction in Europe.[21]

All agenda items, pending or projected, are listed in a daily report issued by the joint secretariat. On 22 April 1986, for example, the report listed eleven items still pending. One was an old issue having to do with the U.S. response to New Zealand's port-access ban. The other ten items were more recent—few stay unresolved for any length of time.

Before the meeting of the Joint Chiefs, the revised agenda is reviewed in a briefing with OP-06 and then with the CNO. (The chiefs may depart from that agenda or, in rarer cases, discard it altogether.) Once they have adopted a position, they authorize a Joint Chiefs memorandum, which is signed by the chairman. This goes to the secretary of defense, then to the National Security Council (which may return it for further comment). After the meeting there is a debrief. The CNO then passes the results down the chain of command, especially action items.[22] The whole procedure is minutely prescribed by the Navy Action Officer's Guide and the Joint Administrative Instruction.[23]

In the Gold Room itself, personalities and interests affect the discussion. Some come less prepared than others, though most do their homework, especially on the issues they feel comfortable with and that are more relevant to their own service and experience.

INTERSERVICE COOPERATION

A spin-off of the team spirit engendered by the Vessey style and by more generous budgets was a greater degree of interservice cooperation. By all accounts, Admiral Watkins played an important role in this development.

General Jones, in the *New York Times* article already quoted (7 November 1982), wrote, "It is no secret that the greatest opposition [to his views] came from the Department of the Navy, just as it did in 1947 and has ever since." Jones attributed that to the fact that navy "is the most strategically independent of the services—it has its own army, navy, and air force. It is least dependent on others. It would prefer to be given a mission, retain complete control over all the assets, and be left alone." By contrast, "the Army is and always has been the most supportive . . . in cross-service activities [because] Army is the least strategically independent service. It depends on the Air Force for much firepower and on the Air Force and Navy for mobility; the Army can, in fact, do very little in isolation. . . ."[24]

That changed between 1982 and 1986, if not before. On 9 September 1982, early in his tenure as air force chief of staff, General Charles Gabriel signed a memorandum of agreement with Admiral Watkins. The two service secretaries also signed it. "There's no break-through there [just in the signing]," said Gabriel. "This has been done by most of our predecessors—the last three or four times at least. . . . The big thing was the execution. He [Watkins] made it a real piece of paper. It was a commitment which we carried through."[25] This was subsequently implemented with ten working groups under flag-level leadership. In 1984, of some 111 exercises, about 46 indicated the possibility of using joint operations.[26] This resulted in, among other things, navy navigators training at air force bases.

A joint navy–air force dispatch from the year before, July 1983, discussing the status of the agreement memorandum, indicated that it had already affected the planning for expenditures of $5.5 billion.[27]

General Gabriel indicated that Admiral Watkins had some difficulty overcoming opposition to the memorandum of agreement and that following up on it required courage:

> He was the first one to allow the U.S. Air Force to have an anti-ship capability on the B-52, the Harpoon. That was a breakthrough . . . I assume that CNOs in the past have figured that that could take a piece of their force structure, if we had a capability with the B-52. [The B-52s for a long while] had been in surveillance operations. But this, now, was a killing capability. [In fleet exercises,] where there are multi-carrier operations, the Air Force provides tankers, AWACs, and F-15s to expand the outer air battle of the fleet. [That] worked very well. That was up in the northwest Pacific and caused lots of excitement and attention among the Soviets as well. [It was] just the beginning of a number of such exercises. And I've said in many speeches that it now has become routine for the Air Force KC-10s or KC-135s, the AWACs, or the F-15s to operate with carrier task forces. It had not been routine before.[28]

General Maxwell R. Thurman (who served a full four years as vice chief of the army) said that Watkins and Gabriel got together first, in 1982, for the purpose of applying air force assets to carrier operations (for refueling) and B-52s to maritime mining. Then in 1983 Gabriel and General John Wickham, who had been classmates at West Point, generated thirty-one initiatives in connection with the joint air-land battle.[29] Watkins and Wickham were working together by 1984; they "converted fast-sealift ships into roll-on, roll-off (RORO) vessels," said Gabriel, "so we could move an Army division faster. We did eight of those and they're available for loading within four days."[30]

General Wickham, army chief of staff, remarked that the army and air force early in his tour as a Joint Chief had looked at duplications and gaps in missions and equipment with an eye toward consolidation. Thirty-five targets were identified. "Just four of them alone," said Wickham, "led to cost avoidance of over a billion dollars." The navy was invited to participate in some of these initiatives, which included sharing close-air support, matching navy sealift capabilities (in terms of ships) with army lighterage and unloading resources. In working together on LOTS (logistics-over-the-shore), the navy bought seasheds and flatracks—devices that fit into container ships and quickly convert them to military use. Similarly, the army bought tugs and barges for quick unloading in nonport areas.[31]

Many interservice initiatives were less newsworthy, but clearly the emphasis was on jointness in these years. The exchange of program budget data was an important step. This was done before programs and budgets were submitted to the Defense Department so that complementary weapons systems and logistics systems could be synchronized. General Thurman dated the new openness to cooperation from December 1984, when the FY 86 proposals were moving forward. Overt proof of cooperation was the assignment of army officers to the navy staff and vice versa. These officers were privy to all the discussions on program and budget or policy that involved their unit. They participated not as observers but as part of the staff.

The impetus continued in 1987. An army information paper in April 1987 listed thirteen joint army-navy projects.[32] These included joint procurement of causeway systems and a logistic support vessel; an increase of the navy's ready reserve force to eighty-two ships, which would be positioned near early-deploying army units; the establishment of qualifications for army helicopter pilots to land on carrier decks; and coordination of the IFF (identification, friend or foe) system.[33] And an OP-64 file memo lists among significant accomplishments the navy's full participation with the Joint Deployment Agency in integrating the movement of national forces to wartime theaters.[34]

By 1986, according to a navy file point paper, the air force was providing over eight hundred tanker sorties a year to support naval transit aircraft and exercises.[35] So this was not token cooperation. And air force B-52s were participating in at least one naval exercise per quarter, as well as in open sea surveillance training. In General Thurman's opinion, "the training had its salutary finale in the 1986 Libyan bombing. The interoperability experience made it smooth as silk."[36]

OPERATIONS

The CNO does not operate forces in a combat sense, though in his role as a Joint Chief he assigns missions to forces. But, as he is responsible for fleet readiness, deployment schedules and operations tempo are his area of concern, and what he does in this regard as CNO will affect what the Joint Chiefs of Staff do.

Before 1979 the operations-tempo requirement was forty-four days deployed, twenty-nine days non-deployed. But the drastic increase brought about by the Indian Ocean commitment in President Carter's time created interlocking problems: more family separation, less meaningful training, fewer quality deployments, less maintenance, and more unbudgeted money spent. By 1986, the continuing expansion of the fleet plus some reduction in requirements allowed the navy to institute a new set of goals. Navy personnel, it was determined, should spend 50 percent of their time homeported, and there should be six-month deployments for ships (around fifty days a quarter deployed and twenty-nine days non-deployed). Flight hours, too, which had exceeded proper standards, were to be cut to twenty-five hours per crew per month. The whole program would be administered with top-level involvement by the CNO and the navy secretary. The reductions would be achieved in part by altering the Joint Chiefs' formal requirements that X number of carriers must always be in Y area. This "flexible operations" concept, proposed by the CNO, was accepted by the Joint Chiefs and the White House, illustrating the link between the CNO's two hats.

The number of navy-related issues considered by the Joint Chiefs is great. Some idea of their scope may be useful. In 1982, the issues included the question of resuming military exports to Argentina, a global contingency-planning mission for the joint rapid-deployment force, navy plans for systems designed under arms control agreements, deployment options, and joint navy–air force efforts to enhance air force contributions to maritime operations.[37] In 1983, they included arrangements for the Mediterranean carrier battle group, development of an unclassified Soviet threat briefing, guidance by the Joint Chiefs on employment for sea-launched land-attack cruise missiles, IFF, safety rules for operations with the Trident backfit FBM weapon system, a basing plan for ships positioned in potential operations areas, the question of what constitutes "strategic sufficiency," Iceland, establishment of the Military Transportation Command, and the conduct of public information programs during combat or contingency military operations such as Grenada.[38]

The CNO is also the agent of the Joint Chiefs for the Incidents at Sea Agreement with the Soviet Union. That agreement, signed in 1972, instituted a much improved situation for Soviet and U.S. forces, which often operate in close proximity and now use direct, navy-to-navy channels of communication.

RULES OF ENGAGEMENT

An important activity for the Joint Chiefs is recommending the ROEs (rules of engagement) for any contingency or operation.

ROEs are almost second nature to the U.S. Navy because the navy is deployed in its likely wartime battle areas in peacetime. So are many marines. Forward-deployed air force and army units, being only minutes away from combat once hostilities are commenced, also appreciate ROEs. But ROEs are not always easy to arrive at. In some instances they require elaborate bureaucratic coordination between the State Department, NATO, and other allies.[39] There are sure to be different points of view on the fine line between preempting an attack before it can be launched (but after the intent to launch is sufficiently clear) and starting hostilities inadvertently.

ROEs, then, are both fundamental to operations and fundamental to policy. This is why Secretary McNamara, at the time of the Cuban missile crisis, felt he should come to flag plot to "fine-tune" the destroyer-line deployment but why CNO Admiral Anderson would not permit him to interfere. McNamara was afraid that the navy would be too aggressive; Anderson was afraid that strict discipline among the deployed units would be jeopardized by well-intentioned but confusing civilian-instituted tactical directions.

Admiral Hayward, as we mentioned in chapter 2, became convinced as commander of the Seventh Fleet that the Pacific ROEs were dangerously inadequate and outdated, having been established in 1962. What motivated him to press for revision was the fact that technology was steadily shrinking warning time. The Soviets made no secret of their eagerness to get in the first shots if war came. Thus Hayward made a specific proposal for revision to the CNO via CINCPACFLT. Captain Ash Roach, who had worked extensively on the problem, tells the tale of what happened next. Hayward became CINCPACFLT, found his memo stagnating in the files, resurrected it with a favorable endorsement, and sent it on to the CNO. A year later he himself became CNO. He inquired about his memo, found it holed up in OP-602, and this time sent it on to the Joint Chiefs. The civilian side of the Defense and State Departments put up roadblocks. Only after Hayward retired was the revision approved.[40]

ROEs have strategic as well as operations and policy implications. Reviewing the war plans, Hayward came to the conclusion that the prospect of fighting the Soviets conventionally had not been thought through.[41] He therefore ultimately found himself arguing for a revised strategy.

What worried Hayward most was that his commanding officers did not have a uniform understanding of the actions they were authorized to take. They were supposed to shoot first if they were in danger, but when were they in danger? Since Soviet doctrine clearly aimed at preemption it was imperative to clarify this point; the effects of delay could never be undone. And what was to happen in the case of an unwarranted preemptive action on the part of U.S. fleet units?

Hayward's proposal, amending and clarifying the rules, magnified civilian fears about losing fine-tuning control in the missile age. (It also took a while for the other services to understand that what was involved was not exclusively a navy problem.) The clearer the instructions, the less the need to query higher headquarters. This concern is understandable (it is what led President Johnson personally to select daily bombing targets in Vietnam), but on the other hand restricting local autonomy to achieve centralized control would inevitably erode the local commander's sense of personal responsibility. As Roach commented, "We were trying to get civilians in policymaking roles sufficiently comfortable with the feeling that their policies would be executed in a militarily correct and efficient manner, and within the parameters of the policy, without having the civilians tell us how to do it."[42]

It is easy to see both sides of this dilemma, for failures attributable to lack of command responsibility have been numerous. Incidents like the Iraqi missile attack on the USS *Stark* in May 1987 or the shootdown of an Iranian civilian airliner by the USS *Vincennes* in July 1988 continually reinforce civilian uneasiness on this point. But too tight a rein by civilians in the chain of command is also a recipe for disaster. Significantly, in the immediate wake of the *Stark* incident the ROEs were further refined by the Joint Chiefs—though the fault was not really with the rules previously in effect, which provided that "aircraft of the belligerent Persian Gulf nations, as well as unidentified aircraft, are all to be regarded as potentially hostile."[43] It is the task of the Joint Chiefs to weigh such risks and make a judgment. This task, along with giving arms control/strategic systems advice (which we shall turn to in chapter 14), is among their most important.

Chapter 13

NAVAL OPERATIONS

In every crisis Secretary of State Henry Kissinger and his successors have asked first, "Where are the carriers?" The operational readiness of the U.S. Navy in the mid-1980s directly affected national security. The navy was the principal instrument the Joint Chiefs and the president had at their disposal. How well did the navy perform? Was there indeed a naval renaissance from the standpoint of combat payoff?

BAD BEGINNINGS

The peace-keeping operation in Lebanon showed with pitiless clarity that something was very wrong with U.S. operations. It led to a series of changes whose efficacy made later operations something to be proud of.

U.S. marines sent to Lebanon in 1982 to keep the peace were given little guidance about what that meant if one or more of the armed groups in Lebanon decided no longer to tolerate their presence. Should they shoot at whoever shot at them? Were they to act, in effect, as belligerents? How involved was the United States willing to get? Who was the enemy? None of this was clear.

Shortly after dawn on 23 October 1983, a truck full of TNT crashed through the entrance to the marine compound at Beirut's airport in a suicide terrorist attack. It blew up headquarters, killing over two hundred marines and sailors. They were easy prey: the guards at the gates of the compound had been given unloaded rifles so that they would not act too hastily and thereby set off a political explosion, and neither deep trenches to obstruct trucks nor a concrete barrier had been erected at the entrance. The United States paid the price for not being prepared.

Another disturbing event occurred in early December of the same

231

year, this time involving the U.S. fleet off Lebanon. Syrian army units ashore fired ten or more missiles and about 750 rounds of antiair fire at a U.S. plane doing reconnaissance at the request of the Lebanese government, and in retaliation a strike was ordered for the *Kennedy* and the *Independence* that resulted in the loss of two jet bombers to primitive shoulder-fired antiaircraft missiles. One pilot died and the other was captured. The following is George Wilson's eye-witness account of the chaos that reigned on the *Kennedy* as the retaliatory strike was being launched:

> Goodman joined Lange on the flight deck, hunted around, and spotted A-6 number 556, one of the bombers belonging to VA-85. He asked his roommate, McNally, what munitions were loaded on it. McNally told him the bomber was the only [one] which had been fully loaded. It held six Mark-83 1,000-pound bombs.
> "Our target is for 83s," Goodman said. "We'll take it."
> Bever and Lieutenant Keith Goeke scouted around the deck looking for a ready-to-go A-6. The only one they could find had a nothing load on it—only two APAMS. There was no more time. They either had to launch or stay home.[1]

They launched.

This chaotic scene had been created by a sudden change of plan from a midday to a first-light launching and the expansion of the mission from an original single strike to three separate targets.[2]

Who was responsible for the fiasco remains unclear to this day. According to fleet scuttlebutt the Joint Chiefs, under pressure, made the late change so that the strike time would synchronize with a White House announcement.[3] Wilson blamed the Joint Chiefs for shortening the preparation time.[4] But Admiral Watkins said flatly that their orders contained no specific time-on-target. Any change would certainly have required a further session of the Joint Chiefs. None took place. He also said that General Vessey, in prior discussions with the Joint Chiefs, had indicated that the only guidance he gave CINCEUR (General Rogers) was "to do it right." Navy file material says specifically that the execution time was to be set by CINCEUR. Vessey told Wilson that, although he wanted a retaliatory strike before too much time had passed, he had " left those details to the theater commander, Rogers."[5]

The second change was to triple the target—again, Admiral Watkins stated, an action neither debated nor approved by the Joint Chiefs. Thus preparation time was shortened by a number of hours while at the same time the mission was broadened. The results: an attempt to change loadings in too short a time, and an attack launched at the wrong time and altitude. Because the sun at first light was not where the planning had assumed it would be, there were shadows on the targets and the U.S. release altitude was 1,500 feet below the usual Israeli minimum. Only twenty-six of the thirty-nine aircraft got over target, and many of them were improperly loaded. A modern carrier is not a munitions 7-11 store where everything is stocked ready to go. It carries many different attack loads, fuzings, and bomb casings. These take time to assemble, move, load, and check. And if a load has to be removed from the plane before the next one goes in, the problem doubles. The time from standby status (including briefings) to specific target launch is twelve full hours. The carriers moreover were vulnerable targets while the mad scramble went on.

Exactly what decisions and whose created this mess is still obscure. Certainly, with the long chain of command from Washington to Lebanon, there were many who could have been at fault.[6]

The difficulty in assigning blame for the two failures in Lebanon increased public furor and led to an investigation of the marine barracks episode that produced the thoughtful Long Commission Report, so named after its chairman, Admiral Robert L. J. Long. The FBI presented to the commission an analysis of the explosive used by the terrorists, a simple device combining bottled propane and something like primer cord. Its yield, already devastating, could be doubled and redoubled merely by adding more bottles of gas. The FBI estimated that the TNT of the explosive used was equal to about eleven Silkworm missiles—about the yield of a small nuclear weapon. So even if the truck had not crashed into the marine compound, it could have caused extensive damage.[7]

The implications of this analysis resulted in renovations at the Pentagon, State Department, and White House, where concrete pots for palms served as barriers. It led also and fairly promptly to the promulgation by the Joint Chiefs, following a navy initiative by Admiral Watkins, of new ROEs. After all, what a truck could do, a small plane or small boat could also do.

Some of the new ROEs were published internationally to warn ships and airplanes to stay clear of situations presenting apparent threats to U.S vessels. HYDROLANT 2420/83 (54, 56), published in December 1983, notified all surface and subsurface craft that U.S. naval forces in the eastern Mediterranean would be conducting hazardous operations for a month, and that they should avoid approaching closer than five nautical miles. VHF channel 16 was specified for communications. HYDROPAC 78/84 (62) of January 1984, which covered the Persian Gulf, Strait of Hormuz, and Gulf of Oman, was more specific: "All surface and subsurface ships and craft" were "to avoid closing U.S. forces closer than five nautical miles without previously identifying themselves," and those who closed "without making prior contact and/or whose intentions [were] unclear" could "be held at risk by U.S. defense measures." A similar notice for airplanes in January 1984 added that aircraft at altitudes less than 2,000 feet "not cleared for approach/departure to or from a regional airport" were to observe the same precautions. No time limit was specified. Each notice ended by saying that no restraint on the international freedom of navigation was intended—these were simply safety precautions.[8]

None of the notices spelled out guidance given in the ROEs to commanding officers whose ships were at risk. That part remained classified.

Peacetime ROEs had by now, under the pressure of events, changed much since the time Hayward was commander of the Seventh Fleet. The *Kennedy* episode led to other changes as well, for example in the navy's approach to tactical air warfare and in the establishment of the "Strike University" at Fallon, Nevada.

STRIKE UNIVERSITY

The Naval Strike Warfare Center at Fallon, Nevada, popularly known as Strike University, was conceived in January 1984. In October of that year the first class arrived. Strike University was an initiative of both the navy secretary and the CNO, who were convinced it was needed right away. Admiral Watkins felt that navy plans briefed to the Joint Chiefs were inadequate compared to those of the air force. "The A-6s were still running Vietnam-type strikes," he said, meaning that the navy was not using the A-6's all-weather capability (the air force was using it well in its F-111s) and was not training for in-and-out night attacks, which were less vulnerable than high-level daytime attacks to radar pickup.[9]

Secretary Lehman claimed to have been the inspiration behind Strike University. His decision, he said, came from two sources. The first was his own flight experience. As a reservist he had flown five missions in Vietnam, and as his knowledge of carrier aviation increased he worried that the bureaucratic inertia of the carrier navy combined with the scarce funding of the 1970s had made for unrealistic tactical training. In Vietnam the navy had done "ridiculous" things such as sending "$20 million airplanes . . . after suspected truck parks."[10] Treating high-cost machines and expensively trained pilots as attrition forces for large daylight saturation strikes made no sense.

Lehman's second reason for wanting a strike center was the poor job against Syrian units in Beirut: "The system produced what it had trained its air wings to do, which was a day alpha strike. And we took 6 to 8 percent attrition, which should not have surprised anyone." Lehman called it a military success in the sense that the bombs hit the target, but the loss of three airplanes and two pilots (one a POW) made it a failure in terms of national purpose. Lehman decided to use the event as a tool for reform.

> I found over the years, as I went from airwing to airwing, that every single airwing had totally contradictory and inconsistent tactical notes, and every time the wing commander changed, every new wing commander developed his own new tactics.[11] And most of it was totally out-of-date: tactics built around dive-bombing, daylight, pop-up, lay-down maneuvers. And they were going to get killed if they ever went against an unattrited [intact] threat.[12]

So Lehman and Watkins called a conference at Fallon. They asked only younger pilots because the old ones were stubborn in their thinking. During the course of the conference Lehman described his plan, patterned after the marine air-warfare training center at Yuma (which had taken the Top Gun setup from the Miramar prototype and revamped it to accommodate attack planes). The Fallon conference proved to be a milestone toward the establishment of greatly improved attack procedures.

Captain Joe Prueher, later commander, Carrier Air Wing 8, became Strike University's first CO in April 1984. Technical Director Dr. Roger Whiteway came in as dean in charge of curriculum development in September. The center's primary mission is the development of strike warfare doctrine and training.

Roger Whiteway recalled how in the 1970s the fighter community had focused on fleet air defense, on protecting the fleet, rather than on how to escort a strike group over land. The escort aircraft would see bogies and peel off and get into a fight, ignoring their escort mission. And they would get shot down. Strike warfare training can be defined in many different ways, but at Fallon it focuses on the air wing of a carrier battle group. An air wing is often better acquainted with Soviet capabilities than its own collective capabilities. Training at the Strike University helps weld the air wing, itself a composite unit assembled from squadrons of different kinds of planes, into a single unit for deployment at sea.

A wing trains at the center for three weeks at a time, usually just before deploying to a ship.[13] Eleven wings a year endure the rigorous course. The heart of this training consists of exercises over Strike University's extensive range. Pilots go on missions that are electronically recorded on the tactical air combat training system (TACTS). With TACTS there is no postmortem argument about what happened. Pilots file into the auditorium and see the entire exercise replayed, blow by blow. With a flick of the wrist the computer screen can be adjusted to display the view from the sky or from the ground. The image is three-dimensional. An individual pilot can also see the view from his own cockpit, fore or aft. He can watch the ground view of his plane as a missile is launched at him and he can watch the missile approaching.

The advanced training phase concentrates on campaign orientation. Pilots are given a battle problem designed to make them think in sequence rather than in single-strike contingencies.

TACTS is a brutally candid record. It demonstrates what happens when pilots make mistakes, and a few demonstrations are usually quite convincing.

THE SUPER-CAG

Prior to the Fallon Conference, and an undercurrent at it, was the Lehman initiative known as the super-CAG. CAG itself is a holdover acronym for commander, air group, which no longer exists. Lehman had come to the conclusion that battle group commanders were not getting the proper advice because they were too concerned with flying strikes rather than with how a whole force was employed. At the conference Lehman explained what he was after. He wanted someone senior to the normal CAG, someone comparable to the CO of a ship, who knew enough to balance out the ship's requirements with air-wing utilization, to act as a super-CAG.

To implement his concept, Lehman made the old CAG the deputy to the super-CAG, responsible for shipboard management routine and seeing that the wing was ready to fly; another "super-CAG" would work with the CO of the battle group, advising him on the use of the air wing.

On a carrier, aircraft (fighters, attack aircraft, helicopters) assembled from various sources come together and form an air wing aboard ship. Some six thousand men live together on the carrier, about half of them ship's company, with a CO and an executive officer running the ship and a CAG running the air wing. The embarked admiral needs the CAG's services while the CAG is planning and then off leading air strikes. Meanwhile, the admiral is commanding the whole operation under a decentralized system. He has a number of subordinates, some on other ships, in charge of different parts of the battle plan. Controlling by negation—that is, stepping in only to countermand if one subordinate commander is proposing to use assets better used by another—he needs expert advice. Without a super-CAG by his side, Lehman thought, he could not do that well. But a super-CAG could easily be an irritant. In effect he would be a second captain working for the flag officer.[14]

Under the old system, said Lehman, the men who advised how to perform strikes had no say in how the wing trained for those strikes.

CAGs were too junior; they were selected for their jobs because of superior leadership of squadrons in operation modes, but

> they were never given a day of intelligence training. They were never made aware of the assets that are available. . . . Their total training to be a CAG consisted of a two-weeks school at Dam Neck and checking out every one of the airplane types they had to fly. They were commanders [in rank] without the depth of experience or schooling they needed to advise. . . . And the way it was set up on a carrier, they worked for the captain of a ship. And the captain of a ship has no time to think about strategy. . . . He doesn't have the time or ability to fuse intelligence and put together an air strike plan. So that admiral, who a third of the time is a surface warfare officer and knows nothing about air strike tactics, is being advised by the ship's captain, based on the advice of a young commander who knows a great deal about flying airplanes and working an air wing, but nothing based on the best intelligence and strategy about what needs to be done.[15]

Air strike plans were the "most important foreign policy moves a President could make and they were essentially being done by kids without training." So Lehman changed that—not to everyone's liking.

This discussion revives several themes encountered earlier in other connections, the first being changes in war at sea. The need to operate a whole battle group, or even two or three, in a threat environment characterized by massive, synchronized Soviet attack, posed new problems for command. We saw this influencing OPNAV reorganization, affecting studies conducted by CEP, and running as a thread throughout various congressional hearings. The second theme is the transformation of a navy formerly fragmented by different approaches in the Pacific and the Atlantic, a navy in which tactics and tactical data varied with the CO and changed when he did. And there is a third: how a navy badly undermaintained and overutilized off Vietnam fell into bad habits—from inadequate contingency plans to inadequate updating of strike tactics—and then was brought up to date.

The super-CAG concept was one element in all of this. From a broader point of view, creating modern command procedures for altered threat environments, designing warfare systems rather than single-platform systems, unifying tactics, formulating uniform tactical data, and bringing the navy's "act" together were all forced on the navy by serious problems requiring effective remedies. The failures off Beirut were the harbingers of the later successes off Libya, in the *Achille Lauro* affair and elsewhere.

Fundamental to all these changes was the navy's utilization of space.

THE NAVY IN SPACE

Among the academic community there has been strong skepticism about extending military competition into space. Among the military, the issue is formulated differently. The military asks whether U.S. efforts are keeping pace with the Soviet exploitation of space for military purposes. Statistics given by Vice Admiral William E. Ramsey, deputy commander in chief, U.S. Space Command, are somewhat startling: between 1980 and mid-1986 the Soviets increased their total number of satellites in orbit from less than 100 to 165 and increased their use of deep space (that is, more militarily secure space) from about 20 to 35 percent of their active satellites in orbit.[16] By 1986 they had the Mir Space Station, had performed docking maneuvers, and were well on their way to a permanent manned presence in space. High-energy lasers were operational at Sary Shagan. The Soviets had the only operational antisatellite (ASAT) system in the world. In the meantime, the total U.S. space effort had failed to keep pace.

As CNO, Admiral Trost made the comparison specific in a speech to the National Security Industrial Society in May 1987: "Despite our successes in the past, despite our superior technological base, we are today farther behind the Soviet Union in the military application of space technology than we were when Sputnik first went up [in 1957]. In short, the Soviets are prepared to go to war in space, and we're not." He compared Soviet spending on space in 1986 with the U.S. effort: $30 billion (USSR) versus $18 billion (U.S.) and ninety-one launches (USSR) versus nine (U.S.). Whereas more than 90 percent of Soviet missions, manned and unmanned, had supported military operations, it was still uncertain whether the U.S. space station would even have a military mission. In almost every category of competition, "the Soviet Union has deployed what we are still discussing."[17] What made this comparison sobering was Trost's other statement:

> Today we know that in wartime, even in a conventional war of limited duration, the two superpowers would fight a battle of attrition in space until one side or the other had wrested control. And the winner would then use the surviving space systems to decide the contests on land and sea. Today, that superpower would probably not be the United States.[18]

Trost was saying that, if in World War II control of the air was a prerequisite for control of the sea or land, today control would be achieved in space.

He was not making these remarks idly. They stemmed from a whole progression of events, technological and bureaucratic changes, new approaches to systems of every kind, new concepts of how a carrier battle group would deploy and fight. We have seen these developments in almost every chapter of this book, beginning with the establishment of OP-094 and OP-095 in OPNAV. The battle commander at sea will fight with a decentralized command structure, but the effort will be governed by communication links from space.

In separate interviews, former Secretary Lehman and former CNO Admiral Watkins made the very point that CNO Trost has made in many speeches: that the United States is technologically superior to the Soviet Union and must maintain and utilize that advantage,[19] especially in space-related research. Indeed, the navy's appreciation of the importance of space had spurred even the financially strained navy of the 1960s and 1970s to put substantial effort in that direction, particularly because the Polaris program required it. By 1987 the navy was the number-one client for space systems, using "roughly 80 percent of [the] assets in orbit or awaiting deployment."[20]

The navy began a formal space systems program in January 1981 to pull together ongoing but scattered efforts. Set up in OP-094, the program was given a broad charter. Its nucleus was satellite communications, environmental and navigational systems, and TENCAP (tactical exploitation of national capabilities). There was also a branch devoted to war plans and policies.

A second major organizational step forward came on 1 October 1983, with the establishment of the Naval Space Command in Dahlgren, Virginia, under the command of astronaut Rear Admiral Dick Truly. The navy was playing a major role also in the new unified U.S. Space Command where, in 1987, Vice Admiral William E. Ramsay, the first navy flag officer with a space specialty, was vice commandant.

Parallel changes in officer career patterns were introduced. Hitherto the space program had involved technically oriented officers or those with engineering backgrounds. Typically, they were not sensitive to the tactical payoffs of space. Now space programs were added to the Naval Postgraduate School curriculum—in 1982, space operations and space engineering, with six officers in each, increasing to about twenty-five in each by 1987. Space subspecialty designations were created to identify the growing community. Space-related billets grew from 170 to over 750 by 1987.[21]

Where the air force tended to view space strategically, the navy's focus was tactical, serving the fleet.[22] A number of steps were taken to increase awareness in the navy of space and of the tactical implications of space to operations. That needed considerable effort in a navy used to thinking in terms of an air ceiling of 60,000 feet. The new frame of reference was 23,000 miles. (As the fleet tactical horizon had expanded outward when over-the-horizon radar was phased in, it had also expanded upward.) The enlargement of the oceanography program, previously noted, was closely associated with this effort. Tactically, a carrier is able to hide in warm and cold eddies, which a good environmental satellite can spot. A satellite capability could sample the ocean's parameters—currents, sea states, velocities, discontinuities in the ocean surface—and report this data, eventually in real time, to oceanographers embarked in fleet units.[23]

Space data bore directly on safety, too. Rear Admiral Richard Macke, CO of the Naval Space Command in 1987, gave a convincing illustration using the north wall of the Gulf Stream.

> That's a very dangerous piece of water—a problem not recognized by those who haven't encountered it. I was on *Nimitz* when we came very close to a collision during alongside refueling when we went through the north wall. Both ships were uncontrollable. It is so sharp and there is such a sheer in current that we went through a major heading change, totally uncontrollable. Knowing where that is, so that you don't blindly stumble into it, becomes a critical piece of information.[24]

To increase this sort of tactical data entailed, in Watkins's words at the commissioning of the Naval Space Command, moving "the sensors from the masthead to the edge of space"—psychologically and physically.[25]

It remains now to see how the efforts we have described have affected naval operations. We shall begin with Grenada, because it represented a watershed and was a large-scale operation that aroused considerable controversy. In this case, as with those that follow, the intent will not be full analysis. Our focus is much narrower: to note how operations changed as the lessons of the past were digested and new technologies incorporated.

GRENADA

Operation "Urgent Fury" was initiated by the National Security Council on 14 October 1983, with additional tasking on 21 October, all of it to culminate in operations prior to dawn on 25 October—what the military calls very short fuze. It was the first joint-service combat undertaking of significant size since Vietnam, which is part of the reason it got so much publicity. Media reporting fell short of accuracy, but for that the military largely had itself to blame; there was no Pentagon media plan, although Grenada was to produce the idea of a pool.

President Reagan's announcement of the U.S. intervention (generally referred to as an invasion in the press) came at about 9 A.M. on 25

October, only two days after the marine bombing in Beirut. The government of Grenada had been overthrown the week before by the New Jewel leftist movement and there were 1,100 U.S. citizens on the small island whose lives, he said, were in jeopardy. A reign of terror was beginning for the island natives into which the Americans might easily be drawn.

Nominally, the U.S. action was taken at the behest of several tiny east Caribbean states that feared the expansion of Cuban influence in their area. From a military point of view, the United States was particularly concerned about the 10,000-foot runway being rushed to completion at Grenada's airport by Cuban combat engineers, purportedly to enhance tourism. With the Soviet-backed Sandinistas in Nicaragua and Castro in Cuba, a new Marxist stronghold in Grenada would complete a triangular area that could be used for the interdiction of resupply forces to Europe in the event of war.

The U.S. landing met determined opposition from the well-armed Cubans in Grenada.[26] U.S. troops included 1,900 marines on their way to Beirut and diverted, about 500 army rangers (light-loaded troops), and the Eighty-second Airborne for reinforcement. The air force used AC-130 Hercules gunships for suppression fire. Some 600 Cuban troops were captured, plus large documentary files showing conclusive evidence of communist involvement in the coup.

The media described this all-service participation as a deliberate, juvenile-level effort of the Joint Chiefs to see that everyone could have a piece of the action. In reference to this criticism Admiral Wesley Lee McDonald, CINCLANT at the time, commented, "Let me assure you as the one who brought the plan to the tank that it wasn't that way at all. It may have come out that way but it wasn't decided that way." The original plan called for the use of marine-navy units, but updated intelligence indicated the need for additional units. There were only three days available. Admiral McDonald was compelled to take some here, some there. The resulting force, though it may have looked too large and motley for the operation, did manage to persuade the Cubans on Grenada that real resistance was useless and to deter further reinforcements.[27] McDonald claimed that the units worked well together, despite some reports to the contrary. He meant they worked well, considering; it would be utopian to expect troops sent suddenly from various geographical locations directly into action without prior training to perform as well as troops used to joint action and trained in it.

The press had a field day reporting stories of officers placing credit card calls to communicate with Washington during the invasion. It was true there was no single, integrated joint-task-force communications plan. This was partly because communications people were left out of the initial planning for technical security reasons—a situation since remedied. The Joint Deployment Agency (JDA) has been given a restricted-access terminal capability so that it can do what it was created to do in 1979—coordinate the rapid deployment of forces.[28]

Probably the greatest military lesson learned from Grenada by the Joint Chiefs was the need to coordinate equipment procurement (including communications equipment) across the services for units that might have to deploy together. Basically, the problem involved different schedules and priorities for purchasing and distributing equipment. Admiral McDonald commented that in Grenada only classified, covered circuits were mismatched—the marines had them, the army units did not. He speculated that army units stationed in Europe at the time, given higher priority for equipment, had probably already been in possession of the new gear.[29]

There was also a public relations lesson to be learned from Grenada: that the media, if excluded from combat zones, might do a great deal of harm by misleading reporting based upon a lack of access to facts or the inability to relay them promptly. There was no easy solution to this. The media could not simply be allowed to mill around in the combat zone or to breach security. Discussions with the media resulted finally in a Pentagon plan whereby a pool would be created and a small group selected to accompany any operation.

THE *ACHILLE LAURO*

The *Achille Lauro*, a 23,629-ton luxury liner flying the Italian flag, was hijacked off the Egyptian port of Alexandria on the night of 7 October 1985 by four heavily armed terrorists from a Palestinian splinter group. The ship set sail for Syria, then Cyprus, but was not granted port rights and returned to Egypt, the terrorists in the meantime killing a 69-year-old disabled American and dumping his body and wheelchair overboard.

The *Saratoga* battle group, Rear Admiral Dave Jeremiah in command, had at the time the only U.S. carrier in the Mediterranean, although there were other U.S. ships off Lebanon. The *Saratoga* was north of Egypt when she got a firm fix on the location of the *Achille Lauro* at about 1800 on 8 October.[30] A destroyer was sent to conduct surveillance from just over the horizon. When the luxury liner entered harbor in Egypt and the terrorists disembarked, the U.S. fleet units returned to normal schedules. At Port Said on 9 October the hijackers surrendered to Egyptian authorities after being promised safe conduct out of Egypt. (The negotiators later claimed they knew nothing of the murder when they made this promise.) The terrorists were permitted to board an Egyptian 737, which took off from Cairo's airport.

On the evening of the tenth the *Saratoga* was heading toward a port visit in Trieste when, at 1844, the chief of staff of the Sixth Fleet ordered her to be ready to launch F-14s and an E-2. After turning south she launched, with the *Yorktown* following her at about 20 knots. At 1917 a second message came ordering the interception of the 737 carrying the terrorists. The aircraft was to be diverted to Sicily. (This was one minute after the E-2 became airborne and almost ten minutes after the first planes were launched.)[31] The *Saratoga* was then at 37°06′N 20°50′E proceeding south. At 1947 the carrier's fighters vectored out, intercepting and positively identifying the 737. One fighter flew close enough to shine a flashlight on its tail, verifying the tail markings and the logo.

According to Jeremiah,

> They [the fighters] were flying lights out, dark cockpit. They took up escort positions. I told them not to begin communicating with the 737 because he was heading west and as long as he continued on that flight path he was headed where we wanted him to go. There was no point in spooking him unless he did something different. So they followed along and two more came in and joined up with them. . . [T]hey did not know we were there. We could see the stewardesses in the cabin moving around, bringing drinks. . . . We're sitting out there and watching all of this and talking to the E-2 and F-14s. . . . As we got to the intercept phase, I moved from the war room to the CIC. . . . Our communications worked excellently in the sense that I was talking to either Admiral [Frank] Kelso or . . . [Vice Admiral Robert] Dutch Schoultz on the same circuit; they were talking to Hank Dorsey who was the J-3 at CINCEUR, and he was talking to Hunt Hardisty who was the J-3 at JCS, and they were talking to Poindexter and Art Moreau.[32]

So all the players, from White House people to the Joint Chiefs, to CINCEUR and the Sixth Fleet, were in direct and immediate contact.

> The aircraft [737] continued west until they [the terrorists] requested clearance to land in Tunis and they were denied this by Tunis. They then attempted to land in Athens and Athens said no. . . . Then they began to fuss around and try, through another airplane, to contact Cairo. At that point I told the E-2 to talk. They told the Egyptian airliner that he was under escort by two F-14s and he was to proceed to [the NATO base at] Sigonella, Sicily. And then the E-2 (one hundred miles away) said, "I'd better turn on my lights so you know where I am." And the F-14s turned on *their* lights.

There was a problem at landing time because the 737 had no clearance. After the E-2 declared an emergency for the 737 it was allowed to land.

The tactical sequence had started at 1844 and by 0141 the last aircraft was back on the *Saratoga*. In that time period the fighters had operated under three different ROEs.[33]

Subsequent events brought additional drama as the Americans and Italians sorted out all the legal angles of the incident. For our purposes, the point is that the episode demonstrated the rapidity with which the U.S. armed forces could respond to an emergency. In execution, this was a one-service affair, but it showed that an all-service command structure need not produce Beirut results when used properly.

LIBYA

The United States has at least three good reasons for tangling with Libya. The first is Muammar al-Qaddafi's sponsorship of international terrorism, in part directed against Americans. Second, Qaddafi, although not a Soviet puppet, has aided the Soviets (at least until the advent of Gorbachev) by fomenting unrest. His outsized investment in modern weapons makes him a threat on the flank of the U.S. Sixth fleet.[34] Third, he established a "line of death" across the Gulf of Sidra at 32°30'N, some eighty-five to ninety miles into international waters, and forbade the U.S. fleet to move south of it. This posed a double challenge by contesting freedom of the seas and encroaching on the only good fleet exercise area in the central Mediterranean.

Three times in recent history the U.S. Navy has contested the line of death. The first incident came in August 1981 when Libyan warplanes challenged U.S. F-14s under then–Rear Admiral James E. Service's command. The Libyan planes were promptly shot down. The other two incidents took place in 1986. What triggered them was the bloody bombings, instigated by Libya, at the Rome and Vienna airports in December 1985. Before midnight of the day of the bombings, Battle Force, Sixth Fleet, had been directed to plan contingency attacks on Libya. Rear Admiral Jerry C. Breast, describing the sequence of events in *Wings of Gold*, writes that Air Wing 13 planned "over 160 combinations of forces and tactics."[35]

By mid-March, with munitions topped off, the fleet was ready to undertake a carefully planned mission moving south across Qaddafi's line. The Sixth Fleet CO, Vice Admiral Frank Kelso, visited the three carriers present—the *America*, *Coral Sea*, and *Saratoga*—to discuss ROEs with each warfare commander and air crew. The ROEs had been discussed by members of the chain of command as high as the secretary of defense and the chairman of the Joint Chiefs.[36] Rear Admiral Jeremiah briefed each squadron CO with special code words for each contingency so that the whole fleet could switch simultaneously to new rules of engagement as often as required. "We knew exactly what to do," said Jeremiah.[37]

The force deployed was substantial, including the three carriers, the

Aegis cruisers *Ticonderoga* and *Yorktown*, and the usual array of escorts. The first force sent across the line, on 24 March, was a three-ship surface action group. This was to proceed within a hundred miles of the Libyan coast, within the area claimed by Qaddafi. In early afternoon the Libyans fired a huge surface-to-air missile against the surface group's combat air patrol. The planes evaded the missiles and responded with a homing, antiradiation missile strike on the Libyan launch site, destroying its antenna.[38] A few Libyan patrol boats ventured out and were destroyed, but the Libyan air force, "very active up to minutes before the missiles were fired, departed overwater air space and never reappeared—to avoid the implication that they were either forced down or shot down."[39]

Libya's next response was the bombing on 5 April of a Berlin discotheque used by American servicemen, which killed one and wounded fifty. Planning for a punitive strike at Libya was speeded up. The *Coral Sea*, which had been heading home, was ordered to return to the central Mediterranean.

The *Saratoga* left the Mediterranean and Jeremiah handed over CTF 60 to Rear Admiral Henry H. Mauz in the *America*. (Rear Admiral Jerry Breast was senior, but his ship, the *Coral Sea*, was already prepared to head home, so tactical command remained with Mauz.)

By 15 April ships were converging at high speed on the launch site. They were scheduled to arrive fifteen minutes before launch time, and thirty-nine navy aircraft from each carrier were to be in position to act in concert with air force F-111s flying from Great Britain.[40] The Defense Department later explained that air force planes had been added because specialized carrier attack aircraft could not reach five targets simultaneously, and because F-111s were especially good, with their terrain-avoidance radar, at low-level precision bombing.

The air force F-111s flew 2,800 nautical miles from their bases in Britain. Refused permission to transit France, they were refueled four times en route—a fourteen-hour round trip. Shortly before they and the navy's A-6 bombers began bombing runs, A-7s and F-18s launched their Shrikes and HARMs to destroy Libyan radars. At 0200 Libyan time the F-111s struck three sites around Tripoli, including the El Azziziya barracks, a home and headquarters for Qaddafi. The A-6s hit two targets in Benghazi. Attacks were made from altitudes as low as 350 feet using laser-guided "smart" bombs.

Qaddafi emerged unscathed but shaken by the attack which, reports said, killed his adopted infant daughter and wounded two of his sons. Although there were fears of a fresh rash of retaliatory violence by Libya, it showed pronounced prudence over the next several years.

Rear Admiral Breast pointed with pride to how minimal the

joint-force problems were here as compared to Grenada, but added that it had taken two and a half months to coordinate the details for Libya, whereas for Grenada there had been less than one and a half days.[41]

The success of the two Libyan operations did depend in significant part on having ample time to prepare, allowing advance agreement on which ROEs to apply in which circumstances. That luxury is not always available in wartime.

PACIFIC OPERATIONS

While at this time the situation in the Mediterranean was volatile, operations in the Pacific were much more low key. The opponent in the Pacific theater was the Soviet Union, and superpower tensions were not translated into the use of force. Here the operational contest was more subtle and restrained and, for reasons of security, much less publicized.

The Pacific–Indian Ocean area is vast—102 million square miles. In 1987 the primary U.S. presence was navy: out of 330,000 U.S. personnel there, 250,000 (including 80,000 marines) were navy. The U.S. Navy had about as many ships (267) as the air force had planes (284). Aircraft in the Pacific fleet numbered about 2,000.[42] These forces were arrayed against a Soviet Pacific fleet that was the largest of the four Soviet fleets. Of its almost 500 combatants, 130 were submarines.

In 1987 Admiral James A. ("Ace") Lyons, Jr., was CINCPACFLT. An outspoken man, he was a favorite of Secretary Lehman and well respected by Admiral Watkins for having had, along with Arthur Moreau and William Pendley, a major impact on the development of the maritime strategy. Lyons was a four-square advocate of forward deployment. He was also very much aware that U.S. alliance obligations with Japan were not reciprocal. Japan would not automatically be involved in hostilities between the superpowers.[43] In the event of war, Japan's reaction would turn on how it viewed its interests and whether U.S. forces could deploy forward and soon enough to assist it. The Chinese had to consider the same question.

Lyons has been involved in OCEAN SAFARI, 1981, when the *Eisenhower* and the *Forrestal* deployed into the Norwegian Sea well forward without being detected by the Soviets. There had now been a parallel operation in the Pacific. The nuclear-powered *Carl Vinson* (which has a normal speed of over 30 knots) had been sent up into the Bering Sea—an action the United States had never taken before.

> The Soviets didn't know where we were for twelve days. They lost us. How do we know that? They were sending out all the reconnaissance aircraft *south* of the Aleutians. We were intercepting them in excess of 200 miles away. The *Vinson* was up in the Bering Sea conducting its exercises—a full battle group—and [it was undetected until] it came down parallel with the Kamchatka Peninsula.

Also, the *Ranger* had been surge-deployed (sent on a non-scheduled deployment) clear across the Pacific undetected, and the *New Jersey* had operated in the Sea of Okhotsk. The *Vinson*, fresh from the Bering Sea, had gone to the Indian Ocean and then back into the Bering Sea.[44] It is under severe weather conditions that nuclear carriers show their value; they are tough ships able to go great distances and still fight. These deployments demonstrated that ability—undetected.

THE LONG ROAD FORWARD

By 1986, the U.S. Navy had come a long way since 1983—materially, in interoperability with other services (and with some allies), and in command and control procedures.

Grenada and Beirut had highlighted problems and pointed the way to solutions. There was a need for a crisis action system, a checklist for joint operations, especially for very rapid response. The military had had "no automated, secure way to exchange data with the Joint Deployment Agency. We developed that," said Admiral Huntington Hardisty, who was on the Joint Staff for nearly two years after Grenada and who became VCNO in 1987. "We also began to streamline command and control." In particular, the Joint Chiefs looked systematically at all areas of the world where a contingency might develop and reviewed command and control arrangements, including joint-task-force planning. By the time of the *Achille Lauro* affair it was possible to act both quickly and effectively. Said Hardisty: "We set everything up [counting from the first contact from CINCUSNAVEUR] within the space of about 45 minutes."[45] Rear Admiral James Dorsey, at CINCEUR headquarters, had passed the order to intercept the Egyptian 737 through CINCUS-NAVEUR, and "twenty-two minutes later they [the intercepting aircraft] were in the air."[46]

New attack training spoke for itself in the Libyan night bombings. Gone was the approach Lehman and Watkins had criticized when setting up Strike University. The concept of "bringing up" the enemy's missile defenses prior to the night bombing was well developed and implemented. And the Libyan operations were real-life scenarios for testing multi-carrier tactics with decentralized subcommands.[47]

The navy had moved far beyond spare parts and personnel shortages, and bungled performances such as the bombing of the marine barracks off Beirut. In the Mediterranean, on the *Coral Sea*, the new F/A-18s bore out what Lehman had told Congress about them. They were "up" and ready to go. Equally important, their equipment worked.[48] And in the Pacific, Admiral Lyons could rest assured that his carriers would not, as in Hayward's day, break down in the middle of an operation.[49]

Quite a change. A naval renaissance.

Chapter 14

THE STRATEGIC DEFENSE INITIATIVE

One of the most dramatic and important changes in national security policy in the 1980s was inaugurated on 23 March 1983, and in it the navy played a key role. Near the end of a major speech on defense and arms control, President Reagan posed a startling question: "What if free people could live secure in the knowledge that their security did not rest upon the threat of instant U.S. retaliation to deter a Soviet attack, that we could intercept and destroy strategic ballistic missiles before they reached our own soil or that of our allies?"[1] Thus was announced a new effort that critics would call Star Wars but which to the national security community would become known as SDI (strategic defense initiative).

What follows is not a definitive history of SDI. Nor is it an attempt to give a comprehensive treatment of the merits of the SDI approach. It is, rather, an account of the navy role.[2]

THE BACKGROUND

Ever since Bernard Brodie wrote at the end of World War II that atomic bombs changed the mission of the military from fighting wars to deterring wars, that word *deterrence* has been prominent in virtually all U.S. doctrine. What does it mean, to deter war? It means in the U.S.-Soviet case to convince the Russians that there is nothing to gain by launching an attack or, specifically, resorting to the use of nuclear weapons against American and allied targets. As the decades rolled by, this thought became packaged in the proposition that no defense was possible and therefore any attack should be met by a punishing counter-attack. If the American people died en masse and the United States was devastated in an attack, the appropriate response was to retaliate with "secure, second-strike" forces such as Tridents. The technology was

248

eminently modern, the thought as old as the Code of Hammurabi: An eye for an eye, a tooth for a tooth.

Deterrence was supposed to be achieved by the enemy's expectation of assured destruction—hence the phrase mutual assured destruction, or MAD. The United States and the Soviet Union went so far in this direction as to renounce or limit the modest defensive efforts technology could provide, signing the ABM (antiballistic missile) Treaty on 26 May 1972 and in 1974 revising it to provide even less flexibility. The United States did away with its ABM deployment in North Dakota, while the Soviets retained and improved their one permitted deployment, a defensive ring around Moscow.

Supporters of MAD spoke of stability as synonymous with equal and mutual vulnerability, especially of urban centers. They opposed moves to defend these targets because the opponent could not then be sure of the other's continued vulnerability. Initially, submarines like Polaris, Poseidon, and Trident, because they were considered second-strike forces hidden away in the ocean depths, were compatible with this concept of one American goat and one Soviet goat, each tethered in the middle of an open field, each an easy target. The first land mobile missiles, hard to find because they moved around, were still not thought inconsistent with the basic MAD concept.

But other technological improvements such as MIRVs (multiple independently targeted reentry vehicles) introduced basic instabilities in the large land-based ICBM leg of the air-land-sea defense Triad. Soviet ICBMs were larger and more powerful than U.S. ICBMs. That made them capable of carrying many MIRVs and gave them more blast effect, raising the possibility that the Soviets would be tempted to knock out a three- or ten-warhead missile with the expenditure of one or two warheads in a preemptive trade. In short, the technological change undermined a number of basic assumptions about the inherent ability of two heavily armed antagonists to rely on the deterrent effects of purely offensive missiles. Moreover, cruise missiles, which could be built out of sight and packed so many in a barn, made true weapons ratios hard to assess. And as sea- and land-based mobile missiles grew more powerful and accurate, they became potential first-strike weapons. All of this highlighted the need to stay within a margin of safety in offensive weapons. Arms control efforts, based on assured units of accounting, became more difficult as there appeared further incentives for an offensive arms race.

There was another problem. MAD repudiated the traditional military wisdom of having a defense. MAD was sensible to military men only when defense was impossible from a technological standpoint. But by the early 1980s the development of third-generation computers, of lasers, and of directed energy beams with combinations of mirrors suggested that a defense might be feasible. So, at the time the cluster of propositions associated with a purely offensive deterrence was encountering roadblocks, some of the difficulties associated with a defense were showing signs of evaporating.

MAD was a proposition hard to justify to the public. Although assured destruction as defined by Secretary of Defense McNamara was subsequently altered by Secretary Schlesinger and then by Secretary Brown in certain respects, in the public's view all the variations arrived at the same dead end. The best one could say for MAD was that it was intended to avert slaughter by threatening slaughter in return. It was not a doctrine compatible with Christian ethical standards, as first Catholic bishops and then leaders of American Protestant denominations began to assert. Any president had to ask himself whether he could in his heart justify an order to retaliate in cold blood. Any member of the Joint Chiefs had to ask himself whether, if he had the power to provide an alternative, he should not do so.

Meanwhile, U.S. fixed-site silos were growing more vulnerable.

THE MX PROBLEM

What we conveniently call the MX problem was, in reality, much more complicated. In bureaucratic terms the issue centered on "the basing mode" question.

Because of improvements in the accuracy of Soviet missiles, the possibility had become real by the early 1980s that the Soviets, in a preemptive strike, could with a minimum expenditure of their ten-warhead MIRVs eliminate many or all Minuteman IIIs. A surprise Soviet attack could conceivably allow the Soviets to ride out an American retaliatory strike with a sufficient arsenal left over to "win" the exchange. Granted, these are rather far-fetched propositions, but Minuteman vulnerability was real enough. In any event, the United States could not simply accept this change, so the MX missile was developed.

The MX was supposed to provide an answer to the problem; powerful enough to destroy hardened Soviet silos, it would prevent any reload capability and limit Soviet follow-on missile assaults—provided, of course, that it survived the initial attack. The MX would be even more useful if fired first. This feature, difficult to overlook, lent fuel to the political arguments that soon proliferated.

The fact that the MX from the Soviet point of view was a first-strike missile was only one part of a serious problem. Given the missile's range, power, and accuracy, it could destroy all Soviet hardened targets (other than mobile or undersea ones). In the abstract calculations of nuclear warfare theorists, this meant that it created instability. In other words the Soviets, being vulnerable, might launch first, and so the Americans would have to be on guard to launch first themselves if necessary.

More concrete was a second part of the problem: where to put the MX and how to base it. Various solutions were suggested, from a "racetrack" to "dense-pack basing." To reduce vulnerability under the first option, the missiles would be housed in shelters laid out in a racetrack pattern. They would be shuttled periodically from one shelter to another, the idea being (like the shell game at the carnival) that the Soviets would use up many warheads hitting shelters in which no missiles were concealed. This would compensate for the instability introduced by MIRVs. Periodically, it was suggested, the shelters could be opened so Soviet satellites could count the missiles to make sure treaty restrictions on numbers were being observed. Here planners began to encounter contradictory goals; they were to hide the missiles but not too well.

Despite these problems, the Carter administration decided to favor the racetrack, or multiple protective shelter (MPS), approach. The decision soon generated stiff opposition from those states in the West where the racetrack would be located. MPS was designed to waste Soviet warheads on empty shelters. What impressed the citizens of potential target areas such as Nevada and Wyoming was how much total Soviet megatonnage the scheme could draw down on them.

When President Reagan assumed office in 1981 he was already on record as opposed to the Carter administration's MPS mode. At the same time he was committed to improving U.S. strategic nuclear capabilities, along with all other significant elements of America's defense. (Since existing U.S. ICBMs lacked sufficient hard-kill capability and were increasingly vulnerable, the MX project could not simply be scrapped.) How was he to reconcile these two stands?

The MX was a reality; it was being produced, and it was not going to be MPS-based. The president's first suggestion to Congress, in October 1981, was to put the MX in existing silos on an interim basis and find a permanent solution by 1984, choosing among defended silos, deep underground basing, or continuous-patrol aircraft.[3] Congress said no, so the president appointed the Townes Commission, which recommended closely spaced (dense-pack) basing. This called for the basing of one hundred MXs close together in super-hardened silos in Wyoming. The Joint Chiefs were split, the air force chief of staff and the chairman in support and the rest opposed. Congress balked, directed that no MX flight tests were to be conducted until the question of basing was settled, and required a report on the whole question by 1 March 1983.

On 3 January 1983 the president created a second commission, the Scowcroft Commission, which concluded that the problem was much broader than MX basing. More immediately, though, they set to work on basing, with the Department of Defense and Joint Chiefs heavily engaged in weighing the various options. Politically, it was far too late to abandon the MX project. It was also widely assumed that doing so would remove pressure on the Soviets to agree to arms control measures. The circle of confusion, somehow, had to be squared, with complicated military, political, technical, and moral considerations reconciled.

INVOLVEMENT OF THE NAVY AND THE JOINT CHIEFS

By early 1983, as the Scowcroft Commission began its work, the Joint Chiefs of Staff had held dozens of meetings devoted to the strategic missile problem. Many of these sessions took place without operational deputies, just with the principals. General Vessey was quoted earlier as saying that for the really complicated issues he did not want the Joint Chiefs responding to various staff proposals but rather wrestling with the issue themselves until they knew what options existed. Then they could use staff. By all accounts, Admiral Watkins played a leading role in these discussions. Both General Kelley and General Gabriel considered that the CNO had a natural bent for strategic analysis.

Admiral Watkins, coming to office in the middle of 1982, could hardly avoid thinking seriously about the strategic controversy. He knew Congress would continue to argue about basing modes. This proved to be the case several months later as Congress mandated that President Reagan, by the March 1983 deadline, would have to come to a decision on what was called the second MX basing mode. Watkins understood that MAD was losing its appeal and utility and felt strongly that it placed the United States inside a Soviet-controlled "strategic cul-de-sac." Furthermore, the entire basing-mode debate was "morally repugnant" to most Americans.[4]

In the summer and fall of 1982 Watkins began to work out his own position, using a small staff group of two or three key people and later asking selected members of his CEP to react. By January 1983, Watkins was convinced that the United States was playing to the Soviet strong suit with MAD and that, as a result, it was no longer a viable long-term strategy. He associated MAD with three problems: the ease with which the Soviets could develop alternative offensive land-missile systems; the political unacceptability in the United States of offsetting the Soviet land-based offensive-systems advantage; and proliferating noncompliance and verification knots. He was thinking more seriously about an alternative to MAD. As he explained to his staff:

> Look, the . . . genius of this country is to take a new technological
> concept (which the Soviets may well have in their minds as we do)
> and build it—field it—which they can't do. So why don't we use our
> applied technological genius to achieve our deterrent instead of
> sticking with an offensive land-based rocket exchange which they
> will win every time? They have bigger rockets, they can lift more
> stuff into space, and they have no political obstacles in basing their
> missiles. We shouldn't continue to play in a game like that.[5]

On 10 January 1983, the chairman and all the Joint Chiefs received
a memo from National Security Advisor William Clark scheduling a
meeting with the president for 11 February. The agenda was to be the
Triad, the MX, and possible basing modes, and each chief was to give
President Reagan his personal views.

Ten days later, on 20 January 1983, Dr. Edward Teller paid
Admiral Watkins an office call that was to have momentous consequences. Teller, "the father of the hydrogen bomb," was a senior
research fellow at the Hoover Institution at Stanford and for many years
had been a moving force at the National Livermore Laboratory administered by the University of California. Staying to lunch, he told Watkins
about a favorite topic of his, a strategic defense concept called Excalibur.[6]

The idea behind Excalibur was to use nuclear-driven X-ray lasers to
destroy ballistic missiles during their boost phase. Interestingly, in the
1950s Dr. Teller had not thought defense possible; he changed his mind
in the 1960s and was confirmed in this change in the late 1970s when
work was begun on the X-ray laser by several physicists. "The X-ray
laser," said Teller, "was a really new idea, an ingenious idea. It looked
like it would work." Nuclear energy would be employed only to get the
beam started; although space-based, the laser was not a nuclear weapon.
Teller spoke of the urgency of taking action; he had encountered much
lethargy.[7]

Watkins argued that it was necessary to think beyond Excalibur.
He did not want to try and sell a specific concept, nor did he feel it was
feasible to think in terms of nuclear trigger devices in space—there would
be too many political obstacles. The point to emphasize was space
defense against ballistic missiles, using conventional means.

As the meeting progressed Watkins became convinced that the
strategic defense approach with conventional means could provide a way
out of the MX basing dilemma by giving the United States a long-range
but believable alternative to simply piling on more and more nuclear
offensive weapons: Teller argued "that we were at the point technolog-
icaly where we could do this. . . . I knew it was the way to go for other

reasons, but I wasn't sure of my technical ground. . . . Just his vibrant, intense feeling about the projected state of technology . . . along with countless prior technology briefings given to all members of the JCS . . . convinced me."[8] The strategic defense approach would not eliminate the basing mode problem, but it could put the controversy into perspective and end a sterile debate. It could be the military man's path to what the arms control advocates so avidly sought: a way to draw the fangs off the weapons that threatened mankind's survival by making the success of a first strike questionable.

Immediately following the lunch with Teller, Watkins directed Rear Admiral Holland and his deputy, Captain Linton Brooks, to develop the concept further in the CNO paper previously drafted for the meeting with the president.[9] During the week of 24 January Brooks, in a presentation to the CNO, made a number of key points: that the CNO should support the Triad, that the United States needed to move beyond the frustrating debate over basing modes, that the strategic moderniza-tion program had restored the credibility of American strategic forces (making the ICBM survivability issue less pressing), that the United States should for the present put perhaps forty MXs in existing silos and push for a long-term strategy based on strategic defense—a position both militarily and morally sound.

The CNO, accompanied by Captain Brooks and Captain Jake Stewart, presented this briefing approach to members of his CEP on 2 February 1983. They agreed that the position had merit, but cautioned the CNO not to oversell it to the president, since the perception would be that the United States already had the strategic defense capability in hand.

THE JOINT CHIEFS BRIEF THE PRESIDENT

Watkins, thus encouraged and cautioned, decided that the next step was to brief his fellow Joint Chiefs. At this point, he still assumed that his proposal would be a personal recommendation only, although he hoped for their endorsement.[10]

On 5 February 1983 the Joint Chiefs met for their forty-third session devoted to strategic issues.[11] It was less than a week before the meeting with the president. The CNO gave his briefing as a sort of dry run before presenting it to the president.[12] Unexpectedly, the Joint Chiefs, with air force General Charles Gabriel in the lead, unanimously adopted his approach as their position. They agreed that Chairman Vessey would give the briefing. Significantly, there was to be no fallback position if the secretary of defense did not concur; their views would, as the law provided, be presented with or without his agreement. The final drafting of the Joint Chiefs' brief was now given to Captain Stewart, with Captain Brooks assisting.

It is important to remember that, although this endorsement of a projected defense was a bold step out of the strategic morass, it was not the centerpiece of the briefing. It was only a part of a comprehensive brief on all aspects of the strategic dilemma. The chiefs were not saying they were ready to make defense the primary strategic response, let alone fund it on any substantial scale.

On 11 February 1983 they, the secretary of defense, and the deputy to the national security advisor met with the president from 1200 to 1330. The ten-page paper from which General Vessey gave his oral briefing followed the general lines of Captain Brooks' original point paper. It began with the Joint Chiefs' statement of support for the Triad and for Peacekeeper (MX) development, plus a continuing research and development effort "on a wide range of alternatives, with more focus on Small Land Mobiles and BMD . . . to facilitate future deployment options" if the Soviets failed to respond to U.S. arms control initiatives. The chiefs made the point, too, that lately the strategic problem had focused far too much on the issue of basing modes and that they would have to "find a better way to present the case in a larger context."

The last section of the briefing paper pointed out the advantages of forward strategic defense:

> —We move the battle from our shores and skies. Thus, we are kept from the dangerous extremes of (a) threatening a preemptive strike, or (b) passively absorbing a Soviet first strike—we have found the middle ground.
> —More moral and therefore far more palatable to the American people. . . .

The oral briefing, like the written draft, said the aim of such a defense was to "protect the American people, not just avenge them."[13] On hearing this, President Reagan said, "Don't lose those words!" They would eventually turn up in his SDI speech.

There was little treatment of strategic defense in the prepared briefing. It was largely devoted to offensive forces. But after explaining the difficulty of keeping up with the Soviet ICBM program, the chiefs, according to Robert McFarlane, an ex-marine who was then deputy national security advisor, concluded:

> "And therefore, Mr. President, we think it appropriate that you begin to consider the applications of defensive technologies." One line in the whole briefing. And I said, "Wait a minute. Are you saying that you think the technology is at hand to possibly prevent ballistic missiles from reaching the United States?" And they said, "Yes,

that's what we mean." And I said, "Stop! Mr. President, do you understand how important a statement that is?"

The President said, "Do you really believe the technology has changed enough to make it possible that we could solve this problem?"

The Chiefs hadn't intended to stress it a lot. They were going to make a mild statement of interest without any implication of major resource investments at the time. But, because of the strategic consequences I believed could flow from it, I interrupted to assure that the President recorded his enthusiasm for the idea with the Chiefs. "This is profoundly important. If it is feasible, we ought to get behind it and get serious about it," and Jim [Watkins] said, "Yes, I believe we should. . . ." The others were less enthusiastic although supportive. The President asked each one in turn and each one in turn said, "Yes, I support a larger effort." . . . The President said, "Let's go back and look at this and get ready to push it hard."[14]

Just how hard (and how quickly) was to surprise almost everyone.

PREPARING THE SDI SPEECH

As with any turning point in national policy, there are always many influential individuals behind it. Describing the sequence by which Admiral Watkins and his chief advisors came to think as they did, or how the Joint Chiefs embraced the defensive option, is only one part of a complex story. We can be sure that SDI had many fathers, that many minds in the government were reacting to the same frustration about strategy in much the same way. Robert McFarlane, one of them, gives much credit to Watkins' role:

The most important contribution he has made in the last four years does deal with SDI. If you've read his material, you're familiar with his motives; but people haven't absorbed how historic a step this is, that it wasn't done frivolously at all, that it was born of intellectual and very rigorous concern on Jim's part about the future of offensive deterrence that he believed strongly was becoming much less stable. When he looked at the Soviet offensive panoply of arms, especially the MIRVed mobile systems, he concluded it was a problem we simply couldn't solve in the traditional offensive offset context. Even though the Navy would have gotten the lion's share of that investment, in Trident submarines. Instead, he said, let's get off this madness of building offensive weapons and see if we can't find a better way. But [Watkins' approach] was both military and moral.[15]

McFarlane himself, along with his assistant and successor, Vice Admiral John Poindexter, played a major role in pushing SDI. He and Poindexter both began advocating the notion of a defense fairly strongly with President Reagan in late 1982. Even before his election, Reagan had heard such views from men like Dr. Teller, but by late 1982 both McFarlane and Poindexter had become convinced that a strategy confined to offense was irreversibly unstable. McFarlane had already tasked his national security staff to work on the defense concept, especially to look at its hardware aspects. He was reassured by their conclusions that the idea of a defense was worth pursuing.

Colonel Gil Rye of the air force became a member of the National Security Council staff in April 1982, specializing in space. He was tasked to create a Reagan space policy, and by July 1982 his work had resulted in National Security Study Directive 42. By December a space strategy was proposed that included some references to space defense. Rye had discussed these ideas with National Security Advisor William P. Clark, Admiral Poindexter, and McFarlane, but had no idea General Vessey and the Joint Chiefs would make the point about strategic defense in their briefing. Rye knew, though, of President Reagan's long-term interest in the problem. He told of Reagan's visit to the Cheyenne Mountain air defense facility when he was still governor of California. After the tour, Reagan turned to the general and asked, "Are you telling me then that we can't defend this country?" When the general told him yes, Reagan was appalled. Never since had he lost interest in the problem or its solution.[16]

In late 1982, McFarlane did not know what the Joint Chiefs' view might be. He was delighted when he found out the direction of Watkins's thinking.

Admiral Poindexter, commenting on the same set of events, indicated that he had known Admiral Watkins had asked his CEP to look at the question. Poindexter, for his part, had asked air force Colonel Richard T. Bovarie, head of the National Security Council defense group, to look at it independently.[17]

> The thing that drove us in this direction was watching this very significant Soviet buildup and the number of new systems they were testing or getting ready to test, and the difficulty we were having with the Congress in terms of getting money for the MX and the ineffectiveness of arms control agreements up to that point—the fact that they were simply controlling increases rather than forcing reductions.
>
> In hindsight, it was pretty clear to all of us that we needed a new solution of the problem. We also at that point did not have the Soviets at the negotiating table and so the idea came to at least the three of us [Watkins, McFarlane, and Poindexter] independently, about the same time.
>
> As I recall, the JCS was doing a review of strategic systems and we were unaware over here that they were looking at this. But in this process of reviewing systems, Jim [Watkins] began to see that this was not going to work, and we could see it over here more from a

political point of view that we weren't going to be able to get MX in any sort of quantities that could compete with the Soviet quantities. So we were all looking for some other way. My staff over here came back to me and said, "Strategic defense looks interesting."

We have a regular program of the President's meeting with the Chiefs about once a quarter. In February of '83 we had a meeting with the Chiefs scheduled. At the time, [army General] Paul Gorman was the assistant to the chairman and, in talking with Bud [McFar-lane] about the agenda for the meeting, Paul revealed that the Chiefs had been thinking about strategic systems and that Jim had appar-ently surfaced with the Chiefs his arguments about strategic defense.

Now, as a corporate body, I think [the Chiefs] didn't realize [at first] how fast we intended to move once they were generally in favor of that. The President had a speech he had to give in March 1983, so what Bud and I decided to do, with Bill Clark's agreement, was to develop a part to go in the speech on what later became the SDI. We didn't tell anyone else [initially] what we were doing. The Chiefs didn't know. Defense didn't know. State didn't know. After we developed the insert, we talked to the President about it. And he agreed; that's what he wanted to do.[18]

The decision to go ahead was made on 19 March. Now began a race against time. Although, as Poindexter indicated, only a small working group dealt with the actual wording, specific individuals had been tapped for consultation—in the navy, the CNO and Captain Stewart.[19] When the Joint Chiefs first looked at the draft they were critical, but as the speech improved they changed their position. The tight deadline and their busy schedules made review a difficult process.[20] The CNO met with General Vessey in the latter's aircraft at Andrews Air Force Base on 20 March for the de facto final approval of the Joint Chiefs.

About a day before the president's speech the insert was sent around to those who had no idea it was coming. Many negative comments came back. But, said Poindexter, "the Chiefs agreed, and [Defense Secretary] Weinberger agreed, although both their bureaucra-cies were battling against it." Poindexter gave Weinberger credit for resisting pressure from some of his principal civilian subordinates. The State Department "was concerned about the impact on the allies, that it would appear as a Fortress America concept, and delink Europe from the United States."[21]

In Poindexter's view, the close-hold approach was unavoidable if the concept was to avoid the "inevitable battering it would have gotten from the bureaucracy, because it was a revolutionary idea." He is probably right in thinking that there would have been a lengthy delay before a consensus emerged. Indeed, the speech on 23 March inaugurated a period of pronounced confusion in official circles. Yet delaying the speech to achieve agreement might well have postponed the initiative indefinitely.

CONTROVERSY

In his speech the president would speak of protecting the American people, not just avenging them. What did this mean? That a foolproof defensive umbrella would be raised over the American people? Or that the defense would create sufficient uncertainty about the utility of a first strike that Soviet leaders would decide against one?

From the outset, concern over SDI's implications was heard abroad at such conferences as that held by the International Institute for Strategic Studies.[22] Well-known European analysts wrote pointed analyses for influential newspapers. Criticism was divided. Some saw SDI as a device to shield the United States and force Europe to serve as the nuclear battlefield. Others saw it as the technical means by which the United States would draw back into a new neutrality and isolationism, leaving Europe to its fate. As we have seen from the record, neither of these criticisms has merit.

At home, in the scientific community, opinion was likewise divided. People of reputation argued both sides, but the majority was opposed to SDI on the grounds that it would never be technically feasible. Many commentators opposed a blank-check approach, "throwing money down the rathole." This criticism ignored the most important point about SDI, that the amount spent only had to be sufficient to maintain momentum. The value of SDI was not achieving the ultimate goal so much as striving for it, for at no stage during development could the Soviets be sure about the utility of a first strike. Neither did the service chiefs want to pour vast sums into the program; they were not looking for something that would interfere financially with their individual service programs.

The media's derision of SDI was a substantial political and intellectual burden for those who had glimpsed a way out of the strategic dilemma and who had dared to propose it. The rather frivolous media label for SDI, Star Wars, grossly libeled a serious issue. The term tended to deflect attention from the complex moral, political, technical, and bureaucratic problems that SDI actually represented. This was especially true for the moral dimension, which had played a prime role in first stimulating thinking beyond the eye-for-an-eye approach in which millions of Soviet corpses would pay for millions of American corpses.

Paul H. Nitze, in an essay prepared for delivery to the Institute for Theology and Peace in Bonn on 6 December 1985, wrote of SDI that the principal impetus behind it was moral. Deterrence through counterstrike was morally acceptable if there was no other way to deter. But if deterrence came primarily through denial to the potential aggressor of the prospect of military success, then greater reliance on defense was the preferable and moral course.[23]

STAFFING AND DEFENDING THE SDI CONCEPT

The new defense program was formalized by National Security Decision Directive 85 on 25 March 1983. National Security Study Directive 6-83, which followed on 18 April, set up studies of the program's technical and policy implications.[24] One of the two policy studies, this one conducted outside the government, looked at near-term intermediate options that came to be perceived as focused on ICBM silo defense. This encouraged critics, who considered SDI a thinly disguised reversal of the 1972 decision not to defend ICBMs. Meanwhile, the CNO became concerned that the lack of a specific organization to manage SDI could easily lead to precoccupation with the technical side plus pressures for near-term deployments to protect silos. He and the other Joint Chiefs were also worried that the program might become a "crash effort" that would drain funds from needed force improvements. When the panel doing the technical study developed two approaches, one limited by funding and the other limited only by technology, the secretary of defense recommended the second approach.

There was a further question of whether SDI should continue to be managed within the Department of Defense. Secretary Weinberger was clearly in favor of this, as he told a meeting of the Armed Forces Policy Council in November 1983. In March 1984 Weinberger appointed air force Lieutenant General James Abrahamson as program manager. An interim charter for the SDI organization (SDIO) was established, and SDIO was designated a defense agency on 23 July.

These changes settled the most important bureaucratic and organizational problems. But, because of the haste with which the program had been announced, it was still not developed enough for a presidential policy pronouncement. Those who had not been consulted at all or consulted late were left free to criticize the program. What was lacking was a well staffed policy paper that would convince the bureaucracy. It had to be simple enough to be understood by the public but not so simple as to invite ridicule.

Admiral Watkins, aware of the gap, made both a staff effort and a public effort to help. Within the navy he had a white paper prepared by Captain Linton Brooks, with inputs from Commodore Roger Bacon, director of the navy's strategic and theater nuclear warfare division,

Captain Mike Hughes, executive director of CEP, and Mr. Fred Hoffman of CEP. He used it as the basis for many of his speeches at the time, which were widely reprinted and distributed to the entire navy flag community.[25]

The white paper was eighteen pages long. It argued that SDI in no way impeded arms control. "Strategic defenses may, in fact, facilitate reaching this goal," it noted. If the Soviets "are unable to kill the Strategic Defense Initiative through propaganda and political pressure, strategic defenses provide an additional incentive for them to negotiate seriously. . . . Much of the controversy over [SDI] results from a confusion of means and ends a misunderstanding of what the United States is attempting to do." Deterrence and arms control were only tools—the means to achieve and maintain security and freedom. They were not ends in themselves. Whatever means achieved those proper ends were valid subjects of inquiry.[26]

The battle in the public forum was heating up. In the face of opposition Watkins felt an early public commitment on his part was required, and only three weeks after the president's speech he delivered a speech to the *Intrepid* museum luncheon in New York. He recounted how the United States had "imposed—unilaterally on ourselves—a freeze in nuclear forces" to which replacing Minuteman I, deploying Poseidon, and producing Trident I were solitary exceptions, while the Soviet Union had moved ahead with the development of eight new nuclear missile systems. The Triad was slipping behind Soviet capabilities. It was this consideration that had led the Joint Chiefs to look at the whole range of responses, including a defense. The president's decision in favor of SDI required "two transitional steps," one mindset, the other technology. "Those who assume the concept will rely on a specific system—and then criticize that system on the grounds that it will not provide perfect defense—have missed the vision and the focus which the President and his military advisors share." Watkins recalled other instances of misguided pessimism: "President Eisenhower was advised that ICBMs were an impossibility less than twenty years before they were capable of delivering weapons over 6,000 miles to within a few hundred feet of their target." If the United States set its mind to it, much was possible; most likely the defense system would one day "incorporate several systems, using different technologies to provide various layers . . . a defense in depth if you will."[27]

A speech given by Watkins in January 1985 was inserted in the *Congressional Record* by Senator Jake Garn of Utah on 29 January. Given originally to the Los Angeles Rotary Club, it is one of Watkins's most eloquent arguments in support of SDI:

. . .our nation has reached a critical crossroads in the nuclear age, with two paths emanating therefrom. One badly worn path leads to continued seeming hopelessness in offensive nuclear arms escalation. The other is fresh and offers new hope of world extrication from the increasingly unpalatable concept of the mutual assured destruction of mankind. . . .

Watkins quoted Weinberger's remark of the month before about "the odd theory that you are safe only if you have no defense whatever." Watkins cited opposition to SDI based on "the false premise that it needs to be perfect. . . ." Even a less than perfect defense, he argued, would critically affect Soviet thinking by denying them "the confidence that they can achieve their goals" by attacking.[28]

Watkins' vigorous defense of SDI brought him letters from influential people posing thoughtful questions or informing him of their own views. In a letter to Colin Gray on 18 May 1984, the CNO thanked him for a copy of Gray's Senate testimony on SDI, agreeing with the thrust of his argument but differing on SDI's implications for terminal defenses for ICBMs: "Until we are certain that point defenses are, in fact, a way-station to the defensive shield . . . we must be skeptical about embracing such near-term defensive steps. The danger is that by focusing on what we know how to do, rather than what we want to do, we will divert resources from the broad, sweeping exploration of new concepts. . . ." Watkins added that if SDI "comes to be seen as simply a repackaging of historic programs for defending land-based systems, we will be unable to sustain the public and Congressional consensus necessary for such a long-range program."[29]

The Los Angeles speech brought more letters. In response to one from Richard M. Blau, a lawyer in Tampa, Watkins claimed that SDI would extend protection to American allies and that arguments to the contrary were typically made by those who assumed SDI would depend on only one type of system, which, they said, could not do the job. "It is important," wrote Watkins, "to realize that we have not yet reached any decision with regard to the architecture of a deployed defensive system. The President has issued a technology and policy challenge, he has not proposed or even requested a system design. We are now engaged in the basic research needed to determine what form any future system might assume." The lengthy letter closed by noting Blau's use at several points of the phrase "defensive nuclear posture." Watkins wanted to make it clear that "the thrust of our research is toward non-nuclear capabilities." There were both technical and policy reasons for that emphasis.[30]

The continuing barrage of questions had ultimately to be answered by the administration. In January 1985 the White House finally issued a pamphlet. For the first time it provided an official, top-level, coherent, and compact rationale for SDI.[31] Using parts of the OPNAV white paper, it focused on the deterrent benefits of this new approach of using defense as a strategic tool to influence Soviet thinking. As we have shown, this point Watkins considered a prime virtue, if not *the* prime virtue of the whole SDI approach.

Once the pamphlet was in print, the president used its themes in public speeches. In a 29 March 1985 speech at the National Space Club, he emphasized the significant point that SDI "is not, and should never be misconstrued as just another [tactical] method of protecting missile silos, [but is] a new kind of deterrence; not just an addition to our offensive forces, but . . . a shield that could prevent nuclear weapons from reaching their targets" and therefore discourage attack in the first place.[32] SDI was a strategic weapon, the president was saying, because it changed the way men thought about war.

This speech by the president, together with the pamphlet, pointed SDI policy in a sound direction, which had the potential of maintaining sufficient public support. In his last months in office, Admiral Watkins made one further effort to develop what he called "a decision roadmap for SDI" that "should focus on technology demonstrations, not interim deployment options." This correctly reflected Watkins concern that there would be increasing pressure to use what was already known about defensive systems and deploy it for quick but fleeting advantage. He wanted instead to maintain public interest and support by carefully spaced demonstrations.

It is very much to the credit of James D. Watkins and his staff, and to the credit of the Joint Chiefs, that they were able to advance a concept that offered hope of an eventual way out of the nuclear morass. While we do not know the motivation behind Soviet actions, it seems reasonable to assume that Mikhail Gorbachev's sweeping arms control proposals in 1987 were made possible at least in part by denying the Soviets the "easy" strategic solution of piling up additional nuclear weapon systems.

SDI, as Watkins many times pointed out, has to survive all kinds of bureaucratic hazards, especially the temptation to deploy existing systems to show that money was well spent. The strategic value of SDI is as much in the research, which introduces basic uncertainty into Soviet war planning, as it is in the results. What, the Soviets must ask, would happen if they launched an attack? It is here that SDI represents an intellectual breakthrough. That recognition of SDI has come slowly can be attributed to decades of American thought devoted to the one-fettered-goat-each approach. In intellectual terms what SDI does is reassess stability, which increases, not with certainty, but with uncertainty.

Chapter 15

CHANGING THE WATCH

The thirtieth of June 1986 was a perfect summer day at the Naval Academy in Annapolis. At the foot of the steps leading to Bancroft Hall, an audience sat expectantly. They were awaiting the traditional ceremony that would mark the navy's transition to new leadership. At exactly 1100 the secretary of defense, the secretary of the navy, the outgoing CNO, and his incoming successor made their appearance. It was time for the changing of the watch. At the end of the ceremony Admiral James D. Watkins, having turned over responsibility to Admiral Carlisle A. H. Trost, read his retirement orders.

And so the uniformed leader of the navy was replaced. The ceremony did not imply a drastic change of course. Such ceremonies rarely do. As one interviewee said in reply to a question about whether Admiral Trost was likely to introduce radical innovation, "Why, he invented the 600-ship Navy we've built. He was the Navy programmer for four years!" The reason is not the navy's supposed conservatism or its inability to shake off bureaucratic shackles. It has to do with the manner in which transition is achieved. Like any military organization, the navy resembles an escalator. At the top, near the stepping-off point, stands the CNO and close behind him his successor, who has an important secondary job as CINCPACFLT or VCNO. A little lower are the barons of OPNAV, the program planner, the warfare czar, the chief of naval personnel. Below them come the captains, including executive assistants, staff for those further up. Farther down are the commanders waiting for promotion. As the escalator cranks forward, those at the bottom rise to the top and those who get off stand by to offer them advice and encouragement. The team is always changing, but at any one time the greater part of it is constant. Thus continuity is ensured while talent is steadily promoted.

THE CHANGE OF COMMAND: NEW DEPARTURES?

That day in late June was the climax of a process of briefing and debriefing as the two admirals and their staffs prepared the transition. Their words during this period of transition were conventional. But, as always at such times, everyone was listening and watching to detect nuances indicating even small course changes.

One of the most interesting of the transition activities was a CEP meeting jointly attended by Watkins and Trost on 18 June 1986. A closed meeting, it provided an opportunity for more than formal rhetoric.[1] Watkins spoke with pride of the renaissance period the navy had entered in the previous few years, of how the Naval War College, parts of CNA, and CEP had helped produce the marked intellectual vigor of navy analysis. He called CEP the "real, long-range planners of the Navy" but cautioned that "a long-range plan written down is a loser"; it needed constant revision.

He cautioned against the public's renewed tendency "to isolate defense as the villain" in the continued battle of the budget, a tendency "that seems to come in five-year cycles." He noted the "vilification of strategy in the press" and added that, even so, "there are a finite number of scenarios you'd better *really* address."

Looking back on his years as CNO, he expressed satisfaction over his role as a Joint Chief, CEP's analysis having given him considerable help in taking a vigorous role on strategic issues. It had been necessary to think ahead, particularly since the Soviets, with their "annual encroachments," were not relaxing their pace of competition against U.S. forces. He mentioned SDI with particular pride. "It was the highlight of my four years—eight of you telling me where I had to round off corners. It was very vital to me at a critical time."

Admiral Trost, in his turn, said his challenge would be to reduce "the amount of downslope until we hit the next cycle." Long-range planning was "not laying out calenders" but setting directions.

Those directions became clear after the change of command, as CNO Trost delivered speeches and flag officers' news grams were sent out.

TESTING THE WATERS

It would not be long before hard choices would have to be made. Among the hardest and least obvious was how many navy personnel to "spend" on education. Ships had to be manned now; study could be postponed. And sending officers who were not the best and the brightest to an institution such as the Naval War College would, in the end, be a waste of time and money.

Admiral Trost, before he became CNO, had often visited the Naval War College and lectured there. He had also served as assistant chief of naval personnel for the officers' programs (PERS-4) from December 1974 to January 1976. In that job he had seen how early reductions in officer strength that accompanied the end of the Vietnam War had wrought havoc with the needs of the system. One fallout was that students at the Postgraduate School and the War College were not competitive in their warfare specialties but were sent because they were available. As a result, there were precious few qualified post-command commanders. "In the seventies, when we went to reestablish [the excellence of] those institutions, we lacked the base from which to do it."[2]

Shortages will always beget pressures, certainly in the area of assignments for "head-and-shoulders" personnel. Admiral Trost recognized the truth of Admiral Hayward's observation about the Strategic Studies Group that taking such officers for schooling always encountered the impatient claims of a host of flag officers who thought they needed their services more. As soon as Admiral Trost took office, to no one's surprise, the chief of naval personnel came under severe pressure to reduce the flow of post-commanders to the War College.

Captain Robert B. Watts, deputy to the president of the college, commented that in the Watkins' years the goal of one hundred naval officers in the senior course had been set and was reached one year, with over ninety in each of the other years. Most significantly, the requirement that of these 65 percent had to be post-command commanders was met every year. "If you use the post-command filter," said Watts, "you've integrated all the other filters the Navy uses to define the right people who have the potential for further leadership and responsibilities. And, if they've been through Newport, they'll be better armed to shoulder those responsibilities." He added that, as a litmus test of the strength of a CNO's support for the college, "there is no more simple statistical test [about] the transition [in CNOs] than those pure numbers and percents."[3]

So there was more than usual interest to see how firm Admiral Trost would be on this point. (His active-navy career had taken him to the University of Freiburg as an exchange student for a short time in 1960, but he had never gone as a student to the Postgraduate School, a command and staff school, or a war college.)

In a decision symbolically significant, Trost agreed to be the speaker at Newport for the convocation that begins each academic year.

On 12 August 1986, after barely a month in office as CNO, he delivered his speech to the new class with a quotation from Michelangelo. Asked about the source of his great works, the artist had shrugged and replied, "Ideas are a natural function of the brain, just as breathing is for the lungs." Did that thought apply to Newport? "In our modern world," Trost said, "ideas are explosive . . . and every military operation demands [these] same 'natural functions of the brain.' " To master the inevitable crises of battle and the preparation for it, we must see "things anew each time and analyz[e] them for what they are." Doing that well is the necessary and "vital gift of command. Those who possess it win. . . . In naval warfare, ideas are the ultimate force multiplier." Trost went on to promise two things: that the Naval War College got the material and personnel support it needed and that the ideas it generated would be put to good use.[4]

Soon thereafter Trost issued a specific directive to ensure that the senior course continued to enroll one hundred commanders and captains and that at least 65 percent of them came from operational command tours. The commitment to send fifty-six post-command officers annually through the eight-week integrated warfare course would be sustained, the goal being that post-command officers would immediately capitalize on their education in follow-on shore tours. "Sending our most promising officers to Newport as both students and faculty," Trost concluded, "is critical to maintaining the revitalized strategic thinking and high caliber leadership required to see the Navy into the 21st century."[5]

STEADY AS SHE GOES!

In December 1986 the new CNO issued a news gram reminding the navy flag community of the dangers of speculating out loud about whether the navy would fall short of its 600-ship goal because of fiscal constraints:

> The size and force structure of a 600-ship Navy is key to America's national defense. . . . It will be in place by 1989 . . . and defines the type of Navy we need in today's strategic environment to execute the Maritime Strategy properly . . . and win. . . . [The] 600 ships and the Maritime Strategy go hand in hand [and] no other service has succeeded in effectively articulating such a strong and comprehensive basis for their entire program structure.

Trost went on to say that the costs of this fleet were well understood and did not exceed what the navy should expect Congress to support, and that any wavering on the part of the navy would create confusion and expose it "to the vagaries of yet another bureaucratic review at a time of increasing fiscal pressures. . . ."[6] And, we might add, once Secretary Lehman resigned, without the help of a very adroit politician.

The CNO was keeping programs on course while encouraging ideas and new thinking. The greatest challenge in this respect was, of course, the maritime strategy. Because, as an idea, it was central to everything, it was inevitably much discussed. The Naval Institute *Proceedings,* for example, had at least seven feature articles on this subject alone between February 1986 and June 1987.

Trost, weighing in to the discussion in January 1987, remarked that much of the loose talk about the maritime strategy confused it "with employment of forces, campaign plans, or the local strategy of battle force or theater commanders."[7] U.S. strategy was directed against a Soviet-orchestrated confederation of powers with totalitarian goals. Although the Soviets did not need a large navy to be secure, they had one, a good one, and it was larger than the U.S. Navy. Moreover, it had improved quickly by stealing U.S. secrets, as the Walker-Whitworth case showed.

The Soviet navy was an increased threat that induced the U.S. Navy to make full use of its assets. And that meant strategy—"not a game plan with the first twenty plays already charted" but a way of looking at the global situation. Trost spoke of the navy's flexibility, its "unique advantage of being able to signal menace without violating sovereignty, and once the need is past, of being able to sail over the horizon without signaling retreat." That was why the navy had been the nation's force of choice in over two hundred crises since World War II.

In the late 1970s, as the concept of the 600-ship navy was developed in response to the navy's mission, the maritime strategy evolved, representing a consensus of professional opinion. Because that strategy was flexible, many critics confused it with a specific employment of forces. But the aim of the strategy was to create doubt in the enemy's mind, not to lay out war plans. Wars were not fought "by automatic, pre-programmed responses under the direction of a video game computer." What the navy actually did in the event of war would depend on how it evaluated the threat. Thus the maritime strategy was the repository of organized thinking about how to utilize U.S. forces to advantage rather than a specific and rigid deployment plan.[8]

Admiral Trost could count on a great deal of momentum coming from the navy's progress in the middle years of the 1980s. What was less certain was the support he would receive from Congress. In October 1986, in an extensive interview he gave to *Sea Power,* many of the problems discussed had that common theme. He called strategic home-porting the navy's number one problem. In the 1960s, with a fleet of almost 1,000 ships, there had had been 65 homeports; now, with 553 ships, there were 34. Almost 50 percent of the active navy was home-ported in Norfolk and San Diego. Congress was beginning to understand this problem. Asked about funding, Trost pointed out how much of the progress made in the previous five years would be destroyed if funding fell beneath a certain level. Congress was considering cutbacks in officer personnel; if it imposed a pro rata cut on all the services of 2 percent, in three years' time the navy would dip below its FY 83 end strength—during which it would increase by 87 ships and more than 20 aircraft squadrons.

Vice Admiral Dudley L. Carlson's testimony to the House on 4 March 1986 indicated that the problem of enlisted strength was becoming more acute.[9] He showed figures for FY 83, 84, 85, and 86 in which the president's budget and congressional authorizations were compared. Although authorized end-strength increased from 560,300 to 581,300, this was 25,300 less than requested and around 90,000 less than had been anticipated by FY 86. Personnel shortages as more ships came on line meant that over 50 percent of navy personnel now spent more than four years at sea for every three years ashore, and eighteen navy ratings were actually spending five years at sea before rotating ashore. Meanwhile, recruiting was meeting numerical goals, but there was some decline in personnel quality from the high years of FY 83 and FY 84. The delayed-entry pool was shrinking. And the population size for young men was shrinking.

One year later, on 4 March 1987, Vice Admiral Carlson's testimony was more disquieting. His statement to the defense subcommittee of the House Appropriations Committee showed the continuing gap between budget requests and the authorized end-strength growth. In FY 83, it was 8,900; in FY 84, 7,400; FY 85, 4,000; FY 86, 5,000; and FY 87, 5,700.[10] These shortfalls affected fleet readiness and shrank the cadre of experienced petty officers. Between FY 83 and FY 86, the average years of service for electronics warfare technicians fell from 10.2 to 9.5.[11] For the third straight year the delayed-entry pool had also declined.

Admiral Trost, in an interview in March 1987, indicated that, although fleet manning had been maintained, the shore establishment "in many cases [was] down to about 75 percent of required manning. This means that fewer people are doing more and more work."[12] When Admiral Trost gave that interview, the Reagan administration defense budget proposal projected a 3 percent annual growth. One year later, the revised plan projected 2 percent. Although between 1981 and 1985 defense spending increased in all the major categories, beginning with 1986, some areas showed increases and others decreases. After that, except for modest personnel increases, all areas showed downward movement.[13] The question was, how far would the down cycle go this time? Would the navy be faced again with the problems of the 1970s?

SECRETARY LEHMAN DEPARTS

John Lehman, as we have seen in these pages, was not an ordinary secretary of the navy. A younger man than most, who held office longer than most, he had the energy (some say, the brashness) to change many traditional navy ways. He was the first secretary within recent memory to be an active, drilling reservist; that experience as well as administration policy made him a strong advocate of the total-force approach. He insisted that reservists must have proper (equivalent) equipment and training to discharge their duties.

In introducing modern business techniques into the navy procurement process, he made defense dollars stretch further while convincing Congress that his program for an expanding navy made sense. There is little question that Lehman's contribution to the achievement of six hundred ships, especially costly units such as large carriers, was critical.

Even in his role as publicist for the navy he attracted consistent media attention. Typical was a *New York Times Magazine* article of 15 December 1985, "The Navy's Brash Leader." In it Bill Keller wrote, "For five years, John Lehman has been the Navy's chief strategist, salesman, personnel manager and purchasing agent. To the annoyance of some senior Pentagon officials, he sometimes seems to be an unguided torpedo . . . enormously self-assured, relentlessly competitive and politically adept. . . ."[14] Norman Friedman was quoted to the effect that "Lehman has given the Navy a rationale . . . but I worry that when he goes, it all falls apart." It is not really correct to attribute the rationale to Lehman, although he has certainly been the articulate spokesman for the rationale; the question is whether Lehman's organizational changes, which concentrated more power directly in the secretary's office, will prove fruitful in the hands of Lehman's successors, not all of whom will share his restless energy. Former Secretary of the Navy Paul H. Nitze raised this issue in 1989. Commenting on the abolition of the Navy Material Command, he wrote, "I believe his decision was ill-advised and will be reversed in time."[15]

On 10 April 1987, some nine months into Admiral Trost's tenure as CNO, John Lehman resigned. His departure marks a convenient place for this book to end.

RETROSPECT

Five distinct themes emerge from the material in this book. One is that the navy since the end of World War II has experienced varied support for its programs. In fact, this has been the case throughout American history. Nor are the intense arguments over what kind of navy to have and what kind of strategy to employ new. (President Thomas Jefferson wanted a gunboat navy scattered along the coast for local defense.) The navy recognizes that the United States is flanked by two oceans, that American defense is made more feasible by supporting allied nations across those seas against continental threats, and that a strong U.S. Navy is indispensable for that purpose; the American people do not always agree. The fight for an adequate navy for the United States has to be refought with every generation.

The attitude of the American people and therefore of the Congress toward U.S. defense needs is cyclical, and not always logical. Admiral Tom Hayward saw clearly at its end that during the Vietnam War a new and formidable challenge to American seapower had risen in the form of a Soviet blue-water navy. This was at a time when the U.S. Navy had used up resources to maintain a rigorous operations tempo at the cost of proper maintenance. And as the budgets shrank with postwar disillusionment, overused equipment could not be replaced. The spare parts were not there, petty officers left in droves.

What had contributed to a situation properly labeled desperate—in which Admiral Hayward as CNO had to invent a new readiness category, "unsafe to steam"—was the navy's own eagerness to do the job asked of it. It is unlikely that the navy will abandon this attitude in the years ahead or that it will not from time to time be overcommitted. That does not mean it will enjoy a sustained level of financial support. History in this sense can be expected to repeat itself.

A review of the CNO posture statements to Congress for FYs 88–91 indicates that this has already been happening. The navy requested (in total obligational authority) $92.5 billion for FY 88, compared with $87.6 billion for FY 89, $89.1 billion for FY 90 , and $93.8 billion for FY 91. Requested aircraft procurement in the FY 90–91 years is 140 airplanes the first year, 193 the second. As Admiral Trost told Congress in the FY 90–91 posture statement, "we are poised today at the top of a roller coaster we have ridden before. . . ."[16] The FY 89 statement spoke of negative growth for three of the previous five years. After a certain point negative growth means stagnation, and stagnation is the forerunner of decline.

The second theme emerging from these chapters is more within the navy's control: its intellectual resources. For it is clear that its use of such resources has by choice vacillated between efficient and inefficient. There are some valid excuses for failures to send enough talented officers to professional educational institutions like the Naval War College, but there can be little excuse for the neglect and misuse of gaming for so many years. It took a long time to right this situation. It would be unpardonable to allow it to degenerate again.

A third theme is the consistency with which the navy has fought for its major programs. The 600-ship navy, as we have shown, was not the idea of a few people in a study or two. Rather, it was the result arrived at by many studies by many people. What varies are opinions about how to distribute platforms among ship types, but the disagreement is minor, usually accounted for by Soviet actions and U.S. reactions. The navy, for example, has never strayed far from the concept of task forces or battle groups centered around large-deck carriers, despite much discussion outside the navy.

The need for a 600-ship navy is based essentially on what it takes to deploy a commanding presence on the seas that flank the North American continent. Geopolitical features, being relatively constant, guide analyses to preferences for large ships capable of extended deployment. Since U.S. ships are expected to be deployed forward, they must be large enough to carry the oil and the munitions and the equipment and the crew to remain at maximum efficiency.

A fourth theme is the cohesive core of the professional U.S. Navy, both enlisted and officer. The monopoly once enjoyed by Annapolis on candidates for flag rank has long since disappeared. But it is still true that for the highest ranks academy graduates predominate.[17] A visit to the Naval Academy museum will illustrate the point. There on display are pictures of graduates presently holding the navy's key three-star and four-star billets.

This group of officers is small—too small, only twenty-nine or thirty active three-star line and seven or eight four-star officers.[18] It is a close-knit group united by strong traditions, most of its members having associated with one other since academy days. They work to suppress the centrifugal forces within the navy—the separate surface, aviation, and submarine communities—and to groom younger talent for top navy posts.

There is an important related point. The outsider thinks of successive CNO regimes as new departures. He sees a Zumwalt as very distinct from a Holloway in style, in emphasis, in personality. To a certain extent that is correct. But offsetting it is something far less obvious. Succession in the navy is not like political succession, where there is one party in power and another waiting in the wings to take over after the next election. What we have, rather, is a group of senior officers who when they take the helm have already been dealing with the same problems at a level not too far below the CNO's. What shapes their different approaches is rarely the wish to see an abrupt change of direction. Rather they encounter changing conditions when confronting the same problems, and this permits certain changes in emphasis.

There was no substantial difference, for example, in what Admirals Holloway, Hayward, and Watkins wanted: a 600-ship navy, improved readiness, an adequate supply of spare parts, and proper compensation. What varied was their opportunities.

It is notable that a concept like the maritime strategy can begin in one regime and be "massaged" in subsequent regimes until it emerges as a significant response to U.S. strategic problems.

Not all is continuity, however. Naval historians have always emphasized the significant role played by individual personalities. Which is our fifth theme.

Another whole book could be written on the interaction between Hayward and Lehman, Watkins and Lehman, Trost and Lehman. Our primary interest has been in reviewing their programs, which has been made possible by access to both the people and the documents. On the personal level it is clear that all three CNOs thought Lehman played personal favorites, and that the professional judgments of an officer's uniformed seniors were taken less seriously than the secretary's own impressions—a problem not new in kind, although perhaps more intense this time. What is more important than personality is a secretary and a CNO's decision to get along so that the navy's business can prosper. Because the fact is that nothing of significance can be achieved unless these two officials work effectively together, not allowing the natural frictions between civilian and uniformed perspectives to intrude on a common view of what benefits the navy and the nation.

The fact that between 1982 and 1986 two remarkably talented men were simultaneously in office, one as CNO, the other as secretary of the navy, helps explain why the navy prospered. There were many outside influences that made the way easier, such as President Reagan's determination to restore a credible U.S. defense posture, the continuity provided by a sensible, effective, two-term secretary of defense, and congressional provision of sufficient funds to implement the navy program. But the navy was fortunate that James Watkins and John Lehman shared the sense of purpose, tenacity of mind, and vision that enabled the navy to forge ahead when the opportunity arose to reap the rewards of patient preparation.

Every tale and every book must be told from some point of view; this one has been told from that of the blue suiters. And with the emphasis being the years 1982–87, these pages have centered on the tenure of James D. Watkins. It is therefore appropriate to conclude with a few words on Watkins and his approach.

He said, in an interview, that the man at the top has to keep in the back of his mind the possibility that those under him are not going to carry out his orders his way. They hear what they want to hear, not what their leader says. On a ship, the CO can see from the repeaters on the wings of the bridge what happens when he gives an order. But "in a bureaucracy, the repeater is in the back of your head." If you forget to check it, though your management chart in Washington shows that everything is fine, out in the fleet you will find that things are a mess.[19]

For Admiral Trost's successors as CNO, it is advice that is not likely to become dated.

APPENDICES

APPENDICES

Appendix A

PRINCIPAL NATIONAL SECURITY OFFICIALS

	President	Secretary of Defense	Secretary of the Navy	CNO
1961	Kennedy	McNamara	Connally	Burke
				Anderson
1962	Kennedy	McNamara	Korth	Anderson
1963	Kennedy	McNamara	Korth	Anderson
	Johnson		Nitze	McDonald
1964	Johnson	McNamara	Nitze	McDonald
1965	Johnson	McNamara	Nitze	McDonald
1966	Johnson	McNamara	Nitze	McDonald
1967	Johnson	McNamara	Nitze	McDonald
			Ignatius	Moorer
1968	Johnson	McNamara	Ignatius	Moorer
		Clifford		
1969	Nixon	Laird	Chaffee	Moorer
1970	Nixon	Laird	Chaffee	Moorer
				Zumwalt
1971	Nixon	Laird	Chaffee	Zumwalt
1972	Nixon	Laird	Chaffee	Zumwalt
			Warner	
1973	Nixon	Laird	Warner	Zumwalt
		Richardson		
		Schlesinger		
1974	Nixon	Schlesinger	Warner	Zumwalt
	Ford		Middendorf	Holloway

Note: Overlaps of tenure not noted.

	President	Secretary of Defense	Secretary of the Navy	CNO
1975	Ford	Schlesinger Rumsfield	Middendorf	Holloway
1976	Ford	Rumsfield	Middendorf	Holloway
1977	Carter	Brown	Claytor	Holloway
1978	Carter	Brown	Claytor	Holloway Hayward
1979	Carter	Brown	Claytor Hidalgo	Hayward
1980	Carter	Brown	Hidalgo	Hayward
1981	Reagan	Weinberger	Lehman	Hayward
1982	Reagan	Weinberger	Lehman	Hayward Watkins
1983	Reagan	Weinberger	Lehman	Watkins
1984	Reagan	Weinberger	Lehman	Watkins
1985	Reagan	Weinberger	Lehman	Watkins
1986	Reagan	Weinberger	Lehman	Watkins Trost
1987	Reagan	Weinberger Carlucci	Lehman Webb	Trost
1988	Reagan	Carlucci	Webb	Trost

Appendix B

A TYPICAL DAILY CNO SCHEDULE

Monday, 7 October 1985

0715	Arrived
0733–0807	DMC; w/no deputy
0830–0850	Operational Intelligence - NCC [National Command Center]
0855–0931	AFPC - 3E912
0944–0953	Captain Dvornik
1034–1136	*Time* interview w/Bruce Von Voorst/OOP
1140–1254	MCPON advisory panel reporting out - CNO's conference room
1244–1358	Lunch w/secretary of the navy/Admiral Moorer - small dining room
1402–1530	CEP task force on personal excellence and national security - CNOCR
1530–1538	Captain Hughes
1545–1719	Navy manning brief w/Rear Admiral Burkhardt/Rear Admiral Harlow/Commodore Kalleres
1719–1722	Rear Admiral Harlow
1730–1751	Vice Admiral Kirksey
1752–1815	Rear Admiral McNamara
1815–1840	Vice Admiral Jones
1847	Departed

Most of the naval officers on this schedule were part of the OPNAV staff. Vice Admiral Jones headed the important OP-06 office, which handled affairs of the Joint Chiefs as well as matters of strategic and international concern. The CNO's executive panel met from 1402 to 1530. Captain Dvornik, Watkins' public affairs officer, met with the CNO to prepare the way for a *Time* interview. Most of the other officers were the heads of OPNAV's major sections.

Appendix C

OPNAV IN 1942

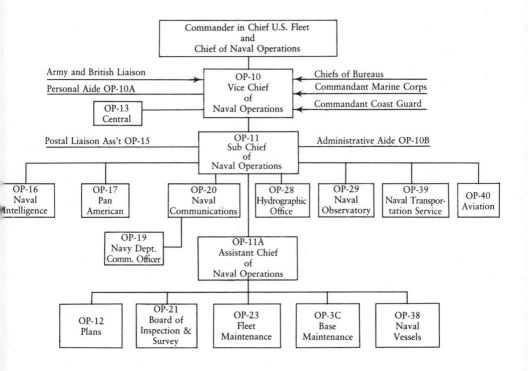

Commander in Chief U.S. Fleet
and
Chief of Naval Operations

Army and British Liaison
Personal Aide OP-10A

OP-10
Vice Chief
of
Naval Operations

Chiefs of Bureaus
Commandant Marine Corps
Commandant Coast Guard

OP-13
Central

Postal Liaison Ass't OP-15

OP-11
Sub Chief
of
Naval Operations

Administrative Aide OP-10B

OP-16
Naval
Intelligence

OP-17
Pan
American

OP-20
Naval
Communications

OP-28
Hydrographic
Office

OP-29
Naval
Observatory

OP-39
Naval Transpor-
tation Service

OP-40
Aviation

OP-19
Navy Dept.
Comm. Officer

OP-11A
Assistant Chief
of
Naval Operations

OP-12
Plans

OP-21
Board of
Inspection &
Survey

OP-23
Fleet
Maintenance

OP-3C
Base
Maintenance

OP-38
Naval
Vessels

Appendix D

OPNAV IN 1985

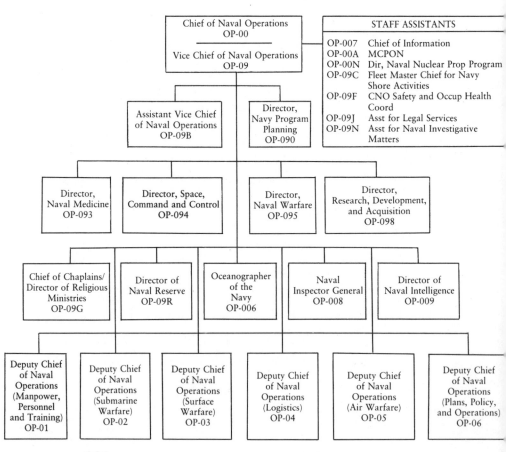

Chief of Naval Operations
OP-00

Vice Chief of Naval Operations
OP-09

STAFF ASSISTANTS	
OP-007	Chief of Information
OP-00A	MCPON
OP-00N	Dir, Naval Nuclear Prop Program
OP-09C	Fleet Master Chief for Navy Shore Activities
OP-09F	CNO Safety and Occup Health Coord
OP-09J	Asst for Legal Services
OP-09N	Asst for Naval Investigative Matters

Assistant Vice Chief
of Naval Operations
OP-09B

Director,
Navy Program
Planning
OP-090

Director,
Naval Medicine
OP-093

Director, Space,
Command and Control
OP-094

Director,
Naval Warfare
OP-095

Director,
Research, Development,
and Acquisition
OP-098

Chief of Chaplains/
Director of Religious
Ministries
OP-09G

Director of
Naval Reserve
OP-09R

Oceanographer
of the
Navy
OP-006

Naval
Inspector General
OP-008

Director of
Naval Intelligence
OP-009

Deputy Chief
of Naval
Operations
(Manpower,
Personnel
and Training)
OP-01

Deputy Chief
of Naval
Operations
(Submarine
Warfare)
OP-02

Deputy Chief
of Naval
Operations
(Surface
Warfare)
OP-03

Deputy Chief
of Naval
Operations
(Logistics)
OP-04

Deputy Chief
of Naval
Operations
(Air Warfare)
OP-05

Deputy Chief
of Naval
Operations
(Plans, Policy,
and Operations)
OP-06

Appendix E

THE NINETY-DAY MESSAGE
7 October 1982

PERSONAL FOR ADMS CROWE, WILLIAMS, FOLEY, MCDONALD; VADM HAYS; INFO
VADM CARROLL; RADMS SHUGART, PALMER, HORNE, DILLINGHAM FROM WATKINS
SUBJ: SPECIAL INTEREST ITEMS (U)

1. EACH OF US ON ASSUMING A POSITION OF NEW RESPONSIBILITY LOOKS FOR AREAS
WHICH MAY REQUIRE SPECIAL ATTENTION TO IMPROVE COMMAND PERFORMANCE.
AFTER LOOKING BACK NINETY DAYS AS CHIEF OF NAVAL OPERATIONS, I HAVE IDENTI-
FIED SEVERAL SUCH AREAS. WHILE THESE IN NO WAY CONSTITUTE AN ALL-INCLUSIVE
LISTING, THEY ARE CLEARLY THOSE WHICH REQUIRE ADDED FOCUS, BUT WITH A NEW
SENSE OF URGENCY, IN ORDER TO ACHIEVE CRITICAL OBJECTIVES. OTHER AREAS I
HAVE HAD AN OPPORTUNITY TO REVIEW (INCLUDING PERSONNEL SUPPORT PRO-
GRAMS) SEEM TO BE WORKING SATISFACTORILY FOR NOW WITHIN THE INSTITUTIONAL
SYSTEM.

2. WARFIGHTING READINESS. OBVIOUSLY WE NEED ADEQUATE NUMBERS OF MODERN-
IZED FORCES TO PREVAIL. BUT BY APPLYING AVAILABLE AND EVER-IMPROVING INTEL-
LIGENCE WE CAN REVISE CURRENT STRATEGIC AND TACTICAL THINKING, INITIATE
TIMELY ACQUISITION OF SELECTED HIGH LEVERAGE TECHNOLOGICAL COUNTERS,
EXPLOIT IDENTIFIED SOVIET WEAKNESSES, AND GAIN FORCE MULTIPLICATION. IN SO
DOING, WE WILL REAP IMMEDIATE DIVIDENDS AT COSTS WE CAN AFFORD, IN CON-
TRAST TO LEANING TOO HEAVILY ON LARGE CAPITAL INVESTMENTS IN HARDWARE—
WHICH WE CANNOT AFFORD. SPECIFIC CONCERNS, NOT NECESSARILY IN PRIORITY
ORDER, ARE:

   A. TECHNOLOGY. FROM OUR SPARSE INVENTORY OF TECHNOLOGICAL
ADVANTAGES OVER THE SOVIETS, WE SHOULD SELECT THOSE THAT CAN PROVIDE
MEASURABLE FORCE MULTIPLICATION (WE HAVE ONLY A THREE-YEAR LEAD IN
EXPLOITING TECHNOLOGY BEFORE SOVIETS USE OUR OPEN LITERATURE TO EMULATE
US). THEN SHARPEN OUR ACQUISITION PROCESS TO INTRODUCE THESE SELECTED
HIGH-PAYOFF-TECHNOLOGY TOOLS INTO FIGHTING FORCES RAPIDLY SO THAT WE
RETAIN OR, IF POSSIBLE, EXTEND THE FEW REMAINING ADVANTAGES WE DO HAVE.

   B. STRATEGY/TACTICS. REVITALIZE NAVAL WAR COLLEGE AS THE CRUCIBLE

FOR STRATEGIC AND TACTICAL THINKING. IN THE NEAR TERM, ROTATE SELECTED POST-COMMAND CO'S THROUGH THE SENIOR COURSE (OR A PORTION OF IT) EN ROUTE TO SUBSEQUENT ASSIGNMENTS. THIS IMMEDIATE INFUSION OF HIGH QUALITY, OPERA-TIONALLY PROVEN PROFESSIONALS INTO THE STUDENT BODY, COUPLED WITH WAR-GAMING EMPHASIS, AN OPERATIONALLY MOTIVATED FACULTY, AND SUPERB RESIDENT CONTINUITY PROVIDED BY OUR NEW STRATEGIC STUDIES GROUP THERE, CAN PROVIDE IMPETUS TO THE LONGER TERM OBJECTIVE OF PROVIDING MANY MORE OPPORTUNI-TIES TO TEST AND HARMONIZE TACTICAL THINKING IN A WIDE VARIETY OF STRATEGIC APPLICATIONS. EMPHASIZE EDUCATING OUR VERY BEST LINE OFFICERS IN UNDER-STANDING THE SOVIET THOUGHT PROCESSES AND WEAKNESSES IN ORDER TO EXPLOIT AND DEFEAT HIM. DETAILS REGARDING IMPLEMENTATION ARE BEING WORKED OUT AND WILL BE PROMULGATED SEPARATELY.

C. OFFICER TRAINING PIPELINE. I FOUND IT OUT OF CONTROL AND EXCESSIVELY INFLATED AT THE EXPERIENCED OFFICER LEVELS. SIGNIFICANT PIPELINE REDUCTIONS RECENTLY DIRECTED WILL NOT ONLY PROVIDE THE SOURCE OF OFFICERS FOR AC-TIONS PLANNED IN PARAGRAPH B ABOVE BUT WILL ALSO ALLOW US TO FILL SOME CURRENTLY GAPPED BILLETS IN KEY FLEET, NAVMAT, JOINT, AND OPNAV ASSIGN-MENTS IN ORDER TO HELP CARRY INCREASED STAFF BURDENS AS WE BRING OUR MODERNIZED NAVY TO THE "600 SHIP" LEVEL.

D. NAVAL RESERVE. WE MUST INTEGRATE RESERVES MUCH MORE INTO OUR WARFIGHTING THINKING. HORIZONTAL INTEGRATION OF NAVAL AIR RESERVE, SIGNIFICANTLY EXPANDED FOUR-BY-TEN PROGRAM AND OTHER SKILL INVENTORY IMPROVEMENTS WHICH CAN PROVIDE DESIRED TRAINED BASE OF RESERVE AUGMEN-TEES, AGGRESSIVE FOLLOW THROUGH ON NEW INITIATIVES IN SURFACE RESERVE PROGRAM, AND ENHANCED AND FULLY INTEGRATED REPAIR CAPABILITY OF RESERVE SIMA'S ALL CONTRIBUTE TO WARFIGHTING READINESS ON M-DAY. ADDITIONALLY, ON MOBILIZATION OR AUGMENTATION BY RESERVES UNDER PRESIDENTIAL CALL-UP AUTHORITY, OUR PEACETIME PERSONNEL READINESS GOAL OF C-2 SHOULD JUMP TO C-1. IT DOES NOT JUMP MUCH AT ALL NOW.

E. INTERSERVICE COOPERATION. SINCE WE WILL FIGHT GLOBAL WARS JOINTLY, WE'D BETTER LEARN TO PLAN AND TRAIN ACCORDINGLY. WE ARE NOT VIEWED AS FULLY COOPERATIVE BY OUTSIDERS TODAY, AND THEY'RE RIGHT. MY RECENT MEMORANDUM OF AGREEMENT WITH CSAF TO IMPROVE TACTICAL AIR SUPPORT OF JOINT OPERATIONS IS ONE STEP IN THE RIGHT DIRECTION; OTHER INITIATIVES ARE UNDERWAY AT CINC AND FLEET LEVELS. JOINT WARGAMING SHOULD BECOME THE NORM. TRANSITION FROM PEACETIME TO WARTIME OPERA-TIONS SHOULD BE POSSIBLE WITHOUT A RIPPLE. IT IS NOT NOW IN TOO MANY CASES. [ONE CLASSIFIED EXAMPLE DELETED]

3. NAVY MANAGEMENT. WE MUST BE SIGNIFICANTLY MORE COST CONSCIOUS AND JUST STEWARDS OF OUR NATIONAL RESOURCES, PARTICULARLY IN HOW WE BUY AND MAINTAIN HARDWARE. THIS IS ESSENTIAL IF WE ARE TO ACHIEVE THE "600 SHIP" NAVY AND ALL IT DEMANDS. IF WE CANNOT FIND IMAGINATIVE WAYS TO REDUCE THE EVER-GROWING COST OF DOING BUSINESS, WE JEOPARDIZE OUR FUTURE FORCE STRUC-TURE. WHILE WE MUST REMAIN A FIRST CLASS NAVY, WE MUST ALSO BE DISCIPLINED ENOUGH NOT TO PRICE OURSELVES OUT OF BUSINESS.

A. COST REDUCTION. I SEE TWO COMPONENTS TO THE PROBLEM OF GETTING OUR COSTS UNDER CONTROL: COST DISCIPLINE AND COST TECHNOLOGY. COST

DISCIPLINE REQUIRES WEAPON SYSTEM CONFIGURATION CONTROL, INDEPENDENT COST ESTIMATING, HARD-NOSED CONTRACTING AND COMPETITION IN A VARIETY OF FORMS, E.G., SECOND SOURCING, CONTRACTING OUT AND UTILIZATION OF MAN-DAY/DOLLAR PRODUCTIVITY COMPETITION AMONG PUBLIC YARDS AND NARFS PERFORMING SIMILAR TYPES OF WORK, ETC. IN THIS REGARD THE RECENTLY SUCCESSFUL EFFORT SPEARHEADED BY SECNAV TO FORCE F/A-18 COSTS FOR FY 82 DOWN TO ACCEPTABLE LIMITS HAS SET AN EXAMPLE FOR ALL OF US TO FOLLOW AS A MATTER OF ROUTINE. SIMILARLY, COST TECHNOLOGY IS A MIND SET WHICH EMPHA-SIZES COST AS A CRITERIA IN DESIGN, OPERATION, AND SPARING A WEAPON SYSTEM. APPLICATION OF COST TECHNOLOGY RESULTS NOT IN MISSILE COMPONENTS DE-SIGNED TO PERFORM AT THE LEADING EDGE OF TECHNOLOGY FOR AN INFINITE LIFE BUT RATHER WITH 100 PERCENT RELIABILITY FOR THE TIME OF FLIGHT, BE IT 30 SECONDS OR 30 MINUTES.

     B. INDIVIDUAL RESPONSIBILITY TO DEFEAT WASTE—HAVING THE RIGHT STUFF IT TAKES TO HOLD OURSELVES ACCOUNTABLE. THE OFTEN-USED PHRASE, "FRAUD, WASTE AND ABUSE" CONNOTES A FELONY IN THE MINDS OF MOST, AND IN THAT CONTEXT A PHRASE APPLICABLE TO ONLY A TINY FRACTION OF THE NAVY. INTENT TO "WASTE" IS CLEARLY NOT THE THRUST OF MY CONCERN. BUT WASTE CAN EASILY AND UNWITTINGLY FLOW FROM BUSINESS MANAGEMENT INEPTNESS, LACK OF A MEASURED AND REALISTIC SENSE OF PROFESSIONAL CYNICISM TO SLICK BROCHUREMANSHIP, LACK OF PERSONAL INVOLVEMENT IN AND COMMITMENT TO CONSERVATION OF RESOURCES, AND THE LIKE. WE NEED TO CONTINUALLY ASK, "HAVE WE REALLY MEASURED OURSELVES AS JUST STEWARDS OF PUBLIC FUNDS?" WHEN A CIVILIAN CONTRACTOR PRESENTS US—THE GOVERNMENT RESOURCE CUSTODIAN—WITH HIS BILL FOR CHARGES WHICH ARE MARKEDLY HIGHER THAN THE LAST ONE, BUT FOR THE SAME PRODUCT OR SERVICE, HOW SENSITIVE ARE WE IN CRITICALLY EXAMINING THE VALIDITY OF HIS BILL AND HIS SO-CALLED "FACT OF LIFE" COST ESCALATION? WE MUST IMBUE OUR MILITARY AND CIVILIAN LEADERS WITH THE QUALITY OF CHARACTER THAT LOOKS UNDER THE RUG AS A MATTER OF PROFESSIONAL CONSCIENCE AND ROUTINE. OUR FIRST INSTINCT SHOULD BE TO REJECT HIS BILL. RECALL HOW WE TOOK THAT APPROACH IN OUR WAR ON DRUGS. SOME SAID WE HAD TO ACCEPT DRUG USAGE AS AN AMERICAN WAY OF LIFE. WE SAID NONSENSE. WE WERE RIGHT. UNWITTING COMPLACENCY TO WASTE IN THE SPECIAL SENSE OUTLINED HERE IS, LIKE DRUG ABUSE, A SOCIETAL PROBLEM WHICH WE CANNOT ACCEPT AS A NATURAL WAY OF LIFE IN THE NAVY. AS IN THE DRUG WAR, WE NEED TO APPLY THE SAME TOUGH, LOOK-UNDER-THE-RUG APPROACH IN OUR ACQUISITION PROCESS, FOLLOW-ON ILS PLANS, AND DAILY OPERATIONAL/ADMINIS-TRATIVE BUSINESS. FOR EXAMPLE, WE CANNOT REMAIN INACTIVE IN THE FACE OF WASTEFUL USE OF GOVERNMENT FUNDS BY PRIME CONTRACTORS, THEIR SUBCON-TRACTORS, OUR OPERATING FORCES OR SUPPORTING SHORE ESTABLISHMENT. WE SHOULD NOT LET OTHERS (E.G. BELTWAY BANDITS OR OTHER CONTRACTORS) MANAGE FOR US THROUGH BENIGN NEGLECT NOR SHOULD WE WAIT FOR AN OUTSIDE AUDIT TEAM OR INSPECTOR GENERAL TO FERRET OUT OUR WEAKNESSES. WE, THE OFFICER CORPS, ARE ACCOUNTABLE UNTO OURSELVES AND OUR SENIOR LEADERSHIP WHEN IT COMES TO OPTIMIZING RETURN OF THE PUBLIC TRUST THROUGH INTOLERANCE OF UNPROFESSIONAL MANAGEMENT OF PUBLIC DOLLARS.

LET'S GET INTO THIS FRAME OF MIND, AND I GUARANTEE THAT THE 600-SHIP NAVY WE ALL SEEK WILL BECOME A REALITY IN THIS DECADE.

4. YOUR THOUGHTS AND ASSISTANCE IN MOVING OUT SMARTLY TO IMPROVE OUR PERFORMANCE IN THE AFOREMENTIONED AREAS WILL BE OF GREAT HELP TO ME. PLEASE WORK THESE PROBLEMS WITH YOUR SUBORDINATES AND READDRESS THIS MESSAGE AS YOU DEEM APPROPRIATE.

5. WARM REGARDS.

NOTES

Where standard sources are utilized in this book, standard citations are given in the notes. Documents and papers are cited by whatever identifying data they carried. That ought, in most cases, to enable the reader to find them once they become available through declassification. Most of these documents and papers are from files of former Chief of Naval Operations James D. Watkins. They were working documents, and only in a very rough sense were they arranged in systematic order. Once a CNO's tour ends, his files are transferred to secure spaces at the Naval Historical Center at the Washington Navy Yard, Washington, D.C. Here they are ultimately sorted and given documentary file numbers that considerably simplify a scholar's task. Such numbers were not available as this book went to press.

All of the tapes are in the same location as the documents. There is a set government procedure for handling, declassifying, and otherwise processing them. Individuals not on active duty when interviewed can, at their discretion, attach specific restrictions to their use.

CHAPTER 1

1. Captain Edward L. Beach, *The United States Navy: 200 Years* (New York: Holt, 1986), 193.

2. Admiral Thomas B. Hayward, "Navy: 3-Dimensional Capability at Sea," *Defense 82* (Washington: GPO, 1982), 13–15, in Colonel William G. Hanne, USA, "A Separatist Case," U.S. Naval Institute *Proceedings* (July 1985): 95.

3. Steven T. Ross, "Chester William Nimitz," in Robert William Love, Jr., ed., *The Chiefs of Naval Operations* (Annapolis, Maryland: Naval Institute Press, 1980), 189 (hereafter cited as Love, *CNOs*).

4. Ibid.

5. Paolo E. Coletta, "Louis Emil Denfeld," in Love, *CNOs*, 194.

6. Ibid., 196. Captain Brown Taylor, in "Controversy in Retrospect," *Proceedings* (July 1962):39–51, stresses that funds were short and jets, needed by both services, required larger carriers.

7. Gerald Kennedy, "William Morrow Fechteler," in Love, *CNOs*, 240.

8. Paul R. Schratz, "Robert Bostwick Carney," in Love, *CNOs*, 246.

9. Ibid., 246–47.

10. Quoted by Schratz, "Robert Carney," in Love, *CNOs*, 247.

11. Ibid. For the whole speech see Robert B. Carney, "The Role of the Navy in Future War," *Naval War College Review* (June 1954).

12. David Alan Rosenberg, "Arleigh Albert Burke," in Love, *CNOs*, 270–71.

13. Ibid., 280.

14. Ibid., 295. For most purposes, the FY or fiscal year can be thought of as one year more than the calendar year.

15. Ibid., 296.

16. Admiral George W. Anderson, USN (Ret.), "As I Recall . . . the Cuban Missile Crisis," *Proceedings* (September 1987): 44. Anderson says that Secretary McNamara came to the Navy Command Center wanting "answers to a lot of highly classified information and there were many people present who were not cleared to hear the answers. So I intervened." Anderson took McNamara aside and told him the story of what was being done. "As we were leaving, McNamara said something like, 'It's all right.' I said, 'Mr. Secretary, you go back to your office, and I'll go to mine and we'll take care of things.' Apparently that got him very provoked. I didn't realize it at the time."

17. House Appropriations Committee, *Hearings on the Fiscal Year 1963 Defense Budget*, 87th Cong., 2d sess., 1962, 66, quoted by Floyd D. Kennedy, Jr., in Love, *CNOs*, 344.

18. Kennedy, in Love, *CNOs*, 344.

19. Ibid.

20. J. Kenneth McDonald, "Thomas Hinman Moorer," in Love, *CNOs*, 359.

21. Ibid., 360.

22. In a debate with the author on the meaning of detente before the New York Militia Association, 1975.

23. U.S. Congress, *Congressional Quarterly*.

24. Norman Friedman, "Elmo Russell Zumwalt, Jr.," in Love, *CNOs*, 369.

25. Elmo R. Zumwalt, Jr., *On Watch: A Memoir* (New York: Quadrangle, 1976), 63.

26. Ibid., 64.

27. The USS *Pueblo*, an electronic surveillance ship patrolling outside North Korean waters, was attacked by North Korean patrol craft on 23 January 1968, boarded, and taken into Wonsan Harbor as a prize.

28. Zumwalt, *On Watch*, 281.

29. Ibid., 338.

30. Taped interview, Admiral Elmo R. Zumwalt, USN (Ret.), Arlington, Virginia, 15 July 1987.

31. Zumwalt, *On Watch*, 167–68.

32. Later, repeated polls of enlisted personnel indicated a clear wish to

return to bell-bottoms. But that was not so in Zumwalt's time. The civilian clothes issue was complicated by limited stowage space aboard ship.

33. Zumwalt, *On Watch*, 172. Direct policy guidance by CNOs is normal enough, but is usually contained in flag officer newsletters.

34. Taped interview, Admiral James D. Watkins, the Pentagon, 24 April 1986.

35. Taped interview, Vice Admiral William H. Rowden, Crystal City, 13 April 1987.

36. Taped interview, Vice Admiral Staser Holcomb, USN (Ret.), San Antonio, Texas, 15 September 1987.

37. Zumwalt tape.

38. Zumwalt, *On Watch*, appendix E, 533.

39. Taped interview, Rear Admiral William A. Cockell, USN (Ret.), President's Office Building, Washington, D.C., 13 July 1987.

40. Speech before the National Naval Officers Association, Philadelphia, 13 July 1985.

41. Taped interview, Captain Ash Roach, USN, JAGC, Naval War College, Newport, Rhode Island, 22 October 1986.

42. Holcomb tape.

43. *New York Times*, 14 February 1976.

44. United Press International, 17 February 1977.

45. Taped interview, former Secretary of the Navy Graham Claytor, Washington, D.C., 20 October 1987.

46. Taped interview, Admiral James L. Holloway III, USN (Ret.), Washington, D.C., 24 April 1986.

CHAPTER 2

1. Department of Defense, *Annual Report, Fiscal Year 1982*.

2. Taped interview, Admiral Elmo R. Zumwalt, USN (Ret.), Arlington, Virginia, 15 July 1987.

3. Admiral James L. Holloway III, "The Aircraft Carrier: An Overview," *Wings of Gold*, special report (summer 1987): 5–7.

4. Taped interview, former Assistant Secretary of Defense Francis West, Monterey, California, 14 August 1987.

5. Taped interview, Vice Admiral John A. Baldwin, Jr., the Pentagon, 21 October 1987.

6. Zumwalt, *On Watch*, 67.

7. Taped interview, Admiral Thomas B. Hayward, USN (Ret.), Honolulu, Hawaii, 20 May 1987.

8. Taped interview, Captain James M. Patton, USN (Ret.), Monterey, California, 14 August 1987.

9. Taped interview, Admiral Robert L. J. Long, USN (Ret.), the Pentagon, 13 July 1987. Long said that "even by the end of the Carter administration it was tacitly understood that the swing strategy was more political than actual."

10. West tape.

11. *Sea Plan 2000*, 1: 8.

12. Ibid., 18–19.

13. Report of the comptroller general of the United States, *How Good Are*

Recent Navy Studies Regarding Future Forces?, 13 February 1980. The document's overall classification is secret; only unclassified sections are quoted.

14. *Sea Plan 2000*, 1: 3.

15. Comptroller general report, 3.

16. West tape.

17. Baldwin tape.

18. Hayward tape.

19. Cockell tape.

20. Taped interview, Rear Admiral Robert C. Austin, Monterey, California, 29 May 1987.

21. Taped interview, Vice Admiral William P. Lawrence, USN (Ret.), Naval Academy, Annapolis, Maryland, 20 September 1986. Admiral Lawrence, a POW from June 1967 to March 1973, served as superintendent of the Naval Academy between August 1978 and September 1981. He was chief of naval personnel from October 1983 until his retirement on 1 February 1986.

22. Briefing paper on navy drug and alcohol abuse, prevention and control program, January 1987 version, slide N6-106. See also the speech by Captain A. Taylor, commanding officer, Naval Drug Rehabilitation Center, San Diego, "The Extent and Consequences of Drug Abuse in the Naval Service," 2, 4 December 1981, CNO's files 11ND-NRDC-5216/1 (rev. 9-79).

23. *Navy Spotlight*, "CNO Speaks on Drug Abuse in the Navy," December 1981, transcript, CNO's files DN43124.

24. "The Navy's War on Drugs," March 1987. Briefing sheet prepared by the Naval Military Personnel Command. Officers and chief petty officers got no second chance.

25. Briefing paper, January 1987, slide N6-157.

26. Briefing sheet, 2. It includes thirty-six hours of prevention and remedial instruction and has an average attendance of fifty-three thousand. Three basic NAVOPS cover the whole program: 29 December 1981 (on drug abuse and urinalysis), 18 April 1984 (on alcohol abuse), and 4 October 1985 (on tightening standards further).

27. Hayward tape.

28. *A Conversation with Admiral Thomas B. Hayward: Naval Preparedness in the 1980s* (Washington: American Enterprise Institute, Studies in Defense Policy, 1981), 3–5.

29. Ibid., 6–7.

30. Senate Appropriations Committee, Hearings FY 1981, 96th Cong., 2d sess., 26 March 1980, 608–19.

31. Cockell tape.

32. Hayward tape.

CHAPTER 3

1. A highly useful source of such data is NAVSO P-3523, March 1986, issued by the Office of the Navy Comptroller, Financial and Statistical Reports Branch.

2. How to count some navy statistics is in dispute. The navy's own commemorative pewter plate, celebrating its 200th anniversary, carries the dates 1775 to 1975, thus including the Continental navy of the American Revolution. Captain Edward L. Beach, in *The United States Navy, 200 Years*, writes that the

navy was founded in 1794. The Navy Department was established by an act of Congress signed by President Adams on 3 April 1798 (Commander Arthur A. Ageton, *The Naval Officer's Guide* [New York: McGraw-Hill, 1943], 22). Jack Sweetman, in his impressive *American Naval History: An Illustrative Chronicle of the U.S. Navy and Marine Corps, 1775 to the Present* (Annapolis: Naval Institute Press, 1984), establishes 13 October 1775 as the date for the founding of the Continental navy, 3 July 1785 for its end; 30 April 1798 for the creation by Congress of the Navy Department and the Office of the Secretary of the Navy; and 28 June 1794 for the first appointment of naval officers. Benjamin Stoddert, on 18 May 1798, became the first secretary of the navy.

3. Taped interview. Ambassador J. William Middendorf II, Newport, Rhode Island, 27 August 1986.

4. Taped interview, Senator John Warner, Vice President's Room, U.S. Senate, Washington, 23 October 1987.

5. Taped interview, former Secretary of the Navy Graham Claytor, Washington, 20 October 1987.

6. Taped interview, Admiral Thomas Moorer, USN (Ret.), Washington, 3 June 1986.

7. Ibid.

8. Statement by Secretary John Lehman to the Senate Armed Services Committee, 2 November 1983. See especially p. 7 of the navy file copy for the quotation and argument.

9. Taped interview, Vice Admiral Staser Holcomb, USN (Ret.), San Antonio, Texas, 15 September 1987.

10. Ibid. Holcomb elaborated his point:

> About the first week that Lehman was in the office as a confirmed secretary, I think at his request, Hayward assembled most of the flag officers who were in Washington into a long and skinny conference room on the fourth floor of the Pentagon. I remember walking down there that day and that room was full. There must have been 75 admirals there—almost every flag officer on duty in Washington—and no room for a stage or platform, just three chairs up at the end. And CNO got up and started to say to the assembled flag officers, "I really don't need to introduce to you the Secretary of the Navy, but I want to tell you that he's here, he's in charge, and he's. . ." Hayward got about that far and John Lehman was out of his chair with his hand on Hayward's shoulder, and literally sat him down and said, "I *don't* need any introduction. I'm the Secretary of the Navy." And he proceeded to give a 20-minute monologue on what was wrong with the Navy, how it had never had a strategic concept, how there was too much systems analysis and not enough operational guts out there. He really gave a terrible put-down to the uniformed leader of the Navy, and you can't do that and expect to have unstinting cooperation and mutual respect. It was not an auspicious start.

Compare Holcomb's statement with what Andy Kerr said in his book, *A Journey amongst the Good and the Great* (Annapolis: Naval Institute Press, 1987), 150:

> The TFX controversy demonstrated how lonely the Secretary . . . can become [if the CNO is on the other side]. The CNO commands almost all of the resources of the navy. The secretary quickly finds himself isolated. Korth described the sensation [as] like the driver of a huge truck that is thundering down the highway. The secretary sits high in the cab, thrilled with the majesty and power of it all. Then suddenly he realizes that his steering wheel is not

connected to anything. Others, down below, are steering the vehicle and deciding where it will go.

11. OPNAV Organizational Manual, revision of 9 October 1985, viii.

12. Love, *The Chiefs of Naval Operations*, xvii. Beach, *The United States Navy*, says that although Fiske and Sims were the frontrunners, Daniels chose Benson as CNO instead (see 411–14).

13. Love, xviii.

14. Ibid., xix.

15. Ibid.

16. See the 1942 OPNAV diagram, appendix C. After Pearl Harbor King did not like the acronym CINCUS ("sink us") and instead called himself COMINCH.

17. Love, xix.

18. CNO as senior uniformed officer by executive order 9635 of 29 September 1945, and by act of Congress on 5 March 1948. By the end of 1986 naval officers had been chairman three times. Admiral Arthur W. Radford was the first, Admiral Tom Moorer the second, and Admiral William I. Crowe the third.

19. Moorer tape.

20. Ibid.

21. Lawrence J. Korb, *The Joint Chiefs of Staff: The First Twenty-five Years* (Bloomington: Indiana University Press, 1976), 5.

22. Admiral Moorer's comment was made in a letter to the author, 13 June 1988. He pointed out, "men's lives are at stake," and added that as a participant in many National Security Council meetings and discussions with the president on highly secretive operations he had not once "seen a service secretary in the same room with the President during the . . . discussions." Lehman (*Command of the Seas* [New York: Scribner's, 1988], 297), commented that in every crisis the service secretaries "were institutionally excluded from the policy process." During Grenada, for example, they "depended on corridor gossip and the press. . . ."

23. Of the CNO's immediate staff, two were of special importance in 1982–86: the public affairs officer and the special counsel. In 1986 Captain Don Dvornik was completing five years' duty with Admiral Watkins. Less often in the CNO's immediate entourage but always consulted was the special counsel, Captain Al Rudy. The Goldwater-Nichols Act of 1986 specified that the navy's public affairs officer billet would be under the secretary.

24. Richard Halloran, "Working Profile: Admiral James D. Watkins: A Week in the Life of a Joint Chief," *The New York Times*, 1 October 1984, section B, 8. Admiral Watkins commented that the article was accurate.

25. Taped interview, Rear Admiral Jeremy M. (Mike) Boorda, the Pentagon, 17 March 1986.

26. CNO's statement before the Senate Armed Services Committee on 9 November 1983 had been through thirteen drafts, the last four of them on 8 November.

27. In 1979 there were fourteen hearings; in 1980, only seven; 1981, sixteen; 1982, ten; 1983, thirteen; 1984, six; 1985, eight. The typical sequence is first for the House and Senate Armed Services Committees to hear the navy posture statement, then for the House and Senate defense subcommittees to look

at budget, and finally for the two seapower subcommittees to hold hearings on special topics like the 600-ship navy and the fiscal year wrap-up.

28. In 1983, OP-906 coordinated OPNAV staffing for congressional issues. To illustrate, in December of that year, both the chief of legislative affairs and the head of the navy's Appropriations Liaison Office (Office of the Comptroller) submitted internal navy briefs on issues likely to be raised by congressional committees. The Legislative Affairs Office submitted eighty-one issues, the Comptroller's Office forty-seven, with more to come. Interestingly, a number of issues actually raised did not appear on either list. In each case, the brief stated the issue, the attitude and interests of committees or members, and the specific questions likely to be raised.

29. What such lists cannot predict, of course, is the relative importance such issues are likely to have. In this case, for example, the issues Congress spent most time on appear in the lists, but there is nothing to show they would be overriding.

Many issues were raised by only a few congressmen or senators—in the SAC 1983 case, eight senators. (Senator Stennis alone raised sixty-one.)

In a comparison of the tracking logs for the armed services committees, the House log for 17 February 1983 listed twenty-nine issues, the Senate committee log listed seventy for 25 February 1982 and eighty-one for 2 March 1983—far fewer issues than either of the appropriations committees listed.

30. Navy log printouts usually indicate the issue number, the name of the congressman initiating a question, the action officer, the date received, the key word, the list of "chops," and forwarding data (for replies).

31. The 1985 diagram is in OPNAVINST 5430.48B, CH-2, 9 October 1985. The 1987 diagram is the same except for the replacement of some staff assistants. Some DMSOs report to both the CNO and the secretary. All DCNO and DMSO authority is subject to CNO and secretary approval when force levels are affected, or certain dollar ceilings are reached, or modernization decisions affecting systems characteristics are made.

32. As CNO, Watkins moved key bureau chiefs like the director of naval medicine (OP-093) into the Pentagon so that virtually all major navy activities were represented in OPNAV spaces by the officer in charge. (There had to be exceptions. Admiral Kinnaird Mckee, commander, naval nuclear propulsion program, stayed in Crystal City; the manpower chief remained a stone's throw away in the Navy Annex.) Watkins also, in conjunction with the secretary, strengthened the position of oceanographer of the navy.

33. Taped interview, Vice Admiral Daniel L. Cooper, the Pentagon, 20 March 1986. Recent 090s, including Hayward and Trost, have had impressive careers.

34. Taped interview, Vice Admiral Robert E. Kirksey and Rear Admiral Lawrence Layman, the Pentagon, 18 March 1986.

35. Taped interview, Vice Admiral James R. Hogg, the Pentagon, 20 March 1986.

36. Senate Appropriations Committee, subcommittee, Hearings FY 81, 96th Cong., 2d sess., 26 March 1980, 650.

37. Taped interview, CNO Admiral James D. Watkins, Newport, Rhode Island, 28 February 1986.

38. Boorda tape.

39. Taped interview, Vice Admiral Bruce Demars, the Pentagon, 19 March 1986, and Vice Admiral Edward H. Martin, the Pentagon, 20 March 1986.

40. Taped interview, Vice Admiral Joseph Metcalf III, the Pentagon, 21 March 1986.

41. Taped interview, Vice Admiral Albert A. Baciocco, Jr., the Pentagon, 19 March 1986.

42. Taped interview, VCNO Admiral James B. Busey, the Pentagon, 4 June 1986.

43. Hayward tape.

44. Lawrence tape.

45. Watkins tape.

46. Taped interview, Vice Admiral Charles Griffiths, USN (Ret.), Fairfax, Virginia, 5 June 1986.

47. Taped interview, Rear Admiral David E. Jeremiah, the Pentagon, 5 June 1986.

48. Taped interview, Vice Admiral William F. McCauley, Norfolk, Virginia, 27 May 1986.

49. Jeremiah tape.

50. Taped interview, John Cardinal O'Connor, Newport, Rhode Island, 7 April 1986.

51. Taped interview, Rear Admiral John McNamara, the Navy Annex, Washington, 19 March 1986.

52. McCauley tape.

53. Watkins tape.

CHAPTER 4

1. Britannica *Book of the Year, 1982* (events of 1981), (Chicago: Encyclopaedia Britannica, 1982), 596.

2. Ibid., *1983* (events of 1982), 590–91.

3. Ibid., 591. Admiral Watkins, reading the draft manuscript. remarked that the bishops had not recognized the USSR as an integral part of the nuclear equation until their third draft. He gave credit for restoring balance especially to the former navy chief of chaplains, then-Bishop John O'Connor.

4. Britannica *Book of the Year, 1984*, 592.

5. James D. Watkins, "The Moral Man in the Modern Military," *Seapower* (December 1982): 17–20.

6. Taped interview, Admiral James D. Watkins, the Navy Yard, Washington, 17 April 1987.

7. Taped interview, Admiral James D. Watkins, Newport, Rhode Island, 28 February 1986.

8. Ibid.

9. Ibid.

10. The initial message, later widely repeated, was classified as confidential. With classified sections deleted, it is reprinted in appendix E. The message went out first as a "personal" for Admirals Crowe, Williams, Foley, McDonald, and Vice Admiral Hays, with "info" to Vice Admiral Carroll and Rear Admirals Shugart, Palmer, Horne, and Dillingham. All quotes in this chapter are from the personal. (One classified section is omitted.)

11. No stenographic or taped record is made of such conferences. The

author was present at this discussion in the president's conference room at the Naval War College.

12. The Naval War College archives include substantial materials on this subject. The author was a chief staffer when these changes were made.

13. Admiral Watkins, reading the draft manuscript, said that by joint he also meant U.S. allies. Certainly including the allies in some coherent way in the maritime strategy was high on his list of priorities.

14. Taped interview, General John Vessey, USA (Ret.), at his home in Minnesota, 22 September 1986.

15. Taped interview, Vice Admiral Henry C. Mustin, the Pentagon, 13 April 1987.

16. Taped interview, Captain Charles H. Kinney, Captain Kathy Laughton, and Mr. Pat Talbot, the Navy Yard, Washington, 18 March 1986.

17. This is from the briefing paper, 8 pages long, dated 1 August 1985 and identified as 1727s. Captain Laughton gave this brief.

18. Ibid., 3.

19. Ibid., 4. There is much detail in the briefing on computer links to other data banks.

20. Ibid., slides data.

21. Kinney interview.

22. Taped interview, Vice Admiral James A. Sagerholm, USN (Ret.), Alexandria, Virginia, 16 September 1986.

23. Taped interview, Admiral James D. Watkins, the Navy Yard, Washington, 15 April 1987.

24. Sagerholm tape. That CNET was also considered overstaffed by Watkins is clear from a preliminary memo to the secretary (ser. 00/5U300160 of 25 April 1985) that suggests a reduction in the layering and cutting of CNET staff positions. The file has no record of a response.

25. Taped interview, Vice Admiral William P. Lawrence, USN (Ret.), Annapolis, Maryland, 17 September 1986. Lawrence was superintendent from 1978 to 1981.

26. Taped interview, Admiral James D. Watkins, the Navy Yard, Washington, 17 July 1987.

27. Lawrence tape.

28. Ibid., Vice Admiral James Stockdale, then president of the Naval War College and a noted war hero, became a member of the academy's advisory committee.

29. Taped interview, Vice Admiral Lando Zech, USN (Ret.), chairman, U.S. Nuclear Regulatory Commission, Washington, 14 April 1987.

30. Taped interview, Admiral Kinnaird McKee, Crystal City, Arlington, Virginia, 15 April 1986.

31. Ibid.

32. He went to OPNAV as a special assistant in navy program planning, directed CEP, spent two years with Submarine Group 8, then served as superintendent of the Naval Academy, as commander of the Third Fleet, and as Rickover's successor.

33. Lawrence tape.

34. Taped interview, Rear Admiral John R. Seesholtz, oceanographer of the navy, Naval Observatory, Washington, 16 April 1987. The budget doubling was in real dollars. Seesholtz mentioned the feat in the 1840s when Commander

Maury created wave and current charts. Captain Jackson of the barque *Wright* took Maury seriously. Using his charts for guidance, Jackson did the Baltimore-Rio round trip—normally 115 days—in 35 fewer days. TESS, the modern version of Maury's charts, is on most carriers now. It was scheduled for installation on about forty major ships.

35. Lawrence tape.

36. The special pay and bonuses issue is complex. Vice Admiral Zech said, "When you increase a bonus there's no problem, but when you decrease [one], that's something different." To stimulate retention, periodic shifts were inevitable (Zech tape).

37. In April 1985 Congressman Aspin, chairman of the subcommittee on military personnel and compensation of the House Committee on Armed Services, held new hearings. The Joint Chiefs testified at length. The *Navy Times*, 15 April 1985, quoted Aspin as calling for a $4 billion cut in the 1986 retirement budget. *All Hands*, March 1987 (no. 840), provided a summary of what came next: the Military Retirement Reform Act of 1986. Admiral Lawrence's discussion concerns those who enlisted after 7 September 1980 and before 1 August 1986, who were to receive, instead of final basic pay, the average of their highest thirty-six months' basic pay. The new law kept that, but reduced cost-of-living adjustments to the consumer price index minus 1 percent per year. Instead of 50 percent of base pay for twenty years and 75 percent for thirty, there would be 2.5 percent minus 1 percent for each year short of thirty, and 75 percent for thirty.

38. One petty officer told the author about a buddy of his who for ten years wore a beard. Suddenly one day, after nine years of marriage, he was beardless. His wife's shocked comment, when she saw him thus for the first time, was, "You're *ugly!*"

39. One reserve chaplain said, in the mid-1970s, that ten years earlier only 20 percent of his congregation's wives worked and church meetings for women were primarily daytime affairs. A decade later only 20 percent did not work, and meetings were held in the evening.

40. *A Nation at Risk: The Imperative for Education Reform*, 26 April 1983, a report produced by a national commission appointed by Education Secretary T. H. Bell.

41. The panel members were Professor Richard N. Cooper, Dr. June Tuefel Dreyer, Dr. David Hamburg, Dr. Joshua Lederberg, Dr. Harrison Shull (chairman), and Mr. R. James Woolsey.

42. CEP Task Force on Personal Excellence, *Final Report*, iv.

43. Ibid., 8.

44. Ibid., 11.

45. Ibid., 9.

46. CNO memo, ser. 00/6U300050, 20 February 1986.

47. Taped interview with Vice Admiral Sagerholm, Alexandria, Virginia, 16 September 1986.

48. Sagerholm tape.

49. Enclosure 1 to CNO memo, 6.

50. Ibid., 2.

51. Ibid.

52. Ibid., 7.

53. CNO memo, ser. 00/6U300055, 25 February 1986.

54. These represented earlier steps in the education area. The math/science

initiatives were ongoing at Great Lakes, Norfolk, Jacksonville, Orlando, Pensacola, and Corpus Christi and used senior navy volunteers. Adopt-a-School, begun in 1982, was operating in San Francisco, Long Beach, and San Diego. The Saturday Scholar program met in Chicago and Pensacola. In 1986 one of the follow-up areas for expanded programs was California, because of interest expressed there and its large navy population.

55. CNO memo, ser. 00/6U300091, 25 March 1986.

56. CNO memo, ser. 00/6U300170, 2 June 1986.

57. CNO memo, ser. 00/6U300174, 5 June 1986.

58. The *Navy Times*, 23 June 1986. Admiral Watkins confirmed that Admiral Trost had gone to the conference to underline his personal interest in the program.

CHAPTER 5

1. Taped interview, former Secretary of the Navy John Lehman, Yorktown, Virginia, 22 October 1987. Watkins recalled Lehman's views on Rickover as "frightening" (taped interview, Admiral Watkins, the Navy Yard, Washington, 17 July 1987).

2. His fourth star was an additional flag billet given to the navy by Congress for this special purpose.

3. See Elmo Zumwalt, Jr., *On Watch*, 98–100. Andy Kerr's version differs in detail (see *A Journey amongst the Good and the Great*, 112).

4. Taped interview, Admiral James D. Watkins, the Pentagon, 24 April 1986.

5. Taped interview, Mr. William Wegner, Fredericksburg, Virginia, 22 October 1987. See also Zumwalt, *On Watch*, chapter 5.

6. Wegner tape.

7. Memo (with italics) from Rear Admiral A. K. Knoizen, chief of legislative affairs, LA-2:SW, 28 January 1982, with broad OPNAV distribution.

8. Wegner tape.

9. Sometime in 1963–64, Dennis Wilkinson, an active-duty officer, had received orders to be Rickover's deputy. Rickover persuaded the secretary to drop the orders.

10. Wegner tape.

11. Ibid.

12. Taped interview, Admiral James D. Watkins, the Pentagon, 24 April 1986. Watkins himself, on another occasion, told of how near he had come to leaving the nuclear navy (taped interview, the Navy Yard, Washington, 17 July 1987):

> Do you know how I knew I had "arrived" with Rickover? I worked with him for three and a half years when I first got here, early 1961. After 18 months I was getting pretty discouraged. I got a call one day from his secretary, to go see him right away. I thought, good God, here we go again. What have I done now? I went up there and he says: "Damn Jack W—. He doesn't know how to write a memorandum. I've been telling him and he doesn't respond. Take this memorandum down there and show him how to write it." I almost fell out of the office backwards. I said with a big smile to myself, "I've made it!" That was as nice a way as he had of telling me, "Watkins, I think you've finally arrived."

13. Watkins tape, 24 April 1986.

14. Wegner tape.

15. Watkins tape, 24 April 1986.

16. These documents are "The Rickover File." They formed a part of the CNO's "sensitive files."

17. Senator John Warner's draft of 23 November 1981, sent to Secretary Lehman, provided for either a three-star or a four-star director. The amended draft, marked 1700, 12/3, is quoted. For the text as issued, see the *U.S. Code*, 1982 ed. (Washington: GPO, 1983) 16:1048–49.

18. Watkins tape, 24 April 1986. Lehman devotes the first thirty-five or so pages of his book, *Command of the Seas*, to a detailed account of how he retired Rickover.

19. Wegner also says, and Lehman confirms this on his tape, that the latter invited him to his office as the time for the final act neared and offered him Rickover's job. Wegner was retired by then. Lehman offered him a return to active-navy status with a civilian rank equivalent to a three- or four-star admiral. Wegner said no, and told Lehman that with all the nuclear ships that existed he would do well to make Watkins CNO.

Asked about the time Rickover was told that he was being retired, Wegner said Rickover "came back from his meeting with [Lehman and] Weinberger [and] told me, to the best of my memory, 'I don't know.' I said, 'Well, what happened?' He said, 'Nothing happened.' " Wegner got the idea that Weinberger had not told him about retirement.

Lehman said he and Weinberger informed Rickover "collectively. Cap said [to him] the President has approved your retirement, . . . he wants you to take a job as his senior adviser for nuclear power on the White House Staff. . . . We tried to sugar coat it . . . and he didn't react at all." Lehman claimed Rickover had not heard the news on television. In an excerpt from his book, *Command of the Seas* (New York: Scribner, 1988), printed in the Naval Institute *Proceedings* (January 1989): 60–64, Lehman made virtually the same claim. He says he informed Rickover on 10 November that he was recommending retirement, and that Rickover was told of the president's concurrence in Weinberger's office on 13 November, with Lehman also present. But the decision leaked from the White House on 9 November. Lehman's description of Rickover's 8 January 1982 meeting with President Reagan includes a quote from Rickover: "Mr. President, that piss-ant [Lehman] knows nothing about the Navy."

20. Watkins tape, 24 April 1986.

21. Ibid.

22. Taped interview with Admiral Kinnaird McKee, Crystal City, 15 April 1986. Admiral McKee was not aware of Watkins's full role in the transition.

23. Memo from Admiral Rickover to the CNO, dated 1 May 1981.

24. CNO letter to Congressman Bennett, 15 February 1985.

25. Ibid.

26. The eulogy text is taken from Admiral Watkins's personal file.

27. Beach, *The United States Navy*.

28. CNO memo, ser. 00/500296, 2 October 1976.

29. Ibid.

30. Ibid.

31. *Navy Times*, 31 December 1975.

32. *Navy Times*, 31 May 1976.

33. San Diego *Union*, 4 June 1976, B13.

34. Washington *Post*, 13 May 1976.

35. Judge Advocate General memo, ser. JAG: 004: WDC: lgf, 12 October 1976.

36. CNO memo, ser. 00/500296, 2.

37. Ibid., 3.

38. Ibid.

39. Judge Advocate General memo, to chairman, Board for Correction of Naval Records, ser. 202/37031, 23 May 1980.

40. See OP-00F memos to CNO, 4 May 1979 (96–79), 8 June 1979 (119–79), 11 July 1979 (141–79), and 27 July 1979 (160–79).

41. Ibid., 4 May 1979.

42. Ibid.

43. OP-00F memo, 8 June 1979.

44. Ibid., 7

45. Admiral James D. Watkins, "The Principle of Command," Naval Institute *Proceedings* (January 1983): 33. The article was based on his mid-October flag officer news gram, 18–82.

46. *Naval Affairs* (May 1984): 10–15. See also CNO letter to all flag officers, 29 September 1982.

47. For instance, *U.S. News & World Report* (27 February 1984): 35–39, ran an article entitled "Can't Anybody Here Run a War?"

48. Commander, Naval Air Force, U.S. Pacific Fleet, to commander in chief, U.S. Pacific Fleet, ser. 011/C310, 16 July 1984.

49. Ibid., 3–4.

50. First endorsement by CINCPACFLT (5830 ser. 03J/685, 13 September 1984) on COMNAVAIRPAC's letter 5830 ser. 011/C310, 16 July 1984.

51. Second endorsement by CNO (ser. 00/4C300598, 9 November 1984) on COMNAVAIRPAC's letter.

52. Flag officer news gram 11-84, 7 December 1984.

53. The new rules were published in ALNAV (all-navy notice) 83 in 1985.

54. See, for example, "The Wrong Stuff," an editorial in the San Diego *Union*, 15 March 1986. Three of the pilots told the Los Angeles *Times* reporter "that they think the Navy overreacted, particularly in light of the shortage of fighter pilots and the costliness of flight training" (Los Angeles *Times*, 13 March 1986).

55. The quote is from para. 2 of CINCPACFLEET 5830 ser. 03J/C157, March 1985, 7th endorsement on Commander Marksbury, investigative report. The precise date in March is blurred on the file copy.

56. Ibid., para 4.

57. All quotes here are from CNO ser. 00/6U300069, 13 March 1986, 8th endorsement on Marksbury, investigative report, 23 April 1984.

Admiral Watkins, reading the first draft discussion of these events, commented that the navy had drifted into this "no-accountability syndrome" and had not really faced it until the *Belknap-Kennedy* collision. Then it had stopped accepting "the cop-out that we were bringing in trash from our society and therefore we have to expect trash in our performance" (taped interview, the Navy Yard, Washington, 17 July 1987).

58. Seventeenth endorsement, CNO ser. 09/300581, 14 June 1982, Captain M. J. Saldana, 451-68-9283, letter NRMC: JC 5830, 15 May 1981.

59. Ibid.

60. Ibid.

61. Second endorsement, CNO ser. 09/5U301257, 9 August 1985, Rear Admiral Stanley J. Anderson, investigative report 5830 ser. NJAG 131.1/11325/5, 13 June 1985.

62. Ibid.

63. The account here is drawn principally from an article by Captain G. B. Powell, Jr., "Accountability Afloat," *Proceedings* (August 1986): 31–35.

64. Ibid., 31.

65. Ibid., 32. The flag mast was held on 14 March 1985.

66. Ibid. The special court-martial was at Pearl between 17 and 26 April 1985. See also 2d endorsement, CNO ser. 09/5U301467, 22 October 1985, concurring, Captain William W. Mathis, investigative report, 19 February 1985.

67. Ibid.

68. Ibid., 33. Quote is from investigative letter report, 14 July 1985.

69. See 4th endorsement, CNO ser. 09/6U301206, 8 August 1986, Commodore B. C. McCaffree, Jr., investigative report, 14 July 1985.

70. The flag officers news gram introduced this quote from the commanding officer, Captain Leuschner, by saying it was "an outstanding example of the bedrock principles upon which our Navy is founded."

71. Captain Ash Roach, memo, 18 April 1986, to Captains Rudy, Sinor, and McCoy.

CHAPTER 6

1. Admiral H. G. Rickover, statement before the House Committee on Armed Services, subcommittee on procurement and military nuclear systems, 16 June 1981, navy file copy, 2.

2. Ibid., 4.

3. Admiral Rickover, statement before the House Committee on Appropriations, defense subcommittee, 5 May 1981, navy file copy, 2.

4. Ibid., 5.

5. Ibid., 14. The entire testimony is a first-class analysis.

6. Senate Committee on Armed Services, Hearings FY 85, 98th Cong., 2d sess., part 2, 875–76. In his book, Secretary Lehman attributes a good deal of the shipbuilding cost problem to Rickover's micromanagement of ship design: "Because of Admiral Rickover's uncompromising standards for quality control (in the view of his admirers) and/or his arbitrary and capricious demands (in the view of his detractors), nearly all the competition had been driven out of supplying components to the nuclear shipbuilding program" (*Command of the Seas*, 17–18). Lehman argues that recurrent changes in orders drove prices higher, in most cases on a cost-plus basis. It is certainly true that Rickover always put safety first.

Lehman (p. 204) comments that in 1980 alone the navy made three thousand design changes to the *Ohio*, under construction.

7. Secretary of Defense Weinberger, letter, 18 July 1983, OASD (PA) PC/2E 777, 1.

8. Committee on Government Operations, report 15, 9 November 1983, 2.

9. House Committee on Armed Services, subcommittee on investigations, 98th Cong., 1st sess., 13 July 1983, from navy file summary. A sheet in navy files (7/18, probably 18 July 1983) indicates that $80,000 was paid for about $4,000

of Federal Supply System parts, including a four-cent diode bought for $110. The sheet emphasizes that it was the navy's own audit that found this.

10. Testimony by Ms. Mary Ann Gilleece, deputy undersecretary of defense, Senate Appropriations Committee, subcommittee on defense, 98th Cong., 1st sess., 4 August 1983.

11. Testimony by Department of Defense Inspector General Joseph H. Sherick, Senate Committee on Appropriations, subcommittee on defense, 98th Cong., 1st sess., 4 August 1983, navy file copy, 1, 5.

12. Department of the Navy, *Fiscal Year 1985 Report to the Congress*, 23.

13. Ibid., 24.

14. "Improving the Acquisition Process," presentation to the Packard Commission by secretary of the navy, 10 December 1985.

15. House Armed Services Committee, seapower subcommittee, 99th Cong., 1st sess., Hearings FY 86, February–April 1985, part 3, 411.

16. Reported in *Aerospace Daily* (9 April 1985): 219.

17. "A First-Year Report for Competition Advocates," competition advocate general of the navy, CAG com. 8, 13 August 1984.

18. Taped interview, Captain J. Ash Roach, Newport, 22 October 1986.

19. Fourth endorsement, 5830 ser. 011/8326, 7 September 1985, para. 2, Commander James R. Lenga, investigative report, 10 August 1985.

20. Taped interview, Commander David Gibbs, supply officer, aboard *Carl Vinson* at sea, 5 October 1987.

21. The spare parts for each type of airplane constituting an air wing are at the base used for that type, on either the Pacific or the Atlantic coast, as the case may be.

22. Fourth endorsement, investigative report, 10 August 1985.

23. Ibid., para. 2b.

24. Notes from discussion with Miramar supply officers, Lieutenant J. B. Hart, Lieutenant Commander George Hartmann, and Lieutenant Commander Cliff Szafran, 7 October 1987. They estimated the number of Miramar's "repairables" to be roughly twelve thousand, the "consumables," about seventy-eight thousand.

25. Fourth endorsement, 10 August 1985, para. 2c.

26. Supply chief, *Carl Vinson*.

27. Gibbs tape.

28. Ibid.

29. Fourth endorsement, 10 August 1985, para. 6.

30. CINCPACFLT 240400Z to the CNO, June 1985.

31. See 3d endorsement, CNO ser. 00/5U300299, 29 July 1985, 18 June 1985.

32. First endorsement, Rear Admiral J. R. Batzler, investigative report, 18 June 1985, paras. 2a, 2b.

33. CINCPACFLT 240400Z, June 1985.

34. Ibid.

35. CNO endorsement, para. 5.

36. Ibid., para. 6. Cassidy, after being relieved, was reinstated with "an administrative letter of instruction."

37. Ibid., para. 10.

38. Commander, Naval Air Force, U.S. Atlantic Fleet, letter, 10 October 1985; Commander, Naval Air Force, U.S. Pacific Fleet, letter, 3 March 1986.

39. Quoted from "Remarks by Admiral James D. Watkins, Air Force Brigadier General Conference, 25 March 1985," navy files. See also CNO ser. 00/5U30033, memo to the secretary of the navy, 25 January 1985.

40. *Navy Times*, 22 April 1985.

41. It was reported that the reorganization was also to make the Office of Naval Technology, Office of Naval Research, and director of Navy Laboratories into one command under the chief of naval research (*Navy Times*, 22 April 1985, 3).

42. *Defense Week*, 15 April 1985.

43. CNO ser. 00/5U300108, letter to secretary of the navy, 20 March 1985, para. 1.

44. CNO ser. 00/5U300140, 5 April 1985, with attached plan. File copy carries Lehman's approval.

45. Taped interview, Vice Admiral William H. Rowden, Crystal City, 13 April 1987.

46. Taped interview, Admiral William N. Small, USN (Ret.), the Pentagon, 15 April 1987.

47. Taped interview, Admiral Ronald J. Hays, USCINCPAC, Hawaii, 21 May 1987.

48. Taped interview, Vice Admiral Glenwood Clark, Jr., Crystal City, 14 July 1987.

49. Secretary of the navy instruction 4210, 20 November 1985.

50. The navy file copy carries no number. At the end the new instruction (4210) is included.

51. "A Formula for Action," Report to the president on defense acquisition, the president's Blue Ribbon Commission on Defense Management, April 1986, 32.

52. For the text, see the *Congressional Record*, House, 99th Cong., 2d sess., 12 September 1986, p. H6846, cols. 2 and 3.

53. Rowden tape.

54. Ibid.

55. Taped interview, former Secretary of the Navy John Lehman, Yorktown, Virginia, 22 October 1987. Lehman had said to the Packard Commission on 10 December 1985 that "gold-plating" was often done because military requirements, in addition to being overstated, were frequently set by the military without first examining commercial specifications that would not require custom tooling and production.

56. Lehman tape.

57. Ibid.

58. Taped interview, Admiral James D. Watkins, USN (Ret.), the Navy Yard, Washington, 17 April 1987.

59. Ibid., 18 September 1986. CNO ser. 00/5U300015, 9 January 1985, set up program coordinators from OPNAV in systems-command program manager offices.

60. Taped interview, Admiral Robert L. J. Long, USN (Ret.), the Pentagon, 13 July 1987.

61. Taped interview, Vice Admiral Richard A. Miller, USN (Ret.), Monterey, California, 28 May 1987.

62. Taped interview, Admiral John G. Williams, Jr., USN (Ret.), Seattle, 19 August 1987.

63. Ibid.
64. Taped interview, Vice Admiral Robert R. Monroe, USN (Ret.), Bechtel Corporation, San Francisco, 12 August 1987.
65. Ibid.
66. *Navy Times*, 22 April 1985, 3.
67. Secretary John Lehman, "Successful Naval Strategy in the Pacific: How We Are Achieving It, How We Can Afford It," *Naval War College Review* (winter 1987): 24–25.
68. Ibid., 25.
69. Ibid., 26.
70. See, for example, *Navy Times*, 22 April 1985, and *Aerospace Daily*, 9 April 1985.
71. Senate Appropriations Committee, defense subcommittee, Hearings FY 87, 99th Cong., 2d sess., 21 February 1986, p. 29 of navy file copy.
72. Ibid., 68–69.
73. Ibid., 69.
74. House Armed Services Committee, defense subcommittee, Hearings FY 87, 99th Cong., 2d sess., 26 February 1986, 477.
75. Ibid., 506.
76. Ibid., 528.
77. Ibid., 506.
78. Ibid., 507.

CHAPTER 7

1. Taped interview, Admiral Isaac C. Kidd, Jr., USN (Ret.), Arlington, Virginia, 29 May 1986.
2. Taped interview, Vice Admiral Robert R. Monroe, USN (Ret.), San Francisco, California, 12 August 1987.
3. Colonel George W. Acree II, et al., *Overview of the Defense System Acquisition Process* (National Defense University Press: Washington, D.C., 1984), 2, updated for Naval War College use by Dr. Maurice Halladay.
4. Monroe tape.
5. Ibid.
6. David D. Acker, "Defense Systems Acquisition Review Process: A History and Evaluation," *Program Manager* (January–February 1984): 5–13, 38.
7. Monroe tape.
8. Ibid.
9. Speech to San Francisco Rotary Club, 3 December 1974.
10. Briefing, by Captain Ernie Tedeschi (OP-355) and Commander Chipp Wilfong (OP-355F), the Pentagon, 23 October 1987.
11. House Armed Services Committee, subcommittee on seapower, Hearings, FY 85, 98th Cong., 2d sess., part 3, 119.
12. Senate Committee on Armed Services, Hearings, FY 84, 98th Cong., 1st sess., part 6, Sea Power and Force Projection, 22 March 1983, 3000.
13. House Committee on Armed Services, subcommittee on seapower, Hearings, FY 85, 98th Cong., 2d sess., part 3, 33.
14. Interview with Vice Admiral Thunman, Pensacola, Florida, 28 May 1986.

15. House Armed Services Committee, seapower subcommittee, FY 85, 38, 45.

16. Ibid., 150. Admiral Walters had earlier said the average follow-on cost of the CG 47 would be $977 million (ibid., 56). This compared with a DDG 51 follow-on cost of $693.

17. Senate Armed Services Committee, FY 84, 3000.

18. Ibid., 3002.

19. Ibid., 3003–4.

20. Ibid., 3003.

21. House Armed Services Committee, FY 85, 45–46. The adverse publicity that accompanied Aegis missile testing was well under way by this time. Navy files contain a letter dated 18 May 1983, from Congressman Bennett, referring to press comments and to earlier letters of his expressing concern about the failure to test against "air-launched, supersonic, sea-skimming" missiles. The 22 June 1983 reply from the CNO was an effective and detailed letter, but it had no effect on press criticism. That reply is still classified.

22. Ibid., 50.

23. Ibid., 209.

24. Ibid., 211. Vice Admiral Monroe, very experienced in this area, commented that

> any system in test and evaluation is going to do a great many things right and some number of things wrong. [Moreover, test and evaluation] is about 10 percent test and 90 percent evaluation. Quite literally, I could take ten new missiles out, get ten failures, and come up with a correct evaluation that said, "This is a very fine missile. Let's buy it." Or, in another program, I could take ten missiles out, get ten successes, and (again correctly) say: "This thing is a dog. Forget it!" In each case the critical issue is the *evaluation* of the successes, failures, and overall performance. It must be done honestly and objectively, by individuals with exceptional combat and operational experience.

Monroe admitted these would be extreme cases, but his point is that it is "easy to write a glowing report about any test result. Or vice versa" (taped interview, San Francisco, 11 September 1987).

25. Ibid., 217.

26. Ibid., 501.

27. Ibid., 506.

28. Ibid., 512.

29. Ibid.

30. Ibid., 513.

31. Ibid., 515.

32. Senate Committee on Armed Services, subcommittee on seapower and force projection, Hearings FY 85, 98th Cong., 2d sess., part 8, x.

33. Ibid., 4345.

34. Ibid., 4348.

35. Ibid., 4349.

36. Ibid., 4386.

37. Ibid., 4387.

38. Taped transcript of 2 May 1984 press conference, the Pentagon.

39. See *Wall Street Journal* and *USA Today*, 3 May 1984.

40. *Washington Times*, 3 May 1984.

41. Senate Committee on Armed Services, seapower subcommittee, 3897.

42. Ibid., 4160.

43. Ibid., 4161.

44. Ibid., 4200.

45. Ibid., 4201.

46. Ibid., 4396.

47. House Armed Services Committee, seapower subcommittee, Hearings FY 85, March–April 1984, part 3, 139. Admiral Thunman, going through the elaborate navy procedures for ship numbering and naming, reached a dead end and simply started calling it SSN 21.

48. Ibid., 4124.

49. Ibid., 4125.

50. House Armed Services Committee, seapower subcommittee, Hearings FY 86, 99th Cong., 1st sess., June–September 1985, document no. 99-33, 148–49. McKee's testimony is interesting but so chopped up by security deletions as to limit quotability.

51. Ibid., FY 84, April 1983, part 4, 644.

52. Senate Armed Services Committee, Hearings FY 85, March–May 1984, part 8, 4127.

53. Ibid., 4132.

54. Ibid., 4133.

55. Ibid., 4137–38.

56. Ibid., 4158.

57. Ibid., 4171.

58. Ibid., 4172.

59. Taped interview, Vice Admiral Thomas J. Hughes, Jr., the Pentagon, 21 March 1986.

60. Navy Department files, ser. 441/3U394641, 27 December 1983.

61. Ibid., CNO message, 7 July 1984.

62. Ibid., originated by OP-03, 24 October 1983.

63. Ibid., ser. 441/3U393439, 16 September 1983.

64. House Armed Services Committee, seapower subcommittee, Hearings FY 86, 99th Cong., 1st sess., February–April 1985, part 3, 12.

65. Ibid., 425.

66. House Appropriations Committee, Hearings FY 86, 99th Cong., 1st sess., March 1985, part 2, 850.

67. House Armed Services Committee, seapower subcommittee, 99th Cong., 1st sess., June–September 1985, 194. The navy's own initial internal estimates of primary costs were less than this figure, at least for basic needs.

68. Ibid., 288–89.

69. Ibid., 289.

CHAPTER 8

1. *Wall Street Journal*, 25 March 1980.

2. Senate Appropriations Committee, subcommittee on defense, Hearings FY 81, 96th Cong., 2d sess., 26 March 1980, 648.

3. Ibid., 722.

4. Ibid., 724.

5. "A Report by Chief of Naval Operations Admiral Thomas B. Hayward,

U.S. Navy, on the Fiscal Year 1982 Military Posture and Budget of the U.S.
Navy." Prepared by Navy Internal Relations Activity, Office of the Chief of
Information, approximately February 1981, 5.

6. Ibid., 18.

7. Senate Appropriations Committee, Hearings FY 82, 97th Cong., 1st
sess., 374. Recall that the navy's FY 81 request under Hidalgo was for $48.9
billion.

8. Ibid., 377.

9. Ibid., 379. The figure of fifteen CVBGs is based on a simultaneous
notional deployment of four in the North Atlantic and Norwegian Sea, four in
the Mediterranean, three in the Indian Ocean, and four in the northwest Pacific.

10. Ibid., 447.

11. Ibid., 455.

12. Ibid., 481.

13. Secretary of the Navy/CNO Report, FY 1983, 4.

14. Ibid., 5.

15. Ibid., 7. Forward strategy is, of course, a key concept in the new
maritime strategy.

16. Ibid., 18.

17. Ibid., 19.

18. Ibid., 19–20.

19. House Appropriations Committee, subcommittee on defense, Hearings
FY 84, 98th Cong., 1st sess., part 2, 387.

20. Ibid., 401–2.

21. Ibid., 395.

22. Ibid., 401.

23. Ibid., 402.

24. Ibid., 428.

25. Ibid., 430.

26. Ibid., 436.

27. Ibid., 437.

28. Ibid., 454–55.

29. House Armed Services Committee, Hearings FY 84, 98th Cong., 1st
sess., "Defense Department Authorization and Oversight," 23 February and 3, 8,
10 March 1983, parts 1, 2, 15, 16, 17: 991.

30. Ibid., 540.

31. Ibid., 622.

32. Ibid., 623.

33. Ibid., 624.

34. Ibid., 459–60.

35. Ibid., 472–73.

36. Ibid., 1001. Vice Admiral Monroe, asked about repeated charges of
major new systems like the F/A-18 being inefficient, said:

> Take the F-4 and, to a lesser extent, the F-14. They are fine aircraft. To get
> them to be fine aircraft in the fleet today, we did it the hard way. We bought
> those airplanes three or four times. We bought them once when they didn't
> work. We bought them again when they wouldn't do the job we wanted
> done. And the third time when they broke. We only bought the *real* airplane
> after years of trial and effort. The fleet is not the place to fix a weapon system
> that doesn't work, is unreliable, cannot be maintained, etc.

The problem here goes back to the milestone and testing questions discussed in chapter 7. During the years when industry is working kinks out of aircraft through development and operational testing, both industry and the service want to be producing *production* aircraft for the fleet. They buy lot 1 of eight aircraft, lot 2 of sixteen, lot 3 of thirty-two, and so forth, all before a production configuration is arrived at. "What do you find when you look five years later?" Monroe asked. "These first several lots of planes are essentially parked somewhere. They can't even be modified adequately to be used in the fleet" (taped interview, San Francisco, 11 September 1987). On the other hand, of course, trial and error cannot be eliminated; it is really a question of who pays for it and how much.

37. Ibid., 1009.
38. Ibid., 1012.
39. House Armed Services Committee, Hearings FY 85, 98th Cong., 2d sess., 23 February and 6 March 1984, parts 1, 2, 7, 8, 9: 534.
40. Ibid., 565.
41. Ibid., 670.
42. Senate Armed Services Committee, Hearings FY 85, 98th Cong., 2d sess., 7 February 1984, part 2.
43. Ibid., 877.
44. Ibid., 892.
45. Ibid., 894.
46. Ibid., 913.
47. Senate Armed Services Committee, subcommittee on seapower and force projection, Hearings FY 85, 98th Cong., 2d sess., 14, 28, 29 March, 5, 11 April, and 1 May 1984.
48. Department of the Navy, Report to the Congress, FY 1986, 4.
49. Ibid., 5.
50. Ibid., 21.
51. Ibid., 25–26.
52. Ibid., 31.
53. Senate Armed Services Committee, Hearings FY 86, 99th Cong., 1st sess., 7 February 1985, parts 2, 5, 6: 963.
54. Ibid., 970.
55. Ibid., 964.
56. Ibid., 987.
57. Ibid., 988.
58. House Armed Services Committee, Hearings FY 86, 99th Cong., 1st sess., 7 February 1985, parts 1, 5, 6: 1. The title for the hearings was "Authorization of Appropriations for Fiscal Year 1986 *and* Oversight of Previously Authorized Programs" (italics added).
59. Ibid., 766.
60. Ibid., 821.
61. Ibid., 970.
62. Senate Appropriations Committee, Hearings FY 86, 99th Cong., 1st sess., 7 March 1985, part 1 (budget overview): 161.
63. Ibid., 314.
64. Ibid., 315.
65. Ibid., 326.
66. House Appropriations Committee, subcommittee on defense, Hearings

FY 86, 99th Cong., 1st sess., part 2: 639. Lehman specified the goal of 50 reserve ships in the 600-ship navy.

67. House Armed Services Committee, Hearings FY 86, 99th Cong., 1st sess., 4 April 1985, part 3: 389.

68. House Armed Services Committee, Hearings FY 87, 99th Cong., 2d sess., 5 February 1986, 2.

69. Ibid., 3.

70. Ibid., 52.

71. Ibid., 53.

72. Ibid., 54.

73. Ibid.

74. Ibid., 195.

75. Ibid., 196.

76. Ibid., 203.

77. Senate Appropriations Committee, Hearings FY 87, subcommittee on defense, 99th Cong., 2d sess., 21 February 1986, 67.

78. Ibid., 72.

79. Ibid., 72, 73.

80. Ibid., 73.

81. Ibid., 113.

82. Ibid., 179.

83. Ibid., 182.

84. Senate Appropriations Committee, subcommittee on defense, Hearings FY 87, 99th Cong., 2d sess., 21 February 1986, 184.

CHAPTER 9

1. Often quoted, this remark is cited in Beach, *The United States Navy*, 330.

2. Rear Admiral Joseph C. Wylie and Rear Admiral Henry E. Eccles are two of the few exceptions. In the intelligence area, there are more books written, though. Captain Robert Bathurst at the Naval Postgraduate School is one author.

3. Zumwalt, *On Watch*, 285. By 1986, when Captain Michael B. Hughes was director, CEP had had seven heads: Kinnaird McKee (September 1970–June 1973), William A. Cockell (July 1973–July 1975), Stewart A. Ring (August 1975–October 1977), Nicholas Brown (November 1977–February 1980), James M. Patton (March 1980–April 1982), and Jake W. Stewart (May 1982–October 1984).

In 1986, the panel had twenty-five members plus ten senior consultants. They represented a broad range of expertise, and many were well known.

4. The account here follows OP-OOK's memo to CNO, 12 May 1986, ser. S368.

5. Ibid.

6. OPNAV instruction 5430.40A, 28 August 1984, para. 7b.

7. The author has attended a scattering of these sessions over a fifteen-year period. The ambiance changes little, and the dialogue is often sparkling: "Arms control is like the bubonic plague; it won't go away, you can't kill the fleas, and you can't get rid of the rats."

8. OP-OOK 20 April 1984, ser. 589.

9. Each group had two four-stars, six other flags (one a rear admiral, the

rest three-stars), and one or more civilians from the panel. The reports of these discussions, still classified, indicate they were frank and pertinent.

10. A few years ago the army overhauled its Carlisle-based think tank for exactly that reason.

11. CNA began at Columbia, moved to MIT, then to the Franklin Institute, to Rochester, and finally to Hudson.

12. "About CNA," an information pamphlet from the Center for Naval Analysis, no date, 2.

13. Up to 15 percent of the research program may be CNA-initiated.

14. Occasionally, as the chairman of one department remarked to me in May 1987, some members of the faculty would like the freedom to conduct entirely disinterested research and publication. So there is some tension the other way around, too. This is not to say, however, that fundamental academic freedom is curtailed.

15. In 1980 the author attended a conference at Monterey during which the then chief of naval personnel explained in exhaustive detail why there were no more officers available for academic programs.

16. This system, the Phoenix System, uses questionnaires to get estimates (mainly from flag officers) of how many given specialists will be needed by the navy in years to come. From this required inventory in given subspecialties, billet numbers are created.

17. "Summary of Subspecialty Categories," Naval Postgraduate School document, Monterey, California, 4 August 1986.

18. Figures were supplied by Captain Howard Venezia, director of programs, Naval Postgraduate School.

19. Taped interview, Rear Admiral Robert C. Austin, Monterey, 29 May 1987.

20. The Naval War College, alone among the services, has two levels: the senior or College of Naval Warfare level and the command and staff level.

21. The author lectured recurrently at all these institutions and for more than fifteen years attended the annual war college meetings (the Military Education Coordinating Council and the Intermediate Military Education Coordinating Council).

22. Taped interview, Captain Timothy E. Somes, Naval War College, Newport, 19 February 1987.

23. The electives program, for example, took up 20 percent of curriculum after the Stockdale changes.

24. Although tabletop gaming was retained and expanded, its role outside education is severely limited. It cannot replace the electronic-computer center.

25. Taped interview, Vice Admiral Thomas Weschler, USN (Ret.), Newport, 19 February 1987.

26. It caused problems, obviously, with the other services. If the navy needed only one course, why did they need two? The Naval War College is the only such U.S. institution that actually has both levels under the same immediate commander. The air force has both at the same base, Maxwell.

27. Weschler tape.

28. Somes tape.

29. Files of the dean of academics, Naval War College. The naval command and staff figures were much more modest, but students rarely had a chance to command before attending Newport. That the navy, even under

reduced budgets, has continued to use the Naval War College properly is clear from the later senior class figures: in August 1988, with 99 navy students, 62 were post-commanders; in November 1988, with 104, 64 were post-commanders; and in April 1989, with 99, 56 were post-commanders.

30. Taped interview, Captain George S. Allen, Newport, 18 February 1987. The interim course was dropped on 1 August 1988 because the flow of post-commanders into the year-long course was now deemed sufficient.

31. See John Hattendorf, B. Mitchell Simpson III, and John R. Wadleigh, *Sailors and Scholars: The Centennial History of the U.S. Naval War College* (Newport: Naval War College Press, 1984).

32. Later William Owens became executive assistant to the VCNO. He was promoted to rear admiral in 1987.

33. Somes tape.

34. Taped interview, Mr. Robert Murray, Harvard, 20 May 1986.

35. Taped interview, Admiral Thomas B. Hayward, Honolulu, 20 May 1987.

36. Ibid.

37. Murray tape.

38. Hayward tape. As of December 1989, a total of thirty-five studies group graduates had entered the flag selection zone and eighteen had been selected. For later studies groups (five through eight), twelve were selected of fifteen in the zone.

39. In a memo from the CNO to OP-01, 20 April 1983, Admiral Watkins said he would stay "personally involved" not only in initial studies group selection but in "follow-on assignments" and that, "as a general rule," those would go to OP-06 and OP-095 billets. Follow-on assignments were made only with his approval. See also a memo from the CNO to the president, Naval War College, and director, Strategic Studies Group, ser. OO/3U3OO345, 12 September 1983, which describes studies group objectives, tasks, and organizational relationships. The document expresses the CNO's strong interest. For example: "No tasking from external sources will be communicated to the SSG except through the CNO." And: "Quarterly, the President of the Naval War College, the Director of the SSG, and the SSG will meet with the CNO, the VCNO (plans and policy), and the Director of Naval Warfare to report on the progress of SSG work and to receive guidance" (para. 3).

The objective was for the studies group to be "the Navy's focal point on framing strategic issues and the conceptualization/development of concepts for naval strategy and tactics."

CHAPTER 10

1. A 1987 Naval War College (war-gaming department) publication, *War Gaming in Newport Since 1887*, says that Colonel Livermore, USA, was playing games at Fort Adams in Newport at that time and that Lieutenant McCarty Little, USN, "drew on his experience." War gaming itself can be traced back to the Prussian *Kriegspiel*.

2. John Hattendorf, B. Mitchell Simpson, III, and John R. Wadleigh, *The Centennial History of the Naval War College*, 41.

3. Sims Hall was built as a barracks for use during World War I. Vice

Admiral John T. Hayward, who retired in 1968, told the author that he had been assigned there more than forty years before, when he first enlisted in the navy.

4. Visitors to Newport can still see some of the original game space in the Naval Command College lecture room.

5. Francis J. McHugh, *Fundamentals of War Gaming*, 3d ed. (Naval War College, 1966), 2–54. The quote comes originally from a lecture Nimitz gave at the Naval War College on 10 October 1960.

6. It seems hard to believe, but the author knows it is fact, that in 1966 the faculty intelligence officer would "brief" students from *New York Times* clippings. He had no real role in the games. The author was able to bring about a change here that led to the sophisticated intelligence inputs of today.

7. Taped interview, Captain Jay S. Hurlburt and Captain Dave C. Klinger, Newport, 17 February 1987.

8. The college, then struggling to improve its image among navy officers, who "went where the action was," nonetheless was grateful for Kidd's support.

9. Hurlburt-Klinger tape.

10. A move encouraged by the author in his role as electives coordinator.

11. Hurlburt-Klinger tape.

12. Taped interview, Mr. Bud Hay, Newport, 19 February 1987.

13. Taped interview, Dr. Robert S. Wood, Newport, 23 May 1986.

14. Technically, the Strategic Studies Group is not an integral part of the war college, since it is directly under the CNO.

15. Data in this paragraph is from the unclassified introduction to "War Gaming at the Naval War College: Significant Issues, July 1985–August 1986," U.S. Naval War College pamphlet, no date. In 1987, the Global games were built one on the other so as to arrive at D+100 over a five-year span.

16. The Japanese dismissed game findings that most closely approximated events at Midway. For further material on war college gaming, see "Annual Report, 1985–86," Center for Naval War Studies, 1986; Peter P. Perla, *A Guide to Navy Wargaming* (Alexandria: Center for Naval Analyses, 1986); and "Selected Bibliography: Game Reports, 1986," Naval War College, War-Gaming Department, 1986.

17. Taped interview, Mr. Robert Murray, Harvard, 20 May 1986.

18. Wood tape.

19. Murray tape.

20. Wood tape.

21. Taped interview, Dr. Marshall Brement, Newport, 9 June 1986. The CNO's personal attention is apparent from the files. His May 1984 message for General Rogers at the European Command declines a studies-group visit until Rogers himself can be there (ser. 042056Z). A memo of 29 January 1985 asks for studies group nominations from senior OPNAV officers but adds, "I will personally select the officers to be assigned" (ser. 00/5U300041).

22. The old wooden minesweepers were fun for weekend reservists—but no one learned very much.

23. Congressional pressure in 1982 was direct and specific. The House Appropriations Committee report for FY 83 said that its "annual mark-up sessions for the last four years" had "been marked by frustration at Navy's disregard for its Reserve component" and "Navy's stubbornness in refusing to comply with Congressional guidance to rectify the situation." This quotation was

included in a draft message for CINCLANTFLT, CINCPACFLT, and CNAVRES (commander, naval reserve) prepared by OP-901R for the CNO's signature.

24. Secretary of Defense Weinberger, in a 21 June 1982 memo to the service secretaries, referred to Defense Department directive 1225.6, which established "that units that [are to] fight first shall be equipped first regardless of component." Each addressee was to formulate explicit guidance. "I believe," wrote Weinberger, "that it would be appropriate for you to insist upon personally approving any deviation. . . ."

25. As early in his tenure as 2 August 1982, Admiral Watkins wrote to Chairman Vessey to ask his help in getting Congress to rectify the shortage of three- and four-star navy billets. "We need this relief now. By the end of next week, two key three-star assignments (one Pacific air and surface forces type commanders) will be filled by two star officers. We have not promoted an officer to three stars in over a year." The navy was still seeking relief when Admiral Kempf was promoted.

26. Curiously, commander, Naval Surface Force, also commands the subsurface force. Admiral Kempf explained: "When nuclear submariners go into the Reserve, they lose their nuclear qualifications and don't go to sea in submarines" (taped interview, Vice Admiral Cecil Kempf, the Pentagon, 20 March 1986). The thought is their knowledge could lose currency and then they would pose a hazard to at-sea operations.

27. There is a clear "audit trail" of messages in the files showing how these changes came about. It begins effectively with the director of naval reserve's memo of 30 June 1983 (ser. 09RA/435-83) saying that "the role of the Naval Reserve forces in the execution of the Maritime Strategy is not well defined," which led to shortchanging in the program-objective-memorandum process. Admiral Trost, then OP-095, concurred.

Follow-up memos in July and September 1983 show progress with the creation of a flag oversight group, a study directive in October (OP-605D/C10975-11, ser. 60/3U410986), and a look at a new reserve mission (095/584-83) in December. A secretary of the navy memo of 22 February 1984, sent to Senator Tower and Congressman Price, enclosed "the first annual Navy report" on reserve progress.

28. Taped interview, Mr. Bill Legg, the Pentagon, 24 April 1986.

29. Ibid.

30. In his February 1981 speech to the Reserve Officers Association, Rear Admiral Palmer noted that two reserve carrier-airborne early-warning detachments had been sent to Iceland on short notice. Their E-2B Hawkeyes were then eighteen years old.

31. In February 1981, VCNO Admiral Watkins, addressing the Reserve Officer Association Conference, noted that the naval reserve had often been overlooked and underfunded because its role in the navy's peacetime mission was small. Watkins added that the reserve was already fully integrated into all major operations plans. A fair appraisal of the real change set in motion can be made by reading Vice Admiral Cecil J. Kempf's testimony to the defense subcommittee of the House Appropriations Committee, 22 April 1986.

32. Reserve figures are from "United States Naval Reserve: A Force on the Move," a pamphlet prepared by the Office of the Director of the Naval Reserve, May 1986, p. 2. Regular figures are from Department of the Navy, "Report to

the Congress, FY 1987," 13. In December 1985, seventy-seven thousand ready reservists *were* on active duty.

33. Department of the Navy, "Report to the Congress, Fiscal Year 1987," 26.

34. "A Force on the Move," 7.

35. OP-09R published a weekly summary of significant naval reserve events for the deputy assistant secretary of the navy, reserve affairs. See 8, 13 February, 22 March, 17 May, 1, 8 August, 27 September, and 13 November 1985, and 16 January and 6 February 1986, for especially interesting summaries.

36. His speeches as head of state sometimes drew generously on his notes from Naval War College lectures, to the delight of all concerned.

37. There had been nine International Seapower symposia at Newport by October 1987 (and some regional spinoffs were organized by other navies). The author was the originator of the formula mentioned. Fifty-four nations were present at the ninth symposium. Typically, at least two-thirds of the delegations are led by CNOs.

38. As a member of the staff of commander, Sixth Fleet (on training duty), the author once participated in a luncheon on the flagship for senior Spanish officials at Majorca. Not only were there no alcoholic beverages, but only one man in the group of eighteen spoke both languages.

39. CNO dispatch 242103Z to the American defense attaché, Madrid, February 1983.

40. Port visits in 1984 included 108 countries. The chart for these shows 24 in the Central American–South American region and 16 on Africa's west coast.

41. CNO ser. 00/5S300062, 13 February 1985.

42. CINCLANT letter to CNO, 20 September 1982.

43. OP-613C/53883/B09567, 30 April 1985.

44. OP-603D, 28 April 1985.

45. CNO message, ser. 081516Z, July 1985

46. See the 603D memo to CNO, 29 August 1985.

CHAPTER 11

1. Neither the word *maritime* nor the word *strategy* appear in the index of Zumwalt's *On Watch*.

2. Admiral Harry Train, CINCLANT from October 1978 to October 1982, dismisses the contribution of the Strategic Studies Group: "They didn't have intellectual discipline and started off with all the wild things" (taped interview, Newport, 16 July 1987). He credits Rear Admiral Bill Pendley (as many do) with "putting the pieces together."

3. Taped interview, former Secretary of the Navy John Lehman, Yorktown, Virginia, 22 October 1987. He said he came into office "with a very clear-cut, simple understanding of what maritime strategy *must be.* . . . I didn't create anything. My strategy is not a new strategy. It is simply applying a little rigorous logic to integrate conceptually the commonsense things that the Navy needs to do in wartime." He told Admiral Watkins in San Diego that if the latter became CNO, his first responsibility would be to put together a maritime strategy. "And the reason I was so strongly for him [Watkins] is that he did think conceptually."

4. John R. Hattendorf, "The Evolution of the U.S. Navy's Maritime Strategy, 1977–1987," unpublished manuscript.

5. Ibid., 100.

6. Ibid., 127.

7. Ibid., 131–32. The briefers for this version were Lieutenant Commander Stanley Weeks and Commander W. S. Johnson. Captain Wylie writes that the original version was about two and a half hours long: "We eventually developed 'tailored' versions from 30 to 90 minutes, with emphasis dependent on the particular audience." They had started with "no particular visions in mind," simply trying to develop a coherent version "of what every naval officer knows intuitively. . . ." (letter to author, 28 June 1988).

8. Ibid., 143. Hattendorf takes this from the OP-603 file, "Memo on Maritime Strategy presentation to SECNAV on 4 November [1982]."

9. By this time three classified versions had been developed; the first was the Weeks-Stanley version, the second the Swartz-Barnett version, the third the Parker-Seaquist version. The mid-1984 (classified) version, OPNAV 60 P-1-84, was distributed under CNO letter ser. 00/45300236, 4 May 1984. The Parker version in January 1985 was briefed to Senator Barry Goldwater and the Senate Armed Services Committee and later to the House seapower subcommittee (see ibid., 180). Admiral Watkins signed it on 1 November 1985 (ibid., 182).

10. White House news release, Long Beach, California, 28 December 1982.

11. Admiral James D. Watkins, "The Maritime Strategy," U.S. Naval Institute *Proceedings*, reprint (January 1986): 12–13. The same point was made to Congress in the hearings of the seapower and strategic and critical materials subcommittee of the House Armed Services Committee in June and September 1985, House document 99-33, 34.

12. House Budget Committee, Hearings FY 84, 98th Cong., 1st sess., 9, 16, 17, and 23 February 1983, 151.

13. Ibid., 200. It is true there was a bow wave. According to Bill Keller, in "The Navy's Brash Leader," *The New York Times Magazine*, 15 December 1985, Lehman and Weinberger agreed early "that the Navy would forgo some budget increases later on in exchange for large increases in the first two years" (38). That led in 1982 to the two *Nimitz*-class carriers, three Aegis cruisers, etc. Lehman (*Command of the Seas*, 174) credited Assistant Secretary George Sawyer with the idea and said that Frank Carlucci proposed going ahead with it, giving more money in the 1983 budget to the navy in return for paying back the exact amount in the 1984 budget. Keller called 1982 "the Navy's most successful year," and when spending was later reduced, "many of Lehman's ships were already rising in the dry docks."

14. House Budget Committee, Hearings FY 84, 174.

15. Ibid., 201.

16. Ibid., 202.

17. Ibid., 203.

18. Ibid., 203–4.

19. Ibid., 204.

20. Ibid., 445.

21. Ibid., 458.

22. Robert W. Komer, *Maritime Strategy or Coalition Defense?* (Cambridge, Massachusetts: Abt Books, 1984), 36.

23. There are different versions of the Nunn-Lehman argument. Admiral

Harry Train, formerly CINCLANT, believes that Lehman, wanting appropriations for two nuclear carriers in one year, did a careful market survey to see what
would appeal to the congressional swing vote. He found "if he could show that
two carriers could go up to the Kola Peninsula and bomb the Soviets into the
stone age before they could enter combat in the North Atlantic, that this would
be a persuasive rationale." Whereupon, says Train, Lehman took the pieces of the
preliminary version of the maritime strategy, "packaged it, and announced this
without ever having consulted with his CINCPAC, Bob Long, or myself." Train
recalls being summoned posthaste from Norfolk to speak about carrier survivability after Lehman had testified to the Senate Armed Services Committee. They
asked him if he would "really do something that stupid," and Train told them
that if it were important enough, he could. But he commented in the interview for
this book, "You can't do it" (Train tape).

According to Lehman, Nunn kept saying that the secretary of the navy was
going to send those carriers up right away to attack the Kola Peninsula. "He was
twisting things around—he'd been listening to all the critics who had bowdlerized
what I said." Nunn could not, when challenged, point out where on the record
Lehman had made such a statement. Nunn called Train and some retired flags to
testify and asked them, "'Do you agree with Secretary Lehman that we should
start a thermonuclear war and send a carrier up the Volga River?' That kind of
thing" (Lehman tape).

24. House Armed Services Committee, seapower and strategic and critical
material subcommittee, Hearings FY 86, "The 600-Ship Navy and the Maritime
Strategy," 99th Cong., 1st sess., 24 June, 5, 6, and 10 September 1985.

25. Ibid., 13.
26. Ibid., 23.
27. Ibid., 32.
28. Ibid.
29. Ibid., 33–36.
30. Ibid., 88.
31. Ibid., 96.
32. Ibid., 171.
33. Ibid., 176–84.
34. Ibid., 186.
35. Ibid., 192.
36. Ibid., 200.
37. Ibid., 201.
38. Ibid., 219.
39. Ibid., 222.
40. Ibid., 224.
41. Ibid., 225.
42. Ibid., 230.
43. Ibid., 231.
44. Ibid., 240–41.
45. *The Defense Monitor* 14, no. 7, 1985.
46. Hearings FY 86,"The 600-Ship Navy and the Maritime Strategy,"
242–49.
47. Ibid.
48. Ibid.
49. Ibid., 253.

50. Ibid., 272.

51. Ibid., 276.

52. Hearings FY 86, "The 600-Ship Navy and the Maritime Strategy," 276.

53. Ibid., 276–77.

54. Ibid., 277–78.

55. Ibid., 281.

56. Ibid., 282.

57. Ibid.

58. Ibid., 283.

59. Ibid., 284.

60. Ibid., 285.

61. Ibid., 286.

62. Ibid., 293.

63. Ibid., 298.

64. Ibid.

65. Ibid., 299.

66. Taped interview, Admiral James D. Watkins, USN (Ret.), Washington, 21 October 1987. Admiral Watkins by this time was the busy chairman of the president's Commission on AIDS.

67. Ibid.

68. U.S. Naval Institute *Proceedings*, special supplement (January 1986).

69. Ibid., 9. The exact number bought by the Soviets, who use various disguised means in their acquisition of U.S. products, cannot be established.

70. Ibid., 10.

71. Ibid., 7.

72. Ibid., 11.

73. Ibid., 12.

74. Ibid., 13.

75. For example, the enclosure to flag officer news gram 1-87 (ser. 00/75300085, 7 April 1987) sums up the basic elements of the strategy this way (italics in original):

— Deals with forces we have *today*.

— Positions forces *far forward*.

— Puts pressure on *Soviet flanks*.

— Uses *no fixed timetables*.

— Permits navy to *make a strategic difference*.

76. Taped interview, Vice Admiral Henry C. Mustin, the Pentagon, 13 April 1987.

77. Watkins tape.

78. White House, "National Security Strategy of the United States," January 1987, 41 pp.

CHAPTER 12

1. Taped interview, Admiral James D. Watkins, the Pentagon, 28 April 1986. In an interview in 1987 Admiral Ron Hays made a parallel observation from the perspective of a unified commander (USCINCPAC). Although under the defense reorganization act of 1986 the CNO had zero responsibility for opera-

tions, was he in fact involved in operations? "Right up to his eyebrow," said Hays (taped interview, Camp Smith, Hawaii, 21 May 1987).

2. The complex and far-reaching changes mandated by the Goldwater-Nichols Defense Reorganization Act of 1986 have been noted occasionally in previous chapters and will be noted here. But, essentially, it is the situation prior to those changes that is of central concern in this book.

3. Taped interview, Admiral Tom Moorer, USN (Ret.), Washington, 3 June 1986.

4. A fact paper from files of the Joint Chiefs of Staff (April 1986) indicates that the number of meetings between the president and the Joint Chiefs has varied from a low of three to a high of twenty-two. The record is as follows: Truman (1948–53), eight; Eisenhower (1953–61), twelve; Kennedy (1961–63), twenty-two; Johnson (1963–69), eighteen; Nixon (1969–74), three; Ford (1974–77), three; Carter, (1977–81), eight; Reagan (1981–86), twelve.

Topics discussed at these meetings are not always available. The list for a thirteen-month period is as follows: February 1983, strategic modernization; April 1983, unknown; October 1983, Far East, defense against ballistic missiles, budget reductions by Congress, and security assistance; March 1984, security assistance and readiness of U.S. forces.

5. Watkins tape.

6. The official files of the Joint Chiefs show, in a memo dated 3 December 1985 (with 1985 data available only through November): General Gabriel, 142.5 days; Admiral Watkins, 138.5 days; General Wickham, 91.5 days; and General Kelley, 85 days. The smaller numbers for Wickham and Kelley reflect, their shorter tenure as chiefs as of that date. The memos are not dated or identified.

7. Watkins tape.

8. Taped interview, General P. X. Kelley, commandant of the Marine Corps, marine headquarters, 17 April 1986.

9. General Thurman said you have to have your answers ready. Taped interview, General Maxwell R. Thurman, vice chief of staff of the army, the Pentagon, 17 April 1987.

10. Reprinted by the House Budget Committee in its 1983 hearings, 57–66, the Jones article is well argued. One can see why it made a deep impression. Certainly Jones is correct on a number of the points, such as the lack of opportunity/attraction represented by duty with the Joint Chiefs of Staff. Jones the official seems to have aroused resentments. One three-star staffer said Jones had his own "kitchen cabinet" and decided issues out of staffing channels. General John Wickham, then army chief of staff, said that, whatever the reason, "the chiefs under Jones were fractious. Bad chemistry" (taped interview, McLean, Virginia, 14 July 1987).

11. Moorer tape.

12. Taped interview, General John W. Vessey, Jr., near Brainerd, Minnesota, 22 September 1986.

13. These are not a reporter's words but his own, from an article "Reorganizing the Joint Chiefs," *Wall Street Journal*, 8 February 1984, 32.

14. Jones would say, and the Joint Chiefs from these years would hotly disagree, that there were few disagreements because the chiefs dodged real issues.

15. Watkins tape.

16. Ibid.

17. Specifically, the Defense Resources Board (DRB). A typical meeting, in

1983, was prefaced by a Joint Chiefs' memo, in this case 3 June, inviting commanders in chief to DRB sessions on 13 and 14 July. "The morning sessions will be devoted [to] your views on the strategy, the adequacy of the POMs to meet that strategy," while the 14 July afternoon session was to "deal with the policy and risk assessment issue book which is intended to establish the overall context [for] detailed force and program decisions. . . ."

18. Vessey tape.

19. Watkins tape. One of Watkins's concerns was that under reorganization, chiefs might not be able to initiate agenda items. He sent sixty-two such memos in his first three years.

20. Watkins tape. Rear Admiral Roger Bacon had the assignment then.

21. Ibid.

22. I am struck, having attended these briefings, with how the emphasis shifts as the briefing (and debriefing) level changes. Those presiding want to know different things or have different interests. Debriefing may bear little resemblance to what went up the briefing chain. This is mostly because the chiefs do not stick with their formal agenda.

23. The number in 1986 was 5711.6G, March 1985, and had two main parts: action processing and administrative procedures for the Office of the Joint Chiefs of Staff.

24. Jones, *New York Times Magazine*, 7 November 1982.

25. Taped interview, General Charles A. Gabriel, McLean, Virginia, 21 August 1986.

26. OP-605D4 point paper, 24 February 1984.

27. The dispatch, which remains classified, is an eloquent rebuttal of critics who think this cooperation is mere facade and that nothing has changed.

28. Gabriel tape.

29. There is a good discussion of this in *Army Times*, 17 March 1986.

30. Thurman tape.

31. Wickham tape.

32. See memorandum marked DALO-TSM, 17 April 1987.

33. There were also programs for joint-force-development education, cross-service participation in budget development, and the exchange of staff officers already mentioned. See memorandum for vice chief of staff, army, 17 April 1987, from army director, strategy, plans, and policy (CF: ODCSLOG).

34. See navy files 5400/ser. 64/6U433935. In 1984 the services conducted seventy joint or combined exercises; in 1985 that figure rose to eighty-three. An undated navy file "talker" listed other joint ventures initiated by the services, including the JRMB already mentioned, a joint electronic warfare center systems-engineering capability, a joint communications satellite center, a joint special operations agency, and a joint-force development process, among others.

35. The cooperation is not just bilateral. For example, the navy identified eleven areas in the thirty-one-point army–air force memorandum of understanding where navy would join in.

36. Thurman tape.

37. CNO memo 56-82, which also carried an air force designation as CSAFM 12-82. It is dated 10 September 1982.

38. All the above is, of course, taken from unclassified listings or summaries. The media (or Grenada) CNO memo is 63-83, 8 December 1983.

39. Navy files contain numerous papers dealing with coordination of ROEs among allied nations.

40. Taped interview, Captain Ash Roach, Newport, 22 October 1986. Captain Roach, assigned to the Office of the Judge Advocate General, international law branch, from 1979 to 1983, had a good deal to do with the handling of the revision.

41. Hayward tape.

42. Roach tape.

43. *New York Times*, 14 June 1987, 8.

CHAPTER 13

1. George C. Wilson, *Supercarrier* (New York: Macmillan, 1986), 136.

2. A package is a given armaments load for a particular type of mission, figured in advance to simplify and expedite the complex business of loading.

3. This rumor may trace back to George Wilson's remark, in another context, that "President Reagan wanted to deliver a political message. . . ." *Supercarrier*, 151. The time change was from 1100 to 0630.

4. Ibid., 155.

5. Admiral Watkins said: "If the Chairman did something it was outside the normal JCS chain. He didn't tell us. All he told us was that he had told Bernie Rogers that the timing of the strike was his, and don't screw it up. We want it done right. No time restrictions. Now, if the White House imposed something on top of that, it's unknown to me. . . . As far as I know, that was a directive in Europe. . . ." Taped interview, Admiral James D. Watkins, USN (Ret.), Washington, D.C., 21 October 1987.

6. Wilson quotes Watkins: "If you find out [whose fault it was] you'll be the first." *Supercarrier*, 155.

7. Taped interview, Professor Jack Grunawalt, Newport, 17 June 1988. Then-Captain Grunawalt served with the Long Commission. The notices to ships and aircraft, in setting restrictions, are typical of U.S. practice since.

8. In an exchange in January 1984, the United States rejected the Soviet protest that the U.S. action curtailed freedom of navigation. (The Soviet "non-paper" and the U.S. "draft non-paper" are discussed in OP-616B memo, 12 January 1984, ser. C1-84/A12449.) In March 1984, the news agency TASS said the Soviets would not recognize the U.S. restrictions (*Washington Post*, 8 March 1984, 27, and *New York Times*, 8 March 1984, 4). Nothing much came of that.

9. Taped interviews, Admiral James D. Watkins, Washington, D.C., 17 April 1987, 17 July 1987, and 21 October 1987.

10. Taped interview, former Secretary of the Navy John Lehman, Yorktown, Virginia, 22 October 1987. Lehman said that A-4s were $0.5 million when the Vietnam War began and $10 million at its end.

11. Admiral Watkins agreed. At Fallon he told the group that navy attack plans coming, say, from OP-60 and from the Sixth Fleet would sometimes be very different.

12. Lehman tape. There were two meetings, the first with the Air Board at China Lake, the second at Fallon.

13. Taped interview, Dr. Roger Whiteway, Naval Air Station, Fallon, Nevada, 5 August 1987.

14. Captain George O'Brien, commanding officer of the *Carl Vinson* (CVN

70), deployed under the new arrangement. He pointed out the serious organizational problems he had encountered but also said that one part of the program was a complete success: using super-CAG as the battle-group strike-warfare commander. He further indicated that the super-CAGs chosen to date were not only very competent but had been given far more extensive training in intelligence and weapons employment. That made a lot of difference in what they could contribute, since they were generally more knowledgeable than their predecessors. O'Brien, on balance, thought the change had more negative than positive effects, particularly on shipboard relations (taped interview, at sea, 6 October 1987).

15. Lehman tape.

16. Speech by Vice Admiral William E. Ramsey to the National Space Club, Washington, 18 June 1986.

17. Speech by Admiral Carlisle A. H. Trost to the National Security Industrial Association Antisubmarine Warfare banquet, 20 May 1987, in *Defense Issues* 2, no. 41: 3.

18. Ibid.

19. Admiral Trost pointed to how quickly Soviet espionage overtakes the U.S. technological lead. John Barron, *Breaking the Ring* (Boston: Houghton Mifflin, 1987), contains a useful unclassified study of the Walker case.

20. Trost speech, *Defense Issues*, 2.

21. Taped interview, Vice Admiral William E. Ramsey, Colorado Springs, 16 September 1987.

22. Taped interview, Rear Admiral Richard C. Macke, Dahlgren, Virginia, 22 October 1987.

23. Ibid.

24. Ibid.

25. The U.S. space commands also keep track of approximately six thousand objects in space in 1987, every one of which has a specific number.

26. The Cubans were there principally to guard and work on the airstrip (long enough for bombers) being rushed to completion.

27. Taped interview, Admiral Wesley Lee McDonald, USN (Ret.), the Pentagon, 18 April 1986. The *Independence* battle group and embarked marines, en route to the Mediterranean, were diverted to Grenada.

28. Taped interview, Admiral Huntington Hardisty, the Pentagon, 13 April 1987.

29. After Grenada Watkins set up a whole new organization for Seal teams and selected the first Seal flag officer so that someone would be defending them in the budget process. Watkins pointed out that the marine unit used at Grenada had been trained to evacuate citizens under difficult conditions, rather than for the assault role they actually undertook. The unit performed well, he said (Watkins tape, 17 July 1987).

30. Taped interview, Vice Admiral David E. Jeremiah, the Pentagon, 15 July 1987.

31. Ibid.

32. Ibid.

33. Ibid.

34. Colonel Qaddafi spent $2.1 billion on military goods and services in 1979 alone. In a nation of 2,933,000 people, that amounts to $716 for each man, woman, and child.

35. Rear Admiral Jerry Breast, "Battle Stations!" *Wings of Gold* (Summer 1987): 26–29, 32.

36. Ibid., and the Jeremiah tape.

37. Jeremiah tape.

38. Ibid.

39. Breast, "Battle Stations!"

40. Videotape (edited) prepared originally by Rear Admiral Breast for his Pentagon debriefing.

41. Breast, "Battle Stations!" 29. He added that more survivable search and rescue, plus more tactical reconaissance, would have been needed if a single blow did not end the affair.

42. Taped interview, Admiral James A. Lyons, Jr., Pearl Harbor, 22 May 1987.

43. Admiral Watkins commented, "It's not just the Aegis system [being made available to Japan that counted]. We exchanged strategic views with Japan" (Watkins tape, 17 July 1987).

44. Lyons tape. See also his interview in the U.S. Naval Institute *Proceedings* (July 1987): 68.

45. Hardisty tape.

46. Taped interview, Rear Admiral James F. Dorsey, Jr., the Pentagon, 23 October 1987.

47. Jeremiah tape.

48. Breast video.

49. Lyons tape.

CHAPTER 14

1. *New York Times*, 24 March 1983.

2. The navy's role is detailed in a classified folder in the OPNAV files. This file memo on SDI includes a careful account of the chronology and steps taken. The author also interviewed people extensively on this subject, including almost everyone present at the Joint Chiefs of Staff meeting with President Reagan on 11 February 1983.

3. CNO OPNAV files, undated cover memo, 2.

4. Taped interview, Admiral James D. Watkins, the Pentagon, 2 June 1986.

5. Taped interview, Admiral James D. Watkins, USN (Ret.), the Navy Yard, Washington, 21 October 1987.

6. Ibid., fn 4. The lunch was also attended by the late Admiral Arthur Moreau, Jr., then three-star deputy chief for plans and policy, Rear Admiral W. J. Holland, director of the strategic and theater nuclear warfare division, Captain John Y. Schrader, and Mr. Peter Mantle.

7. Taped interview, Dr. Edward Teller, Hoover Institution, Stanford University, Palo Alto, California, 28 April 1987. See also Edward Teller, *Better a Shield than a Sword* (New York: Free Press, 1987). The quotations here are taken from the interview tape, but they refer back to the lunch conversation.

8. Watkins tape, 21 October 1987.

9. Brooks, by all accounts, seems to have played a significant role in every subsequent step. The file memo calls this lunch "the CNO's first specific discussion of strategic defense" (ibid., fn 4). Admiral Watkins's memory of the sequence was that the Lin Brooks papers predated this lunch.

10. Ibid.

11. This meeting, as with the previous meetings, was confined to the chiefs.

12. The files date the last revision 1730, 4 February 1983.

13. Page 8 of the file memo.

14. Taped interview, Robert McFarlane, Washington, 25 April 1986.

15. Ibid.

16. Taped interview, Colonel Gilbert R. Rye, USAF (Ret.), Washington, 20 August 1986.

17. Taped interview, Vice Admiral John M. Poindexter, the White House, 3 June 1986. Poindexter himself was not present at the chiefs meeting with the president. Judge William Clark was then national security advisor, but he was also absent that day.

18. Poindexter tape.

19. Rye said that four staff members were tabbed to write the insert—"very compartmented; any outside contacts only through McFarlane." Rye thought that Teller had had little influence on the president's thinking. With x-ray lasers, you are "talking about a nuclear explosion in space," and that "scares me a bit." It would also, he said, violate the Outer Space Treaty (taped interview).

20. Page 7 of the file memo.

21. Admiral Watkins indicated that Weinberger at the very outset did not support the new concept. But he encouraged the chiefs to present it anyway (taped interview, Washington, 28 April 1986). McFarlane said that, if Weinberger was initially opposed, he quickly switched his position to one of support.

22. Especially at the International Institute for Strategic Studies meeting in Ottawa in September 1983 and at Avignon in 1984.

23. The moral dimension of SDI got very little press attention.

24. The technical study was called the Fletcher Study. Two policy studies were conducted, one under Franklin Miller of the Office of the Undersecretary of Defense for Policy and the other by an outside team (the Hoffman Study).

25. "Toward a More Stable World: United States Policy on Strategic Defense," 15.

26. Ibid., 17.

27. Delivered on Wednesday, 13 April 1983. Quotes are from a news release, Office of Assistant Secretary of Defense (Public Affairs), no. 172–83.

28. The speech is in *The Congressional Record*, 99th Cong., 1st sess., 29 January 1985, S820-S823.

29. The letter is marked control no. 452771.

30. Letter, 18 March 1985, replying to Richard M. Blau's letter of 27 February 1985 (no control number).

31. It is entitled "The President's Strategic Defense Initiative." It has a foreword by the president, a statement of policy, and "assertions and facts about SDI." The last part represents an especially good response to critics.

32. Quotation is from a navy file copy.

CHAPTER 15

1. The author was present at the ceremony and bases this account on notes he took and subsequent interviews with participants.

2. Taped interview, Admiral Carlisle A. H. Trost, Norfolk, 27 May 1986.

By coincidence, this interview occurred at the very time Admiral Trost was nominated to be the next CNO.

3. Taped interview, Captain Robert B. Watts, Newport, 17 February 1987.

4. The text used by the CNO carries his editorial changes. Before the words about material and personnel support, the word *all* had been deleted, for prudence's sake. But it indicates his leaning.

5. See flag officer news gram 4-86, 6 October 1986.

6. Flag officer news gram 5-86, 17 December 1986.

7. Admiral Carlisle A. H. Trost, "Looking Beyond the Maritime Strategy," U.S. Naval Institute *Proceedings* (January 1987): 13–16.

8. Ibid.

9. House Appropriations Committee, defense subcommittee, Hearings FY 87, 99th Cong., 2d sess., 4 March 1986. Citations are from a navy file copy.

10. Ibid., FY 88, 100th Cong., 1st sess., 4 March 1987, 7 (navy file copy).

11. Ibid., 11. There was also a 1.1 percent decline in enlistments of upper "mental" groups and a 3.7 percent decline in high-school graduate enlistments (see p. 27).

12. Admiral Carlisle A. H. Trost, "The CNO Answers Your Questions," *All Hands* (March 1987): 6.

13. *New York Times*, 3 April 1988, 5.

14. For Lehman at his most adroit, see the interview in *Armed Forces Journal*, international edition, November 1983. Lehman's successor, James H. Webb, Jr., froze Lehman's final organizational-change orders for careful review. (Lehman had issued twelve far-reaching instructions only days before resigning.)

15. Paul H. Nitze, "Running the Navy," *Proceedings* (September 1989): 77.

16. A Report by Admiral C. A. H. Trost, chief of naval operations, on the posture and FYs 1990–91 budget of the U.S. Navy, p. 36, no date.

17. Of eighty-four active or recently retired three-star and four-star line officers, twenty-four, or 29 percent, were non-academy.

18. On 1 January 1986, for instance, there were (apart from Admiral Crowe), eight four-star and thirty three-star line officers. On 1 April 1986, there were eight four-star and twenty-nine three-star line officers.

In an addendum to flag officer news gram 1-87 (ser. 00/75300085, 7 April 87), Admiral Trost summarized the flag situation. Of the 1,073 flag and general officer billets authorized by Congress, the army had 412, the navy 253, the air force 343, and the marines 65. On a fair-share basis tied to end strength, the numbers would be army 390, navy 284, air force 300, marines 99.

19. Taped interview, Admiral James D. Watkins, USN (Ret.), the Navy Yard, Washington, 17 April 1987.

INDEX

325

330

  and Urgent Fury, 241, 242
Maritime strategy
  and defending Norway, 213–15
  and nuclear war, 215, 216
  criticized, 204–6, 209–11
  delay in evolving, 199
  Lehman explains to Congress,
    211–14
  need for, 69, 70
  presented to Congress, 207, 208
  published, 214, 215
  role of OP-603 in developing, 201,
    202
  Sea Plan 2000 as step toward, 201
  Strategic Studies Group role in,
    185, 202
  tested repeatedly at Newport, 156
Martin, Edward H., 56
Massive retaliation, 8
Math/science volunteer initiative, 84,
  296n, 297n
Maury, Matthew F., 296n
Mauz, Henry H., 245
Melbourne, HMAS, 94
Merchant fleet numbers, 154
Mercier, Mark, case, 102
Metcalf, Joseph, III, 56
Middendorf, J. William, II, 42, 43,
  131, 132
Midway, 100
Milestones, 130, 131
Military Sealift Command, 57
Miller, Franklin, 322n
Miller, Richard A., 121
Miramar affair, 110–13
Missouri, 158
Modular concept, 134
Moffett Field, 111
Monroe, Robert R.
  on abolition of Naval Material
    Command, 121, 122
  on milestone approach to procure-
    ment, 130, 131, 306n, 307n
  and operational testing, 129, 304n
  and problems with systems analy-
    sis, 128
Moorer, Thomas H.
  and Joint Chiefs' role in formulat-
    ing movement orders, 219

on proper role of secretary, 44, 45
  on push-button war, 200
  and reform of Joint Chiefs, 222
  and Secretary Chafee, 43
  and service secretaries, 292n
  tenure as CNO, 11
"Moral Man, Modern Dilemma," 68,
  69
Moreau, Arthur S., Jr., 202, 243,
  246, 321n
Multiple protective shelter basing for
  MX, 251
Murray, Robert, 176, 184–86
Mustin, Henry C., 73, 74, 216
Mutual assured destruction (MAD),
  249, 250, 252
MX problem, 250–52

Naples hospital, incident at, 100, 101
National Conference of Catholic
  Bishops, report, 68
National Security Act of 1947, 5, 44,
  47
National Security Decision Directive
  of 1985, 260
Nautilus, 92
Naval Academy, 76, 77
Naval Air Systems Command, 57, 59,
  100
Naval Education and Training Com-
  mand, 74–76
Naval establishment, figures on, 41
Naval Facilities Engineering Com-
  mand, 57
Naval Intelligence Command, 57
Naval Investigative Service, 74
Naval Material Command
  abolition of, 58, 114
  CNO and secretary concur for dif-
    ferent reasons, 115, 116
Naval Military Personnel Command,
  74, 76
Naval Nuclear Propulsion Program,
  57
Naval Postgraduate School, 35, 166,
  168–71, 239
Naval Reserve, 186–91, 311n, 312n
Naval Reserve Officers Training
  Corps (NROTC), 77

The Naval Institute Press is the book-publishing arm of the U.S. Naval Institute, a private, nonprofit professional society for members of the sea services and civilians who share an interest in naval and maritime affairs. Established in 1873 at the U.S. Naval Academy in Annapolis, Maryland, where its offices remain today, the Naval Institute has more than 100,000 members worldwide.

Members of the Naval Institute receive the influential monthly naval magazine *Proceedings* and substantial discounts on fine nautical prints, ship and aircraft photos, and subscriptions to the Institute's recently inaugurated quarterly, *Naval History*. They also have access to the transcripts of the Institute's Oral History Program and may attend any of the Institute-sponsored seminars regularly offered around the country.

The book-publishing program, begun in 1898 with basic guides to naval practices, has broadened its scope in recent years to include books of more general interest. Now the Naval Institute Press publishes more than forty new titles each year, ranging from how-to books on boating and navigation to battle histories, biographies, ship guides, and novels. Institute members receive discounts on the Press's more than 300 books.

For a free catalog describing books currently available and for further information about U.S. Naval Institute membership, please write to:

Membership Department
U.S. Naval Institute
Annapolis, Maryland 21402

or call, toll-free, 800-233-USNI.

THE NAVAL INSTITUTE PRESS
NAVAL RENAISSANCE
The U.S. Navy in the 1980s
Designed by CR MacLellan and Associates, Baltimore, Maryland

Set in Sabon (text) and Serif Gothic (display) by Byrd Data Imaging, Inc.,
Richmond, Virginia

Printed on 55-lb. Antique Cream and bound in Holliston Roxite B
by Maple-Vail, Inc., York, Pennsylvania